The Senate and the People of Canada

The Senate and the People of Canada

A Counterintuitive Approach to Reform of the Senate of Canada

James T. McHugh

LEXINGTON BOOKS
Lanham • Boulder • New York • London

Published by Lexington Books
An imprint of The Rowman & Littlefield Publishing Group, Inc.
4501 Forbes Boulevard, Suite 200, Lanham, Maryland 20706

www.rowman.com

Unit A, Whitacre Mews, 26-34 Stannary Street, London SE11 4AB

British Library Cataloguing in Publication Information Available

Library of Congress Cataloging-in-Publication Data Available

ISBN 978-1-4985-4793-2 (cloth : alk. paper)
ISBN 978-1-4985-4794-9 (electronic)

∞™ The paper used in this publication meets the minimum requirements of American National Standard for Information Sciences—Permanence of Paper for Printed Library Materials, ANSI/NISO Z39.48-1992.

Printed in the United States of America

For Emilia–who inspires me, always

Contents

List of Figure and Tables

FIGURE

TABLES

Acknowledgments

I am grateful for feedback that I have received on this topic and book throughout the years of its creation. I received invaluable editorial feedback and advice from Daniel Quinlan and Jacqueline Mason and, of course, from the editorial team at Lexington Books, including Joseph C. Parry, Madhumitha Koduvalli, and Emily Roderick. I received both feedback and encouragement from many colleagues, especially (but not exclusively) Patrick James of the University of Southern California, Howard Cody of the University of Maine, George Sulzner of the University of Massachusetts, Christopher Kirkey of the State University of New York at Plattsburgh, Jeffrey Ayres of Saint Michael's College, David Plazek of Johnson State College, Paul Petterson of Central Connecticut State University, and many other fellow scholars whose names I have not mentioned but whose assistance has been, nonetheless, valued.

Additionally, several institutions also provided support and encouragement. The Department of Political Science at Carleton University was especially helpful while I was pursuing this project during part of my time as Fulbright Distinguished Research Chair for North American Integration, including Laura MacDonald and the department chair at that time, Jonathan Malloy. During that time, I received particularly useful feedback and encouragement from my colleague, Gary Levy, who was the Bell Chair in Canadian Parliamentary Democracy and has been a scholar of Canadian Senate reform for some time, exploring ideas that have, often, complemented my own research. I received assistance from the Canadian Parliamentary Library and its director, Sonia L'Heureux and especially useful advice from Meg Russell of the Constitution Unit of University College, London, whose superlative work on reform of the House of Lords provided a good deal of inspiration for my own efforts. That interest in upper house reform began when I was a graduate student at the University of Edinburgh and I am grateful to its Centre for Canadian Studies and the director at the time, Ged Martin, who arranged for me to present my first paper on this subject to the British Association for Canadian Studies.

Additional interest and support came from Canadian public officials. The former Leader of the Liberal Party of Canada and Secretary of State for Global Affairs, the Honorable Stephane Dion, was especially encouraging, consistent with his long-standing interest in this subject. The Honorable Senator Serge Joyal, who has been cited, many times, within this book also offered support and encouragement for my efforts. I am hopeful that their interest may inspire other parliamentarians to consider these "counter-intuitive" recommendations for Senate reform as possible future options for this institution, especially as some of them already appear to have reflected policy directions under the Right Honorable Prime Minister Justin Trudeau, whose father, the Right Honorable Prime Minister Pierre Elliot Trudeau, also indirectly inspired my initial interest in this subject.

Mostly, though, I am grateful to my wife, Emilia. Not only did she tolerate the intolerable amount of time that I spent on this manuscript (including when we were supposed to be on vacation) but she always inspired me to persist with it, even when it encroached upon the attention that I should have been paying to us and our family. She further assisted me, invaluably, with the final edits for the manuscript and she amazes me, always, not only with her superior intelligence and grace but, also, with her persistence and patience, despite her obvious bad taste in men.

Preface

As I have pursued this project, a couple of experiences in my academic development have occasionally been recalled. The first experience occurred when the late teacher and scholar of enormous repute in the field of Canadian politics, Dr. Richard Simeon, held an informal contest among members of the Department of Political Studies at Queen's University (where I was a doctoral candidate at the time) for the person who could provide the best response to the following question: "Have you read X?" The response was supposed to begin "No, but …" My entry broke the rule by stating "Yes, but only because I wrote it." He later indicated that some of the better submissions included "No, but I assigned it for my class," "No, but I cited it," and "No, but I vehemently disagree with it."

The second recollection involves a course I took in the History of Japan as an undergraduate student at the University of Vermont that was taught by another wonderful professor, the late Dr. Peter Seybolt. One of the subjects that we addressed was the decline and fall of the Ashikaga Shogunate and its replacement by the Tokugawa Shogunate. I conceived my own explanation for that pivotal development in Japanese history and I would discuss it in class with the professor, who respectfully yet strongly disagreed with my conclusions. Not surprisingly, a question on that subject appeared within the midterm exam. In my response, I advanced my argument while acknowledging the more conventional interpretation that both Dr. Seybolt and the course textbook had provided. When I received my graded exam, it included a two and a half-page critique of my approach, an acknowledgement that I had recognized and addressed his explanation and approach, and a thorough explanation of the reasons that my conclusions were wrong, followed by my grade—A+.

I often have thought about that contest (a winner was never actually declared) and that undergraduate history course as I have pursued this scholarly project of reform of the Senate of Canada. They taught me two vital lessons about academia and scholarship that have guided me, throughout my career. The first lesson has been the acceptance of divergent conclusions, especially on controversial topics, provided that the scholarly path that leads to those conclusions is grounded upon thorough research, sound methods of analysis, and a meaningful acknowledgment of alternative scholarly approaches and conclusions. The second lesson has been that the academic world is not as idealistic as I would like to believe and even skilled scholars (including policy analysts) often may form critical opinions on something despite having not even examined the actual scholarly position that has been presented.

I have been researching and writing on Canadian Senate reform since I was a master's candidate, working out of the Centre for Canadian Studies at the University of Edinburgh under the excellent tutelage of its outstanding director at the time, Dr. Ged Martin. Over the years, I have found that the response to my research on this subject often depends upon whether the person who is reacting to it already prefers another approach toward Senate reform. In particular, anyone who has insisted as an uncontestable truism that a reformed Senate must be elected or must have dominant provincial participation in the process of selecting Senators often would not only be instantly hostile to my scholarship on this subject but, even in reading it, would appear to miss those sections of my manuscript or presentation in which I did, indeed, address those positions and the arguments upon which they are based. I would receive objections that I had totally ignored the theme of federalism, despite my recommendation for extensive provincial participation in the selection process. I also received a complaint that I had shown "disrespect" for democracy, despite (or perhaps because of) my persistent claims that popular democracy is not the only form of democracy that is relevant to this subject.

Of all the academic subjects on which I have written during my scholarly career, none have proven to be as controversial as Canadian Senate reform—and I have written on several controversial issues. It is, I believe, a peculiar characteristic of this particular subject, which is an excellent example of the tempestuous culture that can pervade academia and public policy. The constitutional proposals relating to the Senate that I have offered have been intended to be highly hypothetical, especially given the extremely difficult political environment for achieving this sort of reform and the tremendous institutional and political obstacles that confront it. Therefore, I have endeavored to construct an idealized model for Canadian Senate reform that is intended to provoke a broader theoretical and comparative analysis of parliamentary upper houses in general, especially (though not exclusively) within the Westminster model. Rather than anachronisms, I have found that these legislative institutions continue to present a potentially positive, supplemental role within parliamentary democracies—provided that they are understood and appreciated within their proper, subordinate relationship to the democratically chosen government and the lower chamber that establishes its legitimacy.

Admittedly, I also have been highly skeptical and critical, at times, when appraising alternative assumptions and declarations concerning Senate reform that I might consider to be not as well conceived or supported by evidence as they might be. The sometimes-bland assertion of some studies that elections offer the only possible source of legitimacy within a democratic system is an example of a claim that I have treated with this sort of critical skepticism. Indeed, I happen to be an extremely strong proponent of liberal democracy—so much so that I disapprove of even electoral attempts to challenge the ultimate popular sovereign authority that is the basis of a parliamentary or a republican system of government. But the argument that the electoral process is the only alternative that can provide a proper role for an institution within a democratic governmental system is one that I have not been willing to accept as an a priori assumption.

I also have been, on occasion, struck by the concerns expressed by colleagues that this model is not useful as an academic exercise because its adoption is politically impractical. Part of my reaction has been a result of the fact that much of this study has been deliberately presented at the theoretical level as a means for contrasting an ideal system with an actual one. However, another part of my reaction has been a result of more pragmatic recommendations that I have made that have been characterized as unrealistic, only to have a version of them (such as the depoliticization of the Senate, the creation of a category of non-partisan Senators, or the creation of a process for securing Senate appointments based upon merit) subsequently adopted, such as reforms that have been introduced by the government of Prime Minister Justin Trudeau. Policy, like politics, can surprise us.

Therefore, I hope that this book is read and assessed in the spirit in which it has been conceived and written—as a critical argument offering an alternative approach to conventional ways of thinking about upper house reform in general and Canadian Senate reform in particular. It may, inevitably, rankle some people who are inextricably committed to a particular path toward this policy area and elicit, therefore, a great deal of umbrage. Hopefully, though, it also may inspire some people to consider the possibilities that are available in this respect. If so, it will have been well worth the effort.

Part I

BACKGROUND, THEORY, AND CONTEXT

Chapter 1

Senatus Populusque Canadensis

INTRODUCTION

The most famous motto associated with the Roman Republic was *Senatus Populusque Romanus*, which was most often represented by the initials SPQR that would appear in various places throughout the city of Rome and the Roman world, including over the doors of the Roman Senate. This motto did not express a subordination of the role of the Senate to the popular assemblies or the subordination of the people to the Senate. It reflected, instead, an uneasy relationship between the popular and non-popular elements of the republic.[1] The first emphasis was upon the role of the Senate that served as the institutional expression of the political primacy of the patrician class of the Roman polity. It reflected the august image of the Senate as an institution of elite interests.[2] That generally august image would become so profoundly noted that its name or initials (SPQR) would be attached to prestigious political chambers, throughout history—even within modern liberal democracies.

The Senate of Canada has been the source of ongoing demands for its reform for most of its existence. Those demands have become increasingly insistent and, even, overwhelming in recent years. Since the introduction of the "Triple-E" reform proposal of the mid-1980s through the increased agitation for reform spurred by scandals of the early 2010s, the insistence that "something must be done" has led to proposals that have not always been as thoroughly thought through to their ultimate results as they ought to be. Arguably, a more comprehensive analysis, detached from political frustration and untested hypotheses, is needed.

The Senate of Canada originally was intended as a chamber of an elite segment of Canadian society, appointed upon a regional basis.[3] This elite group reflected, nonetheless, a sector of the liberal democratic society that had been emerging within British North America, particularly individual business persons and entrepreneurs who had succeeded in a manner consistent with the ideals of the market place and property rights. The fact that it was not an elected body reinforced the concept of this chamber as a representative of a minority interest, as opposed to the majoritarian interests of the popularly elected House of Commons.[4] Although Canada was not a republic, it was not entirely immune from the influence of republican beliefs and values[5] and some of this image of the Senate of Canada could be associated with certain aspects of republican values—though the ultimate deference of the Senate to the will of the Commons clearly reflected the principles of responsible parliamentary government, especially consistent with the Westminster model derived from Britain.

However, as Canada evolved, so did attitudes toward the role and function of a second chamber within its parliamentary system. Like the Roman Senate, the Senate of Canada would remain a distinct political body—one that existed differently than, though not completely apart from, the overall political system. It would serve a function that was related to the democratic system but operated along different parameters. Its role would become complementary to, rather than truly integrated within, the federal and parliamentary systems. It would maintain its dignity but serve, also, as a source of resentment and, even, derision.

This book offers a different way to think about the Senate of Canada and, instead, to contemplate the role that it has and the enhanced role that it could have. Like the Roman Senate, it exists within an often ambiguous and uneasy relationship with the popular institutions of government and the people whom those elected bodies represent. Yet the book will contend that this relationship is an intentional one so attempts to transform the Senate of Canada from its role as a traditional parliamentary second chamber into something else are ill-advised. Instead, this body should follow a path that is more closely tied to the overall theoretical development of the parliamentary upper house. That argument differs, markedly, from many other approaches relating to this Canadian institution but it is the seemingly unorthodox nature of that argument that returns attention to the Senate in terms of its proper place within the Canadian political system and its proper relationship to the extremely diverse regions, provinces, and people of Canada.

THE PREMISE

In 1985, the Legislative Assembly of Alberta convened a special select committee for the purpose of investigating and drafting proposals for reform of the Senate of Canada. The resulting report became the official basis for the recommendation that would become known (and widely popularized, especially among the Prairie Provinces of Canada) as the Triple-E Senate proposal. The three "E's" stood for the themes of equal representation among provinces, elected members of the Canadian upper house, and an effective second chamber in relation to the overall Canadian parliamentary system.[6]

Among the assumptions of this report was the belief that the Senate of Canada was badly in need of repair—by implication, it was broken if not merely "wrong." The report stressed its contention that the Senate needed to reflect its perceived original constitutional mandate of representing regional and provincial interests within the national legislature. One of the conclusions of the report was that the Senate had strayed from this purpose because of the influence of national parties over appointed members who ought, otherwise, to reflect the interests of their respective provinces.[7] One idea for overcoming the partisan influence of these political parties was the basis for a curious suggestion.

> It is recommended that Senators be physically seated by "provincial delegations," regardless of party affiliation. This physical arrangement alone would go a long way towards lessening the role of parties. If Senators are in physical proximity with fellow party members, there would be a strong incentive for them to represent their party in their speeches and provide Government or Opposition perspectives. If they are seated in provincial delegations, they would be inclined to represent provincial viewpoints. The seating in the Senate Chamber should be arranged in a horseshoe or some other appropriate way to reflect the provincial grouping.
>
> Each provincial delegation should select a chairman from its membership. The election of a chairman would strengthen the delegation's image. Senators would see aspiring for the position of regional chairman as a potential career as opposed to the allure of the House of Commons and a possible Cabinet post.[8]

The apparent absurdity of the premise of this specific part of the proposal highlights the general problems of not only the Triple-E concept but of many conventional schemes for reform of the Canadian parliamentary upper house. The belief that the pervasive influence of party and party discipline within a Westminster-model political system such as Canada (which is a necessary feature of that sort of system of responsible parliamentary government)[9] can be overcome by moving furniture is an obvious misconception. The further insinuation that a homogeneous provincial policy somehow can emerge from the suppression of party identification (though some scholars have noted the potential and actual decline of parties in this respect[10]) is another obvious oversimplification.[11] The implication appears to be that if Senators could, simply, stop thinking like Conservatives, Liberals, New Democrats, or other party members and, instead (and equally simply), start thinking like Albertans, Manitobans, Nova Scotians, or other provincial advocates, a natural consensus would emerge in that latter respect. Finally, it appears to be assumed that such an institution should attract politicians with an ambition limited to a regional parliamentarian who would not aspire to national office even if the alternative position became available.

Of course, these recommendations reflect the context and specific political culture that prompted and framed them. Anger over the policies of the government of Prime Minister Pierre Trudeau was intensified by the belief that his Liberal Party was indifferent to the economic and social environment concerns of Western Canada. A consensus of strong opposition to the National Energy Program (NEP) that would, among other purposes, redistribute revenue (enhanced by a "double taxation" mechanism) and control prices for resources such as oil (to the perceived detriment of Western provinces) was not only pervasive within Alberta but, also, an intense symbol of general feelings of political alienation from, and frustration with, the central Canadian government.[12] It therefore appears to reflect a vision that, had such a powerful institution of the central government existed to veto such a program, it could have, somehow, not only thwarted such a scheme but, also, could protect Alberta and its fellow Western provinces from future undermining of their interests. It also suggests a belief that this provincial consensus should, and could, be perpetuated so the traditional contest of parties would be replaced by the more genuine struggle of provincial and federal interests—all facilitated by moving the furniture.

In fairness, this specific suggestion was a small part of a much larger set of recommendations, including elections, increased powers, and equal provincial representation. But this specific example is, remarkably, similar to these other recommendations in an important respect. In general, they appeared to be supported by claims that, typically, were not directly justified by critical assessments of underlying political constructs. They generally did not examine, closely or deeply, the methodical premises of institutional examination, comparative scrutiny, philosophical inquiry, historical background, democratic theory, or other critical contributions to this sort of policy analysis. These recommendations generally appeared to have been grounded in popular perception and intuitive assumptions—in other words, upon the basis of wishful thinking.

Scholarly advocates of the Triple-E proposal and similar approaches to reform of the Senate of Canada have offered a more critical defense and assessment of these ideas.[13] But in many cases, the arguments have been motivated by separate frustrations, especially over themes and issues that are not directly relevant to the institutional role and performance of the Senate,[14] including popular anger over reports of corruption on the part of individual Senators. Reform of the Senate has not been perceived as a means for improving the overall parliamentary system but, instead, as a means toward achieving other political ends. Unfortunately, those ways of approaching the issue of Senate reform frequently result in underestimating or ignoring the true parliamentary context and potential of this political institution. They can fail to appreciate both limits and potential in this respect, simultaneously magnifying the Senate into the cause of, and solution to, the most profound and difficult challenges that the Canadian political system traditionally and consistently encounters. They also can fail to appreciate the fact that the Senate of Canada is, simultaneously, a distinctly Canadian institution and (more widely and equally distinctly) a second chamber of a Westminster-model parliamentary system with both the limits and possibilities that this fact presents.

Proposals for significant reform of the Senate of Canada typically have sought to address the themes of federalism and democracy. The comparative models most often cited for these reform proposals have been the Australian Senate and, to a lesser extent (because it is not part of a parliamentary system), the U.S. Senate.[15] The German Bundesrat also is a frequent object of comparison in this respect.[16] However, given both the institutional nature and purpose of parliamentary systems, generally, and the contentious relationship among various provinces and regions within Canada, agreement on creating a democratically elected Canadian upper house of parliament with strong legislative power appears to be unfeasible. More importantly, such an emphasis misses an opportunity for the Senate of Canada to become more truly (though, perhaps, more modestly than most proposals typically envision) effective in a way that does not undermine the parliamentary principle of responsible government and the broader Canadian principles (especially as constitutionally articulated) of a modern democratic system of government.

THE THESIS

This book departs from many other assessments of reform of the Senate of Canada by placing it within this broader context. Instead of perceiving that institutional body as a potential obstacle or solution to specific political issues and controversies within Canada, this book treats it as part of a broader category of parliamentary upper houses. It considers the wider context and implications of such reform and uses those factors as guiding principles toward formulating its recommendations. It especially emphasizes the purpose and relationship of the upper house within the Westminster model of parliamentary government and the potential for making the particular Canadian manifestation of that tradition function in a truly complementary and effective manner. That perspective is not merely based upon universal norms. It also is grounded upon an appreciation of the nature of the uniquely Canadian political system that it is intended to serve.

As a result, this book arrives at a conclusion that may appear to be wildly counterintuitive. While many other conventional proposals for Senate reform may seek inspiration from more contemporary examples (especially of political systems such as Australia, the United States, and Germany), this study finds inspiration in an institution that is not only old but that typically reflects a popular impression of themes that appear to be much more relevant to ancient and medieval ideals. Furthermore, that model institution frequently continues to be perceived as an institutional bastion of the interests of class and privilege that instinctively appear to be antithetical to the purposes of a modern liberal democracy. That inspiration is the modern British House of Lords.

The thesis for this study, generally stated, is that:

1. Any reform of the Senate of Canada should be undertaken in a manner that is consistent with the evolution of the parliamentary upper house of the Westminster tradition, particularly (but not exclusively) as exemplified by the British House of Lords;
2. It should be further consistent with the evolution of the values of liberal democracy, especially within the principles and scheme of parliamentary responsible government rather than its merely instrumental manifestation of the electoral process;
3. The liberal democratic context that guides its reform should bear a particular relation to the characteristics and challenges of modern Canada;
4. Therefore, a reformed Senate of Canada should remain an appointed body but, to the extent that is feasible, influenced by strong guidelines designed to produce a more diverse chamber, consistent with the unique diversity of Canada;
5. In an idealized version, it would consist of an indefinite number of members and those members would be selected with input from federal and provincial governments, federal Government and Opposition officials, and an independent commission;
6. In its ideal form, its members would exercise (either by express constitutional mandate or, more feasibly, through an unentrenched convention) a suspensive veto with special functions and protections that address the federal, linguistic, and multicultural characteristics of Canadian society;
7. While an actual constitutional amendment to achieve such changes may be highly unfeasible (if not practically impossible), a hypothetical constitutional amendment that conforms to these principles offers a theoretical model against which more modest reforms (or restraint from ill-advised reform) can be measured;

8. Certain reforms that would not require constitutional amendment (based upon internal procedural adjustments or informal agreements that are consistent with unentrenched principles of Westminster-style parliamentary government) could be implemented in ways that draw inspiration from that ideal theoretical model.

The British House of Lords (especially in the form in which it evolved as a result of reforms instituted throughout the 20th century) offers an institutional example that could be a particularly effective model for reform of the Senate of Canada. Using that model as a guide, though, could be considered strongly "unorthodox" because it starkly departs from many of the motives and expectations surrounding Senate reform, particularly involving themes of federalism, democracy, and legislative authority.[17] Meanwhile, the House of Lords traditionally has been associated with themes of aristocracy, inherited (and, later, appointed) office, and limited legislative authority.[18] Its association with class status and privilege, though largely rendered archaic, now, has been deemed to be particularly inappropriate and inconsistent with the values of a liberal democracy, as well as conventional critiques of class politics. Therefore, the House of Lords would appear, at least perfunctorily, to be the antithesis of the sort of model that reformers would want to emulate.

However, the themes that normally prompt desires and ideas for Canadian Senate reform merit reconsideration. For example, the Triple-E approach remains influential as a point of departure for many Senate reform proposals.[19] However, it can be strongly argued that the application of reforms designed to achieve the first two "E's" (equal and elected) are, ultimately, incompatible with achieving the final "E" of effectiveness. That incompatibility arises from two sources: first, it is based upon a lack of appreciation for the actual purpose of an upper house within a modern parliamentary system; second, it seeks to correct perceived conflicts within principle areas of Canadian politics (including the area of federalism) that should be and, often, have been better addressed through other forums and institutions of the Canadian political system. Particularly in terms of those motives and goals arising from Canada's federal system, basing proposals upon a seemingly unorthodox set of expectations relating to the role of the Canadian upper house in this respect also could allow federal politics to be more effectively grounded upon interstate, rather than intrastate, relations.

The House of Lords is the seminal example of a parliamentary upper house. Its evolution not only reflects fundamental changes within British society (including the diminished role of nobility and the class system) but, also, pragmatic experiences in parliamentary development and experience, even at times when it historically resisted those changes.[20] While it is not feasible to ignore controversial areas of Canadian politics (such as federal/

provincial relations and the role of bilingualism) and the reform proposals that they have inspired, it is highly advisable to promote reforms that actually address the primary purpose that *any* parliamentary upper house should address within a modern liberal democracy. The reformed House of Lords also may, at first, seem to be a counterintuitive (and, because of its conservative image, ironically "radical") model for reform of the Senate of Canada. But a critical evaluation of this model and its applicability to the Canadian parliamentary system should reveal important, though often overlooked, institutional lessons and considerations that a truly effective Senate reform ought to include.

THE APPROACH

This book will emphasize the general and specific contexts that have shaped the Canadian political system, the development and activity of the Senate of Canada as a uniquely Canadian institution, and the role and function of the parliamentary upper house as a universal institution. It will include methods of analysis derived from history, political culture, normative political thought, neo-institutional studies, and comparative politics. It also will take into account the particular background of the Senate of Canada, the theoretical premises of second chambers, the needs and aspirations of modern Canadian politics and society, and conventional proposals that have been previously proposed and promoted. The various chapters that follow this introductory one are designed to address this subject in such a systematic manner.

One way to think about the approach of this book is in the sense of someone who would have the power, *deus ex machina*, to descend upon the Canadian political system and its various principal actors and impose one's will upon them. After "knocking some heads together," that mythical authority would decree the ideal constitutional amendment for Senate reform and compel the federal government and all of the provinces to acquiesce in it. That ideal amendment would be based upon the ancient Greek principle of *archē* that reflects those "first principles" that reveal the essence of the thing being described.[21] In this case, the amendment would reflect those theoretical principles that reveal the ideal parliamentary upper house, both in itself and within the context of the political, institutional, historical, philosophical, and legal background that has shaped the Senate as a unique institution of Canada's Westminster model of parliamentary government. That amendment, once enacted, would allow the Senate to function in an optimal manner of the theoretical and contextual spirit that inspired it.

But one should not expect that "first principle" to be emulated as a matter of practical public policy. Therefore, the presentation of an idealized constitutional version of Canadian Senate reform will serve, instead, as a model for assessing this overall political environment. It will be contrasted against proposals for reform that previously have been proposed as well as suggested alternative (in some cases, strongly alternative) approaches for considering other reform measures. Finally, it will be used as a contrasting model for considering more pragmatic proposals for potential Senate reform, especially in the category of non-constitutional amendments that will be offered in the final chapter.

In that spirit, therefore, this book offers a specific, hypothetical, and idealized proposal for an amendment to the Constitution Act of 1867 relating to the power, composition, and functions of the Senate of Canada. That proposal is based upon those theoretical principles and historical developments relating to parliamentary upper houses that will be addressed throughout it. That model for reform also is intended to be, in the spirit of theoretical discourse, an exercise that will permit additional critical analysis. It will be understood that such an amendment almost certainly would never be capable of actual adoption, both because of the strong constraints on the constitutional amendment process within Canada but, also, because of the inevitable opposition of the diverse array of participants within this process (such as both large and small provincial governments), any of whom could block its approval.

With that acknowledgment, this hypothetical constitutional amendment will serve as a guide for a critical assessment. Therefore, chapters found within Part II will each begin by highlighting a select hypothetical constitutional section or clause and the related political theme that is affected by it. That particular part of that model constitutional change will, then, be explained in relation to the most pertinent methods of analysis. Thus the explanatory focus will vary from section to section and, thus, from chapter to chapter.

Prior to presenting that hypothetical constitutional amendment, Part I of the book will emphasize the theoretical, analytical, and historical context that ought to shape a consideration of the various potential approaches to Senate reform. Chapter 2 offers an overview of the overall context that is most pertinent to the reform of the parliamentary upper house within Canada. In particular, it will address the various influences that have shaped the structure and performance of the upper house as a general legislative phenomenon and as a specifically Canadian institution. That assessment will include a brief historical background and development of the upper house of the Westminster model in general and the Senate of Canada in particular. It will offer specific emphasis upon theoretical considerations such as the distinctive communities that these institutions are designed to serve, the reduced role of partisan political behavior that they encourage, their specialized roles and functions, and their relationship to the government of the day and the public that elects that government. It will consider the necessity of including federalism as part of Canadian reform of the upper house and it will acknowledge and assess recommendations that have been made by other noteworthy reform proposals.

Chapter 3 provides an analysis of the relationship of this parliamentary chamber to philosophical and ideological values that have shaped parliamentary development, revealing a pattern of activity that is rooted in political thought and culture. The chapter offers both an overview of these various traditions of thought in this respect and different ways in which they are manifested within the institutional relationship of lower and upper parliamentary chambers. It will emphasize the relationship of the upper house to liberal democratic theory and strongly suggest that, rather than advancing democratic norms and aspirations, an elected upper house actually could easily undermine more profound understandings and applications of democratic principles, especially by challenging the role of the lower house in establishing the legitimacy of parliamentary government as the ultimate institution of delegated sovereign authority.

Chapter 4 will provide historical motivation and setting for the Senate as it was originally conceived and as it initially developed. The Senate of Canada was envisioned as a legislative body that would imitate the House of Lords in certain ways but, also, reflect contemporary themes and concerns of Canadian politics and society in other ways. The intention of the Senate as an elite countervailing force to the popularly elected House of Commons was more than matched by the expectation that it would serve as a forum for regional interests and reflect provincial political objectives. The emphasis upon federalism imitated the example of the U.S. Senate, especially with the understanding that its composition would distinctly contrast with the principle of representation by population found within the Commons. However, during its first decade and beyond, the Senate behaved in distinct ways that reinforce many of the arguments that are offered within this book concerning its present status and future reform, especially regarding its overall deference toward the will of the government as supported by the lower house, its emphasis upon technical improvements of legislation and policy, and its self-conscious identity as a chamber that could reflect a different sort of diverse representation relating to Canadian society.

Chapter 5 will offer a more complete defense of the methodology of this book, especially in terms of its significance for institutional reform policy. It will place the approach of this book within the broader context of neo-institutional techniques that stress the actual influence of behavioralism, history, political culture, and the constitutional constraints of Canada's political and parliamentary system (among other influences) upon the outcomes of these sorts of reforms. It will stress predictable outcomes, including ones based upon rational choice assessments, rather than outcomes based upon assumptions that may not be as well considered or tested, either by comparative and historical example or appropriate theoretical applications.

Part II of the book will focus upon a critical application of this context, especially in terms of the idealized model for improvements to the Senate of Canada. Chapter 6 will be the first chapter that presents this hypothetical and highly theoretical constitutional amendment for reform of this chamber. That model will begin with changes to the formal powers of the Senate. Instead of the current authority that the Senate possesses to reject all legislation (though it is a power that is used extremely rarely), this proposal recommends a suspensive veto relating to non-money legislation (with the exception of bills pertaining to the official languages of Canada) and the power only to delay money bills that have been passed by the House of Commons. That proposal is based, largely, upon the same authority that was imposed upon the House of Lords as a result of the Parliament Bills of 1911 and 1949 and it assesses it in terms of the effect that such a reform has had upon that body in relation to its activity and effectiveness, including in contrast to parliamentary upper chambers that are otherwise empowered concerning legislation and policy, especially in relation to governments and their electoral mandates within the lower house.

Chapter 7 addresses the composition of the Senate. It advocates a body with unlimited (or, more precisely, indefinite) membership, which also is modeled upon the example of the House of Lords. That rationale is based upon factors concerning the diversity of its membership and activities that are hampered by the limited membership of the current Senate of Canada. That rationale also is more apparent in relation to additional concerns relating to the regional allotment of Senators and its association with Canadian federalism. It is further explored in terms of proposals that address the source of these appointments. It recommends that appointments ought to include the input of both federal and provincial authorities by addressing themes relating to the problems of partisanship, federalism, and political diversity. The ultimate purpose of this idealized proposal in terms of federalism is to acknowledge the centrality of that theme to Canadian politics (especially in terms of the need to acquire provincial support for a constitutional amendment) while demonstrating the dominance of interstate federalism in federal-provincial relations, thus critiquing reform schemes that seek to use the Senate as a means for enhancing intrastate federalism. Obviously, in the absence of such a constitutional change (which would be extremely unlikely), these arguments for expanding diversity would not be possible to the extent suggested by this theoretical model. Nonetheless, the underlying significance of this concept remains relevant and will be presented as such through this hypothetical device.

Chapter 8 addresses the contentious issue of maintaining a system of appointment rather than elections for choosing Canadian Senators. While this model will consider specific hypothetical arrangements for ensuring a procedure that allows for the sort of diverse appointments that are mentioned within chapter 6, it will devote particular attention to democratic theory (especially, but not exclusively, in terms of parliamentary democracy) and the counterintuitive claim that an appointed Senate actually is a highly preferable option from that democratic perspective. It will continue that theme by addressing the potentially enhanced role of the Senate as an ombudsman for Canadian society. This chapter will be critical of alternative proposals that insist upon an elected upper house as being essential to a democratic system of government and will, instead, demonstrate fallacies relating to that belief and approach, including the actual performance of elected upper houses. It also will advocate the desirability of ensuring greater variety in Senate appointments from the perspective of Canadian pluralism and the important theme of the country's diversity, including, but not limited to, Canadian multiculturalism. It will strongly assert a contention that, in terms of ensuring parliamentary democracy and promoting a more diverse representation, the appointment model remains a superior option.

Chapter 9 will address the idea of a "double majority" requirement (which previously has been proposed as a constitutional option, especially during the 1980s and 1990s) for legislation dealing with the official languages of Canada. That idea would require that all such votes must receive the support of not only a majority of the Senate but that overall majority must include a majority of Senators who are recognized as Anglophone and a majority of Senators who are recognized as Francophone. The chapter will place that proposal within the context of the importance of language to Canadian politics and its national identity as well as the importance of this theme for Quebec and its political, social, and cultural identity. It will argue that this exception to the suspensive veto may be potentially feasible for a constitutional amendment in this area because it could prove to be particularly desirable for acquiring the support of Quebec as well as for preserving a crucial linguistic compromise in Canada's constitutional development. This chapter also will address other structural features of the Senate, including in terms of its internal business and institutional culture. It will use that discussion to address the possibility and preference for non-constitutional changes that the Senate might be able to pursue (especially in terms of decreasing an environment of partisanship and encouraging the chamber's tradition of constructive improvements of legislation) through less formal political avenues. This chapter also will address a potential oversight role for the Senate in relation to the confirmation of certain executive nominations and the theoretical justification for such a role.

Finally, part III will conclude the book by addressing aspects of the Senate as it currently exists and as it could be practically improved, including an assessment of the actual contribution that it now makes (and could continue to make) to the legislative and policy processes within the Canadian parliamentary system. Chapter 10 will consider specific political events and criticisms relating to the Senate, including scandals arising from the actions of four Senators during the administration of Prime Minister Stephen Harper as well as his attempt to pursue unilateral change to that chamber by the federal government. It will consider whether these incidents provide any truly significant insights into the Senate, its function, and its potential for reform, especially within the context of more profound theoretical and practical understandings of that chamber. Chapter 11 will, then, provide more specific analysis and recommendations concerning the possibility of pursuing non-constitutional reform, particularly within the context of the conventions and other unentrenched features of Canada's constitutional tradition as it relates to the guiding principles of parliamentary government of the Westminster model. It also will raise the possibility that the absence of any formal reform may be preferable to constitutional or non-constitutional options, given the fact that the Senate of Canada already performs a highly positive and constructive (if undramatic) function within the Canadian political process.

DO NO EVIL

It has been suggested in the title of this book and the opening of this introductory chapter that an adaptation of the ancient Roman motto of *Senatus Populusque Romanus* (SPQR) into a modern Canadian version (*Senatus Populusque Canadensis*) might seem to make some sense within this overall context. However, a medieval English motto might be even more appropriate. The words *honi soit qui mal y pense* appear, prominently, on the staff of the Usher of the Black Rod of the Senate of Canada and they have been associated with the Senate. Their translation, "evil be to him who thinks evil,"[22] suggests an interesting perspective in this respect.

Negative impressions of the Senate often have prompted desires for its reform. However, it is arguable that the Senate performs functions that are much more effective and makes much more positive contributions to the Canadian political system and society than popular prejudice may admit. The problem may not be the Senate and its function; it may, instead, be unrealistic expectations and a desire to label the Senate as being, somehow, "evil" (to use a hyperbolic term) in not conforming to those expectations. While some reforms could be made through non-constitutional actions, truly meaningful reform ultimately will require constitutional amendment. Even if it could prove to be feasible, that process certainly would be difficult and, even, strained and avoiding it is politically understandable and, arguably, desirable. But a meaningful attempt at reform, whether through a constitutional amendment process or otherwise, also could provide a forum for airing many of the underlying concerns and frustrations that continue to confront Canada—even if they remain suppressed for the present.

Therefore, Senate reform should not be regarded as a means for "punishing" or "correcting" that institutional body but, instead, as an opportunity for exploring those themes that can make Canada a stronger and more vibrant nation. First, though, it requires a positive approach that is consistent with the motto on the staff of the Black Rod and thinking of Senate reform in terms of the "good" that it does and can continue to do, rather than as a source of "evil" that needs to be repressed. So this book will address this subject from the premise of that motto. It will assume that the Canadian upper house already demonstrates a certain (if modest) level of utility and suitability. Consequently, this book will approach that theme of reform in the spirit of enhancing an institution that already does some good and could do even more good. In that way, alone, this approach might be regarded as being fairly "unorthodox." The positive contributions and potential of the Senate of Canada are, therefore, the ultimate purpose of this book. Achieving that purpose requires a fair and rigorous assessment. This book will attempt to promote that goal.

NOTES

1. Paul A. Zoch, *Ancient Rome: An Introductory History* (Norman: University of Oklahoma Press, 1998), p. 32.
2. Marcus Tullius Cicero, *Selected Works*, Michael Grant, trans. (London: Penguin, 1971), pp. 101–156; S. E. Smethurst, "Cicero and the Senate," *The Classical Journal*, vol. 54, no. 2 (November 1958), p. 75.
3. C. E. S. Franks, *The Parliament of Canada* (Toronto: University of Toronto Press, 1987), pp. 193–194.
4. Randall White, *Voice of Region: The Long Journey to Senate Reform in Canada* (Toronto: Dundurn Press, 1990), p. 64.
5. Peter J. Smith, "The Ideological Origins of Canadian Confederation," *Canadian Journal of Political Science*, vol. 20, no. 1 (March 1987), pp. 10–12, 15–17, 21–23.
6. Alberta Legislative Assembly, *Strengthening Canada: Report of the Alberta Select Special Committee on Senate Reform* (Edmonton: Government of Alberta, 1985), pp. 1–4.
7. *Strengthening Canada*, pp. 4–5.
8. Ibid, pp. 38–39.

9. Robert Michels, *Political Parties: A Sociological Study of the Oligarchical Tendencies of Modern Democracies* (New York: The Free Press, 1968), pp. 78–81; Hans Daalder, "The Rise of Parties in Western Democracies," in *Political Parties and Democracy*, Larry Diamond and Richard Gunther, eds. (Baltimore: Johns Hopkisn University Press, 2001), pp. 40–51.

10. Russell J. Dalton and Martin P. Wattenberg, "Unthinkable Democracy: Political Change in Advanced Industrial Democracies," in *Parties without Partisans: Political Change in Advanced Industrial Democracies*, Russell J. Dalton and Martin P. Wattenberg, eds. (Oxford: Oxford University Press, 2002), pp. 3–18.

11. Alan S. Zuckerman, "Advancing Explanation in Comparative Politics: Social Mechanisms, Endogenous Processes, and Empirical Rigor," in *Comparative Politics: Rationality, Culture, and Structure* (Cambridge: Mark Iriving Lichbach and Alan S. Zuckerman, eds. (Cambridge: Cambridge University Press, 2009), pp. 72–95.

12. Barbara Jenkins, "Reexamining the 'Obsolescence Bargain': A Study of Canada's National Energy Program," *International Organization*, vol. 40, no. 1 (Winter 1986), pp. 146–153.

13. Roger Gibbins and Robert Roach, *A New Senate for a More Democratic Canada* (Calgary: Canada West Foundation, 2010), pp. 3–12; Gordon Gibson, "Challenges in Senate Reform: Conflicts of Interest, Unintended Consequences, New Possibilities," *Public Policy Sources,* vol. 83 (September 2004), pp. 3–34.

14. Robert J. Lawson, "Understanding Alienation in Western Canada: Is 'Western Alienation' the Problem? Is Senate Reform the Cure?" *Journal of Canadian Studies*, vol. 39, no. 2 (Spring 2005), pp. 127–155.

15. This theme is addressed in Michael Lusztig, "Federalism and Institutional Design: The Perils and Politics of a Triple-E Senate in Canada," *Publius*, vol. 25, no. 1 (Winter 1995), pp. 36–39, Peter McCormick, Ernest C. Manning, and Gordon Gibson, *Regional Representation: The Canadian Partnership* (Calgary: Canada West Foundation, 1981), and David E. Smith, *The Canadian Senate in Bicameral Perspective* (Toronto: University of Toronto Press, 2003), pp. 149–158.

16. Frederick C. Engelmann, "A Prologue to Structural Reform of the Government of Canada," *Canadian Journal of Political Science*, vol. 19, no. 4 (December 1986), pp. 672–674; Frederick C. Engelmann, Peter McCormick, and David Elton, *Alternatives: Towards the Development of an Effective Federal System for Canada* (Calgary: Canada West Foundation, 1978).

17. David Elton and Peter McCormick, *A Blueprint for Senate Reform* (Calgary: Canada West Foundation, 1990).

18. Sidney Bailey, ed., *The Future of the House of Lords* (London: Hansard Society, 1954), pp. 19–20.

19. Canada 200 Task Force, *Senate Reform and Constitutional Change* (Calgary: Canada West Foundation, 1992).

20. George Dangerfield, *The Strange Death of Liberal England* (London: Paladin, 1972), pp. 24–26.

21. Barry Sandywell, *Presocratic Philosophy* (New York: Routledge, 1996), vol. 3, pp. 142–144.

22. Stephanie Trigg, *Shame and Honor: A Vulgar History of the Order of the Garter* (Philadelphia: University of Pennsylvania Press, 2012), pp. 49–50.

Chapter 2

A Counterintuitive Approach to Senate Reform in Canada

INTRODUCTION

Proposals for significant reform of the Senate of Canada typically have sought to address the themes of federalism and democracy. In the case of the well-known "Triple E" ("equal, elected, and efficient") proposals of Alberta,[1] the practical effectiveness of the institution also has been a goal, particularly in terms of its ability to challenge the legislation of the government-controlled House of Commons. The comparative models most often cited for these reform proposals have been the Australian Senate and, to a lesser (because it is not part of a parliamentary system) extent, the U.S. Senate.[2] However, given both the institutional nature and purpose of parliamentary systems, generally, and the contentious relationship among various provinces and regions within Canada, a democratically elected Canadian upper house of parliament with strong legislative power is unfeasible. Furthermore, it misses an opportunity to become more truly (though, perhaps, more modestly than most proposals for reform typically would envision) effective in a way that does not undermine the parliamentary principle of responsible government and broader Canadian principles (especially as constitutionally articulated) of democratic government.

Instead, as previously noted, the British House of Lords (especially in the form in which it evolved as a result of reforms instituted throughout the 20th century) offers an institutional example that could be a much more effective model for reform of the Senate of Canada. That model, though, could be considered strange because it starkly departs from general motives and expectations surrounding Senate reform involving themes of federalism, democracy, and legislative authority.[3] Meanwhile, as also noted in chapter 1, the House of Lords traditionally is associated with themes of aristocracy, appointed or inherited office, and limited legislative authority.[4] Therefore, the House of Lords would appear to be the antithesis of the sort of model that reformers would want to emulate.

But if the themes that normally prompt desires and ideas for Canadian Senate reform merit reconsideration, the House of Lords offers the seminal example of a parliamentary upper house that needs to be critically assessed for the overall evolution of that institution to be understood and appreciated in a meaningful way. The House of Lords is the seminal example of a parliamentary upper house. Its evolution not only reflects fundamental changes within British society (including the role of nobility and the class system) but, also, pragmatic experiences in parliamentary development, even at times when it resisted those changes.[5] While it is not feasible to ignore controversial areas of Canadian politics (such as the relative power of provinces and the role of bilingualism) and the reform proposals that they have inspired, it is highly advisable to promote reforms that actually address the primary purpose that any parliamentary upper house is supposed to address within a modern liberal democracy.

So while the reformed House of Lords may, at first, seem to be a counterintuitive model for reform of the Senate of Canada, a critical evaluation of this model and its applicability to the Canadian parliamentary system should reveal some important, though often overlooked, lessons and considerations that a truly effective Senate reform ought to include. Furthermore, although the popularity and legitimacy of the House of Lords among the British public often is uncritically assumed to be low, there is considerable evidence that the image of the House of Lords has risen, especially since the 1999 reforms.[6] This improvement in public perception has included attitudes toward the effectiveness of the British second chamber in addressing policy, even in comparison with the elected House of Commons.[7] While popular opinion remains mixed within Britain, including many people supporting an elected House of Lords[8] (and opponents of the aristocratic Lords can be vocal but, also, often admit to positive features of that chamber[9]), support for its current role also exists[10] and populist attitudes should not be automatically assumed to prevail within that country—or, necessarily, within Canada.

BACKGROUND TO THE SENATE OF CANADA

The Senate of Canada has been subject to criticism and proposals for reform since its inception. Its most prominent predecessor was the colonial Legislative Council of Canada, which succeeded legislative councils for Upper and Lower Canada that had been created by the British government under the Constitutional Act of 1791. The original conception was to create a body that would review bills passed by the elected (through a limited franchise) members of the respective legislative assemblies. The Legislative Council was modeled upon the House of Lords in function, though not in composition, as its membership was not restricted to the nobility and, in general, members of this body frequently enjoyed a background and status similar to members of the lower house. Counselors were not conceived as being, strictly speaking, legislators but as advisors to the executive (much like members of the Executive Council) and were intended to serve as a "check" upon the more popular proclivities of the lower legislative body.[11]

Appointments to the Legislative Councils of both of the two largest provinces became dominated by small segments of the ruling families of both provinces: the Family Compact in Upper Canada and the Château Clique (consisting of the families of British mercantile families but, also, of some French *seigneurial* families) in Lower Canada. The result was a predictably conservative second chamber that was, often, friendly to the Governor but hostile to the elected chamber. At the same time, though, the Governor became increasingly dependent upon the Legislative Assembly for his essential support, thus leaving the Legislative Council relatively politically isolated. Furthermore, its 1849 rejection of a money bill adopted by the elected Legislative Assembly resulted in widespread support for its reform.[12]

In 1856, a bill was passed to make the Legislative Council elected and the composition of the upper house became similar to the composition of the lower house. Emboldened by that electoral mandate, on many occasions (including a supply bill in 1859), the Legislative Council directly opposed legislation passed by the Legislative Assembly, raising the possibility of long-term deadlock. Conflict also became more likely as the partisan characteristics of both chambers became more pronounced, especially when different factions controlled different chambers. Despite the disrepute that the Legislative Council often experienced as a result of these conflicts, there was no mention of abolishing it. The fundamental idea that a Westminster system must be a bicameral one appeared to prevail.[13]

As the idea of creating a permanent union of the British North American provinces, endowed with domestic self-government, became increasingly attractive, its legislative structure (upon which its government would be based) became an increasing concern. British North America lacked a land-based (with the exception of the early *seigneurs* of New France) and hereditary aristocracy. Therefore, it was not feasible to transfer the House of Lords model, directly, to the Westminster system that the Fathers of Confederation envisioned. Nonetheless, in that spirit, they sought to create an upper house of that system that reflected its general principles, though not its parochial features. The upper house would not be a mirror of the lower house; its members would represent a distinct segment (if not constituency) of the country.

Therefore, the Senate was intended to reflect elite interests (including successful entrepreneurs) that, like its neighbor to the South, had been instrumental in bringing this new country to the brink of economic viability as an autonomous (if not yet fully sovereign) political society.[14]

That distinction is significant. The Canadian House of Commons was intended to reflect the popular will and (in the spirit of British political developments) become the prime source of political legitimacy for Her Majesty's Government for Canada. Initially, in contrast to the House of Commons, the Canadian Senate's membership was dominated by elites with backgrounds in manufacturing, commerce, trade, banking, and large-scale agriculture. Over time, this aspect of the Senate's composition would be reflected, as well, by the members of the lower house so both chambers would come to have a composition that would reflect an economically elite bias.[15] But the principle that the membership of the Senate should not be a mere cipher of the House of Commons but ought to reflect a different constituency remains a foundational ideal.

The body that was created was intended to address concerns relating to regional representation, centered upon the two largest former provinces of Canada East (formerly Lower Canada and later to become, as it previously had been known, Quebec) and Canada West (formerly Upper Canada and later to become Ontario) plus the much smaller Maritime Provinces. A strong representation of, and protection for, the Francophone community, centered in Quebec, provided a particularly strong focus in that respect. Therefore, the final design of the Senate that emerged from those deliberations would establish a relatively fixed number of appointed Senators (an allowance was made for a few additional appointments under certain circumstances) who would have the same formal powers as the House of Lords, plus particular responsibility for certain private bills (such as divorce bills) and other parochial concerns.[16]

During the next century and a half of its existence, the Senate largely confined itself to the role of revising, amending, and improving legislation. Indeed, between 1867 and 1993, only seventeen House of Commons bills had been either blocked or attempted to be blocked by the Senate.[17] Most of its useful functions occurred outside of the direct legislative process. The Senate became particularly active in terms of public discourse, including an energetic period of investigative committees during the 1960s and 1970s. It very rarely opposed legislation and, when it did, never in a manner that undermined the overall democratic mandate of the government. It also was active in facilitating private interests, including as a liaison between business and government.[18]

Ironically, it was the perceived reticence of the Canadian Senate in its potential political role that led to one of the most outspoken calls for its reform—one that actually called for it to become more politically active and powerful than it has been.[19] Nonetheless, the actual role that the Senate has assumed has been consistent with the evolving expectations of the parliamentary upper house—expectations that are tied to foundational principles that bear examination in order to place this subject within a more meaningful and broad-ranging context. That role has largely continued within the unreformed Senate of the current century.

PARLIAMENTARY UPPER HOUSES IN THEORY

This conception was consistent with a traditional understanding of the role of a legislative second house. The idea of a "chamber of sober second thought" has been attributed to assemblies among early Germanic peoples. One account indicates that members of certain tribes, when considering an important matter, would conduct two assemblies in order to reach a decision. During the first assembly, they would consume alcohol so their deliberations would not lack "vigor" or "imagination." The second deliberation would occur during the next day, without alcohol, in order to reconsider the decision that they made when they were inebriated. That second counsel would not, necessarily, reject the first one but it typically would modify or amend aspects of the initial decision that might have seemed to be a good idea when inspired by drink but that might not appear to be most wise or prudent from the perspective of a clear mind.[20]

While that account provides an interesting (and possibly apocryphal) anecdote to explain the traditional reference to a legislative upper house as a deliberative body of "sober second thought," a more profound consideration of the theoretical arguments in favor of a second legislative chamber would be more instructive. The predecessor of the first legislative upper house, the House of Lords, was the council of leading members of the nobility who advised the medieval English king. This council was modeled upon the early medieval political custom, which was adapted from the practice of the Saxons, of an assembly of "wise men" or *witan* who advised their leader. This practice evolved into the establishment of the Witenagemot, an consultative body that eventually evolved within England, under William the Conqueror, into the *Curia Regis* or King's Court and which (along with the 13th-century development of the Barons of the Exchequer to advise the king on financial matters as well as the rise of other institutions of noble advisors) gradually evolved into the institution that would become the modern House of Lords.[21]

The evolution of the parliamentary system (especially upon the basis of the Westminster model) resulted in certain consistent features of an upper house. If the two chambers resembled each other, too closely, in purpose, composition, and function, bicameralism would be a redundant exercise.[22] It is this sense of difference that is essential for approaching upper house reform (including the Senate of Canada) in a truly effective manner.

Distinctive "Constituencies"

The most conspicuous and important of these distinctions is its "representation." As the parliamentary lower house increasingly became associated with representation of the broad social community (with or without a principle of popular representation), the upper house became a repository of representational difference—a transition that was anticipated to become more diverse through direct appointments.[23] The distinctive nature of that representation would vary among political systems: in England and, later, Great Britain, the upper house represented the landed aristocracy; in the United States, it was created to represent the state governments; in Australia, it was created to represent the states as electoral constituencies; in Japan, Italy, France, and other countries, it represents broader and/or specialized constituencies, including distinctive regions within an otherwise unitary system. Typically it would be practically restrained or legally forbidden from opposing the will of the lower house, especially once those chambers became associated most closely with, representation upon the basis of popular sovereignty.[24]

Interestingly, this perspective is consistent with aspects of modern republican thought—in particular, the good of the commonwealth and virtual representation. That last concept inspired political institutions that provided a means for different constituencies to participate (even if only indirectly) in the collective process of government.[25] In its modern adaptation, republican principles have inspired political institutions (as will be discussed in greater detail within chapter 3) that are designed to be inclusive of the representation of minority constituencies. Simultaneously, they are designed to prevent an unchecked authority of popular representation. In that sense, an unelected upper house is not anti-democratic but frequently seeks to prevent democratic institutions from overwhelming the interests and participation of segments of society not reflected by a popular majority.[26]

A somewhat simpler way of expressing that distinction between lower and upper legislative chambers may be the trend that the lower house is based upon a principle of representation by population while the upper house is consciously based upon "something else."[27] Upper houses are particularly prominent in providing this sort of representation within federal systems, especially in terms of subunit states and their particular interests. They also can promote the political and policy interests of the respective subunit governments—indeed, the U.S. Senate originally had been conceived as performing that precise role.[28] But, as in the American example, that role generally falters and subunit governments promote their interests, more effectively, through direct interaction with the central government.[29]

Therefore, the "something else" that has an even greater potential for representation by an upper house can be the multifaceted demographic of the overall society.[30] Institutions such as the Canadian Senate, even in an unreformed composition, have demonstrated a capacity for serving this purpose, such as a greater capacity to include women, the indigenous peoples of Canada, other ethnic and cultural groups, and individual persons who have made a distinctive contribution to Canada but who, otherwise, would have difficulty being elected to federal offices that remain dominated by middle-aged white men.[31] Interestingly (and for many people, ironically and surprisingly), the second chamber that has demonstrated a notable capacity in this respect is the British House of Lords—a feature that some reformers of that upper house have recognized and would like to enhance.[32]

Originally, the "something else" that the House of Lords represented was the titled aristocracy and, particularly, the agrarian sector of the economy that it traditionally dominated. That role began to diminish during the latter part of the 19th century[33] and, eventually, it disappeared during the 20th century, especially in the wake of economic shifts, the introduction of the suspensive veto, the creation of life peerages (including the severe restriction on participation by hereditary peers), and procedural innovations. Now, rather than being a "house of peers" or a "body of retired politicians," the upper house can be perceived as a "house of pluralism." The elevation of people who have distinguished themselves in many different professions, activities, or as representative of particular (and, often, underrepresented) groups within society has been a distinctive feature of the House of Lords that grew throughout the 20th century (especially through the appointment of life peerages[34]) and continues to serve an important function in the 21st century.[35]

Appointed chambers, such as the House of Lords (though it still retains some hereditary membership as well) generally are well positioned to serve this sort of consociational function, much as government cabinet appointments often have provided within many different political systems, including Canada. This reflection of diversity can be directed toward regional, ethnic, gender, linguistic, professional, social, and many other features of society. Upper houses can be particularly effective in providing this sort of representation when the electoral system fails to produce an accurate reflection of society in this respect and its visibility, at the center of the political system, enhances its significance at a national level. Politically, they can serve as a useful source of cabinet ministers from underrepresented geographical and demographical areas. They also provide opportunities to represent minorities, sometimes for constraining the potentially overbearing or abusive will of democratic majorities (consistent with republican principles) found within the lower house and government.[36]

Of course, the "something else" as originally conceived for the Canadian Senate was regional representation. It was not tied, directly, to a representation of provincial governments (unlike American state governments, which initially were responsible for sending Senators to the U.S. Congress, rather than popular elections, which were only introduced through by the 17th Amendment to the U.S. Constitution in 1913[37]) but it has come to be associated with federalism in that way. However, as this book will argue, a more meaningful role for both the British and Canadian upper chambers has been to provide a parliamentary forum to reflect the growing diversity of their respective societies, especially in a manner that their respective elected parliamentary chambers have been less successful in achieving.

Reduced Partisanship and Broader Public Interest Role

Members of upper houses typically behave in a less obviously partisan fashion than their counterparts in the lower house, especially within Westminster systems that are guided by the principle of "responsible government" upon which the power of the government rests. However, even in non-parliamentary systems, the upper house may be observed to behave in a manner that is considered to invoke more decorum and reduced degrees of overt partisan expression. That sense of decorum was considered to be an important, though largely idealized, feature of the Senate under the Roman Republic—a feature that Cicero highlighted in his speeches attacking Mark Antony before that body.[38] The U.S. Senate traditionally has embraced that image (at least in terms of the decorum of its internal proceedings), though the ultimate result of the process usually is a partisan outcome.[39] Parliamentary upper houses are even more inclined toward that perception and role.[40] Even elected parliamentary upper chambers, such as the Australian Senate, have demonstrated reduced partisanship.[41] This characteristic can be linked to the professional diversity that this sort of chamber can reflect. The appointment of members upon the basis of distinguished accomplishments in public service (e.g., former government officials and senior civil servants) and the private sector has been facilitated by this practice. This factor lends itself to conditions that arguably lead to the encouragement of legislative and extra-legislative activity that transcends conventional politics.

An interesting symbol of an inclination toward non-partisan accommodation within the upper house is the Cross Benches of the House of Lords. The reservation of a specified, and prominent, location for those peers also has been useful for distinguishing those members of the upper house who have been elevated in consideration of distinctive service to the country, especially in offices that have served the public good outside of the conventional political process. Australia's upper house also has adopted this practice of distinguishing independent and minor-party members found within both chambers of the federal parliament, as well as among state legislatures of that country.

Specialized Roles and Functions

Upper houses typically are identified through specialized functions. Although they play a role in the legislative process, within parliamentary systems they generally (with the notable exception of Italy) are expected or required to defer to the overall legislative authority of the lower house. As a result of that deference, the upper house typically focuses its practical energy upon specific aspects of the process, often in an indirect or supporting role. The informational and publicizing work of investigative committees is an excellent example, particularly as those same committees in the lower house often are constrained by more partisan considerations.[42]

Unless it is intended to mirror the legislative activity of the lower house (like the U.S. Senate), an upper house should address other legislative and political activities that enhance the political process in ways that the lower house finds more constrained or difficult to do. One feature that often has been noted is the capacity of the upper house to engage in less partisan committee activities. Those committees typically pursue activities that result in constructive revision of legislation that has been sent to it from the lower house—partly a result of a sense of distinctiveness from the political class that occupies the lower chamber.[43]

In that respect, the upper house also can serve an effective ombudsman role. Its members often have more latitude and time to provide assistance to citizens' groups, individual advocates, or members of the public seeking information or assistance.[44] Of course, members of that chamber also may become involved in lobbying efforts that, again, are not constrained by government positions or policy, which can be perceived in a negative way, especially by the general public. Furthermore, second chambers often are assigned (constitutionally or in practice) special roles that are associated with guarding constitutional principles, human rights, and the integrity of the judicial system.[45] This sort of specialized function can be powerful.

Separation from the Government

The upper house of a parliamentary system, especially within the Westminster model, characteristically has a more distant relationship with the government of the day than the lower house. This distinction results from the fact that, under the principles of responsible government, the political survival of a government is not dependent upon or, even, affected by the actions of the upper house—again, chambers such as the Italian Senate represent an exception to this trend. "Strong" bicameral systems are not inconsistent with parliamentary government *per se* but only with "minimal winning cabinets" and the executive dominance that they support.[46]

This situation allows the upper house and its members to become disentangled from the political pressures and constraints that the lower house and its members generally experience (including protecting private and minority interests in a manner that members of the lower house frequently feel constrained to do[47]), particularly within a parliamentary system. Party discipline must be enforced within the first chamber in order for a parliamentary government to maintain its ability to govern. Furthermore, that party discipline and the loyalty that it demands are prerequisites for ministerial advancement within a government, thus imposing additional constraints upon legislative activity that actually make members of that lower chamber (which serves as the conventional institutional route to political advancement, especially of a ministerial nature) less independent and, thus, much less effective as individual legislators.[48]

Parliamentary second chambers, whose members frequently (but not always) have an extended tenure of office, generally are not as dependent upon the government and its executive leadership for their positions. Although political patronage often accounts for initial nominations or appointments to that body, members of upper houses tend to be less susceptible to the pressures exerted by the head of government, who also happens to be head of the governing political party.[49] Members of that chamber, including members from the government party, are freer to take actions that may not accord with current government policy without the risk that a "rebellion" would entail for their counterparts in the lower house.[50] That characteristic has been described as the capacity to "embarrass" the government (especially over initiatives that are not part of its electoral mandate and may meet with general public disapproval) and it has been noted as being particularly strong within non-elected chambers.[51] This condition creates opportunities for increased freedom of political activity, including of the legislative, publicity, and investigative sort associated with the theme of "specialized roles and functions."

These theoretical attributes of the upper house, especially from a parliamentary perspective, are critical considerations for any reform plan. Unless the objective is to create an effective rival of the lower house and, consequently (at least for parliamentary systems), the government, the most effective role for an upper house is to address political activities that complement and enhance, rather than mirror, the legislative process. That chamber can serve additional political and social functions, including affirming pluralism within society, publicizing the governmental process and citizens' interests, and investigating policy topics and implications in a more independent setting.

NEO-INSTITUTIONAL CONSIDERATIONS

Political institutions can, by themselves, shape political behavior. Many proposals for reform of political institutions (including the Senate of Canada) focus upon expected policy outcomes, rather than broader considerations of the effect of institutional change as an influence by itself. [52] Much of this Senate analysis has emphasized formal structure and process that, while highly useful, is consistent with a traditional approach that is limited to describing origins but not considering outcomes. Both aspects of this approach need to be given more attention from both a theoretical and a practical perspective.

Institutional culture is one of those considerations. Institutions can shape, and be shaped by, political culture. As explained within chapter 4, part of that institutional culture can be shaped by the distinction between a presidential system of non-responsible government and a parliamentary system of responsible government. Canadian politicians adhere to the rules of that system of government (and Canadian citizens expect them to adhere to those rules) because of the strength of the institutional culture that the system imposes upon them.[53] The expectations that are, consequently, created by them result in a pressure to conform that occurs not only within Canada but across various political systems.[54]

One of these expectations is the affect that appointment, as opposed to election, can have upon members of the upper house of a parliamentary system. Elected office confers a sense of "mandate" upon the office holder, while appointment in one chamber in relation to an elected chamber imposes a sense of "constraint." That factor also has contributed to reluctance, even among reformers, to introduce elections for parliamentary second chambers.[55] Consciousness of the exclusive electoral mandate of the British House of Commons evolved into a strong convention within the House of Lords during the latter part of the 19th century and, when it was violated, prompted a sense of public outrage that facilitated the threat of strong and unusual political action, culminating in the enshrining of that convention within the Parliament Act of 1911, as well as a more informal yet still powerful articulation of that principle within an agreement that would become known as the Salisbury Convention (an agreement that the British upper house will not oppose legislation that is part of a current government's electoral mandate)[56] and which is addressed in greater detail within chapter 10.

The relationship between this approach and rational choice theory suggests a systemic tendency to seek alternative institutions for promoting certain goals—which second chambers can provide.[57] A meaningful assessment of this claim requires additional data but the principles it describes appear, even in the absence of that data, to be a reasonable approach to exploring the potential affect that institutional reform may have upon political behavior. Some of that assessment can be derived from a consideration of other institutional factors, including the federal system of shared sovereignty that has been traditionally tied to the creation of the Senate.

Federalism

Bicameral systems typically are designed to address a fundamental feature or division within a society. In the case of Canada, the system was designed to address the regional distinctions among Lower Canada, Upper Canada, and the peripheral Maritime Provinces. Eventually, this focus would be augmented by the more specific role of the provinces within the Canadian federal system. Therefore, it is practically impossible for any proposal for substantial Senate reform to ignore the demands of federalism and the aspirations of the federal subunits.[58]

The Senate of Canada originally was conceived, in part, as an institutional representative of regional interests. It has been suggested that its composition was deliberately intended to reflect and, in some way, extend the role that Legislative Councils had played for the pre-Confederation provinces. Those provincial councils had been abandoned with the interesting exception of Quebec. Members of the Quebec provincial upper house represented the same 24 districts that were the basis for the appointment of Senators from that province to the Canadian upper house. Ultimately, though, that regional balance for the country was replaced with a more specific emphasis upon provincially allotted seats, though that provincial representation was constitutionally framed in a regional context—a framing that may have been critical to the ultimate success or failure of those negotiations.[59] Thus the relationship between the Canadian Senate and its federal system (superficially similar to the U.S. Senate and, arguably, the Senate of Australia) has remained an inextricable association, especially for reformers.[60]

Beyond this parliamentary institution, two approaches (which are elaborated within chapter 7) have emerged for addressing the overall relationship between Canada and its provinces: interstate federalism and intrastate federalism. The former model is grounded upon relationships *between* central and subunit governments, requiring negotiation of different objectives upon the basis of competing areas of sovereign authority, often through executive[61] and judicial institutions.[62] The latter model is one in which the subunit governments are provided direct representation *within* the institutions of the central government so they can influence the decisions and preferences that the central government pursues within the realm of its sovereign authority,[63] which is an arrangement found within the German federal system[64] and often pursued through political parties.[65] Bicameral legislatures often provide for some measure of intrastate participation of subunits, such as the original purpose of members of the U.S. Senate (prior to the shift toward their popular election as a result of a constitutional amendment in 1913) as representatives who were selected, directly, by their respective state governments.[66]

Reform of the Senate of Canada that could obtain a level of support necessary for the requisite constitutional amendment would, inevitably, need to include provisions related to enhancing its role in relation to intrastate federalism, though such extensive reforms could detract from an emphasis upon interstate federalism that is more appropriate (as argued within chapter 6) to the context of the evolving nature of Canadian federalism.[67] In fact, it has been suggested that plans for reform of the Senate that emphasize its role in facilitating federal relationships would become a distraction from more effective means of addressing those relationships.[68] Nonetheless, that association has proven to be so firmly rooted that it probably would be practically impossible to obtain constitutional consensus or even informal political agreement on any such plan that did not attempt to deal with greater provincial input—if not the more contentious desire of smaller provinces to achieve greater representation for themselves within that reformed upper house.

CONVENTIONAL REFORM PROPOSALS FOR THE SENATE OF CANADA

The earliest reform proposals for the Senate of Canada focused especially upon regional representation. This issue was exacerbated by the addition of new provinces, not only expanding current regions (such as the Maritime Provinces) but creating new regions in the Prairies and the Pacific Coast. Meanwhile, the two largest and most dominant provinces, Ontario and Quebec, retained their constitutional status as distinct regions, despite an increasing tendency among citizens of the other regions to regard these two provinces, jointly, as constituting a Central Canada region that share economic advantages over the "periphery" of the country.[69]

Nonetheless, as already noted, any reasonably successful proposal for a constitutional amendment or, even, an informal political arrangement relating to Senate reform would need to include some provision for intrastate federalism. The federal government's most comprehensive Senate reform proposal was contained in Bill C-60 in 1978. This proposal was based upon recommendations made by the Pepin-Robarts Task Force on Canadian Unity under the government of Pierre Trudeau. It was prompted by, and part of, a broader constitutional strategy to address federal-provincial relations through general institutional reform as part of a scheme to adjust the division of powers within the country.[70] The report's conclusions called for the transformation of the Senate into a new second chamber to be called the House of the Federation. It addressed provincial concerns by stipulating that half of the members of this new upper house would be appointed by provincial governments and the other half by the House of Commons—in reality by the government.[71]

Bill C-60 also addressed concerns about greater regional and provincial representation by providing for over-representation of smaller provinces, though Quebec and Ontario would continue to dominate the distribution of seats. In terms of legislative powers, a complex scheme of suspensive vetoes would be introduced, depending upon the nature of the legislation and its relationship to federal and provincial interests. It also introduced the previously mentioned "double majority" procedure requiring a majority of both Anglophone and Francophone members for passage of any legislation dealing with official languages.[72] Ultimately, this scheme was abandoned for lack of support among many provinces, which perceived it as solely a federal conception and project.[73] This scheme was inspired (especially in terms of its complex diversity of suspensive veto schemes) by the German upper house, the Bundesrat, with membership of varying numbers (depending upon state populations) is appointed by the respective state (*länder*) governments, though that model ultimately failed to be adopted by Canadian reformers.[74]

Despite the failure of Bill C-60, the model of the Bundesrat has inspired other schemes for Senate reform in Canada.[75] However, it has been noted that this particular bicameral scheme may not translate well to the Canadian political system as it was created to reflect the particular political culture of post–World War II German federalism. In particular, it has been cited as an example of a consociational model that is much more familiar to Germany (and certain other countries) than it is to Canada. Also, it may focus upon a form of intrastate relationship between the federal and provincial governments that could pose a series of other potential problems and distract attention from the more useful work that a reformed Canadian upper house could do.[76]

As asserted previously, perhaps the most well-publicized Senate reform proposal has been the so-called "Triple-E" plan that was created, and has been most strongly (but not exclusively) embraced, by Alberta governments. Variations of the plan have been proposed since its genesis (especially the 1985 recommendation of the Alberta Select Committee on Senate Reform)[77] but its essential features have included equal representation for each province (with lesser representation for the federal territories), direct elections for Senators within each province, and power to oppose non-budget and taxation legislation, especially an outright veto over bills that affects provincial jurisdiction.[78] Another Alberta select committee modified that final "E" by shifting to a suspensive veto the powers of this reformed Senate over ordinary (non-money) legislation except for ones that affect provincial jurisdictions.[79]

The initial event that prompted the development of the Triple-E plan was the 1980 adoption, by the Trudeau government, of the National Energy Policy that would increase federal regulation and revenue over the energy sector, including Alberta petroleum—an initiative that was perceived as part of a broader shift in federal economic strategy.[80] That incident, however, symbolized larger grievances of regional alienation and resentment over the demographic and economic dominance of central Canada and its resultant dominance over federal legislation, policy, and public administration.[81] The demand for equal (or, at least, more equitable) representation among the provinces (rather than merely among the regions) has become not only a primary demand for such reform but, also, a practically non-negotiable feature. It is a feature that the large provinces of Ontario and Quebec would be extremely unlikely to accept, thus making the possibility of enshrining this proposal within a necessary constitutional amendment equally unlikely. Nonetheless, the Triple-E proposal has remained one of the most consistently recognized and promoted recommendations for Senate reform, making it extremely difficult to ignore within the context of the broader deliberations on this subject.[82]

One of the recommendations that emerged from the Charlottetown Accord, which attempted to balance conflicting demands and goals of the Western provinces (particularly the Prairie Provinces) and Quebec (especially its desire for constitutional recognition as a "distinct society"), was yet another proposal for Senate reform. In many ways, it imitated the Triple-E proposal, particularly in recommending equal provincial representation in the Senate and that Senators be chosen through a process of either direct or indirect election at the provincial level. It also adopted the House of Federation plan that would require a "double majority" of votes by Anglophone and Francophone Senators for language legislation—with failure to achieve such a double majority constituting an absolute veto of that legislation. It also proposed a scheme for guaranteeing representation of aboriginal Canadians within the Senate. In terms of the powers of this reformed upper house, it advanced a version of the suspensive veto that would require a deliberate override by the House of Commons, the ability to delay money bills, and an absolute veto over energy legislation. The overall failure of the Charlottetown Accord resulted in the abandonment of this proposal as well.[83]

The inclusion of a provision for an elected upper house (either directly by the public or indirectly through provincial legislatures) reflected the powerful political appeal of the electoral process as a component of any Senate reform proposal. The demand for an elected Canadian upper house (similar demands have been raised regarding the upper house in other countries, including the United Kingdom) has been supported by the claim that such elections would confer legitimacy upon that chamber. Any other arrangement would be regarded by many critics as being unacceptable because it would "undemocratic."[84]

The most common counter-argument to that demand has been expressed in terms of a different concept of legitimacy—this one associated with the parliamentary principle of "responsible government." An elected Senate would be able to oppose the government that, under this system, derives its authority from the will of the elected House of Commons. The inability of the government to pass its principal legislation would render it unable to function and, thus, compel it to resign.[85] But if that government continues to enjoy an electoral mandate in the lower house, any alternative government also would be unable to exercise power. The result would be an ungovernable system or, at best, frequent and potentially distracting national elections. The Australian "Governor General's Crisis" of 1975 in which this very situation occurred when the Australian Senate defeated legislation passed by the House of Representatives (thus initiating a controversial dismissal of the government and a contentious election) is a particularly prominent example of this concern.[86]

The suspensive veto (which the Australian Senate does not exercise) offers a response to that objection. However, even a weakened upper house has been statistically proven to promote parliamentary government instability through delaying legislation and policy implementation.[87] Furthermore, the use of elections as a means for selecting representatives to the second chamber fails to address another significant complaint of critics of the Canadian upper house: its "elite" dominance. The composition of the Senate has been, historically and currently, dominated by men from the high end of the nation's economic stratus, especially (but not exclusively) over-representing the business community.[88]

A typical populist argument is that elections would make it more likely that Senators who are more representative of "ordinary Canadians" would become members. That argument ignores the fact that the demographic and professional composition of the Senate has largely mirrored the composition of the elected House of Commons. Furthermore, the currently appointed Senate has been more effective (if only marginally) in providing representation for indigenous Canadians, women, and other minority groups. The idea that elections (which generally can be successful contested only by people with the requisite background and resources) will produce "non-elite" Senators requires much more analysis than most criticisms provide—not to mention the very use of "elite" as a pejorative term, rather than as a description of high-quality preparation and ability to assume office and exercise political responsibility.[89]

Numerous other recommendations have been made for variations of Senate reform in Canada. A thoroughly comprehensive exposition and critical assessment of all of these recommendations would be too expansive to be feasible within the context of a single chapter. However, a summary of this body of scholarship and policy proposals reveals similar patterns in their overall approaches.[90] Some of the most important studies were composed during the early and middle 20th century and have included overviews of the history, structure, and work of the Senate, including Robert A. MacKay's *The Unreformed Senate of Canada*[91] and F. A. Kunz's *The Modern Senate of Canada*.[92] A more pointed critique of this chamber was offered in Colin Campbell's *The Canadian Senate: A Lobby from Within*, which drew negative attention to the lobbying efforts of many Canadian Senators and the subsequent liaison function that many Senators were found to have served between the government and various business interests. This activity, Campbell has claimed, undermines certain liberal democratic principles and expectations especially equal treatment of all citizens (and not just for privileged interests) and non-preferential access to the governmental process, thus raising doubts about the legitimacy of even a reformed Canadian upper house.[93]

A series of governmental (including legislative) recommendations also have been made. In addition to the ones that have already been addressed, the Canadian Parliament's Molgat-Cosgrave Report suggested that Senate reform should deemphasize the theme of federalism and, instead, focus upon Canada's "natural communities" while empowering the upper house through the suspensive veto.[94] The earlier Molgat-McGuigan Report challenged the idea of an elected upper house and argued that such a body would fail to achieve diversity in representation.[95] The Beaudoin-Dobbie Report was more specific and ambitious, recommending a system of proportional representation but with a scheme to exclude direct involvement of political parties.[96] It also recommended the suspensive veto and double majority options.[97]

Other work on this subject has placed it more firmly within its larger political context. In particular, C. E. S. Franks has been diligent in noting the institutional consequences, anticipated and unanticipated, of Senate reform, including its preparatory role in the process of examining legislation.[98] His research has placed this subject within a broader critical perspective, noting, especially, the relationship between the Senate and the principles of parliamentary government, including the effect of elections for the Senate on voter participation, political influence through campaign contributions, and party loyalty.[99] He also has addressed the potential problems of approaching federal-provincial relations from that basis, including an exacerbation of an asymmetrical relationship in this respect as well as the potential effect upon conflict between these two sovereign levels of government.[100]

Likewise, Donald Smiley and Ronald Watts provided a comparative analysis of this subject in *Intrastate Federalism in Canada* (originally a report for the Royal Commission on the Economic Union and Development Prospects for Canada) that raised similar questions and addressed the prospect of reforms that could improve the desultory record of the current Senate in facilitating federal-provincial relations, especially in comparison to the practical successes of executive federalism.[101]

A particularly difficult problem encountered by all Senate reform proposals is the need to accomplish most conceived changes through the very difficult constitutional amendment process. Reforms that do not require constitutional amendment (such as informally accepting the results of provincial elections through federal appointment of the successful candidate of such a process) have experienced only limited success. Most serious recommendations on this subject must take into account the need to propose changes that can achieve a consensus of acceptance among the various provinces, groups, and other interests, as well as the federal Canadian government and the Canadian populace in general. The ongoing cleavages within Canadian society and among its different regions pose a formidable obstacle to that ultimate goal. The hypothetical constitutional amendment proposed by this book is, therefore, offered solely as an *ideal* model that reflects the theoretical principles and lessons associated with parliamentary upper houses in general. The additional proposal for an informal agreement, consistent with the spirit of Canada´s unentrenched constitutional tradition, may present a more feasible possibility within the final chapter.

THEORY AND CONTEXT MATTER

Reform of the Senate of Canada, if it is to be truly meaningful and successful, cannot merely react against specific grievances. This reaction has been particularly apparent during the series of corruption charges that plagued that body in relation to certain Senators (especially appointees of Prime Minister Stephen Harper) who were accused of abusing their living allowances, expense accounts, and other institutional benefits.[102] Of course, corruption in office is not unique to any political institution and the Canadian political system (including its House of Commons) historically has experienced its own problems in that respect.[103] The Triple-E proposal is another example of a reform approach that is, arguably, more reactive (initially in response to the federal government's energy policies that greatly angered voters in Alberta but, also, as a response to political marginalization throughout Western Canada) than proactive.

Upper house reform ought to commence from a perspective of opportunity, rather than mere disgruntlement. Instead of addressing those aspects of the Senate of Canada that are perceived to be "wrong" or "broken," a better starting point might be to focus upon both those features that do appear to function in a positive and constructive manner (especially in terms of contributing to the overall function and purpose of parliamentary democracy) and which also have the potential to perform in a more effective manner—again, from the perspective of parliamentary democracy and the way it is intended to function. That approach also needs to take into consideration the specific themes that have dominated Canadian politics and society and consider ways that this sort of reform can truly complement broader goals of political harmony and efficacy without unnecessarily disrupting its functionality.

This book offers an approach that is particularly conscious of the institutional constraints and opportunities offered by the fact that Canada's political system is an example of the Westminster model of parliamentary government. It perceives the Senate as an institution that can make appropriately deferential and complementary contributions for reconciling challenging themes that Canada perpetually encounters, including in terms of federal tensions, multicultural aspirations, bilingual accommodations, and the overall goal of achieving a strong parliamentary democracy that does not undermine its own central premise of responsible government. In order for any reform proposal to achieve good, it also should seek to avoid doing unnecessary harm. Therefore, it is advisable to consider, further, the theoretical application, institutional approach, and historical context that any reform proposal should include.

NOTES

1. Canada 2000 Task Force, *Senate Reform and Constitutional Change* (Calgary: Canada West Foundation, 1992).

2. This theme is addressed in Michael Lusztig, "Federalism and Institutional Design: The Perils and Politics of a Triple-E Senate in Canada," *Publius*, vol. 25, no. 1 (Winter 1995), pp. 36–39; Peter McCormick, Ernest C. Manning, and Gordon Gibson, *Regional Representation: The Canadian Partnership* (Calgary: Canada West Foundation, 1981), and David E. Smith, *The Canadian Senate in Bicameral Perspective* (Toronto: University of Toronto Press, 2003), pp. 149–158.

3. David Elton and Peter McCormick, *A Blueprint for Senate Reform* (Calgary: Canada West Foundation, 1990),

4. Sidney Bailey, ed., *The Future of the House of Lords* (London: Hansard Society, 1954), pp. 19–20.

5. George Dangerfield, *The Strange Death of Liberal England* (London: Paladin, 1972), pp. 24–26.

6. Alexandra Kelso, "Reforming the House of Lords: Navigating Representation, Democracy, and Legitimacy at Westminster," *Parliamentary Affairs*, vol. 59 (2006), pp. 563–581.

7. Meg Russell, *Reforming the House of Lords: Lessons from Overseas* (Oxford: Oxford University Press), pp. 238–253.

8. Patrick Brione, "Survation Polling for *Daily Mirror* Shows Support for the House of Lords but Also Reform," *Survation*, July 30, 2015, http://survation.com/public-still-support-reform-for-house-of-lords/.

9. Bagehot [editorial], "A Democratic Embarrassment," *The Economist*, June 13, 2015, http://www.economist.com/news/britain/21654084-house-lords-aged-over-crowded-and-increasingly-effective-democratic-embarrassment.

10. Peter Oborne, "Ed Miliband's Plan for an Elected House of Lords Would Mean an Upper House Dominated by Ukip," *The Telegraph*, November 3, 2014, http://www.telegraph.co.uk/ news/politics/ukip/11205797/Ed-Milibands-plan-for-an-elected-House-of-Lords-would-mean-an-upper-house-dominated-by-Ukip.html; Ipsos MORI, House of Lords Survey, December 13, 2007, https://www.ipsos-mori.com/researchpublications/researcharchive/250/House-of-Lords-Survey.aspx.

11. Phillip Alfred Buckner, *The Transition to Responsible Government* (Westport, CT: Greenwood Press, 1985), pp. 275–276.

12. Bruce Hodgins and Don Wright, *Federalism in Canada and Australia: The Early Years* (Waterloo, ON: Wilfred Laurier University Press, 1978), pp. 25–28; Robert A. MacKay, *The Unreformed Senate of Canada* (Toronto: McClelland and Stewart, 1963), pp. 20–32; Alan L. Hayes, *Anglicans in Canada: Controversies and Identity in Historical Perspective* (Urbana: University of Illinois Press, 2004), pp. 60–62.

13. Edward Kylie, "Constitutional Developments, 1840–1867," in *Canada and Its Provinces* (Toronto: University of Toronto Press, 1914), vol. 5, pp. 139–141; George R. Parkin, *The Makers of Canada: Sir John A. MacDonald* (Charleston: Bibliobazzar, 2009), pp. 74–75.

14. Desmond Morton, *A Short History of Canada* (Toronto: McClelland and Stewart, 2006), pp. 92–93; Frederick Vaughan, *The Canadian Federalist Experience* (Montreal and Kingston, ON: McGill-Queen's University Press, 2003), pp. 56–64; MacKay, pp. 32–50.

15. Colin Campbell, *The Canadian Senate: A Lobby from Within* (Toronto: MacMillan, 1978), pp. 125–127.

16. Robert MacGregor Dawson and Norman Ward, *Dawson's The Government of Canada* (Toronto: University of Toronto Press, 1987), pp. 189–190.

17. J. Lynch-Staunton, "The Role of the Senate in the Legislative Process," *Canadian Parliamentary Review* (Summer 2000), pp. 10–14.

18. F. A. Kunz, *The Modern Senate of Canada* (Toronto: University of Toronto Press, 1965), pp. 262–266; Smith, pp. 110–119.

19. Lusztig, pp. 38–39.

20. Kunz, p. 4; Bailey, p. 7. This example and metaphor was repeated by Sir John A. Macdonald during the debates on the creation of the Senate of Canada, *Parliamentary Debates on the Subject of the Confederation of the British North American*

Provinces: Third Session, Eighth Provincial Parliament of Canada (Quebec: 1865), pp. 35–36.

21. William Stubbs, *The Constitutional History of England* (Oxford: Clarendon Press, 1887), vol. 1, pp. 138–141.

22. S. C. Patterson and A. Mughan, eds., *Senates: Bicameralism in the Contemporary World* (Columbus: Ohio State University Press, 1999), pp. 3–9.

23. Ivor Jennings, *The Approach to Self-Government* (Cambridge: Cambridge University Press, 1956), p. 113.

24. *World Directory of Parliaments* (Geneva: Inter-Parliamentary Union, 1999).

25. Per Mouritsen, "Four Models of Republican Liberty and Self-Government," in *Republicanism in Theory and Practice*, Iseult Honohan and Jeremy Jennings, eds. (London: Routledge, 2005), pp. 17–38.

26. Philip Petit, *Republicanism: A Theory of Freedom and Government* (Oxford: Oxford University Press, 1997), pp. 171–205.

27. Saul Levmore, "Bicameralism: When are Two Decisions Better than One?" *International Review of Law and Economics,* vol. 12 (1992), pp. 145–162; Gerhard Loewenberg and Samuel C. Paterson, *Comparing Legislatures* (Boston: Little, Brown, 1979), p. 121; George Tsebelis, "Decision Making in Political Systems: Veto Players in Presidentialism, Parliamentarism, Multicamearlism, and Multipartyism," *British Journal of Political Science*, vol. 25, no. 3 (July 1995), pp. 309–310.

28. James Madison, "Federalist No. 51," in Alexander Hamilton, James Madison, and John Jay, *The Federalist Papers*, (New York: SoHo, 2010), pp. 149–150; Thomas H. Hammond and Gary J. Miller, "The Core of the Constitution," *American Political Science Review,* vol. 81 (1987), pp. 1,155–1,174.

29. Peter Aucoin, "Regionalism, Party, and National Government," in *Party Government and Regional Representation in Canada* (Toronto: University of Toronto Press, 1985), p. 150.

30. Meg Russell, "What are Second Chambers For?" *Parliamentary Affairs*, 54(2001), pp. 443–446.

31. MacKay, pp. 159–160; Smith, pp. 80–83.

32. Royal Commission on the Reform of the House of Lords, *A House for the Future* (London: Her Majesty's Stationery Office, 2000), p. 8; Meg Russell, *Reforming the House of Lords* (New York: Oxford University Press, 2000), pp. 101–102.

33. Walter Bagehot, *The English Constitution* (Oxford: Oxford University Press, 2001), pp. 94–96.

34. Peter Dorey and Alexandra Kelso, *House of Lords Reform since 1911* (New York: Palgrave Macmillan, 2011), pp. 100–115.

35. Russell, *Reforming the House of Lords*, pp. 101–102.

36. Arend Lijphart, *Patterns of Democracy* (New Haven, CT: Yale University Press, 1999), pp. 203–211.

37. Jay S. Bybee, "Ulysses at the Mast: Democracy, Federalism, and the Sirens' Song of the Seventeenth Amendment," *Northwestern University Law Review*, vol. 91, no. 1 (1997), pp. 515–517; Todd J. Zywicki, "Beyond the Shell and Husk of History: The History of the Seventeenth Amendment and its Implications for Current Reform Proposals," *Cleveland State Law Review*, vol. 45, no. 1 (1997), p. 169.

38. Marcus Tullius Cicero, *Selected Works*, Michael Grant, trans. (London: Penguin, 1971), pp. 101–156; S. E. Smethurst, "Cicero and the Senate," *The Classical Journal*, vol. 54, no. 2 (November 1958), p. 75.

39. W. A. Peffer, "The United States Senate: Its Privileges, Powers, and Functions, Its Rules and Methods of Doing Business," *North American Review*, vol. 167, no. 501 (August 1898), pp. 178–181; Bruce Jennings, "The Institutionalization of Ethics in the U.S. Senate," *Hastings Center Report*, vol. 11, no. 1 (February 1981), pp. 6–7.

40. Smith, pp. 85–86.

41. Stanley Bach, Politics and Platypus: *The Australian Senate in Theory and Practice* (Canberra: Australian Senate, 2003), p. 55; Hugh V. Emy, *The Politics of Australian Democracy* (Melbourne: Macmillan, 1974), pp. 455–492

42. Russell, "What are Second Chambers For?" pp. 451–453.

43. Gerhard Loewenberg and Samuel Patterson, *Comparing Legislatures* (Boston: Little Brown, 1979), p. 121.

44. C. E. S. Franks, *The Parliament of Canada* (Toronto: University of Toronto Press, 1989), pp. 168–169.

45. Meg Russell, "Responsibilities of Second Chambers: Constitutional and Human Rights Safeguards," in *Second Chambers*, Nicholas D.J. Baldwin and Donald Shell, eds. (Abingdon, Oxfordshire: Frank Cass, 2001), pp. 61–76.

46. Arend Lijphart, *Democracies: Patterns of Majoritarian and Consensus Government in Twenty-One Democracies* (New Haven, CT: Yale University Press, 1984), pp. 101–104, 219–220; K. C. Wheare, *Legislatures* (New York: Oxford University Press, 1963), pp. 205–206.

47. R. H. MacKay, "To End or Mend the Senate?" *Queen's Quarterly*, vol. 71 (1964), pp. 287–296.

48. Peter H. Russell and Lorne Sossin, *Parliamentary Democracy in Crisis* (Toronto: University of Toronto Press, 2009), pp. 151–154; Torbjörn Bergman, Wolfgang C. Müller, Kaare Strøm, and Magnus Blomgren, "Democratic Delegation and Accountability: Cross-National Patterns," in *Delegation and Accountability in Parliamentary Democracies* (Oxford: Oxford University Press, 2003), pp. 179–184.

49. Smith, pp. 136–140.

50. Russell, pp. 446–449.

51. Philip Norton, "Achieving Accountability," *The House Magazine*, vol. 28, no. 1, 29 (March 2003), pp. 34–36.

52. James A. Bill and Robert L. Hardgrave, Jr., *Comparative Politics: The Quest for Theory* (Washington, DC: University Press of America, 1981), pp. 3–6.

53. James T. McHugh, *Comparative Constitutional Traditions* (New York: Peter Lang, 2003), pp. 43–44.

54. John W. Meyer, John Boli, and George M. Thomas, "Ontology and Rationalization in the Western Cultural Account," in *Institutional Environments and Organizations*, W. Richard Scott and John W. Meyer, eds. (London: Sage, 1994), pp. 16–24

55. Peter Dorey, *The Labour Party and Constitutional Reform* (Baingstoke, England: Palgrave Macmillan, 2008), pp. 100–140.

56. Vernon Bogdinor, *The New British Constitution* (Portland, OR: Hart, 2009), pp. 16–18.

57. M. J. Trebilcock, D. G. Hartle, J. R. S. Pritchard, and D. N. Dewees, *The Choice of Governing Instrument* (Ottawa: Economic Council of Canada, 1982), pp. 22–25.

58. Jean-Charles Bonenfant, *Le Senat dans le federalism canadien* (Ottawa: Commission Royale d'Enquete sur le Bilingusime et le Biculturalisme, 1966), pp. 136–137.

59. P. B. Waite, "Edward Whelan Reports from the Quebec Conference," *Canadian Historical Review* (March 1961), pp. 23–45.

60. D. A. Soberman, "Canada's Institutional Deficit," *Queen's Law Journal,* vol. 6 (Spring 1983), pp. 205–207.

61. Thomas R. Klassen and Steffen Schneider, "Similar Challenges, Different Solutions: Reforming Labour Market Policies in Germany and Canada During the 1990s," *Canadian Public Policy*, vol. 28, no. 1 (March 2002), pp. 64–66.

62. Benjamin Spencer, "Jurisdiction to Adjudicate: A Revised Analysis," *University of Chicago Law Review*, vol. 73, no. 2 (Spring 2006), pp. 637–646.

63. Donald V. Smiley and Ronald L. Watts, *Intrastate Federalism in Canada* (Toronto: University of Toronto Press, 1985), pp. 5–16.

64. Ronald L. Watts, *Executive Federalism: A Comparative Analysis* (Kingston, ON: Institute of Intergovernmental Relations, 1989), pp. 11, 16–17; Kalssen and Schneider, p. 66.

65. Richard Simeon, *Federal-Provincial Diplomacy: The Making of Recent Policy in Canada* (Toronto: University of Toronto Press, 2006), pp. 328–329.

66. Jeffrey Parker, *Comparative Federalism and Intergovernmental Agreements* (New York: Routledge, 2014), pp. 176–178; Lewis L. Gould, *The Most Exclusive Club* (New York: Basic Books, 2006), pp. 30–31, 54–55.

67. Smiley and Watts, pp. 36–39.

68. Herman Bakvis and Roselle Hryciuk, "An Experiment in Intrastate Federalism: The Cabinet Committee on Canadian Unity," in *Canada: The State of the Federation, 1993*; Ronald L. Watts and Douglas M. Brown, eds. (Kingston, ON: Institute on Intergovernmental Relations, 1993), pp. 137, 143–144.

69. Brian L. Scarfe, "Redistributing Elected Senate Seats for Regional Balance," *Canadian Public Policy*, vol. 10, no. 2 (June 1984), pp. 245–246.

70. Michael Howlett, "The Politics of Constitutional Change in a Federal System: Negotiating Section 92A of the Canada Constitution Act (1982)," *Publius*, vol. 21, no. 1 (Winter 1991), pp. 130–132.

71. Jean-Luc Pepin and John Robarts, *Report on the Task Force on Canadian Unity* (Ottawa: Queen's Printer, 1978), ch. 7.4.

72. Pepin and Robarts, ch. 5.

73. Smith, pp. 52–53.

74. Smiley and Watts, pp. 121–123.

75. British Columbia, *Constitutional Proposals: Reform of the Canadian Senate* (Victoria, 1978), paper 3, ch. 8; Campbell, pp. 161–162.

76. F. Leslie Seidle, Senate Reform and the Constitutional Agenda: Conundrum or Solution?" in *Canadian Constitutionalism, 1791–1991*, Janet Ajzenstat, ed. (Ottawa: Canadian Study of Parliament Group, 1992), p. 98; Richard Simeon,.

77. Legislative Assembly of Alberta, Special Committee on Senate Reform, *Strengthening Canada: Reform of Canada's Senate* (March 1985).

78. Peter McCormick, Ernest C. Manning, and Gordon Gibson, *Regional Representation: The Canadian Partnership* (Calgary: Canada West Foundation, 1981).

79. Canada West Foundation, *Renewal of Canada—Institutional Reform* (Calgary: Canada West Foundation, 1992), pp. 9, 12–14.

80. Bruce G. Pollard, "Canadian Energy Policy in 1985: Toward a Renewed Federalism?" *Publius*, vol. 16, no. 3 (Summer 1986), pp. 164–167.

81. Smith, pp. 91–92.

82. Michael Lusztig, "Federalism and Institutional Design: The Perils and Politics of a Triple-E Senate in Canada," *Publius*, vol. 25, no. 1 (1995), pp. 35–50.

83. Government of Canada, *Shaping Canada's Future—Together* (Ottawa: Queen's Printer, 1991).

84. Roger Gibbins, *A New Senate for a More Democratic Canada* (Calgary: Canada West Foundation, 2010), pp. 3–4.

85. Paul Warwick, *Government Survival in Parliamentary Democracies* (Cambridge: Cambridge University Press, 1994), pp. 28–32.

86. Zelman Cowen, "The Office of Governor General," *Daedalus*, vol. 114, no. 1 (Winter 1985), pp. 127, 144–146; Pepin-Roberts Report, pp. 13–14.

87. James N. Druckman, Lanny W. Martin, and Michael F. Thies, "Influence without Confidence: Upper Chambers and Government Formation," *Legislative Studies Quarterly*, vol. 30, no. 4 (November 2005), pp. 532–535.

88. Franks, *Parliament of Canada*, pp. 193–194.

89. David C. Docherty, "The Canadian Senate: Chamber of Sober Second Reflection or the Loony Cousin Best Not Talked About?" *Journal of Legislative Studies*, vol. 8, no. 3 (April 2002), pp. 32–33.

90. Smith, pp. 47–63; "Senate Reform in Canada," http://www.rhondaparkinson.com/senate-reform.htm; F. Leslie Seidle, "Strengthening Canadian Democracy," Institute for Research on Public Policy, http://www.irpp.org/research/research_project.php?page=2&ResearchCode=Strengthening%20 Canadian %20Democracy.

91. MacKay, pp. 33–40.

92. Kunz, pp. 15–19.

93. Campbell, pp. 33.

94. *Report of the Special Joint Committee on Senate Reform* (Ottawa: Queen's Printer, 1984), pp. 24–25, 28–30.

95. Molgat-McGuigan Report, 1972, p. 35.

96. Beaudoin-Dobie Report, 1992, pp. 45–48.

97. Ibid, pp. 52–55.

98. C. E. S. Franks, "Not Dead Yet But Should It Be Resurrected? The Canadian Senate," in Patterson and Mughan, eds.

99. Franks, *Parliament of Canada*, pp. 188–194.

100. Ibid., p. 200.

101. Smiley and Watts, pp. 3–15.

102. Leslie MacKinnon, "Senate Votes to Suspend Brazeau, Duffy, Wallin," *CBC News: Politics*, November 5, 2013, http://www.cbc.ca/news/politics/senate-votes-to-suspend-brazeau-duffy-wallin-1.2415815

103. Kenneth M. Gibbons and Donald C. Rowat, eds., *Political Corruption in Canada: Cases, Causes, and Cures* (Toronto: McClelland and Stewart, 1976), pp. 2–17; Michael M. Atkinson and Maureen Mancuso, "Do We Need a Code of Conduct for Politicians? The Search for an Elite Political Culture of Corruption in Canada," *Canadian Review of Canadian Studies*, vol. 18, no. 3 (September 1985), pp. 476–479.

Chapter 3

The Upper House as a Belief

INTRODUCTION

The subsequent evolution of the parliamentary upper house tended to be prompted by different philosophical considerations. Initially, it reflected conservative principles that also were consistent with the general development of the English and, later, British unentrenched constitutional tradition. This body tended to serve to slow and modify change, whether it was the emergence of a more centralized political system, extension of Tudor absolutism, the emerging power of a market-based economy and its representatives within the House of Commons, or the expanding influence of the electoral franchise—an influence that was spread to other parliamentary upper houses, though that particular philosophical motive also waned in the modern period.

The emergence of modern republican ideals also has influenced the institutional development and purpose of upper houses, including parliamentary ones, in ways that can be as relevant to non-republics as they are to societies that are more clearly associated with republican political principles. Utilitarian theories have provided notable insight into the role, purpose, and application of this institution, especially in terms of its practical functionality. Furthermore, liberal and liberal democratic ideas have contributed to this discourse, profoundly, including in terms of the unintended implications of reforms and elimination of this sort of body within the wider context of effective popular sovereignty. In order to consider this sort of reform in a meaningful way, it is important to understand this foundation.

The specific Canadian context for this influence also is significant. Although many modern accounts of Canadian political thought emphasize the influence of the communitarian tradition within Canadian society and its political system, other influences are significant and, arguably, dominant as well. In particular, a strong liberal influence has been historically present and continues to pervade the country. Furthermore, classic conservative values have been associated with Canada's social and political development. Utilitarian principles can be linked to the institutional and policy development of the political system and its outcomes and, even, the desire to apply republican concepts has maintained a presence among certain Canadian reformers and other political advocates.

Those complementary and competing philosophical systems are vital for understanding the context in which the parliamentary upper house has been created and evolved within Canada. The Senate was not created or shaped within a philosophical vacuum. Therefore, its reform cannot be properly understood or achieved in the absence of a meaningful understanding of that context. That consideration frequently is ignored or (arguably worse) assessed in terms of an attachment to a rudimentary and, often, overly simplified interpretation of democracy and democratic beliefs.

Therefore, it is necessary to assess the various traditions of political thought that have shaped the understanding and application of the parliamentary upper house in a universal sense and could be particularly relevant for informing the different approaches toward reform of the Senate of Canada. In particular, it is useful to focus upon those influences that have been responsible for the shaping and critique of this political institution within the broader advancement of modern parliamentary government. It is further necessary to assess that universal development from the perspective of the specific framework of Canadian political thought, especially in terms of its motivations and expectations. From that approach, it should be possible to envision a much more meaningful justification for Senate reform that is both truly appropriate and truly effective.

ANCIENT PHILOSOPHICAL AND POLITICAL ANTECEDENTS

When addressing modern political institutions (especially Western ones), attention often is drawn to ancient Greece and, more specifically, ancient Athens. This interest tends to be especially true in terms of the development of democratic norms and governments. The evolution of Western political thought, especially relating to the conspicuous presence of Plato and Aristotle, often draws attention to such potential origins.[1] While a truly meaningful application of this ancient influence may not be genuinely applicable to the development of modern parliamentary government, its institutions (such as the upper house), and its values, an examination from that perspective could prove interesting.

Plato famously rejected democracy as a suitable form of government. He argued that the ideal republic should be governed by those persons who had demonstrated the necessarily superior characteristics for that purpose, leading to his theoretical description of the philosopher king.[2] This ideal became the basis for his categorization of five regimes of government, each one degenerating from the superior previous one. The best regime was, he argued, an aristocracy that was ruled by the absolute authority of those persons who demonstrated the qualities that qualified them for that status—thus basing his concept of aristocracy more firmly upon a form of merit rather than mere birth into a particular class. The next best regime, a timocracy, would include a broader array of different classes of persons in the governing process, including ones deemed to be inferior to the aristocracy but superior to the largest spectrum of the population of the *polis*, including the poor.[3] This regime arguably provides a basis for conceiving various political bodies that can represent distinctive constituencies and interests—including, presumably, separate legislative chambers.

Therefore, at this point, a division of government into institutional bodies would become significant. Solon's constitution for Athens included the *Boule*, which was a council of 400 (later 500) members who were required to belong to the higher property classes. Additionally, the members of the *Boule* were chosen, equally, for the various tribes of Athens. This body established the agenda that the *Ecclesia* (in which all Athenian male citizens could participate) would consider. It also increasingly assumed administrative functions (especially in terms of the daily functioning of the *polis*), including the routine investigation of public officials prior to, and after departing, an executive office.[4]

These functions also were consistent with Aristotle's theory of mixed constitutional government, which formed his basis for the concept of the polity as superior to a mere rule of the *demos*.[5] His emphasis was upon the division among deliberative, magisterial, and judicial governmental institutions but he also addressed different forms of deliberation that could be more or less exclusionary, thus suggesting the possibility of distinct deliberative bodies that further represented the *polis* as a whole rather than merely the majority of citizens that typically consisted of the poorest class.[6] The assignment of distinct classes of citizens to the *Boule* and the *Ecclesia* suggests a similar understanding and approach in which, it could be inferred, these two bodies served as a practical "check" on their respective power with the *Boule* serving a part within that constitutional arrangement that could be vaguely compared to the role that the parliamentary upper house would come to play.[7]

However, the *Boule* was not an "upper house" in the modern or parliamentary sense. Furthermore, the ancient Greek interpretation of democracy was not confined to the process of popular election or the simple rule of the majority of a highly restricted category of citizen. For example, while the *Eccelsia* was open to the participation of all male citizens, members of the *Boule* were selected upon bases that might, superficially, suggested some of the features associated with the Senate of Canada (such as tribal representation and the capacity to constrain the deliberations of the popular assembly) but, in reality, reflected a far more parochial theory of democratic government as well as an ancient attempt to achieve the sort of balance that Aristotle identified with a polity.[8] Therefore, in order to understand the Canadian Senate and all parliamentary upper chambers in a realistic and meaningfully theoretical manner, it is necessary to explore the contributions that modern political thought has made to its development. Although the most important ideological context for that examination ultimately must be a liberal democratic one, other contributions toward that overall understanding also need to be included. Indeed, rather than beginning with liberal democracy, it is reasonable (given the institutional nature of the upper house) to begin with the modern ideological tradition that chronologically precedes it.

MODERN IDEOLOGICAL INFLUENCES ON THE PARLIAMENTARY UPPER HOUSE

Classic Conservative Influence

Conservatism has become, as an ideological tradition, misunderstood, especially as it has been conflated with other political ideals and movements. Although it often is applied to attachments to *laissez-faire* economic policies and the extolling of moral virtue in the contemporary sense, those tendencies actually can be more closely associated with other ideological traditions (including classic liberalism) than with conservatism in its truest sense. That distinction is vitally important for understanding both the influence of conservatism upon the parliamentary upper house and its role in shaping Canadian society and politics, especially among its framers, many of whom reflected (as emphasized from a traditional interpretation) an elite perspective of 19th-century imperial Britain and the earlier legacy of New France.[9] Therefore, a more profoundly accurate and meaningful manifestation of this ideological tradition should be distinguished from its more current and colloquial expression by labeling it in terms of its "classic" version and interpretation.

"Classic" conservatism refers to one of the earliest ideological developments of the modern period. It developed as a reaction to fundamental changes that were responsible for the emergence of modern society. During the 16th and 17th centuries, it served as a sort of philosophical bridge between the medieval and modern communities of Europe. Its relationship to the growing dominance of the marketplace was particularly conspicuous. Early conservatives were not, necessarily, opposed to the marketplace or the political changes that it prompted but sought to manage the enormous changes that it heralded through various means. In particular, conservatives often counseled caution and prudence in relation to embracing these changes, often by maintaining traditional institutions and practices that would inspire a measure of stability and control, even as profound social, political, and economic transformations occurred. Thus early expressions of conservatism as a modern ideological often were associated with a continued attachment to certain practices and institutions associated with the medieval period, including the trappings of feudalism.[10]

Conservatism, from this tradition, emphasizes the importance of stability, security, and a social and political structure that permit change but within an environment that will manage the disruptive effect of such change. As a result, it often has been associated with patriarchal principles and systems that provide a hierarchical and persistent presence, including in relation to political power. More consistently, though, it tends to value the role of tradition, itself, as a source of continuity that reinforces stability, peace, and prosperity, especially by avoiding conflict between various groups and cleavages within society.[11]

The parliamentary upper house has been associated with this conservative influence, even aside from the promotion of aristocratic interests that historically have been an understandable image of the House of Lords. That upper house, even prior to emerging as a legislative chamber, also was perceived as performing a "conservative" role in the sense of serving as a constraint upon the actions of the sovereign government. Nonetheless, its role was, predominantly, advisory, even after the emergence of a group of non-noble representatives that would begin to deliberate as a separate institutional body during the early 14th century. It was the emergence of a "chamber of the commoners" that would cause the assembly of peers to assume its distinct place as an "upper" legislative body, especially in response to the gradually increasing authority of the "lower house" as its role of representing moneyed interests and the necessary governing revenue that would emanate from those interests increased its influence over governing policy and the legislation necessary to enact it. Once that role for the House of Commons had become firmly established during the 16th and, especially, the 17th centuries, a role for the House of Lords that would be consistent with distinctly conservative principles also would be established.[12]

That conservative role would manifest itself in terms of the tendency of that body toward constraint, caution, and prudence. Even after Oliver Cromwell abolished the House of Lords following his success in winning the English Civil War and establishing a republican Commonwealth of England (largely because that chamber was inevitably dominated by Royalists), he eventually found it necessary to create a new parliamentary second chamber in order to curb the potential for "extreme" behavior within the House of Commons.[13] Although the House of Lords would continue to advance the interests of the English and, later, British aristocratic class and the agrarian sector of the economy that supported the landed aristocracy, even until the early 20th century, this more generally conservative role would become a defining feature of its relationship to the House of Commons, especially as the lower house gradually became more reflective of the emergence of a popular sovereignty.

This conservative role was not, necessarily, anti-democratic. The House of Lords did oppose the extension of the franchise during the 19th century (especially as many of the "rotten" and "pocket" boroughs of the rural regions were controlled by peers) but much of its activity in response to the policies and legislation of the House of Commons reflected conservative ideological principles that were developed during the 17th and 18th centuries.[14] Some of that sentiment reflected general skepticism concerning human nature of the sort explained in the writings of Thomas Hobbes (though whether he should be considered to be a conservative or early liberal philosopher is a matter of debate) in response to a perceived need to impose limits upon certain aspects of political behavior. Hobbes emphasized the need for people to accept, through a social compact, unconstrained sovereign authority.[15] However, to the extent that the sovereign requires assistance in the tasks of government, the counsel of non-elected members of an established elite (rather than the pronouncements of an assembly of many, often self-interested, persons who are subject to popular opinion) could be regarded as desirable.

> A man that doth his business by the help of many prudent counsellors, with every one consulting apart in his proper element, does it best; as he that useth able seconds at tennis play, placed in their proper stations. He does next best that useth his own judgement only; as he that has no second at all. But he that is carried up and down to his business in a framed counsel, which cannot move but by the plurality of consenting opinions, the execution whereof is commonly, out of envy or interest, retarded by the part dissenting, does it worst of all, and like one that is carried to the ball, though by good players, yet in a wheelbarrow, or other frame, heavy of itself, and retarded by the also by the inconcurrent judgements and endeavours of them that drive it; and so much the more, as they be more that set their hands to it; and most of all, when there is one or more amongst them that desire to have him lose.[16]

Later conservative opinion would be able to respond directly to the role of the upper house within an evolving parliamentary system. Edmund Burke perceived the lower house as being, essentially, "counterpoised" by the upper house.[17] His conservative interpretation emphasized a role that was intentionally complementary, stabilizing, and, even, holistic.

> This government of reference is a trustee for the whole, and not for the parts. So is the other branch of our public council, I mean the House of Lords. With us the king and the lords are several and joint securities for the equality of each district, each province, each city. When did you hear in Great Britain of any province suffering from the inequality of its representation, what district from having no representation at all? Not only our monarchy and our peerage secure the equality on which our unity depends, but it is the spirit of the House of Commons itself. The very inequality of representation, which is so foolishly complained of, is perhaps the very thing which prevents us from thinking or acting as members for districts.[18]

This influence of conservative thought upon this particular institutional political development would not be confined to a defense of a privileged aristocracy. The general function of extending deliberation upon the adoption of legislation, policy, and other political decisions is consistent with the premises of that ideological tradition. Maintaining a sense of institutional continuity within the history of a political system also is a feature of conservative thought that often is reflected in the ongoing presence of an upper house. An inclination toward prudence, even in relation to the mandate of a parliamentary majority government, further reflects that influence.[19] That influence certainly can be detected in relation to the Canadian upper house, especially as a chamber that originally was intended to include business elites, a tempering influence upon the popularly elected lower house, and a structural reflection of the British model that helped to inspire it. However, while that conservative influence has been particularly prevalent throughout much of the history of parliamentary upper house in general, it is not the only philosophical influence that is reflected by it, particularly in the modern period.

Liberal and Liberal Democratic Influence

The fact that the Canadian political system is, consistent with Western industrial societies in general, a liberal democratic one demands that the role and reform of the Senate should be considered within that ideological context. Despite the wide variation in democratic theory, it is the liberal variation that is most relevant to this particular consideration. Of course, liberalism preceded the rise of liberal democracy so it is important to understand the former ideological tradition prior to appreciating the broader implications of liberal democratic approaches toward parliamentary reform of this nature.

Liberalism is the ideological tradition that arose from the emerging dominance of the modern market place. Its values emphasize, therefore, the ideals of individualism, freedom, and autonomy that are necessary for a market economy to function.[20] Most importantly, arguably, is the central role that property—both in an economically tangible and philosophically abstract sense—has played in shaping liberal ideology and the relationship that it would develop with the democratic process and its overarching goals. Furthermore, the relationship between freedom and individual property interests (especially as articulated through the modern concept of civil rights and liberties) would have a particularly profound effect upon the understanding of the role of government in general.[21]

John Locke emphasized limited government and property rights. The latter emphasis indicated a seminal shift in the image and purpose of government in general. The delegation of sovereign authority to the government would no longer be associated with the absolute authority of an external sovereign but would originate within the interests of each property-bearing member of society. The purpose of government would be the maintenance of freedom, including (perhaps especially) against its own delegated power and mission. Therefore, both of these considerations of limited government and property rights have been relevant to the development of the modern legislative upper house.[22] Locke was not entirely enthusiastic about the legislative role of government but he did emphasize its purpose in restricting the potential excesses of the political executive.[23] The most important consideration was the recognition of the central importance of property as a defining characteristic of those persons who create the social contract through which they would leave the state of nature and live within a shared society. Any governmental design would need to accept this central premise and other liberal scholars would emphasize similar expectations.[24]

The parliamentary upper house has been historically accepted as a body that represents an elite (including an economically elite) constituency. The express inclusion of a property qualification for Canadian Senators within the Constitution Act of 1867 demonstrates a stark commitment to that ideal.[25] But the evolving perception of the role of the Senate as a potential obstacle to an unfettered parliamentary executive is, arguably, an even more significant development in this liberal expectation. This perceived development has been especially pertinent in relation to the strengthening of party discipline within the Canadian lower house and the subsequent expansion of prime ministerial authority that became particularly notable during the latter part of the 20th century. In that sense, the upper house becomes a counterweight to the executive (rather than a competitor with another legislative actor) and it is potential threat to the property rights of citizens.[26] Although that role would become more closely associated with the development of a judiciary with increased constitutional responsibility, this liberal role of the upper house still could find relevance in the general expectations that accompanied its initial creation and development.

Classic liberals have emphasized rights over popular sovereignty. The idea that a sovereign citizen would be best situated for the protection of those same rights and the promotion of other liberal principles (such as individual autonomy) would evolve through the development of liberal democratic ideals and institutions. A meaningful understanding of the significance of democratic institutions within this context would be based upon the distinction between elections as ends in themselves and as a true institutional expression of a recognizable and unchallenged popular will. Adding the democratic process to every government position (such as the judiciary and the civil service) did not necessarily reinforce democratic principles.[27]

In fact, the establishment of a rival institution to a legislative body that had been delegated ultimate responsibility for expressing the overall sovereign could create conflict and confusion. Furthermore, it could misinterpret the distinction of a liberal democracy as one that expresses a popular will but, also, limits that will according to its original delegation from an association of individual sovereigns. As a result, the elected government of a liberal democracy, while expressing the popular will, should not be confused with an absolute and unchecked sovereign authority. Constitutional principles would establish those limits and other institutions could serve to reinforce them.[28]

John Stuart Mill described the role of the second chamber in relationship to those liberal democratic principles. He noted the difficulty of a body in competition to a popularly elected legislature for that purpose, particularly when it represented a parochial interest of that society. Nonetheless, the liberal theme of limited government on behalf of the sovereign people and each sovereign individual person needed to be retained. Therefore, while the democratic will needs a check upon it, the inclusion of a competing democratic institution is not, necessarily, the best approach—even though the alternative might be a worse option.

> That there should be, in every polity, a centre of resistance to the predominant power in the Constitution–and in a democratic constitution, therefore, a nucleus of resistance to the democracy–I have already maintained; and I regard it as a fundamental maxim of government. If any people who possess a democratic representation are, from their historical antecedents, more willing to tolerate such a centre of resistance in the form of a Second Chamber or House of Lords than in any other shape, this constitutes a stronger reason for having it in that shape. But it does not appear to me the best shape in itself, nor by any means the most efficacious for its object. If there are two houses, one considered to represent the people, the other to represent only a class, or not to be representative at all, I can not think that, where democracy is the ruling power in society, the second House would have any real ability to resist even the aberrations of the first. It might be suffered to exist in deference to habit and association, but not as an effective check. If it exercised an independent will, it would be required

> to do so in the same general spirit as the other House; to be equally democratic with it, and to content itself with correcting the accidental oversights of the more popular branch of the Legislature, or competing with it in popular measures.[29]

Although Mill did not exhibit a fondness for the House of Lords, he also demonstrated an appreciation for the proper liberal democratic parameters of the relationship between the upper and lower houses of a national legislature. Other liberal democratic scholars have addressed the role of the legislature in a similar fashion.[30] That constitutional approach will prove particularly relevant to the context of Canada's liberal democratic institutions as well, especially in terms of the potentially strong conflict that an elected upper house could pose to the broader principles of parliamentary democracy and the legitimacy of its elected governments.

Democratic theory, which had experienced different interpretations that had evolved for millennia, would evolve with the eventual dominance of liberal ideological values, especially as the extent of the property-bearing members of society would expand to include, eventually, practically all of its populace. Within the context of liberal democracy, however, democratic theory bears particular importance from a procedural perspective. This aspect of the issue is especially important because of reform proposals that insist upon an electoral element in the choosing of members of the upper house and it is addressed in much greater detail within another chapter of this overall study. Meanwhile, though, it is useful to provide a few general observations relating to this normative and applied relationship within the dominant ideological tradition of liberal democratic thought.

Procedural democracy is a useful and, ostensibly, necessary manifestation of the desire to reflect and protect the will and interests of the *demos* as a whole. Procedural democracy is predicated upon the ideal that members of society should remain the ultimate determiners of the political will.[31] A problem may occur, though, when democratic preferences are in conflict with each other. Furthermore, that conflict can undermine the expert advice and transformation of will into action that non-democratic actors can provide. The lack of an electoral mandate does not, in itself, negate the democratic role that non-elected officials and institutions may contribute. Therefore, democratic institutions typically do not represent the will of all (or, at least, all recognized full members of society) and, often, fail even to reflect a true majoritarian interests but only reflect the will of a plurality of those members of society.[32]

The important consideration at this point is the relationship, within a liberal democracy, between the representation of a sovereign populace and the liberal values that it is intended to sustain. That consideration should be applied toward the potential reform of the Senate of Canada. The role of the parliamentary upper house can be particularly significant for addressing the relationship between majoritarian and individualist motivations that liberal democracy seeks to reconcile. That consideration also has been addressed within another important philosophical tradition that is especially relevant to the aspirations of a political community.

Modern Republican Influence

Republicanism in the modern sense represents an adaptation of ancient principles (especially associated with ancient Rome) that has inspired many features of modern political development, especially within Western societies. In particular, it emphasized the standards of civic virtue, civic duty, the good of the commonwealth, and virtual representation. That last concept inspired political institutions that provided a means for different constituencies to participate (even if only indirectly) in the collective process of government.[33]

Canada was not designed to be a republic in either the ancient or modern sense and its founders had little inclination to make it one.[34] Nonetheless, an examination of this tradition of political thought is relevant for appreciating some of the theoretical influences that may have shaped, or could be invoked to shape, the development of its parliamentary institutions, including its upper chamber. In its modern adaptation, republican principles have inspired political institutions that are designed to be inclusive of the representation of minorities. Simultaneously, they are designed to prevent an unchecked authority of popular representation. In that sense, republicanism is not anti-democratic. Instead, it seeks to prevent democratic institutions from overwhelming the interests and participation of segments of society not reflected by a popular majority.[35] This desire previously was found in Aristotle's approach to a mixed government that seeks to avoid the shortcomings of different political systems by combining their best features.

> On the other hand, that some should deliberate about all is oligarchical. This again is a mode which, like the democratical has many forms. When the deliberative class being elected out of those who have a moderate qualification are numerous and they respect and obey the prohibitions of the law without altering it, and any one who has the required qualification shares in the government, then, just because of this moderation, the oligarchy inclines towards polity. But when only selected individuals and not the whole people share in the deliberations of the state, then, although, as in the former case, they observe the law, the government is a pure oligarchy. Or, again, when those who have the power of deliberation are self-elected, and son succeeds father, and they and not the laws are supreme- the government is of necessity oligarchical. Where, again, particular persons have authority in particular matters- for example, when the whole people decide about peace and war and hold scrutinies, but the magistrates

> regulate everything else, and they are elected by vote- there the government is an aristocracy. And if some questions are decided by magistrates elected by vote, and others by magistrates elected by lot, either absolutely or out of select candidates, or elected partly by vote, partly by lot- these practices are partly characteristic of an aristocratical government, and party of a pure constitutional government.[36]

The legislative upper house is a prime example of that republican perspective. Montesquieu emphasized the need for a separation of powers and responsibilities in order to achieve those objectives. Further, he advocated a division within the legislature in order to prevent its dominance by a single constituency (such as the popular will) or perspective.

> When the legislative and executive powers are united in the same person, or in the same body of magistrates, there can be no liberty; because apprehensions may arise, lest the same monarch or senate should enact tyrannical laws, to execute them in a tyrannical manner …
>
> There would be an end of everything, were the same man or the same body, whether of the nobles or of the people, to exercise those three powers, that of enacting laws, that of executing the public resolutions, and of trying the causes of individuals.[37]

Interestingly, Montesquieu included the republican principle of having particular institutions that represent particular constituencies, including in relation to an aristocratic constituency. His approach was not a defense of aristocracy as much as it was an acknowledgement of the desirability of grounding this system upon a broader basis than the mere will of the majority.[38] That perspective is important for understanding not only some of the subtler premises of republican theories of government but, also, of the constructive function that second chambers can provide in promoting those values of enhancing the participation of the commonwealth as a comprehensive whole.

> [T]here are always people in the state who distinguish themselves through birth, wealth, and prestige (honor). If they were to be subsumed in the people, however, the common freedom would be their undoing, and they would have no interest in defending freedom, because most decisions would be directed against them. Their share in legislation, therefore, must take account of their special interest.[39]

Republican principles also have emphasized virtual representation—not in the sense that the British used it to defend the lack of direct representation of the American colonists within the Parliament at Westminster but in a sense that is closer to Edmund Burke's characterization of representation that was borrowed from republican principles. Burke argued that legislative representatives should not seek to reflect direct public opinion but, rather, to develop a deliberative consensus of the common good among competing broad constituencies of the society.[40] Furthermore, this virtual representation could include special consideration for elites within society. This "elevation of the best men," as American framers such as Adams, Jefferson, and Hamilton expressed it, would be vital to the advancement of republican government.[41]

The representation of virtue that had been so emphasized within ancient republics often was replaced (such as in the American example) with the representation of interests. This recognition of social homogeneity helped to redefine the notion of virtual representation, especially in contrast to direct representation.[42] Elite members of a particular interest could reflect the goals and opinions of those members of society who shared their interests. In a broader sense, the initial concept of the U.S. Senate as a representative of the interest of state governments within the federal system was reflected by the fact that Senators would not be subject to direct popular election but to selection by their respective state governments.

While a republican interpretation of the upper house appears to be most applicable to the U.S. Senate, these concepts have been relevant to the development of the upper house within non-republics, including parliamentary systems. In particular, they resonate for federal political systems, including Australia and Canada. The idea that the upper house of a legislature should not replicate the representation of the lower house but should reflect a different type of representation (such as particular interests and constituencies, elite opinion, or the good of the "common weal," free from the vagaries of direct popular delegation) in the interest of stability has proven to be a consistent argument in the formation and evolution of this institution.[43]

This philosophical influence also is relevant in terms of the republican theme of "virtual representation." It provides for a principle of inclusion. Certain distinct groups and people may be significant within society and, thus, should be included within the political system and process. However, elections that reflect the will of the majority might not be able to include their presence within democratically representative institutions. Therefore, the upper house can offer a potential political institution for that purpose.[44] This republican principle has been present within the experiences of both ancient Rome and the United States[45]—the latter including its Senate and, particularly, its appointed Supreme Court.[46] It may resonate, also, with an appointed body, such as the Senate of Canada. Not only was the Canadian upper house intended to represent certain business and elite economic interests through its property qualification but it also was intended to represent certain regions in a disproportionate manner.

Republicanism has exerted an influence beyond those political systems that have consciously chosen to embrace its nomenclature and virtues. The desire to replace the hereditary monarch (or her appointed representative) with an elected head of state within Commonwealth countries such as Australia (and, even, within Canada) might appear, on one level, to be a merely cosmetic institutional manifestation of republican rhetoric, especially given the republican emphasis upon distinct separation of powers within a governmental structure. But such sentiments also reflect the meaningful appeal of republican values, even within a parliamentary context and especially for societies that have self-consciously become more broadly inclusive, such as Canada in the 21st century. Republican approaches toward parliamentary structures, including the upper house, offer relevant insights into the current function and potential reform of these institutions that may inspire and guide them in meaningful ways.

Utilitarian Influence

Likewise, the absence of a direct link between other philosophical traditions should not be discounted in assessing institutional reform. This relationship is especially relevant in terms of the utilitarian tradition. Although it has been particularly associated with movements for political and legal reform in Britain during the late 18th and early 19th centuries, its appeal continues to be a pervasive presence among modern political systems, including Canada.[47] While its focus is, ostensibly, practical, its appeal also has had an indirectly moral element, particularly in relation to its desire to promote and secure human happiness.

Utilitarianism found considerable inspiration in the social reforms and ideals proposed by the 18th-century Italian scholar, Cesare Beccaria. However, it achieved its most complete expression through the writings of Jeremy Bentham and James Mill, as critiqued and further expanded by additional theorists (including John Stuart Mill) onward from the mid-19th century. Its essential premise is an *ontological* one. It is based upon the claim that the one feature that all humans share is that they all pursue pleasure and avoid pain. That premise is an appealing one because it allows for subjective interpretations of "pleasure" and "pain"—whether a person finds accumulating wealth or dispersing wealth to be pleasurable constitutes, in both instances, a legitimate expression of "pleasure." According to this premise, a government should seek to maximize human pleasure and minimize exposure to pain—an approach that is the basis, among other reforms, of modern theories of proportionality and deterrence (rather than retribution) within penal law.[48]

The application of utilitarian principles has been extended to various aspects of society, the economy, law, and politics. This philosophical method has been promoted by its adherents as a basis for a universal advancement of human happiness. It has had a strong influence upon the development and advancement of public policy and political improvement. Indeed, the practical ends of political institutions have been a particular focus of utilitarian ideas and analysis.[49] Jeremy Bentham was strongly critical of institutions that were not grounded upon principles of practical usefulness, especially in terms of simplicity of function and effect. He was particularly critical of the role of the upper house within both parliamentary and republican systems of government.

> It may further be suggested that in a federal system the necessity for the existence of two chambers is not so obvious as is commonly supposed, for the interests of the component units can be secured by means other than a second chamber, as, for example, by rigid constitutional guarantees. The existence, too, of political parties on a national scale has to a considerable extent lessened the rôle of the second chamber as the special protector of territorial units. This is actually the situation now in the United States, Canada, and Australia.[50]

Bentham was adamantly opposed to any sort of second legislative chamber, including elected ones. From his perspective, a second chamber was not only superfluous but it also interfered with the popular chamber's ability to express, most directly, the greatest good, delayed useful legislation and policies, served particular, rather than general, interests, and provided an additional source of corruption.[51] Bentham's objections to bicameral government was grounded upon its supposed inefficiency, lack of transparency, and his fear that it would use a power of veto in a purely obstructionist fashion.[52] These objections also were inspired by the specific example of the House of Lords in its role of defending aristocratic principle in the guise of mature deliberation.[53] They also, obviously, could apply to the perspectives of critics who advocate the abolition of the Senate of Canada.

> *Objection the Second—Needlessness.* Yes, needlessness—utterly needless—may be seen to be this institution. No benefit in any *determinate* shape having ever been held up to view as resulting from it—if then, to satisfy the reader of the needlessness of it—and thence, as below, of the perniciousness of it—anything further can be done—it must be by looking out for such *supposable* benefit as the nature of the case may be capable of suggesting.[54]

Etienne Dumont represented a "second generation" of utilitarian thought that was somewhat less focused upon promoting pleasure as it was in avoiding pain. His perspective was inspired by actual events of precipitous action in eliminating an otherwise useful second chamber.[55] Nonetheless, his opinion was supported by a theoretically sound utilitarian basis and it has interesting implications for arguments concerning the function of bodies such as the

Canadian Senate in relation to its role in amending and improving legislation, as an ombudsman, and as a body that could be particularly effective in scrutinizing as well delaying, rather than defeating, legislation and executive action through potential processes such as a suspensive veto.

> This division is a certain method of preventing precipitation and surprise. It is true, that in a single assembly, rules may be established which prescribe multiplied examinations, according to the importance of the business; and it is thus that we find in the House of Commons *three readings,* three discussions, at different intervals—discussion in committee, article by article; report of the committee, examination of this report: petitions from all who are interested; appointment of a day for considering these petitions. It is by these general precautions, and others like them, that the danger of surprise is obviated, and maturity of deliberation secured.
>
> This is true: but a single assembly may have the best rules, and disregard them when it pleases. Experience proves that it is easy to lay them aside; and urgency of circumstances always furnishes a ready pretext, and a popular pretext, for doing what the dominant party desires. If there are two assemblies, the forms will be observed; because if one violate them, it affords a legitimate reason to the other for rejection of everything presented to it after such suspicious innovation.
>
> Besides, multiplied discussions in a single assembly do not present the same security as those which take place among different bodies. Diversity of interests, of views, of prejudices and habits, are absolutely necessary for the examination of objects under all their relations. Men who act long together contract the same connexions and modes of thinking, a spirit of routine and of party, which has its natural correction in another association.
>
> A second assembly may therefore be considered as a tribunal of appeal from the judgment of the first.[56]

A third generation of utilitarian thought would give additional consideration to the utility of a legislative upper house. The role of these institutions in complementing the democratic process (rather than competing with it and the government to which it delegates ultimate sovereign authority, as an elected Canadian upper house very well might) would continue to be considered from this perspective. It still provides a method that is regarded as a suitable means for ensuring that legislative and other policy outcomes are consistent with an overall approach to achieving a rational and maximum good for society as a whole.[57] The fact that this interpretation is regarded as being perfectly consistent with liberal and liberal democratic principles and goals requires a more thorough understanding of that broader ideological context.

Communitarian Influence

The development of a communitarian tradition of modern political thought has been particularly noted within Canada.[58] It also has been tied to central themes of Canadian constitutionalism, including bilingualism, multiculturalism, gender equality, indigenous rights, and the overall increasingly diversity of Canadian society and its implications for Canadian public policy.[59] The general relevance of communitarian thought, in this respect, requires an assessment of its particular potential relevance to the subject of upper house reform. That assessment is challenging, however, because communitarian thought tends to emphasize the role of society and its populace over the role of political systems. Communitarianism offers a particularly pointed critique of the liberal tradition and its approach to government that is, nonetheless, important to understand in order to address the broader subject of the role (if any) of the upper house.

Communitarianism does not, necessarily, reject the entirety of the values of the liberal democratic (nor, even, of the liberal) tradition. It does reject the liberal emphasis upon individual rights and liberties, particularly when they are regarded as being inalienable. Instead, it stresses the context of community in the creation, function, and identity of human life.[60] Various schools of communitarian thought have differed from each other in terms of explanation and emphasis. However, they agree upon the essential ideal of the primacy of beliefs and values that are shaped within the public space of the political and social community. Individual rights are not entirely abandoned (though they are regarded as not being inalienable but, instead, being created by social consensus) but they are not accorded primacy over formulations of the common good.[61]

There are a couple of implications of communitarian thought that are indirectly relevant to the theme of political institutional reform. First, it emphasizes the desires of the community as a whole so it is less inclined to impose limitations upon those desires by "checking" the authority of political bodies (especially legislatures) that represent the general community. Second, it tends to favor the political goals and beliefs of smaller and more coherent, rather than larger and more diverse, communities.[62] The first implication can be associated with the concept of the "general will" as developed by Jean Jacques Rousseau. His belief that true sovereignty resides within an indivisible people prompted the further belief that the institutional expression of that sovereignty should not be divided, either—including among competing legislative bodies. Even when practically necessary to delegate certain responsibilities to smaller bodies, a higher authority, representing the whole sovereign people and its general will, should prevail. Interestingly, he drew upon the example of the Westminster model of parliamentary government (despite the fact that it was bicameral) to illustrate this argument.

> Ce changement de relation n'est point une subtilité de spéculation sans exemple dans la pratique : il a lieu tous les jours dans le parlement d'Angleterre, où la chambre basse, en certaines occasions, se tourne en grand comité, pour mieux

> discuter les affaires, et devient ainsi simple commission, de cour souveraine qu'elle était l'instant précédent ; en telle sorte qu'elle se fait ensuite rapport à elle-même, comme chambre des communes, de ce qu'elle vient de régler en grand comité, et délibère de nouveau sous un titre de ce qu'elle a déjà résolu sous un autre.[63]

The second implication concerning the preference for smaller, rather than larger, communities emphasizes the importance of representing particular communities and segments of a larger population. The socially constructed preferences for public policy are much easier to discern and articulate at a more local level. Furthermore, smaller communities are more cohesive and participation by average members is much more likely, especially at a meaningful level of contribution to the discussion and decision-making process as it affects everyday life.[64] However, the scale and scope of the issues and challenges that face even a local community make it necessary to engage in broader discourse, including at the national and, even, international levels. Therefore, the community cannot dispense with the political system at the national level.[65]

Communitarians contend that formulations of the public good do not emerge from political competition but through social discourse. Without a social articulation of the good, a normative standard upon which to base it is impossible.[66] A strong influence in communitarian thought in this respect is the writings of Georg Friedrich Wilhelm Hegel with his arguments concerning the impossibility of identifying and applying a normatively neutral foundation for developing public policies that serve this greater good. That discovery of an overriding good (including in terms of national well-being) enables persons and groups with different ethical perspectives and ideological preferences to arrive at a principled, rather than merely prudential, consensus. That approach requires a platform for deliberation.

Communitarian thought does not, typically, address these sorts of specific structural manifestations of a national dialogue. Interestingly, though, Hegel's focus upon uncovering the collective values that inform public policy at this level offers a way to understand both an institutional expression of this development and a role for the second chamber of a legislature. Hegel suggested that the political community at this level should be understood in terms of a collection of groups and interests that might be neglected or, even, ignored by a political system that is responsive only to the overall majority of a population.[67] That outcome would not only be bad for those neglected groups but, also, for the overall society. Therefore, he was inclined to favor a more complex political and legislative structure that would provide access to other influences that inform the whole community, rather than merely its majority.

> Now Hegel accepts that positions in the civil service should be open to all those qualified to fill them. But he does not deem it necessary that *all* positions of political power should be open to everyone. In particular, he believes that seats in the upper house of parliament should be reserved for members of the agricultural or landowning estate who inherit their property through primogeniture. The reason for this is that, if laws are to safeguard all the interests and needs of citizens, they must be debated and enacted not only by representatives of the corporations in civil society, but also by citizens who are 'independent of … the quest for profit … [and] of the favour of the executive power and of the masses,' and who are informed above all by an abiding sense of dependence on, and gratitude toward, *nature*. The role of the upper house is thus to make sure that legislation is determined not just by commercial interests and the interests of the executive, but by the interests of those who work, and care for, the land. …
>
> As Rawls points out, the upper house of the Hegelian legislature clearly violates the principle of fair opportunity and restricts the right of all citizens to run for every political office. What Rawls fails to note, however, is that Hegel imposes this restriction because he wants to ensure that ecological intuition plays as much a role in the legislative process as commercial understanding.[68]

Hegel's approach presents an interesting challenge to the institutional implications of communitarian thought, particularly at a national level. The role of the parliamentary upper house can be particularly well-suited to meeting that challenge. It requires, though, a use of that institution that reflects a particular interpretation of the common good that is more than merely majoritarian. Because the communitarian tradition has received relatively strong interest within Canada, that interpretation may be particularly relevant and, simultaneously, delicate to justify, philosophically. In particular, the relationship between group interests (which has been an ongoing and prominent theme of Canadian politics) and the representation that a reformed Senate could, potentially, provide could be extremely relevant to the method by which Senators are chosen. Input, in that respect (including for the principal linguistic communities of Canada) could be as important or more important than direct legislative activity. Therefore, a more parochial examination of the role and reform of the parliamentary upper house from the perspective of Canadian political thought is necessary.

THE SENATE IN THE CONTEXT OF CANADIAN POLITICAL THOUGHT

The purpose and values of a second chamber are necessarily linked to the system of ideas and beliefs that initially motivate them. This relationship is true in general terms and it is especially relevant in Canadian terms. The creation and development of the Senate of Canada did not occur in a vacuum, either politically or philosophically. Therefore, in addition to understanding and appreciating the overarching philosophical and ideological traditions that inform the function of the parliamentary upper house in general, it is important to understand this development and the context of its potential reform within the specific context of Canadian political thought and culture, as F. A. Kunz observed within his historical critique of the Canadian upper house.

> [T]here can be nothing surprising about the genuine hostility of eighteenth century radical thinkers to a legislative institution whose chief function, by general admission, was to resist democratic aspirations. It must have been particularly appalling to believers in an indivisible national unit as expressed through the philosophical idea of the general will and its corresponding political notion of popular sovereignty. They could hardly be enamoured of the idea of checks and balances, which was aimed at checking precisely what they were trying to set free.[69]

Thus the Senate of Canada often has been associated with this anti-populist and anti-democratic tendency. Yet despite the tendency to ascribe Canadian political thought to a relatively simple identification with a single tradition (such as communitarianism), it has lacked an overarching framework to structure its analysis. That indifference does not indicate, necessarily, that such an analytical structure is superfluous. The lack of consistency in terms of approaches to this area arguably results in a haphazard exploration of the historical and present significance of Canada's political ideas and values. Some authors have emphasized the importance of the elite/mass dichotomy that makes political culture subservient to the exercise of power by a "confraternity of power" whose interests, rather than broader ideals, are the actual source of broadly held political values.[70] Other authors have emphasized a classic class analysis that subsumes, more starkly, the role of political culture and other social and political institutions to the larger dynamic of class struggle and dominance.[71] Nonetheless, applying the concept of an identifiable tradition of political thought to Canada remains an important intellectual and practical focus.[72] A greater appreciation of the true relevance of Canada to its tradition of political thought might be strengthened greatly by the imposition of a broad and overarching normative framework that could facilitate theoretical comparisons and evaluations.[73]

A seminal explanation of Canada's dominant political culture and values was the result of the "fragment theory" developed by Louis Hartz. "New World" societies resulted, Hartz argued, from the colonization of particular, culturally homogeneous groups who infused their values into the economic and political practices and institutions of their "new" societies. This process resulted, according to Hartz, in the emergence of a dominant ideological consensus within these societies. For example, the dominant American ideology, according to Hartz, was a libertarian liberalism that reflected the experiences and beliefs of 17th-century English dissenters and entrepreneurs who fled the economic restrictions and political and religious oppression of their former society.[74]

The Hartzian model was applied to Canada, especially through the work of Kenneth McRae and, later, Gad Horowitz. It was used to confirm a desired image of a Canadian political culture that was distinct from the overwhelming presence of the United States. It divided Canadian political thought into distinct Anglophone and Francophone components. The Anglophone component identified a less individualistic, more class conscious, and more stratified Canadian political culture than its supposedly libertarian neighbor to the South. That image would contribute to an interpretation of the Senate of Canada as a guardian of increasingly anachronistic class interests. The Francophone component identified an allegedly quasi-feudal, hierarchical society that reflected the pre-revolutionary values of 16th-century France. The model was appealing because it was so simple and comprehensive.[75] It also had an arguable appeal for some of the arguments in favor of the adoption of the Senate of Canada, particularly in terms of the property qualifications that distinguished this second chamber as a representative of an elite class of a stratified society. The allocation of senatorial appointments within Quebec according to distinct districts that were, in turn, based upon the semi-feudal divisions of New France offers a seeming confirmation of that cultural influence.

This model, however, sought to associate the development of Canadian political thought with the development of American thought by attributing both to parallel defining "moments" that were historically linked. The American "moment," as previously noted, was the American Revolution, from which event the country's political institutions emerged. The Anglophone Canadian "moment" became the migration of Tory Loyalists from the United States, following their post-revolutionary ejection. This focal point of the historical development of Canadian political thought would prove to be inadequate for interpreting the dynamic nature of Canada's cultural development, especially during the late 20th century.[76] Indeed, this approach to historical identification and theoretical explanation would prove to be too simple for a meaningful appraisal of the political thought of both societies, but especially for Canada. It also would diminish the effect of continental influences that would affect the cultural development of both countries. The fact that the framers of the Senate of Canada were, in certain specific respects, deliberately conscious of the U.S. Senate as a model and inspiration (especially in terms of the more elevated status of American Senators and the role that they were intended to play in representing the interests of the states and their respective governments) also should be noted in that respect.

Subsequent Canadian political theorists attempted to confirm this dominant difference of Canadian political thought by exploring the alleged nature of its less individualistic, and even less liberal, social, economic, and political norms. Such an emphasis might have skewed assumptions relating to the purpose of the Senate of Canada as a stabilizing and counter-democratic institution. An influential early scholar who sought to affirm this image was George Grant. His book, *Lament for a Nation*, encouraged a defense of the Anglophone Canadian nation from the *laissez-faire* dominance of corporate America. This approach is reflected in the desire to portray Canada as being influenced by classical conservative forces.[77] Gad Horowitz offered this perspective as a way to explain the easier acceptance of socialism within Canada which, like classical conservatism (as opposed to the classical liberalism that often has been inappropriately labeled "conservative") subordinates individual identity to broader, collective identities and goals.[78] Seymour Martin Lipset echoed that theme in his cross-cultural analysis of Canada and the United States. His empirical surveys led him to conclude that Canada represents a more deferential, class-conscious, and conformist polity than its fiercely individualistic southern neighbor.[79] Lipset later acknowledged, however, that institutional (especially parliamentary) factors may be more responsible for this economic development than purely ideological explanations can provide.[80] It also is appealing in the more specific attempt to explain the development of the Canadian upper house in terms of classic conservative explanations of its purpose and function—explanations that often resonated with commentators during its early years of existence.

The more recent interest in communitarian influences upon Canadian political thought has become the most significant manifestation of this trend toward an anti-individualist definition of fundamental Canadian ideological values. This tradition emphasizes the relative powerlessness of isolated persons who lack connection with, and commitment to, their political community. Therefore, it favors the cooperative process of democratic processes and policies over the atomistic tendencies of a strong tradition of individual civil rights and liberties. Authors such as Charles Taylor have been especially prominent in this respect. His writings, as well as other communitarian critiques of traditional liberalism, have provided a theoretical support for certain collectivist "experiments" within the Canadian political process.[81]

For example, the identification of a so-called "collective rights" tradition within Canadian constitutionalism provides a political and legal manifestation of this development. This legal tradition borrows strongly from the argument that Canadian political thought should reflect, within the country's political institutions, the dominance of communitarian, over libertarian, values. It contends, therefore, that the rights of groups, exercised as groups (such as labor unions) should supersede individual rights within Canada.[82] However, most allusions to collective rights really are expressions of individual rights under a collective label.[83] This attempt to construct a communitarian-based constitutional tradition contradicts many of the libertarian values that have been embraced by the Canadian Charter of Rights and Freedoms.[84]

A traditional liberal influence within Canadian society often has been overlooked or downplayed, including in terms of parliamentary development and, more specifically, the purpose and function of the Senate of Canada. But historical debates regarding economic reciprocity reflect a strong current of *laissez-faire* economic values and traditional liberal values that lean toward a libertarian variation of liberal ideological influence within Canada.[85] Even the right to strike has been defended, within Canada, in terms of an individual freedom of association.[86] The Canadian Senate's image as a chamber to represent business and other economic interests is consistent with that same influence. The claim that Canada's early development constituted a reaction against developments within the United States has been strongly criticized as being too simple and, perhaps, forced.[87] Many early Canadian colonists shared the dissenting values of their American counterparts. The United Empire Loyalists were not as different, ideologically, from the American revolutionaries as some historians uncritically have assumed. Their differences often were motivated by specific economic or political considerations. They disagreed with the institutional and strategic aspects of the American Revolution, while sharing many of the same objections to British interference with certain economic and political liberties.[88]

Many people in Great Britain shared the ideological vision of the American colonists, while remaining loyal to British political institutions; many Loyalists could be characterized in the same manner. The Upper Canada Rebellion reflects many political demands that were based upon traditional liberal beliefs, especially regarding economic and political freedom. The concept of political deference to imperial authority can be explained in terms other than classical conservative adherence to order and stability. Fears regarding American invasion may have become increasingly elite motivated, especially after the Anglo-American War of 1812, while a variety of economic considerations may have provided a strong motivation for maintaining imperial connections, leading to a traditional assertion that the settlement of Upper Canada, as spurred by United Empire Loyalists, introduced an essentially conservative dynamic to Canada's historical development,[89] though other historians have been skeptical of that assumption.[90] Therefore, the reference to peace, order, and good government within the Constitution Act of 1867 may reflect nothing more than the "harm principle" that was advocated by the great utilitarian and libertarian theorist, John Stuart Mill.[91] Likewise, the

Senate of Canada may have been conceived as a practical complement to, rather than opponent of, the elected lower house.

Much like the establishment of a Canadian upper house that found at least part of its inspiration from the House of Lords, the "peace, order, and good government" reference may have been necessary to appease nervous colonial officials and politicians in Westminster. It is tempting to interpret such a passage, broadly, but it needs to be appreciated within the context of the document, and the constitutional institutions that it established, as a whole.[92] Developments of the 20th century, as well as increased contact and cooperation with the United States, have allowed classical liberal values to permeate Canadian society and its political system, including the Senate. Increased global trade has strengthened free-market sympathies. Anti-capitalist trends in places like Saskatchewan and Alberta, as recorded by Lipset and C. B. Macpherson, were not so different from agrarian movements in the United States, especially during the Progressive era, for agrarian and single sector economic movements of a collectivist nature often were, like in the United States, demographically and regionally isolated.[93] The challenge of fascism inspired both a global human rights tradition and a greater appreciation of libertarian values throughout the Western world, including Canada.[94] The Trudeau era demonstrated a strong endorsement of traditional liberal values, even as Canadian sympathies for promoting the communal image of Canada increased.[95]

The Senate of Canada could not fail to be influenced by those same developments, even while its formal structure remained relatively stable. Canadian political thought should be understood in terms of a competition of basic ideological and cultural values that occurs within both society and government and extends to the practical functioning of its political (including legislative) institutions. The essence of this competition should make reference to the complimentary and conflicting goals of liberal *and* democratic values within the broad ideological tradition of liberal democracy. This competition arguably occurs within many, if not most, liberal democratic societies.[96] This struggle pits the desire for individual freedom against majoritarian policy goals. Many communitarians, in fact, may be motivated by a desire to secure a condition of individual autonomy by controlling their environment which, they assume, a majority of the members of their community share.

An institutional consequence of that dichotomy is a tendency to find ways to lessen the dominance of political bodies that represent the will of the electoral majority (or, frequently, an electoral plurality) and advance the interests of either a general minority or distinct categories and groups within society. From a Canadian perspective, this dichotomy may be reflected by the central and dominant role of the government's mandate as provided by the House of Commons, on the one hand, and the constitutional and popular desire to ameliorate that overwhelming dominance, on the other hand, through competing institutions. The role of the Supreme Court of Canada in determining the constitutional limits of legislative and executive authority within the country (though technically inconsistent with the Westminster principle of parliamentary supremacy) offers one such reflection of this latter desire. The Senate of Canada has provided a potential source for that same desire, especially in terms of the motivations and ideas that have characterized many reform proposals.

THE INSTITUTIONAL EXPRESSION OF POLITICAL THOUGHT

The normative context of political thought, though frequently overlooked, is a vital component of a broader political analysis. Certain subjects cannot be properly understood or appreciated without a similar understanding and appreciation of the beliefs, principles, and values that provide the context from which they emerge and which shape them. Politics does not occur within a value-neutral vacuum. Likewise, political practices and institutions have a normative foundation that is essential for understanding them in a meaningful way and for affecting meaningful change in relation to them.

Two such contexts need to be considered in relation to the overall subject of this study. The parliamentary upper house, as a general institutional presence within the history of the parliamentary system of government (particularly, though not exclusively, in terms of the Westminster model) can be explained in terms of multiple philosophical and ideological traditions. The Canadian parliamentary system is the product of an even more specific heritage of political thought and ideals. That specific heritage, though, is not homogeneous and the identification of those traditions and values that are most relevant to its institutions and their development can be contentious. Nonetheless, it is possible to identify ideas and trends that are especially relevant to that system and, particularly, relevant to its parliamentary upper house. The absence of that sort of consideration and analysis raises the distinct possibility that a critical discussion of the true purpose and reform of that institution risks being incomplete or, arguably, even superficial.

Therefore, a critical evaluation of the parliamentary upper house, in particular, and the Canadian Senate, in general, from the perspective of political theory and philosophy should be an essential component of this broader goal. It does not provide, by itself, a sufficient basis for this overall analysis, as other chapters within this study clearly indicate. Nonetheless, it is a vital part of a critical whole that contributes to a necessarily comprehensive approach, especially for avoiding the consequence of basing such a crucial appraisal and reform upon unchallenged assertions, superficially held principles, and, possibly, mere wishful thinking. As a complement to other aspects of this overall analysis and assessment, it should not be discounted. Relationships between aspects of these traditions of political thought and potential options for reform of the Senate of Canada have been observed within this chapter and they should be remembered (even when they are not specifically noted) as distinct models and proposals for that reform are presented and considered throughout this book.

NOTES

1. Arthur Herman, *The Cave and the Light: Plato* versus *Aristotle and the Struggle for the Soul of Western Civilization* (New York: Random House, 2014), pp. 27–22.
2. Plato, *The Republic*, C. D. C. Reeve, trans. and ed. (Indianapolis: Hackett, 2004), ch. 7; R. W. Sharples, "Plato on Democracy and Expertise," Greece and Rome, vol. 41 (April 1994), pp. 51–54.
3. Plato, ch. 8; Mark Blitz, *Plato's Political Philosophy* (Baltimore: Johns Hopkins University Press, 2010), pp. 166–190.
4. Josine Blok, "Citizenship, the Citizen Body, and Its Assemblies," in *A Companion to Ancient Greek Government*, Hans Beck, ed. (Oxford: John Wiley and Sons, 2013), pp. 161–175; P. J. Rhodes, *The Athenian Boule* (Oxford: Oxford University Press, 1985), sec. 2.
5. Andrew Linott, "Aristotle and Democracy," *Classical Quarterly*, vol. 42, no. 1 (1992), pp. 115–118.
6. Aristotle, *The Politics*, Carnes Lord, trans. and ed. (Chicago: University of Chicago Press, 2013), book IV, parts XIII–XIV; Kevin M. Cherry, "The Problem of Polity: Political Participation and Aristotle´s Best Regime," *Journal of Politics*, vol. 71, no. 4 (October 2009), pp. 1,406–1,421.
7. R. K. Sinclair, *Democracy and Participation in Athens* (Cambridge: Cambridge University Press, 1988), pp. 73–105.
8. Aristotle, *The Constitution of Athens*, Thomas J. Dymes, trans. (Omaha: Gryphon Editions, 2014), sec. 7; James Lindly Wilson, "Deliberation, Democracy, and the Rule of Reason in Aristotle's Politics," *American Political Science Review*, vol. 105, no. 2 (May 2011), pp. 268–271.
9. A. H. U. Colquhoun, *The Fathers of Confederation: A Chronicle of the Birth of the Dominion* (Toronto: Glass, Brook, and Company, 1916), pp. 1–11.
10. Jerry Z. Muller, Conservatism (Princeton, NJ: Princeton University Press, 1997), pp. 32–77.
11. Russell Kirk, *The Conservative Mind: From Burke to Eliot* (Washington, DC: Regnery, 1985), pp. 3–11.
12. A. F. Pollard, *The Evolution of Parliament* (London: Russell and Russell, 1964), pp. 120–124.
13. M. Guizot, *History of Oliver Cromwell and the English Commonwealth* (London: Richard Bentley, 1854), vol. 2, pp. 347–359.
14. Corinne C. Weston, "Salisbury and the Lords, 1868–1895," *The Historical Journal*, vol, 25, no. 1 (March 1982), pp. 103–107.

15. Quentin Skinner, "Hobbes on Sovereignty: An Unknown Discussion," *Political Studies,* vol. 13, (1965), pp. 213–218.
16. Thomas Hobbes, *Leviathan*, ch. 25 (near end).
17. Edmund Burke, *Reflections on the Revolution in France*, J. G. A. Pocock, ed. (Indianapolis: Hackett, 1987), p. 39.
18. Burke, p. 165.
19. Herman Finer, *The Theory and Practice of Modern Government* (London: Methuen, 1962), pp. 400–403.
20. Stephen Gardbaum, "Liberalism, Autonomy, and Moral Conflict," *Stanford Law Review*, vol. 48, no. 2 (January 1996), pp. 385–417.
21. Charles Larmore, "Political Liberalism," *Political Theory*, vol. 18, no. 3 (August 1990), pp. 339–360.
22. James Tully and Quentin Skinner, *An Approach to Political Philosophy: Locke in Contexts* (Cambridge: University of Cambridge Press, 1993), pp. 9–70.
23. Lee Ward, "Locke on Executive Power and Liberal Constitutionalism," *Canadian Journal of Political Science*, vol. 38, no. 3 (September 2005), pp. 719–744.
24. Matthew H. Kramer, *John Locke and the Origins of Private Property* (Cambridge: Cambridge University Press, 1997), pp. 15–36.
25. MacKay, pp. 45–47.
26. Meg Russell, "What are Second Chambers For?" *Parliamentary Affairs,* vol. 54 (2001), pp. 451–453.
27. Gerry Mackie, "Schumpeter's Leadership Democracy," *Political Theory*, vol. 37, no. 1 (February 2009), pp. 138–141.John Stuart Mill, *Considerations on Representative Government* (Amherst, NY: Prometheus Books, 1991), pp. 256–258, 275–278.
28. Bernard Crick, *Democracy: A Very Short Introduction* (Oxford: Oxford University Press, 2002), pp. 69–76.
29. John Stuart Mill, *Considerations on Representative Government* (New York: Harper and Brothers, 1862), ch. 13, para. 5.
30. William H. Riker, "The Justification of Bicameralism," *International Political Science Review*, vol. 13, no. 1 (January 1992), pp. 101–116.
31. Kurt A. Raaflaub and Robert W. Wallace, "'People's Power' and Egalitarian Trends in Archaic Greece," in *Origins of Democracy in Ancient Greece*; Kurt A. Raaflaub and Josiah Ober, eds. (Berkeley: University of California Press, 2007), pp. 22–48.
32. Robert Dahl, *A Preface to Democratic Theory* (Chicago: University of Chicago Press, 2006), pp. 63–89.
33. Per Mouritsen, "Four Models of Republican Liberty and Self-Government," in *Republicanism in Theory and Practice*, Iseult Honohan and Jeremy Jennings, eds. (London: Routledge, 2005), pp. 17–38.
34. Desmond Morton, *A Short History of Canada* (Toronto: McClelland and Stewart, 2006), pp. 44–45.
35. Philip Petit, *Republicanism: A Theory of Freedom and Government* (Oxford: Oxford University Press, 1997), pp. 171–205.
36. Aristotle, *Politics*, Book 4, pt. XIV.
37. Montesquieu, *De l'esprit des lois*, Victor Goldschmidt, ed. (Paris: Flammarion, 1993), book XI, ch. 6.

38. Thomas L. Pangle, *Montesquieu's Theory of Liberalism: A Commentary on the* Spirit of the Laws (Chicago: University of Chicago Press, 1973), pp. 48–106.

39. Montesequie, book XI, ch. 6.

40. Edmund Burke, *The Philosophy of Edmund Burke: A Selection from His Speeches and Writing*, Louis I. Bredvold and Ralph G. Ross, eds. (Ann Arbor: University of Michigan Press, 1970), pp. 147–149.

41. Jean Yarbrough, "“Representation and Republicanism: Two Views,”" *Publius*, vol. 9, no. 2 (Spring 1979), pp. 80–81.

42. J. R. Pole, *Political Representation in England and the Origins of the American Republic* (Berkeley: University of California Press, 1971), Gordon Wood, *The Creation of the American Republic: 1776–1787* (Chapel Hill: University of North Carolina Press, 1969).

43. Thomas H. Hammond and Gary J. Miller, "The Core of the Constitution," *American Political Science Review*, vol. 81, no. 4 (December 1987), pp. 1,169–1,170.

44. Gordon S. Wood, *The Creation of the American Republic, 1776–1787* (Durham: University of North Carolina Press, 1998), pp. 181–188.

45. Yarbrough, pp. 77–98.

46. William J. Daniels, "The Geographic Factor in Appointments to the United States Supreme Court, 1789–1976," *Western Political Quarterly*, vol. 31, no. 2 (June 1978), pp. 226–237.

47. Blaine Baker, "Strategic Benthanism: Rehabilitating United Canada's Bar through Criminal Law Codification, 1847–1854," in *Essays in the History of Canadian Law: A Tribute to Peter N. Oliver*, Jim Phillips, Roy McMurtry, and John Saywell, eds. (Toronto: University of Toronto Press, 2008), pp. 257–318.

48. J. C. C. Smart and Bernard Williams, *Utilitarianism: For and Against* (Cambridge: Cambridge University Press, 1973), pp. 3–9.

49. Jonathan Riley, "Utilitarian Ethics and Democratic Government," *Ethics*, vol. 100, no. 2 (January 1990), pp. 335–348.

50. Lewis Rockow, "Bentham of the Theory of Second Chambers," *American Political Science Review*, vol. 22, no. 3 (August 1928), p. 581.

51. Jeremy Bentham, "To His Fellow Citizens of France on Houses of Peers and Senates," in Jeremy Bentham, *The Works of Jeremy Bentham*, vol. 2, John Bowring and Richard Smith, eds. (Edinburgh: William Tate, 1843), pp. 419–450.

52. Jon Elster, "What´s Everybody´s Business is Nobody´s Business: Bentham on Political Assemblies," pp. 26–28, http://www.afsp.msh-paris.fr/activite/groupe/grpp/grpp131010textes/ s3elster.pdf

53. Jeremy Bentham, *A Fragment on Government* (London: T. Payne, 1776), ch. 3, para. 8–19.

54. Bentham, p. 422.

55. J. Elster, "La nuit de 4 août 1789:Une étude de l'interaction sociale dans la prise de décision collective," *Revue Européenne des Sciences Sociales,* vol. 45 (2007), pp. 71–94.

56. Jeremy Bentham (*lacunae* of Etienne Dumont), "An Essay on Political Tactics," in Jeremy Bentham, *The Works of Jeremy Bentham*, vol. 4, John Bowring and Richard Smith, eds. (Edinburgh: William Tate, 1843), ch. 1, sec. 5.

57. J. H. Burns, "Utilitarianism and Democracy," *Philosophical Quarterly*, vol. 9, no. 35 (April 1959), pp. 168–169.

58. Robert Meynell, *Canadian Idealism and the Philosophy of Freedom: C. B. Macpherson, George Grant, and Charles Taylor* (Montreal and Kingston, ON: McGill-Queen's University Press, 2011), pp. 215–230.

59. Olive Patricia Dickason, *Canada's First Nations: A History of Founding Peoples from Earliest Times* (Oxford: Oxford University Press, 2002), pp. 298–342; Eve Haque, *Multiculturalism within a Bilingual Framework: Language, Race, and Belonging in Canada* (Toronto: University of Toronto Press, 2012), pp. 9–30; Jaquetta Newman and Linda White, "The Women´s Movement in Canada," in *Gender and Women´s Studies in Canada: Critical Terrain*, Margaret Hobbs and Carla Rice, eds. (Toronto: Women´s Press of Canada, 2013), pp. 656–668.

60. Stephen Mulhall and Adam Swift, *Liberals and Communitarians* (Oxford: Blackwell, 1997), pp. 102–126.

61. Amy Gutmann, "Communitarian Critics of Liberalism," in *Communitarianism and Individualism*, Shlomo Avineri and Avner de-Shalit, eds. (Oxford: Oxford University Press, 2002), pp. 120–136.

62. Charles Taylor, "No Community, No Democracy," in *The Communitarian Reader: Beyond the Essentials*, Amitai Etzioni, Andrew Volmert, and Elanit Rothschild, eds. (Oxford: Rowman and Littlefield, 2004), pp. 27–43.

63. Jean Jacques Rousseau, *Du Contrat Social*, Bruno Bernardi, ed. (Paris: Falmmarion, 2012), p. 188.

64. Michael Walzer, "The Communitarian Critique of Liberalism," *Political Theory*, vol. 18, no. 1 (January 1990), pp. 9–11.

65. Michael J. Sandel, *Justice: What's the Right Thing to Do?* (New York: Farrar, Strauss, and Giroux, 2009), pp. 244–268

66. Allen E. Buchanan, "Assessing the Communitarian Critique of Liberalism," *Ethics*, vol. 99, no. 4 (July 1999), pp. 852–882.

67. Alexander Kaufman, "Hegel and the Ontological Critique of Liberalism," *American Political Science Review*, vol. 91, no. 4 (December 1997), pp. 807–817.

68. Stephen Houlgate, "Hegel, Rawls, and the Rational State," in *Beyond Liberalism and Communitarianism: Studies in Hegel's Philosophy of Right*, Robert R. Williams, ed. (Albany: State University of New York Press, 2001), pp. 256–257.

69. F. A. Kunz, *The Modern Senate of Canada* (Toronto: University of Toronto Press, 1967), p. 13.

70. John Porter, *The Vertical Mosaic: An Analysis of Social Class and Power in Canada* (University of Toronto Press: Toronto, 1965), pp. 533–557.

71. Walter Clement, *The Canadian Corporate Elite: An Analysis of Economic Power* (McClelland and Stewart: Toronto, 1975).

72. David Bell, "Political Culture in Canada," in *Canadian Politics in the 1980s*, Michael S. Whittington and Glen Williams, eds.(Methuen: Agincourt, ON, 1984), pp. 155–174.

73. Janet Ajzenstat, "Doing Canadian Political Thought," *Journal of Canadian Studies*, vol. 26, no. 2 (Summer 1991), pp. 5–6; Peter Smith, "Some Observations on the Revival of Canadian Political Thought," *Journal of Canadian Studies*, vol. 26, no. 2 (Summer 1991), pp. 3–6.

74. Louis Hartz, *The Liberal Tradition in America* (Harcourt, Brace and World: New York, 1955).

75. Kenneth D. McRae, "The Structure of Canadian History," in *The Founding of New Societies*, Louis Hartz, ed. (Harcourt, Brace, and World: New York, 1964), pp. 219–234.

76. Gad Horowitz, *Canadian Labour in Politics* (University of Toronto Press: Toronto, 1968), pp. 29–44.

77. George Grant, *Lament for a Nation* (McClelland and Stewart: Toronto, 1970), pp. 68–87.

78. Horowitz, pp. 33–35.

79. Seymour Martin Lipset, *Revolution and Counterrevolution* (Basic Books: New York, 1968), pp. 12–44.

80. Seymour Martin Lipset, "Canada and the United States: The Cultural Dimension," in *Canada and the United States: Enduring Friendship, Persistent Stress* (Prentice-Hall: Englewood Cliffs, NJ, 1985), pp. 109–160.

81. Charles Taylor, "Alternative Futures: Legitimacy, Identity, and Alienation in Late Twentieth Century Canada," in *Constitutionalism, Citizenship, and Society in Canada*, Alan Cairns and Cynthia Williams, eds. (University of Toronto Press: Toronto, 1985), pp. 183–229; Avigail I. Eisenberg, *Reconstructing Political Pluralism* (State University of New York Press: Albany, 1995), pp. 9–22.

82. Allen Buchanan, "The Role of Collective Rights in the Theory of Indigenous Peoples' Rights," *Transnational Law and Contemporary Problems*, vol. 89, no. 3 (Spring 1993), pp. 89–108; J. Angelo Corlett, "The Problem of Collective Moral Rights," *Canadian Journal of Law and Jurisprudence*, vol. 7, no. 2 (July 1994), pp. 237–259; Will Kymlicka, "Liberalism and the Politicization of Ethnicity," *Canadian Journal of Law and Jurisprudence*, vol. 4, no. 2 (July 1991), pp. 239–256; Leslie R. Shapard, "Group Rights," *Public Affairs Quarterly*, vol. 4, no. 2 (Summer 1990), pp. 299–308.

83. Donald J.C. Carmichael, Thomas C. Pocklington, and Gregory E. Prycz, *Democracy and Rights in Canada* (Harcourt, Brace, Jovanovich: Toronto, 1991), pp. 1–19.

84. M. James Penton, "Collective versus Individual Rights: The Canadian Charter of Rights and Freedoms," in *The U.S. Bill of Rights and the Canadian Charter of Rights and Freedoms*, William R. McKercher, ed. (Ontario Economic Council: Toronto, 1983), pp. 179–182; James T. McHugh, "The Illusion of Collective Rights in Canadian Constitutional Jurisprudence," presented to the annual conference of the New England Political Science Association, Springfield, MA, May 1996.

85. William Christian and Colin Campbell, *Political Parties and Ideologies in Canada* (McGraw-Hill Ryerson: Toronto, 1983), pp. 45–51.

86. David M. Beatty, *Putting the Charter to Work* (McGill-Queen's Press: Montreal and Kingston, 1987), pp. 116–132.

87. F. D. Forbes, "Hartz-Horowitz at Twenty," *Canadian Journal of Political Science*, vol. 20, no. 2 (Summer 1987), pp. 292–296.

88. W.L. Morton, *The Canadian Identity* (University of Wisconsin Press: Madison, 1961).

89. J.B. Brebner, *Canada: A Modern History* (University of Michigan Press: Ann Arbor, 1960), pp. 105–108.

90. R. Cole Harris and John Warkentin, *Canada Before Confederation* (Oxford University Press: New York, 1974), pp. 110–166; W.L. Morton, *The Kingdom of Canada* (University of Toronto Press: Toronto, 1963), pp. 174–176; W.G. Shelton, "The United Empire Loyalists: A Reconsideration," in *Readings in Canadian History: Preconfederation*, R. Douglas Francis and Donald B. Smith, eds. (Holt, Rinehart and Winston: Toronto, 1990), pp. 234–243.

91. John Stuart Mill, *On Liberty*, Elizabeth Rapaport, ed. (Hackett: Indianapolis, 1984); C. B. Macpherson, *The Life and Times of Liberal Democracy* (Oxford University Press: Oxford, 1977), pp. 25–37.

92. Peter Hogg, *Constitutional Law of Canada* (Carswell: Toronto, 1985), pp. 12–20.

93. C.B. Macpherson, *Democracy in Alberta* (University of Toronto Press: Toronto, 1955), pp. 3–28.

94. Max Wyman, "Tomorrow's Rights in the Mirror of History," in *Civil Liberties in Canada*, Gerald L. Gall, ed. (Buttersworth: Toronto, 1982), pp. 26–50.

95. Christina McCall Newman, *Grits* (Macmillan: Toronto, 1982).

96. Giovanni Sartori, *The Theory of Democracy Revisited* (Chatham House: Chatham, NJ, 1987), pp. 3–20.

Chapter 4

Historical Continuity of the Senate of Canada

THE SENATE AND CONTINUITY

The political activities and behavior of the Senate of Canada have been criticized both for their potential power to overrule the elected House of Commons and for their apparent lack of "effective" output. Those criticisms may reflect fundamental changes in parliamentary government that have occurred throughout its history. They also may reflect expectations of the Senate's constitutional architects and a consistent response to conventions that have informed appropriate roles for the parliamentary upper house, especially within the context of the evolution of parliamentary democracy and the Westminster model.

The fact that the Senate of Canada was not intended by its framers to be "elected" or "equal" does not necessarily negate efforts to transform it in that manner. But it can be argued that the Fathers of Confederation and their contemporaries did intend for the Senate to be "effective." Yet the definition of "effectiveness" among this political institution's designers differed, significantly, from the expectations of some current reformers. During its developmental years, the Senate of Canada demonstrated an appreciation of conventions that were shaping modern parliamentary democracy and the theoretical and practical role of a parliamentary upper house that continues to guide its institutional function and behavior.

The expectations accompanying the Senate's immediate predecessors, its own creation, and its first decade of existence under both Conservative and Liberal administrations reveal a historical political body that behaved in a manner that appears to be remarkably similar to much of its current activities. In order to appreciate the unreformed Senate of today, it is useful to examine its past—particularly its early years. The first decade of its existence is particularly suitable, not only because those years were formative ones but, also, because they spanned a period that included changes in government (resulting in a majority of Senators belonging to the opposition party), enormous infrastructural development of the country, significant policy pursuits, and the establishment of an initial direction for the new political system.

Expectations for an Upper House for British North America

As indicated within chapter 2, the Senate of Canada was a successor to the concept of the Legislative Council that had been introduced by Britain within its North American colonies. Of the various philosophical understandings and motivations relating to the purpose of a second chamber (as addressed within chapter 3), the classic conservative British model understandably prevailed when politicians initially conceived of a Canadian parliamentary upper house.[1] Simultaneously, it was consciously part of a still-emerging liberal democratic parliamentary system. That role of the parliamentary upper house in general was intended to ensure that democratically elected governments, while effective, were restrained by considerations of other interests. Those ideological expectations and influences would evolve and change but its role in shaping institutional expectations would continue to influence its development.[2]

While other philosophical influences on the development of the upper house would become increasingly relevant during the 20th century, the bridge that this conservatism provided with an increasingly liberal, though still prudent, Britain of the 18th and early 19th centuries influenced the treatment of its empire, including the changing imperial marketplace.[3] This perspective was present within the colonial governments that emerged at that time, especially Upper and Lower Canada.[4] That transitional early 19th century would be eclipsed by a growing desire for both unity and truly responsible government. Therefore, the lack of an electoral mandate did not negate the role that a non-elected Senate was intended to contribute to this liberal democratic system.[5]

The Senate was not intended to be a mere continuation of the Legislative Councils that had, during the mid-19th century, frequently sought to curtail or undermine more representative bodies. Simultaneously, though, because democratic institutions typically do not represent the will of all and, often, fail even to reflect true majoritarian interests, the Senate's role can be interpreted as an acknowledgment of that factor, especially its role in protecting liberal concepts of property interests and rights.[6] As indicated within chapter 2, the role of the upper house would increasingly shift from serving the interests of the leading families of their respective societies toward broader political goals. By the 1860s, those inclinations would be evident within both the creation and the early activity of the Senate of Canada.

CONSTITUTIONAL CONCEPTION

The first decade of the existence of the Senate of Canada (roughly from 1867 to 1878) offers an instructive period for explaining its early political establishment, its initial constitutional role, its formative membership, and the expectations surrounding them. Certain case studies, during this period, may be especially revealing in this respect. But the Senate was not created as a novel institutional concept. Therefore, it is important to consider its pre-Confederation background before assessing its initial years of existence as a clue to its later development and current status.

As the idea of creating a permanent union of the British North American provinces, endowed with domestic self-government, became increasingly attractive, the structure of its legislative system, upon which its government would be based, became a growing concern. British North America lacked a land-based (with the exception of the early *seigneurs* of New France) and hereditary aristocracy. Therefore, it was not feasible to transfer the House of Lords model, directly, to the Westminster system that the Fathers of Confederation envisioned. Nonetheless, in that spirit, they sought to create an upper house of that system that reflected its general principles, though not its parochial features. Therefore, the upper house would not be a mirror of the lower house; its members would represent a distinct segment (if not constituency) of the country. The Senate was intended to reflect the elite interests of an entrepreneurial class that, like its neighbor to the South, had been instrumental in bringing this new country to the brink of economic viability as an autonomous (if not yet fully sovereign) political society.[7]

That distinction is significant. The House of Commons was intended to reflect the popular will and, in the spirit of political developments in Britain, become the prime source of political legitimacy for Her Majesty's Government for Canada. Initially, in contrast to the House of Commons, the Canadian Senate's membership was overwhelmingly dominated by elites with backgrounds in manufacturing, commerce, trade, banking, and large-scale agriculture. Over time, this aspect of the Senate's composition would be reflected, as well, by the members of the lower house so, now, both chambers have a composition that reflects an economically elite bias.[8] But the principle that the membership of the Senate should not be a mere cipher of the House of Commons but ought to reflect a different constituency (interestingly, consistent with republican principles of "virtual representation" that will be addressed elsewhere within this book) remained a foundational ideal for that chamber.

The body that was created was intended to address concerns relating to regional representation, centered upon the two largest former provinces of Canada East (formerly Lower Canada and to become, again, Quebec) and Canada West (formerly Upper Canada and to become Ontario) plus the much smaller Maritime Provinces. A strong representation of, and protection for, the Francophone community, centered in Quebec, provided a particularly strong focus in that respect. Therefore, the final design of the Senate that emerged from those deliberations would provide for a relatively fixed number of appointed Senators (an allowance was made for a few additional appointments under certain circumstances) who would have the same formal powers as the House of Lords, plus particular responsibility for certain private bills (such as divorce bills) and other parochial concerns.[9]

The Charlottetown Conference was a relatively brief preliminary meeting held by the future "Fathers of Confederation." Its main result was the establishment of the formula that would be adopted for the formal discussion and negotiation of a union of the British North American colonies. The importance of a parliamentary upper house to these delegates was evidenced by the fact that six of the fourteen days of that conference were spent discussing the upper house, though the specific content of those discussions remains vague.[10] The subsequent Confederation Debates that took place in Quebec in 1864 indicate that a primary motivation behind the creation of a Canadian upper house was the maintenance of institutional ties to the British government and its Westminster model.

The assumption was that this parliamentary chamber would need to be British in nature and design and, therefore, imitate the House of Lords as much as was feasible within the Canadian context.[11] But a secondary, and almost equally important, motivation was to use the upper house as a forum for addressing the concern of the separate provinces within this impending federal union.[12] This concern was particularly acute among the Maritime Provinces, whose smaller size would make them susceptible to political domination by the colonies that were destined to become the provinces of Ontario and Quebec.[13] Despite the fact that the United States would have provided a more appropriate model for this consideration, it was seldom formally mentioned except in general terms and its own upper house was never specifically referenced as a model for the Canadian upper house.

CONSTITUTIONAL CONSTRUCTION

A preliminary copy of the British North America Act that was drafted in January 1867 specified that the members of the new Canadian "Legislative Council" would have all of the rights, responsibilities, privileges, powers, and duties of the House of Lords, except for the judicial functions that the British upper house traditionally exercised.[14] A brief debate relating to this proposal in the House of Lords indicated general approval of the idea of modeling the Canadian upper house upon itself as a means of preserving the traditions and conventions of the British constitutional tradition within a Canadian environment.[15] However, some Canadian politicians were not, necessarily, as enamored of this direct influence, though they remained committed to the general principle of maintaining a bicameral parliamentary system for this new union. J. H. Cameron, for example, warned of the danger of imposing British traditions too closely upon a Canadian political culture that had not incubated some of the same traditions and circumstances of the British model, including the lack of a distinctly aristocratic class and its associated interests.[16] The future Prime Minister, John A. Macdonald, emphasized that concern when he noted that the members of this Canadian upper house would be "men of the people, and from the people."[17] Nonetheless, he invoked the example of the House of Lords in certain respects, especially as an example of general restraint in its relationship with the lower house—a restraint that should prevent it from opposing the will of the lower house and the government that it supported, particularly in the presence of a clear popular mandate.[18]

Meanwhile, the Governor-General of the Province of Canada (and future Governor-General of Canada), Charles Stanley, Viscount Monck, was concerned that members of a Canadian upper house might behave like common politicians of that country and comport themselves with less-than-acceptable dignity, relative to the distinction that this chamber implied. Therefore, he recommended to the British Secretary of State for the Colonies, the Earl of Carnarvon, that members of the Canadian second chamber should be made baronets or received some other title that would be consistent with the status of this institution—a suggestion that also was made by John A. Macdonald.[19] As Joseph Cauchon noted, "they [members of the Canadian upper house] will not, like the House of Lords, have privileges to save from destruction."[20] But despite the general acknowledgment that there would be no hereditary or, even, formally privileged Canadian class upon which its parliamentary upper house would be based (or which would serve as its primary constituency), an assumption also could be detected that such a chamber should be dominated by the propertied interests of the new country. At the Quebec Conference, John A. Macdonald had been explicit on this point when he stated that "there should be a large property qualification for the upper house, which is then representative of property," though delegates from Prince Edward Island and Newfoundland (neither of whose provinces initially would become members of this Confederation) succeeded in having the property qualification for membership in the Canadian upper house lowered to the still-considerable sum (for that time) of $4,000.00.[21]

The remaining concerns relating to the creation of a Canadian parliamentary upper house focused upon the subjects of protecting the Francophone minority, the number of its members, the method for selecting its members, and its ultimate authority in relation to the lower house and the government that this lower chamber would support. Many Francophone delegates to the Quebec Conference expressed concerns that representation within the second chamber, even if it was equally divided among the provinces, would still leave them vulnerable to the majority status of Anglophone delegates from across the new country. This concern was particularly acute as these delegates had been assured that the upper house would serve as an institutional source of protection for language and cultural rights within Canada.[22]

A related concern was the quasi-judicial role that was projected for the upper house in confirming divorce litigation in the form of private bills. The majority of Francophones were Roman Catholics and that church was anxious that its position on such matters could be disregarded by the non-Catholic majority that would dominate this chamber as well as the country.[23] This concern was alleviated, somewhat, by the fact that the Province of Quebec would have an overwhelming Francophone majority and the Francophone representation within the lower house would be sufficiently strong to compel elected federal governments to be sensitive to the needs of this linguistic minority.[24]

Sir John A. Macdonald engaged in a particularly pointed address of the issue of the formal powers of the Canadian upper house. He was concerned by a recommendation that this new chamber should not be restricted in the number of its members. That recommendation was prompted, directly, by the example of the political crisis concerning the Reform Bill of 1832,[25] when the British government persuaded the monarch to create a sufficient number of new peers in order to overcome (the language used in reference to it was to "swamp") an obstructive House of Lords when it proved to be determined to oppose the will of the government, the lower house, and overwhelming public opinion.[26] Macdonald countered that such a move would make the upper house redundant. Simultaneously, he also asserted that this chamber would respect the ultimate popular will that served as the basis for the representation of the lower house.[27] But the popular mandate, though a prime importance, should not be the sole source of political power within a country that would be as diverse as this one was projected to be.

> There would be no use of an upper house if it did not exercise, when it thought proper, the right of opposing of amending or postponing the legislation of the lower house. It would be of no value whatever were it to be a mere chamber for registering the decrees of the lower house. It must be an independent house … preventing any hasty or ill-considered legislation which may come from that body, but it will never set itself in opposition against the deliberate and understood wishes of the people.[28]

The final, vital question of the method of selection for membership in the Canadian upper house was based upon two main alternatives: election or appointment by the Crown. Although addressed by many of the participants in the Confederation Debates, the arguments in favor of, and opposed to, each alternative were, generally, consistent. The principal argument in favor of an elected upper house was that it would keep it responsive to the needs and wishes of the populace. The U.S. Senate was cited as an example of such a chamber, which was held to be an excellent illustration of an institution that successfully checked the "rash tendencies" of its respective lower chamber, the House of Representatives.[29] But these arguments were overwhelmed by the support for the alternative of appointment. An elected upper house was regarded as being inconsistent with British constitutional conventions that provided the foundation for this new political system.

Furthermore, the experience of an elected upper house within the legislature of Canada in 1856 was cited as an example of its defects, especially because its perceived obstructionism (even in matters relating to the budget) had been justified by the fact that it was an elected chamber. Concerns about the effect of elections upon imposing party discipline, patronage, and electoral corruption also were cited. Meanwhile, the independence of peers within the House of Lords was cited as an example of the independence that members with an indefinite tenure (whether by heredity or appointment) would enjoy while, also, being acutely aware of the legitimacy of the elected chamber in a manner that would temper the political behavior of its members and lead to restraint when appropriate.[30]

Even George Brown, Editor of *The Globe* and often supportive of populist sentiment, warned that an elected Canadian upper house could demand equal authority with the lower house over supply bills[31] while John A. Macdonald noted that an elected upper house would be susceptible to party discipline, internal patronage, and partisan opposition to the government mandate in the lower house.[32] George Etienne Cartier perhaps best summarized the opposition to a Senate with an elected membership and other institutional features designed to make it an effective "check" on the lower house and government when he observed that "We, who had the benefit of being able to contemplate republicanism in action during a period of eighty years, saw its defects, and felt convinced that purely democratic institutions could not be conducive to the peace and prosperity of nations."[33]

FORMATIVE YEARS: 1867–1878

Once those matters were resolved, public discussion relating to the proposed Canadian upper house virtually disappeared, reflecting a general concurrence with Macdonald's vision for the Canadian upper house as part of a broader Westminster-style system of government.[34] The early decades of the

Senate of Canada would establish the pattern for its practical powers and performance. It also would reveal certain interesting tendencies, especially in relation to general theories concerning the purpose and role of parliamentary upper houses in general.

Concerns about the Senate's response to having a majority of its members belong to the Opposition were tested when the Liberal Party won the election of 1874, replacing the Conservative government under Prime Minister Macdonald. The new Prime Minister, Alexander Mackenzie, was concerned about having his party's agenda frustrated in the Senate and, for that reason, he had requested that the Colonial Minister in London, Lord Kirby, endorse his request that the Governor-General appoint an additional number (as many as six) of Senators above the limit ordinarily established under the British North America Act. When Lord Kirby refused to make this recommendation, many Senators took advantage of the incident in order to state their own vision of the Senate's proper constitutional role. The Leader of the Conservative Party in the Senate, Alexander Campbell, strongly expressed his belief that the Senate would never oppose the clear will of the people, especially as it lacked an electoral mandate of its own and it, unlike the House of Lords, was not an institution of "caste and privilege which none of our people are imbued with." Other Senators from both parties expressed similar beliefs within the context of this particular discussion.[35]

It was not, however, the restraint otherwise shown by the Senate that was telling but the reason for that opposition that revealed an important pattern of behavior for that body that would typify its overall behavior in subsequent years and indicate its relationship to the general pattern of parliamentary upper houses. The Senate demonstrated this resolve during the next several years of Liberal rule. The Senate's Conservative majority acted against the Liberal government's policies in only two significant instances: one involving a government contract and the other one involving active opposition to government legislation in only one major incident. In both cases, popular opinion was the single most common rationale that Senators invoked in support of their actions. Senate opposition to the Georgian Bay Railway contract (which would have resulted in the construction of an expensive branch of the main transcontinental line that would have served an isolated area) had been expressed through an address of the Senate to the Governor-General, requesting that he lay before the Senate copies of correspondence between the federal government and the provincial Government of Ontario concerning land grants to the company that constituted the private party. The address was approved without division after a long debate and the government soon abandoned the proposed contract.[36]

When the Liberal Secretary of State, Senator Scott, insisted that Senate pressure had not been responsible for the government's withdrawal of the

Georgian Bay contract, Senator Dickey retorted that "the vote of the Senate on that occasion was not only in accordance with the sentiment of the country, but also with the action of the Government, afterward."[37] Other Senators also contended that the only reason they felt confident in acting as they had done was because of public opposition to this contract.[38] But the most conspicuous action on the part of the Senate during this period was in relation to another proposed branch of the transcontinental railway—this one to be constructed between the Vancouver Island communities of Esquimalt and Nanaimo. The enacting legislation for this undertaking was supported not only by the Liberal government but, even, by John A. Macdonald, now the Leader of the Loyal Opposition in the House of Commons.[39] However, a great deal of public opposition existed, particularly because this railway branch was described as superfluous, unacceptably expensive, and not specifically required by the political agreement that had brought British Columbia into Confederation. Nonetheless, although rigorous debate over the enacting legislation had been anticipated in the Senate, the actual defeat of the legislation (which subsequently was not reintroduced in the House of Commons) in April 1875 was unexpected.[40]

The Governor-General, Lord Dufferin, had long been contemptuous of the Senate, describing it as "an absurdly effete body, and given no sign of life since I have been in the country." He had supported Prime Minister Mackenzie's previous effort to appoint additional Senators, especially as he disliked the Senate's ability to defeat government legislation within the context of responsible parliamentary government.[41] Surprisingly, though, Lord Dufferin believed that the Senate's rejection of this bill was defensible, especially as it appeared to have been motivated by strong public opposition to it.

> I hope you will not think that I have expressed too strongly my own opinion that you would not compel the Senate to come back upon their vote. ... Moreover, constituted as the Senate is, and with its numbers fixed, it would have been out of the question to have allowed a vote of the nominated chamber to have overthrown a popular Minister, who commanded an overwhelming majority in the House of Commons. Now the case is different. Mackenzie's many blunders, and above all the degree to which his party has been implicated in electioneering malpractices, and the Big Push Letter, are really I believe producing a reaction against the Grits.[42]

This sort of rationale would be invoked in many examples of the Senate's contributions to the parliamentary process relating to government policy and legislation. This openly declared respect for the electoral mandate of the government through the lower house was an acknowledgement not merely of the conventions that have guided the Westminster model in general but, also, of the inherent danger of an upper house that might presume to oppose the will of that lower chamber in an illegitimate manner. It also reveals a level of self-awareness concerning the restrained and complementary role in which an upper house ought to engage according to theories of both the role of upper chambers, generally, and parliamentary responsible government in particular.[43]

Another characteristic of the Senate of Canada during these early decades was a relative demonstration of specialization and expertise among its members. Unlike the members of the House of Commons, who were becoming increasingly professionalized as politicians, Senators were not distracted by the need to secure election to their tenured parliamentary positions, nor were they as likely to be as engaged in partisan activities as their lower house colleagues—though two early Prime Ministers of Canada (Sir John Abbot and Sir Mackenzie Bowell) had been Senators. Although members of this upper chamber did not develop the sort of social and professional diversity, in this respect, that would characterize the House of Lords (especially following the introduction of life peers and, particularly, "people's peers") this distinction was notable and it arguably influenced its approach to its parliamentary role and responsibilities.[44]

RATIONALES FOR SENATE BEHAVIOR

Public opinion was the single most common defense that Senators employed when addressing public bills, including government legislation. In those rare occasions when it appeared possible that government legislation actually could be defeated, this rationale was particularly prominent as a defense of such actions, such as when the Conservative Senate Opposition Leader, Sir Alexander Campbell (who had been the law partner of Sir John A. Macdonald) asserted that the membership of the Canadian upper house, though unelected, was affected by the same "social winds" as the general public—a sentiment with which his fellow Senators appeared to concur.[45] That statement was made during a debate on a motion to congratulate the British Colonial Minister, Lord Kimberly, for refusing a request by the Liberal Prime Minister Alexander Mackenzie to summon additional Senators to Parliament, consistent with section 26 of the British North America Act of 1867.

A memorandum on this subject clearly indicated Mackenzie's concern was that Opposition Senators might interfere with government legislation and his belief that section 26 had been included within the British North America Act in order to address just such a potential situation. However, Lord Kimberly rejected the request, asserting that it should apply only to situations in which an actual and serious parliamentary impasse occurred.[46] The Senate responded to this incident by proposing an address to the Colonial Minister.

The ensuing debate on that motion provided Senators with an opportunity to explain and interpret their parliamentary role and legislative function, especially in response to the way it was perceived in the press and by the general public. Campbell, who also was the former Postmaster General for Canada, echoed the assertion of Sir John A. Macdonald during the Confederation Debates that the Senate was a chamber of "caste and privilege which none of our people are imbued with."[47]

However, Campbell did acknowledge that it was institutionally possible for the Canadian upper house to frustrate the popular will of the lower house, though it would be contrary to the constitutional spirit of the Canadian parliamentary system. He conceded that, under such circumstances, the creation of additional Senators would be appropriate. Nonetheless, he contended that such a move should occur only if the Senate action clearly contravened the popular will or public interest.

> It is a provision analogous (so far as the circumstances of this country will allow any provision to be analogous) to a similar provision in England to the reserve power subsisting in the Crown to create peers of Great Britain, a power to be used only in the event of an actual difficulty occurring in the actual administration of public affairs insoluble by other means.[48]

Campbell's Conservative colleague, Senator Robert Duncan Wilmot of New Brunswick, seconded both the motion and its sentiment that the independence of the Senate benefited the general public. He also warned that the ability to "swamp" the Senate with additional members would undermine its ability to protect the interests of the regions of Canada, especially the smaller provinces. This connection between the "public interest" and the interest of the electorate within individual provinces also was made by other Senators during this debate.[49]

During the first decade of its existence, Senators were conspicuous in defending the institution and its behavior upon the basis of reflecting the public will, public interest, and the evolving role of the upper house within a British-style parliamentary democracy. Senators also could assert (as will be addressed) a specialized status, independence, and expertise in certain areas as a justification for technical improvements, targeted scrutiny and, occasionally, opposition to specified policies and legislation. A particularly notable case study of this political attitude and approach presented itself in 1875.

ESQUIMALT AND NANAIMO RAILWAY BILL

A branch of the transcontinental railway system was promised to the people of Vancouver Island as part of the agreement for them to join with the mainland territories of British Columbia in 1866. It also had been understood as a condition for this part of British North America to accede to Confederation in the following year and, subsequently, for British Columbia to join Canada as a province in 1871.[50] Despite that assurance, railways within the province had come under strong scrutiny, especially following scandals involving the Canadian Pacific Railway (which had achieved its charter for the transcontinental railway after having provided a large donation to the Conservative Party's election fund) that ultimately resulted in the fall of the first Conservative government under Sir John A. Macdonald and the coming to power of the first Liberal government under Alexander Mackenzie.[51]

This debate was related to the Senate's ultimately successful opposition to the Esquimalt and Nanaimo Railway, which was the only significant legislative defeat that a government experienced in the Senate during its first decade of existence. The defeated legislation, in 1875, was a proposed bill for the construction of a branch of the transcontinental railway that was intended to be built between the Vancouver Island communities of Esquimalt and Nanaimo. Interestingly, the bill had been supported in the House of Commons by the Leader of the Opposition, Macdonald, who had been a strong proponent of the overall project. The fact that his Conservative Party had developed a strong base in British Columbia also may have influenced his support for the bill. However, opponents of the bill had argued that the acquisition of these public lands was superfluous, unacceptably expensive, and not specifically required by the agreement that brought British Columbia into Confederation.[52] The bill's defeat received strong objections in British Columbia and even led to demands that the province withdraw from Confederation.[53]

Conservative Senators thus defied the leadership of their party in defeating this legislation. It had been anticipated that the Senate would debate the bill in a vigorous manner but its outright defeat was unexpected and it became a source of indignation for both the Liberal government and the leadership of the Conservative opposition. As previously mentioned, the Governor-General, Lord Dufferin, though generally contemptuous of the Senate, conceded to the British Colonial Secretary, Lord Carnarvon, that public opinion had given that action considerable moral support.[54] Much of the Senate debate over the bill centered upon the economic and certain technical aspects of the controversy, as well as the relationship between this proposed branch line and the political agreement that had promised to connect British Columbia to the rest of Canada via the overall Canadian Pacific Railway system. In this way, the debate in the Senate was much like the debate in the House of Commons. However, in the Senate, the Conservatives were aware of two additional factors: though in opposition, they controlled a majority of seats in the upper house and the general mood of the country appeared to support their antagonism toward the bill.

A highly significant expression of this Senate opposition was the fact that it took the form of an amendment to the bill that was passed by the Commons that did not defeat it, outright, but required it to be delayed for further consideration until the next session of the current Parliament. Senator James Cox Aikins of Ontario retroactively explained this rationale in terms of a lack of a popular mandate for the bill, specifically justifying this approach when he asserted that the "Government has no right to assume an obligation of this kind and pledge the faith of the country to this measure."[55] Senators from British Columbia were, understandably, upset by this amendment and favored passage of the bill in order to ensure the transportation link between that province and the rest of the country.[56] Nonetheless, the amendment to delay the bill (effectively resulting in its immediate defeat) was easily passed. Even while upbraiding the Senate for this action, George Brown, though a staunch ally of the Liberal government, admitted that it probably enjoyed a consensus opinion of support from the Canadian electorate.[57]

This episode reflects two conventions that would continue to guide the political and constitutional development of the Canadian Senate: first, it was a highly selective action that was primarily justified upon the basis of its lack of a government electoral mandate; second, the *de facto* defeat of the bill assumed the form of a *de jure* "delay" that would permit the House of Commons to reconsider it—in other words, the application of a virtual "suspensive veto." In summarizing his support for this amendment that he had moved and that the Senate was on the verge of adopting, Senator Carrall, though a member of the Conservative Party, was careful to defend that action in terms that were highly cognizant of the context of parliamentary democracy within which it occurred. Of course, it could be claimed that his action was almost certainly motivated by partisan goals and calculations. But the fact that he felt compelled to justify it within a broader context that was highly aware of the circumstances and consequences of Canada as an evolving democracy and institutional practitioner of the Westminster model of government, nonetheless remains significant.

> I believe that the majority of this House will agree with me that the policy of the Government, or the no policy of the Government with respect to the Pacific Railway from its inception down to the present hour, has not given satisfaction to the people of Canada. … If I thought the vote for my resolution would have the effect of overthrowing the Government, I would hesitate to press it. [But] as I think the country is misrepresented I have not the slightest doubt, and I would point out, as a proof, to the result of nearly every new election since the General Election, which shows a rapid growth of absolute want of confidence in the Administration of the Day. I think this debate has elicited a great deal of information on the subject, and when the outside public reads the reports, it will, perhaps, have the effect of maturing public opinion, and forming some sound

policy upon which the railway scheme could be based that would be acceptable to the entire Dominion.[58]

Self-interest cannot be dismissed as a motivation for this action on the part of the Senate, especially given the ties to railway businesses, interests, and investments among many Senators at this time. But the rarity of an outright defeat of government legislation (in an area in which it enjoyed not only an electoral mandate, at least indirectly, and the support of the Leader of the Opposition) indicates that a strong defense was needed to justify this action. Yet those rationales were not confined to this exceptional case; they revealed themselves in other ways during this initial decade of the Senate's existence.

APPEALS TO PUBLIC OPINION AND POPULAR SUPPORT

Senate scrutiny and other legislative activity found expression in relation to other policy areas. For example, the Supreme Court Bill of 1875 aroused much controversy in the Canadian upper house. Much of the debate considered the legal and administrative problems of establishing a Supreme Court for the country.[59] However, such arguments were supplemented by the concern for the effect of such legislation upon the public, though they ultimately manifested themselves in the form of improving amendments rather than opposition to the bill, itself.[60] This approach is indicative of a pattern that would dominate the institutional behavior of the Senate—not only throughout this initial period but throughout its subsequent historical development as well.[61]

That pattern was strongly evident in the Senate's approach to legislation and parliamentary business such as its scrutiny of the Treaty of Washington in 1871, particularly relating to trade and fishing agreements with the United States.[62] Although the ratification of the treaty was the prerogative of the British government (as part of its continued imperial jurisdiction, following Confederation, over external Canadian affairs), the Parliament of Canada reviewed the treaty in order to provide an opportunity for public inquiry and the Senate was active in that role—with Senators such as George William Allan of Ontario noting that "there is a natural feeling on the part of anyone who is here in a representative capacity to state for the information of those whom he represents, the reasons that influence him to vote for a measure on which there may be a considerable diversity of opinion."[63]

It is particularly interesting to note the reference to a "representative capacity" from an appointed Senator in this instance. This sort of language was used by Senators, frequently, during this period and it appears to have been used for two purposes: stressing the relationship between Senators and the provinces and regions from which they were appointed; justifying their legislative activities in terms of a claim to reflect public sentiment in some manner. The latter justification understandably could be perceived to be a rationalization intended to defend the actions of a political agent who lacks an electoral mandate. But the very fact that such a rationalization even would be felt to be advisable, if not necessary, suggests the strong legitimizing influence of parliamentary democracy as a firmly established feature of Canadian political culture by this time.

Therefore, it was not unusual for Senators to defend their actions in reference to popular support, such as Senator Alexander Vidal's motion to adopt a report on the Prohibitory Liquor Law of 1873 (upon the basis of a supporting petition of 36,000 signatures) that was further supported by Senator Bill Flint of Ontario who cited this public expression as justification for establishing a select committee of the Senate on the subject. Likewise, in 1876, Senator James Dever of New Brunswick inferred that shifts in public opinion between elections ought to serve as a basis for scrutinizing the Courtenay Bay extension of the Canadian Pacific Railway.

> The motion which I have the honor of introducing is one in which I am most anxious every member of the Senate will take a deep interest, inasmuch as it relates to a portion of a great public work, known as the Intercolonial Railway, of this Dominion—a work to which each of us, as well as every individual in this country, is contributing a large share of their means, and thereby necessarily called on to see that none of those means are squandered or misused in the construction of any part of that property by anybody, much less by the Government the country has entrusted with its care.[64]

Even the Senate debate on the admission of British Columbia into Confederation was subject to populist appeal. The Senate insisted that the enacting bill should have been introduced into both parliamentary chambers, simultaneously, both out of respect for the privileges of the Senate and as a means of providing a more effective debate for the greater information and benefit of the public.[65] Even in the area of business and industrial policy in which many Senators could claim a particular prerogative of expertise and interest, recourse to public support also was expressed, as can be noted in the general tenor of a debate to delay passage of the Mechanics Bill of 1876.[66] A more pointed example of this rhetorical approach to legislation can be observed within the debate regarding the Marine Electric Telegraph Bill of 1875, particularly when Senator William Miller of Nova Scotia spoke in favor of its passage.

> There is a great public measure necessary in the interests of the country, and I would say of humanity—a great public amelioration, unanimously approved by

> the popular voice, and sent for ratification in this House, and I do not believe that the efforts of London or New York capitalists, the lobbying or wire-pulling of any "ring," will prevail in the Senate against the wishes and interests of the people, by defeating this Bill, and preventing the passage of an Act imperatively demanded by the public well-being.[67]

The Senate appeared to have an appreciation of its proper constitutional role as determined by unentrenched convention as much, or even more so, than by the formal powers provided to that chamber by the British North America Act—regardless of whether or not the majority in that house was from the same party as the current government. The Senate clearly preferred to behave as a parliamentary institution that could assist the government in tempering and improving legislation and policy,[68] often with the claim of rejecting (whether or not it was genuinely felt) partisan preferences in favor of a role that benefited the country and its people as a whole—a role that also had been conceived by its framers.[69] This assertion, prominently advocated during the Confederation debates, was reiterated, forcefully, by Senator Alexander Campbell when speaking on behalf of the Loyal Opposition during the debate on the reply to the Speech from the Throne for the first session of the new Liberal government.

> [T]he usefulness of the Senate will be to bring about the wishes of the people as brought forward by the other House. Although the Senate is independent of the popular voice, there is no such distinction between them and the other branch of the Legislature as to justify them in taking up the exalted position which the House of Lords sometimes assumed. Experience has shown that we ought to defer to the opinions of the people in all matters related to their welfare, and the Ministry who had that experience, and had public opinion so unmistakenly pronounced in their favour had a great public duty to perform. ... [W]e will not meet with any factuous [sic] opposition arising out of a spirit of warfare. We will be glad to assist the Government in perfecting those measures that might be submitted for the consideration of the Senate.[70]

This expression should, nonetheless, be contrasted with the belief, also frequently expressed within that chamber, that the Senate, while refusing to undermine the government, also should not merely provide a passive confirmation of public legislation. That belief was given a particularly poignant expression by Senator John Sewell Sanborn when he urged his colleagues to assume a more critical position in relation to the Offenses Against the Person Bill of 1869. Even though this policy reflected a priority for the government of his own party, Senator Sanborn asserted that the Canadian upper house had a constructive role that complemented the lower house.

> If we sit here simply as a recording House and allow Bills to pass through clause after clause without one scarcely knowing anything about them, leaving the

> responsibility of them upon members of the Cabinet who are with us, the country will begin to remark what advantage have we in choosing men of experience as Senators? What advantage is it to have them assemble, year after year, if they are merely to take the Bills of the Commons and pass them to the Governor-General to be sanctioned. This is a very utilitarian age, and while appointed we need to make sure of our ground and maintain that standing and respect before the country which our position demands, and which as the second House of Parliament we ought to take. We must discriminate in our views in legislating, and not let legislation pass merely as a matter of course. If it passes with our approval, it ought to pass with our intelligent approval.[71]

This attitude reflected a similar sentiment that was emerging, simultaneously, within the House of Lords as it was adjusting to the late-19th-century evolution of parliamentary democracy. Like its British model and counterpart, the Canadian Senate had become highly aware of the paramount importance of the electoral process and the legitimacy that it conferred upon the parliamentary system as a whole. The need to defer to the mandate of the electorate and public opinion (or, at least, to appear to defer) accompanied a general restraint in the legislative behavior of the upper house, an increased emphasis upon technical and other improvements to policies and bills, and an image of conspicuous scrutiny within the overall political process—a general trend noted within bicameral systems of the Westminster model during this period.[72]

SENATORS AND THEIR EXPERT BACKGROUNDS AND SPECIALIZATIONS

One other feature of the Senate that emerged during these first years of its existence was the manner in which its composition differed from the House of Commons. This characteristic reflected that theoretical category of the upper house as a chamber of "something else"—a political institution that represents a constituency that is not based upon the general population of society or, more specifically, the electorate.[73] Although in its early years the Senate did not reflect the sort of diversity that has become a more pronounced characteristic of upper houses in the 21st century (as addressed elsewhere with this book), its membership was self-consciously distinct from the House of Commons in a manner that appears to have been, at least somewhat, intentional.

The Fathers of Confederation intended the Canadian parliamentary upper house to possess a membership that would differ from the members of the lower house. The Senate initially was envisioned, at least partially, as an institution that would represent the interests of a more affluent section of

Canadian society and the economic sectors from which that wealth was generated.[74] Unlike the House of Lords, it would not reflect the medieval and agrarian legacy of an aristocratic class. Instead, like its neighbor to the South, affluent Canadians frequently achieved their success through the development of natural resources, trade, transportation, finance, and an emerging business sector and industrial capacity. Therefore, a certain level of logic might have directed the constitutional framers to conceive of the Senate (in the spirit of an upper house as an institution representing "something else") as a chamber that could promote the interests of that numerically small but powerful "constituency."[75] The fact that many early appointees to the Senate shared this background and expertise also led it, at times, to exert more scrutiny and activity in policy and legislation that were deemed particularly relevant to the new country's economic stability and future. Despite being, overall, deferential to the mandate of the government as reflected by the House of Commons, Senators did appear to recognize and claim this greater expertise as a means of enhancing their influence within the overall parliamentary and political process.[76]

The fact that a Senator was required to possess net assets of at least $4,000 (as previously noted, a considerable sum at the time) was indicative of this expectation. Although many members of the House of Commons also might reasonably be expected to be persons of financial means with interests and expertise derived from these sectors of the Canadian economy, the institutional constraints of party discipline and parliamentary process of the lower house would undermine the independent expression of that expertise and individual interest. As a result, the legislative participation of members of the House of Commons (at least overtly, though not necessarily excluding influence exerted within the party caucus or through other informal networks) would likely be reduced to support for official party policy.[77] Senators did not experience such constraint and, additionally, spent less time on parliamentary responsibilities, thus permitting them to devote more attention to the areas of their own areas of economic and other interests and expertise.[78]

F. A. Kunz has provided a particular critical historical appraisal of the composition of the Senate of Canada in terms of the business and other professional backgrounds of its members. During the latter part of the 19th century (including its early years), the Senate was dominated by members with business-related backgrounds—a trend that would continue through the middle of the 20th century and, according to Kunz, prove instrumental in shaping the role of the Senate as a source of active lobbying for business, industrial, and related economic interests. During the early decades of his study, Kunz concluded that 25% of all Senators had strong connections to manufacturing, 16% of them were merchants, and 7% of them had strong backgrounds in finance and banking, accounting for nearly half of the membership of that chamber. While Kunz has emphasized the negative implications (especially in terms of the promotion of self-interest) of this characteristic, it also became a basis for constructive interjections by Senators into the policy and legislative debates that were especially significant during the political system's early years.[79]

Railway legislation offers one of the best examples of the sorts of issues in which Canadian Senators had an opportunity to make practical parliamentary use of their professional diversity and expertise, especially in proportion to the time devoted to other policy areas during this period. During the debate on the admission of British Columbia to Confederation in 1871, economic issues, especially concerning the transcontinental railway, dominated the proceedings in the upper house. Senators appeared to be especially well-versed in the facts and figures concerning the economic implications of this issue—a characteristic that frequently was displayed throughout the proceedings of the Senate on several policy and legislative topics. An excellent example of this participation is the speech of Senator Robert Duncan Wilmot of New Brunswick who, despite being a member of the governing Conservative Party (he would become a Minister without Portfolio in a future Macdonald cabinet) and a strong advocate of Confederation, expressed doubts concerning the government's plan to link British Columbia by rail to the rest of the country. He was well-known for his concerns relating to patronage and he noted his own experience with railway planning and construction in New Brunswick during the 1850s.[80] From that experience, he emphasized the technical difficulties that the current government plan would need to overcome if its policy were to be successful.

> Whatever the House may do, I must enter my protest against such a suicidal policy. We have already had a little experience in the way of railway construction. I have been a member of a Committee formed on the motion of my honorable friend to the left [Hon. Mr. Wark], to enquire into matters connected with the Intercolonial Railway. I have seen that the expenditure on that road, in connection surveys alone, has amounted to $1,200 a mile—any railway engineer, who understood his business, would perform the same work for $500 a mile. ... We have had some experience in New Brunswick with respect to the construction of railways. The honourable member from St. John [Hon. Mr. Hazen] and myself were members of a Government who entered into a contract with an English firm, of which the late Mr. Brassey was a member, to build a railway from St. John to Shediac, and the westerly to the American boundary. The province agreed to take £1,200 stock per mile in the Company, and advance, as a first mortgage, £1,800 more—altogether £3,000 per mile. Unfortunately, for the country, that Government was displaced. ... They [the new government] thought that the road could be built for a smaller sum, and they agreed to buy out the English company for £90,000 sterling. The eventual result was that the

road cost $43,000 a mile cash paid. Instead of a charge on the province as was originally contemplated, of $12,000 per mile.[81]

Senators expressed disagreements within their own parties and their own provinces and regions concerning the implications of the admission of British Columbia. Senator William Miller was opposed by Senator Robert B. Dickey, both of Nova Scotia, concerning the fiscal assessment of this policy. His speech reveals, again, a technocratic tone that was much more indicative of Senate debates than often found among the participation of individual Members of Parliament within the lower house.

> I cannot agree with my honourable colleague from Nova Scotia [Mr. Miller], who put down the cost of the Central Pacific Railway at $32,000,000 to the United States Government; for on reference to an authority on the subject, I find that line of 1,774 miles, gave a large subsidy equal to $52,800,000 besides a guarantee for interest on an equal amount, and all this irrespective of the lands for alternate 20 mile sections. ... We have every reason to suppose that ... we would be landed in an expenditure of at least $150,000,000. The companies in the United States had, doubtless, some additional capital besides the Government assistance, which amounted to nearly $60,000 a mile. We are now asked, under these circumstances, to construct the work in ten years. ... The House will see that one of the greatest difficulties we would have to encounter would be the cost of getting up supplies and materials along the route—the iron, say 100 tonnes per mile.[82]

Of course, many participants in this debate had personal interests in the outcome of this policy, especially regarding railway contracts. That characteristic has been famously observed among legislators within other political systems (including upper houses), especially in terms of promoting personal financial interests.[83] Nonetheless, the fact that these Canadian Senators presented their experience and expertise as a distinct advantage to their participation within the legislative process in these policies areas is consistent with this particular characteristic of the parliamentary upper house as it evolved. Senator Donald McDonald, a leading Ontario Liberal and associate of Alexander Mackenzie, claimed this advantage in support of his arguments during this debate, despite the fact that the decision regarding "Section Fifteen" of the transcontinental railway could result in an awarding of the contract to his brother-in-law, Joseph Whitehead and the appointment of his own son as Whitehead's nominal partner—admittedly on behalf of himself. Similar advantages were sought by Conservative Senators John Sutherland of Manitoba, Frank Smith of Ontario, and David Lewis Macpherson of Ontario, though these obvious conflicts of interest were, retrospectively, presented to the Senate as advantages in terms of illuminating the debate with invaluable knowledge, background, and insight.[84]

Opposition to the Esquimalt-Nanaimo branch railway, ultimately resulting in the defeat of that bill in the Senate, largely was based and justified upon these claims of expert opinion on the part of Senators, even though personal interest often was involved. Expert testimony concerning the costs of this venture were prominent within this debate, such as the estimates provided by Senator James Cox Aikins of Ontario, who disputed the government's cost projections as being grossly and irresponsibly inflated. The tone and emphasis of the debate differed, markedly, between the two parliamentary chambers; while the debate in the House of Commons emphasized the political consequences of the branch line for British Columbia's full integration into Confederation, the Senate debate tended to focus upon the economic implications.[85] Even Senators from British Columbia, such as Robert William Weir Carrall (who nonetheless indicated his intent to support the government on this bill) were highly critical of expenditures that were deemed to be frivolous, extravagant, and irresponsible.[86] Other railway bills received similar scrutiny from the Senate during this period, such as a Motion for Correspondence concerning the Georgian Bay branch of the Canadian Pacific Railway.[87]

But railway legislation and policies were not the only areas in which the Senate was particularly active. In other areas relating to business and industry, the Senate devoted a relatively large proportion of its attention to careful examination and critical appraisal. For example, during the debate on the Quebec Trinity House and Harbour Bill of 1875, the speeches of Senator Luc Letellier de Saint-Just of Quebec (a strong political ally of Prime Minister Mackenzie) and Senator David Macpherson of Ontario (a strong political ally of the Leader of the Opposition, John A. Macdonald) supported a major amendment by Senator Thomas Ryan of Quebec to grant greater representation on the Quebec Harbour Committee to the Quebec Board of Trade. Although this amendment was acknowledged as potentially benefiting Senator Ryan and his own business interests, the business expertise of these Senators was considered to be sufficiently impressive to result in non-partisan support for the measure from both sides of the chamber.[88] The Marine Telegraphs Bill of 1875 was another example of this trend when Senator William Miller of Nova Scotia (a future Speaker of the Senate) objected to foreign investment in a Canadian communication company, prompting both interest and deference to his perceived background in this area among his fellow Senators.[89] When the Liberal government was coming under increased political criticism concerning its fiscal policies in 1878 (in anticipation of a general election), the Senate was chosen as the venue for countering this criticism. Despite the constitutional convention that primary responsibility for money bills should belong to the House of Commons, the government deliberately chose the Senate as the forum that would initially address these criticisms (vigorously led by Senator George Brown) concerning its fiscal policies, ostensibly because of its image of expertise, a less-conspicuously partisan environment, and professionalism in this area.[90]

The professional background of Senators lacked the diversity that it would begin to develop, later in its history. As Colin Campbell has famously noted, the tendency of the Senate to be dominated by members with strong business and financial backgrounds and expertise would be perceived as having a corrupting influence upon that chamber's political behavior.[91] Nonetheless, it also provided a source of informal strength and influence for the Senate in certain areas of policy and legislation. Much of that influence was not exhibited on the floor of that chamber but, instead, through its less conspicuous but highly influential committee system.

Senate Committees

Much of the development of the Senate's approach toward legislation and policies occurred in committee. Arguably, the most active and influential of these bodies during this early period was the Senate Committee on Banking, Commerce, and Railways. Newspapers such as *The Globe* reported on the proceedings of Senate committees with particular attention to this one during this period as it was the most active one of them, even when compared to committees of the House of Commons. During the debate on supply during the 1875 session, Senator Dickey made particular reference to this activity while defending the activities of the Senate and emphasizing its influence. In particular, he noted that "While at my desk, this morning, I have glanced over the minutes of our proceedings during the Session, and I find that, while we have rejected [only] three public bills from the House of Commons, we have materially amended no less than twenty-six sent to us for concurrence, independently of the large number of Bills amended in the Banking and Private Bills Committee [cheers]. These facts speak in trumpet tones of the necessity of a Second Chamber."[92]

This activity was consistent with the spirit of revision and technical improvement that had been originally perceived to be the most appropriate role for the Canadian upper house. The committee system appears to have greatly facilitated that activity, especially in support of crucial but, often, mundane minutiae that transformed broad policy ideas into viable programs and services.[93] In that capacity, the Senate often found itself the recipient of projects of a technical and non-partisan nature that the government and the House of Commons could not find either the time or the inclination to pursue.[94]

One striking example of this delegation of policy was the program that the government entrusted to the Senate for establishing a uniform standard of weights and measurements for the country. Canada was among the first countries to adopt, officially, the metric system and the Senate used this system as a guide in considering the Weights and Measures Bill of 1872. Most of the consideration of this bill took place in a special committee, resulting in a thorough study and recommendations that had been accomplished in an apparent spirit of cooperation.[95] Senator Letellier de St-Just's proposal to add water measurements to the scope of the bill's content, for example, was accepted readily by his colleagues from all parties.[96]

Another example of this Senate activity was the creation of a select committee to reform and improve statistics gathering in Canada. Again, the account of these proceedings provides a strong impression of non-partisan cooperation in the pursuit of this technically challenging mandate. Challenges to the motion to create the committee were limited to an examination of alternative approaches to the method that the committee might use in addressing this subject.[97] The Senate committee system appeared to be a particularly appropriate venue for this sort of unexciting but, nonetheless, very important activity.

Even committee proceedings relating to the supply bills sent to the Senate from the House of Commons displayed some of these characteristics. The Senate normally was very circumspect in its treatment of this legislation, primarily in observance of the convention that supply should be a prerogative of the lower house and the government that it supported.[98] Still, these proceedings, though normally brief, provided Senators with opportunities to address concerns and make recommendations in specific areas in which they had a particular interest or expertise. For example, Senator Campbell took advantage of the debate on the Supply Bill of 1874 to discuss, in some detail, the clause in the bill concerning additional government expenditures on the Baie Verte Canal.[99] In a similar manner, Senator Macpherson raised specific questions relating to the budget for the Georgian Bay branch of the intercontinental railway,[100] while Senator James Skead of Ontario addressed concerns on the effect of government policy on the economy of the Ottawa Valley during consideration of the supply bill in 1877.[101] Given the very brief amount of debate normally allotted to supply bills on the floor of the Senate (in one instance, the entire Senate debate on the supply bill lasted little more than an hour[102]), committee review offered an important opportunity for Senators to scrutinize the complexities of this legislation and offer particular critiques and recommendations.[103]

The committee system would become increasingly important to the operation of the Senate, throughout its history. These early years demonstrated the usefulness of committees to the Senate as it began to focus upon the details of legislation and policy, including implementation and other areas. This aspect of the Senate's function often was neither dramatic nor contentious but it could be highly useful, especially in complementing the broader policy interests of the lower house,[104] as the activities of other parliamentary upper houses also have demonstrated.[105]

SUBSEQUENT DEVELOPMENT

During the latter 19th and early 20th centuries, the Senate continued to be dominated by members who had business and commercial backgrounds, including Senators with a background in the agricultural sector of the economy. This composition contrasted with the composition of the House of Commons, which was dominated by various persons with professional and administrative backgrounds, especially in the law.[106] This level of specialization and expertise may have contributed to the Senate's particular activity in areas relating to commerce and transportation during its early decades, including legislation relating the Canadian railways. Often, this expertise could be quite detailed and pointed, as revealed during the debates concerning the admission of British Columbia into Confederation, during which some Senators would reveal a particularly detailed knowledge of technical facts and arguments in relation to the impact of British Columbia on the Canadian economy.[107]

Self-interest obviously could have played a part in this approach—the participation of Senator David Lewis Macpherson (who had been an executive of the Grand Trunk Railway prior to Confederation) in the debates concerning the intercontinental railway is a good example.[108] Other examples of the interjection of this expertise (such as contemporary assessments concerning trade reciprocity with the United States)[109] also can be assessed in a similar manner. But the fact that this expertise was exhibited during these early decades of the Senate's existence is indicative of a pattern of behavior that is consistent with broader theories of the modern purpose and role of the parliamentary upper house, as articulated elsewhere within this book.

During the next century and a half of its existence, the Senate's political record found it behaving in a similar manner. It largely has confined itself to the role of revising, amending, and improving legislation. Most of its useful functions have occurred outside of the direct legislative process. The Senate became particularly active in terms of public discourse, including a particularly active period of investigative committees during the 1960s and 1970s. It very rarely opposed legislation and, when it did, never in a manner that undermined the overall government mandate. It also was active in facilitating private interests, including as a liaison between business and government.[110] Ironically, its perceived reticence in its potential political role that led to one of the most outspoken calls for its reform—one that actually called for it to become more politically active and powerful than it has been.[111]

Nonetheless, the actual role that the Senate has assumed has been consistent with evolving expectations of the parliamentary upper house—expectations that are tied to foundational principles of political philosophy that bear examination to place this subject within a more meaningful and broad-ranging context. That role has continued within the unreformed Senate of the current century.[112] It has continued to engage in technical improvement of legislation, oversight of public activity, advancement of various interests, and public investigation of the policy process. These activities are consistent with broader theories of the function and purpose of the upper house as described within this book. They were not merely the product of a gradual development; these institutional traits and behaviors emerged during the initial years of the Senate of Canada.

PLUS C'EST LA MEME CHOSE

The first decade of the existence of the Senate of Canada is remarkable for the manner in which much of its activities and behavior resembles the most recent decade of its existence and the decades between them. That chamber has remained extremely reluctant to oppose any public legislation, especially if it results from a clear electoral mandate on the part of the government. Its membership also has peculiar features that reflect greater potential for diversity through the appointment process, whether for a self-aggrandizing purpose or in pursuit of other broad goals of the nation and its political system. But it also has been active in scrutinizing, critiquing, amending, and, otherwise, improving legislation and policies. That activity has become especially effective within the context of the Senate committee system—a trend that can be traced to these early years of its existence and initial development.

This early historical record lacks the breadth that can lend itself to meaningful quantification. However, as an examination of select cases suggests, the Senate of this first decade already possessed a strong sense of its identify and mission that remarkably resonates within subsequent decades, including recent ones. Although the scope of its activity and specific concerns has, obviously, changed over time, certain consistent patterns of behavior appear to have been established during this initial period of the Senate's history. That historical example may provide a useful tool in support of a broad and critical analysis of the current Senate of Canada in consideration of its potential reform or other options for its future.

The Senate of Canada was never intended to be a co-equal chamber of the Canadian parliamentary system, despite its superficial construction as a parliamentary chamber with formal procedures and powers that are, on the surface, identical to the House of Commons.[113] Assumptions to the contrary not only may be neglectful of important aspects of the historical record but, also, may be grounded upon a formal-legal approach toward this political institution that reflects the fundamental weakness of that traditional and, frankly, archaic method of political analysis. However, that particular weakness should not dissuade alternative uses of institutional analysis, especially from the developing and much more sophisticated field of neo-institutionalism. That approach offers highly relevant and useful critical perspectives that can build upon this historical foundation. It merits, therefore, further consideration, which the next chapter will address.

NOTES

1. George Ross, *The Senate of Canada: Its Constitutions, Duties, and Powers Historically Considered* (Toronto: Copp Clark, 1914), pp. 252–255.

2. Phillip Alfred Buckner, *The Transition to Responsible Government* (Westport, CT: Greenwood Press, 1985), pp. 275–276.

3. Sanford Lackoff, "Tocqueville, Burke, and the Origins of Liberal Conservatism," *Review of Politics*, vol. 60, no. 3 (Summer 1998), pp. 435–464; Herman Finer, *The Theory and Practice of Modern Government* (London: Methuen, 1962), pp. 400–403.

4. Angus Hopkins, "'Parliamentary Government' and Victorian Political Parties, c. 1830–c. 1880," *English Historical Review*, vol. 104, no. 412 (July 1989), pp. 641–645.

5. Desmond Morton, *A Short History of Canada* (Toronto: McClelland and Stewart, 2006), pp. 92–93; Robert A. MacKay, *The Unreformed Senate of Canada* (Toronto: McClelland and Stewart, 1963), pp. 32–50.

6. Robert Dahl, *A Preface to Democratic Theory* (Chicago: University of Chicago Press, 2006), pp. 63–89.

7. Desmond Morton, *A Short History of Canada* (Toronto: McClelland and Stewart, 2006), pp. 92–93; Frederick Vaughan, *The Canadian Federalist Experience* (Montreal and Kingston, ON: McGill-Queen's University Press, 2003), pp. 56–64.

8. Colin Campbell, *The Canadian Senate: A Lobby from Within* (Toronto: MacMillan, 1978), pp. 125–127.

9. Robert MacGregor Dawson and Norman Ward, *Dawson's The Government of Canada* (Toronto: University of Toronto Press, 1987), pp. 189–190.

10. P. B. Waite, *The Charlottetown Conference* (Ottawa: Canadian Historical Association, 1970), pp. 3–11.

11. MacKay, p. 46.

12. Jean-Charles Bonenfant, *Le Senat dans le federalism canadien* (Ottawa: Commission Royale d'Enquete sur le Bilinguisme et le Biculturalisme, 1966), p. 137.

13. G. P. Browne, ed. *Documents on the Confederation of British North America* (Toronto: University of Toronto Press, 1969), pp. 97–98; P. B. Waite, "Edward Whelan Reports from the Quebec Conference," *Canadian Historical Review*, vol. 42, no. 1 (March 1961), pp. 23–45.

14. Browne, pp. 233–234.

15. *Hansard* (House of Lords), Third Series, February 19, 1867, p. 560.

16. *Parliamentary Debates on the Subject of the Confederation of the British North American Provinces* (Quebec: Hunter and Rose, 1865), Third Session, Eighth Provincial Parliament of Canada, p. 973—hereafter referenced as the *Confederation Debates.*

17. *Confederation Debates*, p. 38.

18. *Confederation Debates*, p. 35; Joseph Pope, *Memoirs of the Right Honourable Sir John Alexander Macdonald, GCB* (London: Edward Arnold, 1894), vol. I, pp. 235, 277.

19. W. L. Morton, *Monck Letters and Journals, 1863–1868* (Toronto: McClelland and Stuart, 1970), p. 65; Pope, vol. I, pp. 391–392.

20. *Confederation Debates*, p. 701.

21. Browne, pp. 31, 120; F. A. Kunz, *The Modern Senate of Canada* (Toronto: University of Toronto Press, 1965), p. 11.

22. *Confederation Debates*, pp. 570, 624, 692–694, 842, 973.

23. Letter to the Editor, *Le Canadien*, March 6, 1865.

24. *Confederation Debates*, p. 185.

25. Ibid., p. 495.

26. Colin Matthew, *The Nineteenth Century: The British Isles, 1815–1901* (Oxford: Oxford University Press, 2000), pp. 8, 26.

27. *Confederation Debates*, pp. 36–37.

28. Ibid., p. 36.

29. Browne, p. 138; *Confederation Debates*, p. 513; Pope, vol. II, p. 233.

30. Ibid., pp. 35–37, 88, 117–118, 1,009; Charles Tupper, *Recollections of Sixty Years in Canada* (London: Cassell, 1914), p. 41.

31. Ibid., p. 88.

32. Ibid., pp. 35, 1,009.

33. Ibid., p. 59.

34. Charles Tupper, *Recollections of Sixty Years in Canada* (London: Cassell, 1914), p. 41.

35. CO 42: Dufferin to Kimberly, dispatch no. 302, December 29, 1873; *Debates and Proceedings of the Senate of the Dominion of Canada* (Ottawa 1877), March 19, 1877, pp. 194–197; Eugene Forsey, "Alexander Mackenzie's Memoranda on the Appointment of Extra Senators," *Canadian Historical Review*, vol. 27, no. 2 (June 1946), pp. 189–194.

36. *Debates and Proceedings of the Senate*, March 6, 1876, pp. 52–68.

37. Ibid., March 19, 1876, p. 214.

38. Ibid., pp. 207–208.

39. Garth Stevenson, Ex Uno Plures: *Federal-Provincial Relations in Canada, 1867–1896* (Montreal and Kingston, ON: McGill-Queen's University Press, 1993), pp. 327–328.

40. Desmond Morton, *A Short History of Canada* (Edmonton: Hurtig, 1985), pp. 88–89.

41. C. W. deKiewiet and F. H. Underhill, eds., *Dufferin/Carnarvon Correspondence* (Toronto: Champlain Society, 1955), p. 81; W. S. Wallace, "Edward Blake's Aurora Speech," *Canadian Historical Review*, vol. 2, no. 2 (July 1921), pp. 249–271.

42. Frederick Hamilton-Temple-Blackwood, Marquis of Dufferin, and Henry Herbert, Earl of Carnarvon, *Dufferin/Carnarvon Correspondence: 1874–1878*; C. W. deKewiet and F. H. Underhill, eds. (Toronto: Champlain Society, 1955), pp. 278–279.

43. MacKay, pp. 39–41; Joseph Pope, *Documents on the Confederation of British North America*, G. P. Browne, ed. (Toronto: McClelland and Stewart, 1969), pp. 45–46.

44. Kunz, pp. 66, 212.

45. *Debates and Proceedings of the Senate of the Dominion of Canada*, March 19, 1877 (Ottawa: Queen's Printer for Canada, 1877), p. 197.

46. CO 42: Kimberly to Dufferin, dispatch no. 302, December 29, 1873, quoted in Eugene Forsey, "Alexander Mackenzie's Memoranda on the Appointment of Extra Senators," *Canadian Historical Review*, vol. 58, no. 2 (June 1946), pp. 189–194.

47. *Debates and Proceedings of the Senate*, March 19, 1877, p. 196.

48. Ibid., p. 202.

49. Ibid., pp. 203–206.

50. Donald F. MacLachlan, *The Esquimalt & Nanaimo Railway—The Dunsmuir Years: 1884–1905* (Vancouver: British Columbia Historical Railway Association, 1986), pp. 12–16.

51. Richard Gwyn, *Nation Builder: Sir John A. Macdonald: His Life, Our Times*, vol. II: 1867–1891. (Toronto: Random House, 2011), pp. 200–202; P. B. Waite, *Macdonald: His Life and World* (Toronto: McGraw-Hill Ryerson, 1975), pp. 101–104.

52. Desmond Morton, *A Short History of Canada* (Edmonton: Hurtig, 1985), pp. 88–89; W. A. Taylor, *Crown Land Grants: A History of the Esquimalt and Nanaimo Railway Land Grants, the Railway Belt, and the Peace River Block* (Victoria: British Columbia Crown Land Registry Services, 1997), p. 4.

53. MacLachlan, p. 16.

54. *Dufferin/Carnarvon Correspondence*, pp. 278–279.

55. *Debates and Proceedings of the Senate*, April 6, 1876, pp. 191–195.

56. Ibid., March 20, 1876, pp. 159–174.

57. *The Globe*, April 8, 1876, p. 2, column B.

58. *Debates and Proceedings of the Senate*, April 6, 1876, p. 280

59. Michael John Herman, "The Founding of the Supreme Court of Canada and the Abolition of the Appeal to the Privy Council," *Ottawa Law Review*, vol. 8, no. 7 (Winter 1976), pp. 12–13.

60. *Debates and Proceedings of the Senate*, April 5, 1876, pp. 727–729, 733–738.

61. David E. Smith, *The Canadian Senate in Bicameral Perspective* (Toronto: University of Toronto Press, 2003), pp. 85–86.

62. A. P. Cockburn, *Political Annals of Canada* (London: Stanley Paul, 1909), pp. 405–409; L. O. David, *L'Histoire du Canada depuis la Confederation* (Montreal: Librarie Beauchemin, 1909), pp. 39–51.

63. *Debates and Proceedings of the Senate*, May 28, 1872, p. 148.

64. Ibid., March 7, 1876, p. 78.

65. Ibid., March 21, 1871, pp. 97–110.

66. Ibid., April 3, 1876, pp. 274–277, April 4, 1876, pp. 291–292.

67. Ibid., March 10, 1875, p. 359.

68. Kunz, pp. 112–114.

69. *Confederation Debates*, pp. 22–23, 35–39; Pope, vol. I, pp. 45–46.

70. *Debates and Proceedings of the Senate*, March 30, 1874, p. 6.

71. Ibid., June 4, 1869, p. 264.

72. Alpheus Todd, *Parliamentary Government in the Colonies* (London: Longmans, Green, and Company, 1929), vol. I, p. 6.

73. Saul Levmore, "Bicameralism: When are Two Decisions Better than One?" 12 *International Review of Law and Economics* (1992), pp. 145–162; Gerhard Loewenberg and Samuel C. Paterson, *Comparing Legislatures* (Boston: Little, Brown, 1979), p. 121; George Tsebelis, "Decision Making in Political Systems: Veto Players in Presidentialism, Parliamentarism, Multicamearlism, and Multipartyism," *British Journal of Political Science*, vol. 25, no. 3 (July 1995), pp. 309–310.

74. MacKay, pp. 36–37.

75. Kunz, p. 67.

76. Harold D. Clarke, Colin Campbell, and Arthur Goddard, eds., *Parliament, Policy, and Representation* (Toronto: Methuen, 1980), pp. 1; Kunz, p. 212; MacKay, p. 37.

77. Robert J. Jackson and Michael M. Atkinson, *The Canadian Legislative System* (Toronto: Macmillan, 1974), pp. 96–98.

78. Campbell, p. 2.

79. Kunz, p. 66, including table VII.

80. Irma Coucill, *Canada's Prime Ministers, Governors General, and Fathers of Confederation* (Markham, ON: Pembroke, 2005), p. 178.

81. *Debates and Proceedings of the Senate*, April 3, 1871, p. 168.

82. Ibid., April 4, 1871, pp. 197–198.

83. Neil MacNeil and Richard A. Baker, *The American Senate: An Insider's History* (New York: Oxford University Press, 2013), pp. 14–34.

84. *Debates and Proceedings of the Senate*, May 9, 1878, pp. 1,002–1,004; Royal Commission on the Canadian Pacific Railway, *Report*, "Papers of Sir John A. Macdonald Connected with the Awarding of Section Fifteen of the Canadian Pacific Railway," (Ottawa, 1877), vol. I, pp. 79–81, 85, 89; Pierre Burton, *The National Dream* (Montreal: McClelland and Stewart, 1971), pp. 15, 71, 81, 87, 149, 240, 245–246, 281.

85. *Debates and Proceedings of the Senate*, March 30, 1876, pp. 222–227, March 31, 1876, pp. 241–243.

86. Ibid., April 6, 1875, pp. 739–741.

87. Ibid., March 6, 1876, pp. 52–68.

88. Ibid., April 7, 1875, p. 749; Robert Bruce Bell, John Newton, and Sandford Fleming, *Report on a General Scheme of Improvements for the Harbour of Montreal* (Montreal: Commission of Engineers, 1877), pp. 163–164.

89. Ibid., March 10, 1875, pp. 359–360.

90. J. M. S. Careless, *Brown of the Globe* (Toronto: Macmillan, 1963), pp. 353–354; *Debates and Proceedings of the Senate*, March 21, 1878, pp. 219–232.

91. Campbell, pp. 32–36.

92. *Debates and Proceedings of the Senate*, April 7, 1875, pp. 754–755.

93. Frederick C. Englemann, "A Prologue to Structural Reform of the Government of Canada," *Canadian Journal of Political Science*, vol. 19, no. 4 (December 1986), pp. 677–678.

94. Henry S. Albinski, "The Canadian Senate: Politics and the Constitution," *American Political Science Review*, vol. 57, no. 2 (June 1963), pp. 381–382.

95. "Senate Memoranda to His Excellency the Governor General," Ottawa 1873.

96. *Debates and Proceedings of the Senate*, June 11, 1872, pp. 184–186.

97. Ibid., February 18, 1875, pp. 57–63.

98. *Confederation Debates*, pp. 35–37; Jackson and Atkinson, pp. 97–98; MacKay, p. 49.

99. Ibid., May 23, 1874, pp. 359–362.

100. Ibid., April 7, 1875, pp. 755–756.

101. Ibid., April 28, 1877, p. 491.

102. Ibid.

103. B. J. Roberts, "Canada's Budgetary System," *Annals of the American Academy of Political and Social Science,* vol. 107 (May 1923), p. 206.

104. Kunz, pp. 262–266; Smith, pp. 110–119.

105. Gerhard Loewenberg and Samuel Patterson, *Comparing Legislatures* (Boston: Little Brown, 1979), p. 121; Meg Russell, "What are Second Chambers For?" *Parliamentary Affairs,* vol. 54 (2001), pp. 451–453.

106. Campbell, p. 2; Robert J. Jackson and Michael M. Atkinson, *The Canadian Legislative System* (Toronto: macmillan, 1974), pp. 96–98.

107. Pierre Berton, *The National Dream* (Montreal: McClelland and Stewart, 1971), pp. 87, 149, 240, 281; David E. Smith, *The Canadian Senate in Bicameral Perspective* (Toronto: University of Toronto Press, 2003), pp. 132–133.

108. Berton, pp. 15, 71, 81; *Debates and Proceedings of the Senate*, May 9, 1878, pp. 1,003–1,004.

109. L. O. David, *L'Histoire du Canada depuis la Confederation, 1867–1887* (Montreal: Librarie Beauchemin, 1909), pp. 39–51; A. P. Cockburn, *Political Annals of Canada* (London: Stanley Paul, 1909), pp. 405–409.

110. Kunz, pp. 262–266; MacKay, pp. 110–119.

111. Lusztig, pp. 38–39.

112. James T. McHugh, *In Another Place: Three Case Studies in the Development of the Upper House of Parliament within the Westminster Model of Government* (Edinburgh: University of Edinburgh M. Litt. Thesis, 1986), pp. 60–80, 98–112.

113. Patrick Malcolmson and Richard Myers, *The Canadian Regime* (Toronto: University of Toronto Press, 2012), pp. 129–132.

Chapter 5

Assessing Reform—Neo-Institutional and Related Strategies

Given the theoretical, historical, cultural, political, and other considerations that have been addressed by the previous chapter, it is appropriate to offer a formal proposal for the sorts of constitutional changes that these considerations suggest within the context of Canadian politics and society. Unlike a traditional institutional (also known as formal-legal) approach, these recommendations will apply neo-institutional, political culture, power-elite, and other social science methods and theoretical considerations that anticipate political outputs in terms of broader theoretical ideas and the actual performance of similar institutions. The intent is that this overall approach will take into consideration the potential outcomes of this sort of reform in a manner that will conform to the outputs that social science disciplines and their methods provide for the purpose of sound public policy analysis.

In other words, rather than pure speculation, this approach seeks to provide an assessment that is based upon meaningful evidence and analysis. This approach is, therefore, especially appropriate from a comparative perspective as it seeks to draw from the actual experiences of upper houses within other political systems. For example, rather than assume that elections uniformly strengthen all political institutions of a democracy, it will consider different theories and models of democracy and democratic government, especially from a parliamentary perspective. Rather than assume that the effectiveness of a political institution relies upon its absolute power, it will assess levels of political activity and efficacy that result from different distributions of, and even limitations upon, its formal authority. Rather than assume that federal relations are improved through a central institutional approach, it will consider historical trends in those relationships that suggest the primacy of an alternative approach. Even if supporting data is somewhat limited, it will seek to demonstrate anticipated effects whenever possible.

This context is consistent with the development of various methods of neo-institutionalism, which treats political institutions as political actors in themselves and asserts that they are influenced by the same factors as other political actors, including history, culture, and the guidance of rational choice alternatives. Neo-institutional considerations are particularly pertinent and offer a rationale for addressing Canadian Senate reform through this instrument of a hypothetical constitutional amendment. Those considerations have been mentioned, in general terms, within the previous chapter. However, their implications may be much more important than many reform proposals have suggested. Therefore, a further explanation of neo-institutional analysis appears to be warranted as it will consider specific models of that approach that are relevant to the overall political context from which this proposal ultimately is derived.

THE REASON THAT POLITICAL INSTITUTIONS MATTER

Many proposals for reform of political institutions (including the Senate of Canada) focus upon expected policy outcomes, rather than broader considerations of the effect of institutional change as an influence by itself.[1] Reform of the Senate of Canada has been expected, within many proposals, to result in an upper chamber of the Canadian Parliament that will be much more conspicuous in its contribution to the government and politics of Canada, especially (though not exclusively) in relation to intrastate federalism. Many of these ideas within this hypothetical model for reform, the non-constitutional recommendations that follow that model, and the analysis that supports them have emphasized formal structure and processes that, while highly useful, are consistent with a traditional approach to political science that can be limited to describing origins but not considering outcomes. They are based upon assumptions about the nature and function of certain types of institutions that have not necessarily been tested, let alone demonstrated. They result in assumptions that make certain reform options appear to be axiomatic when, in fact, the ultimate outcomes could be highly dubious.

For example, the Triple-E approach to Senate reform is based upon certain assumptions that frequently have not been challenged and, therefore, tend to be accepted as truisms. The belief in "equality" among the provinces is based upon a symmetrical assumption regarding the origins (if not the actual nature) of Canadian federalism as well as an assumption that intrastate, rather than interstate, federalism is the most acceptable constitutional and political forum for addressing the relationship between the central and provincial governments.[2] The proposal for an "elected" Senate is based upon an assumption that, within a democratic political system, elections generally are the only legitimate means for conferring political roles upon all participants within the governmental process. According to this assumption, imposing an electoral process automatically makes any political institution better. The assumption of providing a measure of "effectiveness" has been based upon a desire to enhance the capacity of the Senate to affect or, possibly, prevent legislation of the lower house, especially as initiated by the government of the day.

Reforms of political bodies such as the Canadian Senate traditionally have been driven by a formal-legal analysis, also known as the "old" institutionalism. This traditional approach is positivist in nature, relying upon empirical observation and description of the institutional structures and the formal rules upon which they are based.[3] But Senate reform appears to fit, more specifically, into a structuralist model that has had more success in being accepted among more recent scholars, despite being associated with that "traditional" formal-legal approach to social science research that has been, largely, set aside by scholars since, at least, the 1970s.[4] The classic textbook on the subject of Canadian government by Robert MacGregor Dawson is an excellent example of that approach, including in terms of its limitations, even in its updated editions.[5] For a long time, it was considered to be *the* classic text on the general subject of Canadian politics and government, even though its approach was largely descriptive in nature. While it did offer analysis, that analysis often was guided solely by the ostensible description of the institutions and the context in which they were examined, including a bias from a centralized perspective derived from its reliance upon the British North America Act (as it was known at the time) as its primary descriptive source. Those limitations should not negate its strengths in presenting a historical institutional approach to Canadian government that was informative and well-integrated. But it did lead to exaggerations of certain political features, such as the dominance of the central government within the federal system and the contribution of the Senate toward the overall governmental process.[6]

That approach, though ultimately set aside by later scholars, concealed informal features of these bodies that often are overlooked, even though they can provide useful insights.[7] In particular, the tendency for this "old institutionalism" to be presented from a comparative perspective has been especially useful for clarifying features of a political system that might not be appreciated or, even, noticed by observers from within the system.[8] The fact that the Senate of Canada is an intrinsic part of a parliamentary system often requires such a comparative perspective in order to gain a realistic appreciation of the potential advantages and problems associated with specific reform proposals. That claim is relevant not only in terms of contrasting it with a non-parliamentary system (most notably, the United States and its presidential and bicameral system) but, also, with other parliamentary systems (especially, but not exclusively, Westminster systems such as Britain and Australia) that can reinforce understandings of its essential workings and provide cautionary tales concerning the sort of upper house reforms that have been advocated for the Senate of Canada.

The "old" institutionalism has not been completely lacking in providing a foundation for a sophisticated analytical development within the social sciences. Those origins often are traced to the seminal work of Max Weber and other pioneering social scientists. The Weberian approach to institutional studies, in particular, has emphasized the significance of legal orders and conventions—a factor that may be underappreciated among current scholars and policy makers and that is particularly relevant to Canadian Senate reform. The emphasis upon constitutional convention within this approach is particularly significant because it explains the power of institutions in terms of motivations other than the more basic political emphasis upon coercion or other variations of force.[9] These motivations result in a regularity of behavior and a readily recognized mechanism that offers a strong explanation for compliance with the expectations of political conventions. In many respects, it orients behavior among participants within the overall political system, especially ones that are derived from the Westminster model. Other examples of this "older" version of institutionalism have offered additional useful insights, especially for explaining the way in which institutions influence social participation and communication by channeling efforts and informing expectations.[10]

RATIONAL CHOICE AND BEHAVIORALIST APPROACHES

The limited scope of formal-legal methods and other expressions of the "old" institutionalism caused it to be increasingly neglected during the latter part of the 20th century. However, lingering appreciations of its usefulness and the sustained presence of formal institutions that frame the political system and its processes have prompted a renewed interest in a modified version of this traditional analytical approach. In fact, this interest has grown to the point that, in recent years, the "new" institutionalism (particularly the variant identified as "historical institutionalism") has vied with behavioralism and rational choice theory as a "research pillar" of political science.[11] It has emerged in the form of state theory (appreciating that the use of the term "theory" may be contested in a strict sense in this context)[12] in identifying those institutions that are specifically political and assessing the work of politics within them.[13] The relationship with rational choice theory appears to be particularly useful because it explains the role of institutions in relation to final goals and outcomes. This approach has been influenced, in this respect, by economists who have added to those assessments a measurement of success that motivates participants to act in ways that often require cooperation and an adherence to certain collective expectations of conduct.[14] While often not dealing with state structures, rational choice institutionalists have made an important link between institutions and goals, including through the development of a motivational analysis.[15] This relationship treats institutions as a structural context that influences optimal choices for achieving those goals and, then, guides the path to take in reaching those ends.[16] The relationship with behavioralists is tied to a mutual desire to construct a theory that can inform specific structural concepts, including institutional reform.[17] That relationship has contributed to a recasting of group behavior and the policy choices that emerge from it in institutional terms.[18]

These approaches are relevant to considerations of Canadian Senate reform. Rather than focusing upon the formal role of the Senate in terms of voting on legislation or representing regions and provinces, this approach assesses its actual function in terms of activities such as amending legislation (particularly "technical" and "improving" amendments), ombudsman functions, and advocacy. Measurements of relative success are modified through those approaches, both in terms of the outcomes that are assessed (such as the quality and quantity of amendments) and the methods used to attain them (such as less partisan and cooperative behavior) as well as the way in which the structure and formal powers of the Senate are related to those outcomes. The "effectiveness" of the Senate is not assessed in terms of formal powers (such as a *de facto* capacity to block legislation) but in terms of behavior that is consistent with the actual development of the parliamentary upper house in complementing the process and achievements of the overall political process, including in ways that are not indicated by its formal institutional structure.

A CRITICAL CONTEXT OF HISTORY

Historical institutionalism is one of three variations of the new institutionalism that has been particularly useful for assessing phenomena such as the reform of political bodies.[19] In its origins, it drew upon the structural functionalist theory that emphasized the interrelationship of various parts of a political system.[20] Consistent with group theory, it perceived the role of institutions in providing a "stage" for the interaction and competition of groups that established parameters for political competition.[21] Structural functionalist explanations of the state were strongly influenced by Marxist analyses of the active role that state institutions perform in support of class interests.[22] That influence was particularly important for studies of the Canadian state that sought to transcend the strict formalism that previously had been so prominent.[23] Historical institutionalists can explain political behavior in terms of "calculus" or "culture." The calculus approach emphasizes human behavior that is motivated by strategic calculation. It is based upon the assumption that political actors behave strategically by choosing a particular preference function. They choose among options within the institutional structure in which they find themselves. These political institutions affect this behavior by providing the actors within them varying degrees of certainty concerning the anticipated behavior of other political actors within the same structural context. The institutions are grounded upon rules and expectations that permit actors to predict actions and responses as a part of a wider anticipation of strategic interaction.[24]

This approach can be useful in relation to the Canadian Senate in terms of the context of the overall Westminster system and its conventions. The norms of behavior of parliamentarians inform overall political behavior, especially in terms of the influence that reasonably can be brought to bear upon a government while refraining from undermining the concept of responsible government that allows the overall system to function. Therefore, a Senate with powers that could be disruptive in this respect (consistent with the "effective" goal of a proposed Triple-E Senate) could be, ultimately, contraindicated by the calculus upon which its reform is based—provided that the calculus is based upon a reasonable expectation of policy influence, rather than merely a frustration of political activity at the federal level.

CULTURAL ANALYSIS

The cultural approach stresses the extent to which choices and other political behavior are informed by a "worldview" that, while still rational and strategic, emphasizes patterns that are established within the institution and reaffirm their understanding of their cultural and political environment and its associated values. In this way, they create a path for achieving their goals. From the perspective of this approach, a course of action depends on the interpretation of the overall situation, rather than on purely instrumental calculation of ends and means. Therefore, political institutions provide "moral or cognitive templates" that inform both understanding and the response to that understanding. Political actors are intrinsically connected to their respective institutions and its symbols and routines that affect their perception of themselves, the institution, and their strategic environment. The institutions thus define the self-identity of the political actors and the legitimacy of the goals that they seek to attain.[25]

This approach may be useful in explaining the emphasis upon the "elected" goal of a proposed Triple-E Senate, given the liberal democratic context within which any parliamentary reform goal is couched. In a larger sense, it could explain the general insistence that Canadian Senate reform absolutely must include some sort of electoral scheme, due to the often unchallenged assumption that all institutional changes within a liberal democratic system must involve this most basic symbol of self-referential legitimacy. Simultaneously, it can be used to demonstrate that different understandings of democratic governance (including parliamentary democracy) may be inconsistent or, even, incompatible with the concept of an elected upper house. It also can be used to indicate the relevance of the British heritage in developing the Canadian parliamentary upper house, thus reinforcing the appropriateness of the House of Lords as a potential reform model.

CULTURAL-COGNITIVE APPROACH

Thus, while institutions can shape political culture, they are, more often, shaped *by* the political culture—even in ways that might, overall, be contrary to other substantive goals of truly effective reform. That conflict is particularly apparent in relation to the subject and the various proposals for reform of the Senate of Canada. Of three identified analytical "pillars" of institutions, the third such pillar, the "cultural-cognitive" one, is particularly significant in this respect. Its assumptions include a reference to an internal logic of institutions that tends toward orthodoxy and indicators that reflect, and are shaped by, shared beliefs and a "shared logic of actions."[26] In the case of Canadian Senate reform, part of that institutional culture can be shaped by the overall category of democratic government, such as the distinction between a presidential system of non-responsible government and a parliamentary system of responsible government. Political actors tend to interact with these institutions in ways that appear to bind their behavior. In this sense, a predictive evaluation of the effect that reform of political institutions will have can be guided through an application of rational choice theory.

Formal institutions need to be examined along with informal institutions in the form of norms and values.[27] That interdependence of formal and informal institutional influences has been recognized, even within an organizational framework.[28] Rules, roles, and reasons have featured prominently in that assessment because of the way they constrain political behavior, even in the pursuit of power and other, more specific goals.[29] Indeed, for rational choice theorists, rules provide the context within which optimizing decisions occur.[30] The recognition of political roles as attached to particular institutions also constrain behavior of the actors within them, due to a social, as well as political, expectation of their proper reaction to those roles—an understanding also known as the motivational approach.[31]

The informal role of the backbencher within the lower house of a parliamentary system (including both the Canadian and British House of Commons) offers a good example of this sort of analysis. These elected members are related to the larger tasks associated with that body: checking the executive, producing future ministers, maintaining the legislative process, and addressing grievances. Those expectations constrain behavior by backbenchers in other areas (such as taking non-partisan, independent action on government legislation) and compel them to find indirect means to achieve their overall political ends.[32] Likewise, members of the parliamentary upper house (including both the Canadian Senate and the British House of Lords) typically perform political roles that constrain their behavior, especially in relation to the electoral mandate of the government, regardless of certain other formal provisions to the contrary, such as the Canadian Senate's formal authority to reject government legislation. The willingness to assume a more aggressive role within the legislative process as a result of changed mandates or formal powers might be undermined by long-standing constraints associated with that institution and its members. Consequently, the cultural-cognitive approach can be used to explain the relative lack of success that can occur when certain institutional reforms fail to account for these persistent constraints, including proffered changes to the Senate of Canada such as the introduction of an elected mandate or veto powers over certain categories of central government legislation.

UNENTRENCHED CONSTITUTIONAL MODEL

One of the most important, but often overlooked, institutional constraints in relation to parliamentary institutions (especially within the Westminster tradition) is the concept of an unentrenched convention—as opposed to an "unwritten convention," the term "unentrenched" refers to the absence of a constitutional device (such as a formal amending process) that legitimizes constitutional change.[33] While this feature is particularly relevant to the unentrenched British constitutional tradition (parts of which are grounded upon written documents) and its specific parliamentary system, it is, also, relevant to Canada. The Canadian constitutional tradition can be described as being "partially entrenched" because its entrenched documents (specifically the Constitution Acts of 1867 and 1982, which became constitutionally entrenched as a result of the amending formula of the Constitution Act of 1982) do not specify the rules of parliamentary government. The Constitution Acts do not formally articulate concepts such as a "vote of confidence," "fallen government," or, even, the office of prime minister. Yet Canadian politicians adhere to those rules.[34] Furthermore, Canadian citizens expect them to adhere to those rules because of the strength of the institutional culture that the system imposes upon them and the expectations that are, consequently, created by them, resulting in a sociological and psychological imperative to conform that occurs across various political systems.[35]

The Westminster system is grounded upon traditions, historically evolved habits, practical guidelines, and customary behavior. They create a scenario within which political actors understand and conduct their relationships to the other political actors and the political system as a whole.[36] Much of that scenario is understood, rather than formally expressed.[37] The concept of an unentrenched constitutional system is one that often baffles observers who live in countries that not only have entrenched constitutional documents to guide their respective political systems (such as the United States) but who rely upon the legal construction of such a constitutional document in order to frame much of their political competition. In terms of the Westminster model, it is based upon conventions that are not only honored by custom but, also, required by necessity.[38] A failure to abide by a constitutional convention (such as government that refused to call new elections or resign after having lost a "vote of confidence") ultimately could make the entire system unpredictable and, thus, unworkable.[39] Neo-institutionalism is based upon similar principles to understanding political activity within a political system.

PARTIALLY ENTRENCHED CONSTITUTIONAL MODEL

Canada has a constitutional system that can be described as "partially entrenched." It is informed by legal documents (again, most notably the Constitution Acts of 1867 and 1984) that cannot be amended or rescinded except through a difficult and relatively comprehensive scheme (which is the very basis for the concept of constitutional entrenchment) but it also is guided by conventions and other informally understood practices that are not contained within those entrenched documents.[40] Despite the absence of guidelines to explain, for example, the role (let alone the existence) of a prime minister, responsible government, the criteria that constitute a "fallen" government, and other key features of parliamentary government, the presence of these guidelines, symbols, and constraints are very real and powerful.[41] They also inform and direct all political behavior within the Canadian system through political institutions that cannot be understood, properly, unless they are analyzed within that context.[42]

That understanding ultimately is grounded upon the identification of the parliamentary system's definitive, sovereign source. The evolution of the Westminster system has reflected shifts in sovereign authority, even while the institutions, themselves, have remained in place.[43] During the medieval period and into the early modern period, that sovereign authority for the English political system was vested in the monarchy. During several centuries, that authority shifted to a popular sovereignty. Ultimately, any political activity, particularly within the processes that legitimate the parliamentary system, is directed toward, and controlled by, that central truth.[44] The Canadian parliamentary system is a recipient of that heritage, despite the fact that, during its early decades in the latter part of the 19th century, an unelected upper house with formal veto powers lingered in that perceived role. However, the absolute legislative dominance of the lower house soon would prevail in parliamentary systems throughout the world and the role of the upper house would shift along with that development.

INSTITUTIONAL CULTURE AND THE WESTMINSTER MODEL

A problem with many plans for reform of the Senate of Canada is that they do not appear to be constructed in relation to that institutional construct. The Canadian parliamentary system is, ultimately, geared toward, and constrained by, its sovereign source. Therefore, dividing the expression of that sovereign source within the institution of Parliament, itself, could be, at best, confusing and, at worst, irreparably divisive. An elected Senate, with its own mandate, could feel free to undermine the electoral mandate of the House of Commons and, thus, the government that depends upon the support of the House of Commons for its own mandate (let alone functional ability) to govern. Likewise, a central institution that is not, ultimately, governed by a concept of representation-by-population but can be challenged by a body that is "equally" representative of the electoral mandates (directly or indirectly) of smaller, as well as larger, political subunits faces a similar challenge to the functionality and legitimacy of the entire system. Therefore, an "effective" Senate, in which effectiveness is measured in terms of the capacity to nullify or, otherwise, curtail the policy decisions of the House of Commons, easily could undermine the effectiveness of (or, even, disable) the parliamentary system as a whole.

Of course, the presidential-congressional system of the United States actually is grounded upon that very assumption; its republican institutions are derived from a theory of the "separation of powers" that is intended to provide a level of immobility into the political system on behalf of the popular sovereign and the political subunits that also represent them—a classic example of the principle of non-responsible government. A parliamentary system is grounded upon very different principles of responsible government—principles that function, best, within an environment of predictable legislative support and, thus, depend upon certainty of outcome in order to operate, properly or at all.

But even within a hierarchically structured parliamentary system, other institutional variables must be taken into account within this analysis of the norms and values that guide, and ought to guide, the operation of the political system and the behavior of the actors within it. Federalism, as already inferred, is the most significant institutional variable that can alter these norms. The lack of a single sovereign focus (and its distribution among different levels of shared sovereign authority) introduces ambiguity into the process and the rational choices that are made within it. The significance of deviations in norms that are attributable to that situation should not be downplayed under any circumstance.[45] The fact that the Canadian parliamentary system (especially the Senate) explicitly has focused upon that feature is particularly significant, especially as it tends to divide the focus of the political system between national interests (often associated with "high politics") and more parochial interests at the subunit level.[46]

Nonetheless, even such an important variable must be placed within the overall institutional context of the Westminster system and its controlling conventions, especially when considering reform of one of its central institutional features. The fact that political subunits are represented within central institutions is a departure from the normal conventions of the Westminster model that has changed the dynamic of Canadian politics in this respect, especially in terms of the introduction of an element of intrastate federalism to a system that initially evolved within a highly centralized context.[47] That factor also should be noted within the context of a neo-institutional analysis of a subject such as Canadian Senate reform. Likewise, it also has provided misleading accounts of the role and power of the Senate, reflecting the exaggerated expectations (though not, allegedly, by the Fathers of Confederation) in relation to that chamber and its role within the federal system.[48]

The Westminster parliamentary system, as it has institutionally evolved, is practically identical in its general norms and practices (except in relation to federalism) between Britain and Canada. Those institutional norms that govern its operation emphasize the role of the sovereign (symbolized in both cases by the Crown) and the relationship of political actors toward it. Government ministers are held accountable to the sovereign and that accountability is supervised by the lower house of Parliament, whose mandate is a reflection of that sovereign authority. The behavior of other political actors (including unelected judges and civil servants) responds, accordingly, in relation to these other actors and the overall sovereign authority.[49] Therefore, rational choices in the quest for power and specific goals also are guided by that context and all formal and informal political behavior within this system also is derived from that environment.

The role of the Westminster model in developing reform proposals for the Senate of Canada illustrates the overarching relevance of these neo-institutional considerations. It also highlights the importance of taking into consideration the broader context of history, political culture, federalism, and other aspects of the overall setting in which not only the Senate of Canada but all parliamentary upper houses have been shaped. The subsequent chapters of this book will make reference to these features and will apply them in a manner that is consistent with neo-institutional methods and objectives. By framing these ideas in the guise of a hypothetical constitutional amendment, this proposal will provide a framework for this varied analysis and justification for the options that are proffered. Hopefully, it also will present this theoretical model for Canadian Senate reform in a way that will encourage thoughtful consideration of both its potential promises and consequences in this respect.

FRAMEWORK OF THIS PROPOSAL

The specific theoretical model for reform of the Senate of Canada will, as already explained, assume the form of a hypothetical and idealized amendment to Canada's Constitution Act of 1867. It will emphasize changes to the current constitutional sections dealing with the Senate, including those parts that will be retained, eliminated, and altered. In relation to each specific recommendation, an analysis and commentary will engage in a justification and discussion of those choices. Those sections will make reference to the themes that have been raised within the second chapter as well as concepts and approaches that have been addressed within this chapter. That model will be followed by a chapter offering arguably more attainable, non-constitutional recommendations for reform that are, nonetheless, informed by the theoretical model of the hypothetical constitutional amendment.

The effect of that particular presentation is to frame the current discussion and future considerations from the perspective of active public policy development. Framing legal discourse requires a thoughtful consideration of the political context in which it is framed. Often, that context is a highly practical one, as politicians seek to reflect current public opinion and appeal to popular impressions of current political controversies. It also must account for the desires and goals of other political elites, especially in relation to alternative schemes for Senate reform that have been offered for many decades. In the Canadian context, all of these considerations must include the various perspectives and objectives of the provinces and their respective governments and leaders.

While the hypothetical constitutional amendment that will be presented is intended to offer an idealized model, based upon broad theoretical understandings, the non-constitutional recommendations that will be subsequently offered must be more practical in this respect. Most Canadian constitutional amendments require the approval of the Canadian government and at least seven of the ten provincial governments, provided that those provinces represent at least 50% of the country's population—with unanimous provincial support required for constitutional changes specified within section 41 of the Constitution Act of 1982 that may be relevant to certain aspects of Senate reform.[50] Therefore, any proposal for an actual constitutional amendment must accept those considerable constraints. These considerations must account for the need to propose changes that, unless they can achieve a consensus among the various provinces, groups, and other interests (as well as the federal Canadian government and Canadian populace), should seek institutionally more informal, yet still theoretically sound, objectives.

Therefore, although the Senate's role in relation to Canadian federalism is not as prominent a feature of this proposal as it has been for many other proposals, it cannot be ignored—especially if, for no other reason, the approval of the provinces is necessary for the successful navigation of the process of constitutional amendment. That factor is, therefore, included within this analysis. Ultimately, though, the hypothetical constitutional amendment differs, significantly, from other, more conventional approaches. It draws, therefore, upon a different feature of the public policy process: the use of the process to think, critically, about the choices that are available and the rationale for the ones that have been adopted, particularly when they challenge the public to contemplate the subject in a radically different way.

Each chapter of part II of this book will address a different section (or multiple sections that are thematically related to each other) of the Constitution Act of 1867 as related to the Senate. It will indicate its hypothetical and theoretically based alterations as edits to that constitutional document to facilitate an understanding of these specific changes and their relationship to the current powers, rules, structure, and status of the Senate. Those paragraphs that represent parts of this proposed constitutional amendment will be presented in a distinctive manner within the text:

> Relevant sections of the Constitution Act of 1867 are presented within double-indented paragraphs and extra spacing in order to distinguish them from the commentary that surrounds them. *Those sections or clauses that would be newly added are indicated in italics.* ~~Sections, clauses, or language recommended for repeal are represented with crossed-out script~~.

General analyses relating to these constitutional proposals will be provided before, after, and between the various constitutional clauses of this proposed amendment. It also is intended to promote clarity for assessing the specific concept that is being proffered for discussion. The overall effect of this format is intended to facilitate critical analysis. It also is intended to distinguish this hypothetical amendment from the rest of the chapter.

CAUSE AND EFFECT

Neo-institutional methods do, indeed, require a demonstration of cause and effect in the relationship between institutional structure and political activity. Any prediction concerning the outcome of changes to the institution of the Senate can only be demonstrated through actual examples. While some data will be presented within chapter 7 relating to a limited experiment in holding "consultative elections" in support of Senate nominations, extremely little evidence from within the Canadian system is available to indicate the effect that various reforms might have.

Therefore, the only meaningful evidence of this potential effect will be presented from a comparative perspective. Data from the experiences of pertinent upper houses such as the House of Lords and the Australian Senate will, when appropriate, be cited for this purpose. Among these examples, statistical trends relating to the introduction of the suspensive veto for the House of Lords will be assessed within chapter 5, an assessment of trends in the diversity of appointments since the introduction of Life Peers and the appointment of "People's Peers" will be addressed within chapter 6, and a particularly important case study of the effect of the elected Australian Senate upon parliamentary government will be offered within chapter 7.

But neo-institutional analysis cannot always provide a thorough assessment of the results of these sorts of changes, especially when they have not yet been put into effect. Comparative examples of success and failure are important but they generally cannot be comprehensive, given the cultural and cognitive differences and constraints previously discussed. As other studies have indicated, very specific evidence of this sort can be very difficult to parse.[51] Furthermore, neo-institutional results are not limited to statistical evidence, though that exclusive assumption sometimes is mistakenly made.[52] Therefore, a neo-institutional approach also must provide a best estimate that draws upon theoretical predictions as well as empirical demonstrations, including ones that are not, by necessity, quantifiable.

So this reform proposal, as framed within this book, offers a suggested ideal model that remains aware of these institutional considerations while it seeks to inspire and guide other proposals—including ones that may be unfavorably inclined toward the assumptions upon which it is grounded. Understandably, it is not intended to be a politically attainable amendment to the Constitution Act of 1867. Ultimately, it is intended as an exercise in applied theoretical inquiry that, hopefully, will influence the ongoing political discourse of a challenging, sometimes divisive, and always highly interesting and relevant subject of Canadian public policy, now and in the future.

NOTES

1. James A. Bill and Robert L. Hardgrave, Jr., *Comparative Politics: The Quest for Theory* (Washington, DC: University Press of America, 1981), pp. 3–6.
2. Alain-G Gagnon, *Le Fédéralisme canadien contemporain: Fondemants traditions institutions* (Montréal: Les Presses de l'Université de Montréal, 2006), pp. 15–17; Dmitry Anastakis and Penny Bryden, *Framing Canadian Federalism* (Toronto: University of Totonto Press, 2009), pp. 186–187, 202.
3. Albert Broderick, *The French Institutionalists: Marice Hariou, Georges Renard, Joseph T. Delos* (Cambridge, Ma: Harvard University Press, 1970), pp. 5–7.
4. B. Guy Peters, *Institutional Theory in Political Science: The "New Institutionalism"* (London: Continuum, 2005), pp. 8–9.
5. Robert MacGregor Dawson and Norman Ward, *Dawson's the Government of Canada* (Toronto: University of Toronto Press, 1987).
6. Alan C. Cairns, "Alternative Styles in the Study of Canadian Politics," *Canadian Journal of Political Science*, vol. 7, no. 1 (March 1974), pp. 103–107.
7. Gabriel A. Almond and James S. Coleman, *The Politics of the Developing Areas* (Princeton, NJ: Princeton University Press, 1960), pp. 6–7.
8. Ronald H. Chilcote, *Comparative Inquiry in Politics and Political Economy* (Boulder, CO: Westview, 2000), pp. 9–10, 72; B. Guy Peters, *Strategies for Comparative Research in Political Science* (New York: Palgrave Macmillan, 2012), pp. 7–9.
9. Max Weber, *The Theory of Social and Economic Organization*, Talcott Parsons, ed. (New York: Free Press, 1964), pp. 56–77.
10. Chalres F. Andrain and David E. Apter, *Political Protest and Social Change* (New York: New York University Press, 1995), pp. 136–140; S. N. Eisenstadt and L. Roniger, Patrons, Clients, and Friends: *Interpersonal Relations and the Structure of Trust in Society* (Cambridge: Cambridge University Press, 1984), pp. 1–18; Philip Selznick, "Institutionalism 'Old' and 'New,'" *Administrative Science Quarterly*, vol. 41 (1996), pp. 270–277; Arthur L. Stitchcombe, *Information and Organizations* (Berkeley: University of California Press, 1990), pp. 17–20, 314–315.
11. Shu-Yun Ma, "Political Science at the Edge of Chaos? The Paradigmatic Implications of Historical Institutionalism," *International Political Science Review*, vol. 28, no. 1 (January 2007), pp. 63–64; Peters, *Institutional Theory in Political Science*, pp. 47–49.
12. Russell Keat and John Urry, *Social Theory as Science* (New York: Routledge, 2011), pp. 3–8.
13. Patrick Dunleavy and Brendan O'Leary, *Theories of the State: The Politics of Liberal Democracy* (New York: New Amsterdam Books, 1998), pp. 3–17; Theda Skopcol, *States and Social Revolution* (Cambridge: Cambridge University Press, 1979), pp. 3–19, 284–293.

14. Ronald H. Chilcote, *Theories of Comparative Political Economy* (Boulder, CO: Westview, 2000), pp. 149–156; Thráinn Eggerston, *Economic Behavior and Institutions* (Cambridge: Cambridge University Press, 1990), pp. 1–10.

15. Martin Hollis and Steve Smith, "Roles and Reasons in Foreign Policy Decision Making," *British Journal of Political Science,* vol. 16 (1986), pp. 276–278.

16. Jan-Erik Lane and Svante Ersson, *The New Institutional Politics: Performance and Outcomes* (New York: Routledge, 200), pp. 35–36.

17. Kathleen Thelen and Sven Steinmo, "Historical Institutionalism in Comparative Politics," in *Structuring Politics: Historical Institutionalism in Comparative Analysis*, Sven Steinmo, Kathleen Thelen, and Frank Longstreth, eds. (Cambridge: Cambridge University Press, 1992), pp. 3–8.

18. Suzanne Berger and Michael J. Piore, *Dualism and Discontinuity in Industrial Societies* (Cambridge: Cambridge University Press, 1980), pp. 8–12.

19. Peter A. Hall and Rosemary C. R. Taylor, "Political Science and the Three New Institutionalisms," *Political Studies*, vol. 44, no. 5, pp. 937–939.

20. Sven Steinmo and Kathleen Thelen, *Structuring Politics: Historical Institutionalism in Comparative Analysis* (Cambridge: Cambridge University Press, 1992), pp. 2–8.

21. Mehran Kamrava, *Understanding Comparative Politics: A Framework* (New York: Routledge, 1996), pp. 43–48; Robin Blackburn, *Ideology in Social Science* (New York: Pantheon, 1972), ch. 11; Peter B. Evans, Dietrich Rueschemeyer, and Theda Skopcol, "On the Road Toward a More Adequate Understanding of the State," in *Bringing the State Back In*, Peter B. Evans, Dietrich Rueschemeyer, and Theda Skopcol, eds. (Cambridge: Cambridge University Press, 1999), pp. 347–366.

22. Theda Skopcol, *Social Revolutions in the Modern World* (Cambridge: Cambridge University Press, 1997), pp. 55–71.

23. Leo Pantich, "The Role and Nature of the Canadian State," in *The Canadian State: Political Economy and Political Power*, Leo Panitch, ed. (Toronto: University of Toronto Press, 1977), pp. 9–12.

24. James March and Johan P. Olsen, *Rediscovering Institutions: the Organizational Basis of Politics* (New York NY, Free, 1989); Hall and Taylor, pp. 938–939.

25. March and Olsen, pp. 939–940.

26. W. Richard Scott, *Institutions and Organizations: Ideas and Interests* (London: Sage, 2008), pp. 50–51, 56–59.

27. Donald D. Searing, "Roles, Rules, and Rationality in the New Institutionalism," *American Political Science Review*, vol. 85, no. 4 (December 1991), pp. 1,241–1,243.

28. William G. Ouchi and Alan L. Wilkins, "Organizational Culture," *Annual Review of Sociology,* vol. 11 (1985), pp. 458–468.

29. James G. March and Johan P. Olsen, "The New Institutionalism: Organizational Factors in Political Life," *American Political Science Review,* vol. 78 (1984), pp. 734–749.

30. Kenneth A. Shepsle, "Studying Institutions: Some Lessons from the Rational Choice Approach," *Journal of Theoretical Politics,* vol. 1 (1989), p. 135.

31. Martin Hollis and Steve Smith, "Roles and Reasons in Foreign Policy Decision Making," *British Journal of Political Science,* vol. 16 (1986), pp. 270–276.

32. Searing, pp. 1,252–1,253.

33. William Roberts Clark, Matt Golder, and Sona L. Golder, *Principles of Comparative Politics* (London: Sage, 2013), pp. 706–707.

34. James T. McHugh, *Comparative Constitutional Traditions* (New York: Peter Lang, 2003), pp. 43–44.

35. John W. Meyer, John Boli, and George M. Thomas, "Ontology and Rationalization in the Western Cultural Account," in *Institutional Environments and Organizations*, W. Richard Scott and John W. Meyer, eds. (London: Sage, 1994), pp. 16–24

36. R.A.W. Rhodes, John Wanna, and Patrick Weller, *Comparing Westminster* (Oxford: Oxford University Press, 2009), pp. 45–77.

37. A. V. Dicey, *Introduction to the Study of the Law of the Constitution* (*Indianapolis*: Liberty Fund, 1982), pp. 277–315.

38. Jeffrey Jowell, "The Rule of Law Today," in *The Changing Constitution*, Jeffrey Jowell and Dawn Oliver, eds. (Oxford: Clarendon Press, 1989), pp. 3–23; Fredeick Maitland, *The Constitutional History of England* (Cambridge: Cambridge University Press, 1948), pp. 281–288; Margaret H. Olgilvie, *Historical Introduction to Legal Studies* (Toronto: Carswell, 1982), pp. 203–266; Owen Hood Phillips and Paul Jackson, *Constitutional and Administrative Law* (London: Sweet and Maxwell, 1987), pp. 41–82; S. A. de Smith, *Constitutional and Administrative Law* (London: Longman, 1971), pp. 43–66.

39. Geoffrey Marshall, *Parliamentary Sovereignty and the Commonwealth* (Oxford: Clarednon Press, 1984), pp. 3–18.

40. McHugh, pp. 83–84.

41. Peter Hogg, *Constitutional Law of Canada* (Toronto: Carswell, 1977), pp. 196–197.

42. Andrew Heard, *Canadian Constitutional Conventions: The Marriage of Law and Politics* (Oxford: Oxford University Press, 1991), pp. 2–7, 3–15; Gregory S. Mahler, "Canada: Two Nations, One State?" in *Political Culture and Constitutionalism: A Comparative Approach*, Daniel P. Franklin and Michael J. Baun, eds. (Armonk, NY: M. E. Sharpe, 1995), pp. 56–76.

43. Mark Bevir and R. A. W. Rhodes, The State as Cultural Practice (Oxford: Oxford University Press, 2010), pp. 157–160.

44. William Stubbs, *The Constitutional History of England* (Oxford: Clarendon Press, 1880), vol. I, pp. 597–605.

45. Stein Rokkan and Derek Urwin, "Centres and Peripheries in Western Europe," in *The Politics of Territorial Identity*, Stein Rokkan and Derem Urwin, eds. (London: Sage, 1982), pp. 11–13.

46. Jim Bulpitt, *Territory and Power in the United Kingdom* (Manchester: Manchester University Press, 1983), pp. 235–236.

47. Jennifer Smith, "Informal Constitutional Development: Change by Other Means," in Herman Bakvis and Grace Skogstad, eds., *Canadian Federalism* (Oxford: Oxford University Press, 2002), pp. 45–50.

48. Michael Rush, "The Canadian Parliament and the Federal System," in *Canadian Federalism: Past, Present, and Future*, Michael Burgess, ed. (Leicester: Leicester University Press, 1990), pp. 148–151.

49. Geoffrey Marshall, *Constitutional Conventions: The Rules and Forms of Political Accountability* (Oxford: Clarendon Press, 1986), ch. 4.

50. Katherine Swinton, "Amending the Canadian Constitution: Lessons from Meech Lake," *University of Toronto Law Journal*, vol. 42, no. 2 (Spring 1992), pp. 140–144.

51. Meg Russell, *The Contemporary House of Lords: Westminster Bicameralism Revived* (Oxford: Oxford University Press, 2013), p. 59.

52. Peters, *Institutional Theory in Political Science*, p. 90.

Part II

APPLICATION AND IDEALIZED CONSTITUTIONAL REFORM

Chapter 6

Constitutional Amendment, Part I

Legislative Powers

OVERVIEW

The first part of the counterintuitive approach that this book offers addresses the third of the three "E's" of the Triple-E concept, which is the concept of "effectiveness." Its conclusions are based upon the theoretical and comparative framework of the parliamentary upper house that has been previously assessed. It particularly relies upon the comparative example of the House of Lords, especially in terms of actual changes in political behavior that have resulted from particular institutional changes. That sort of analysis is the essence of a neo-institutional approach. However, other analytical considerations also are relevant to this overall proposal, as will be recognized throughout this process.

The overall theoretical model, framed as a constitutional amendment to the Constitution Act of 1867 within this chapter and the subsequent three chapters, will emphasize (as also alluded within the thesis statement found within the first chapter) the following hypothetical reforms:

1. The substitution of the current legislative power of the Senate with a suspensive veto that will permit delay but not outright defeat of government legislation;
2. Unlimited numbers of Senate appointments with compensation for parliamentary activity to be based upon a stipend for actual performance;
3. Adjustments to the ratio of regional and provincial representation;
4. Guidelines for the appointment of a more consciously diverse Senate, including structured input from a non-partisan appointments commission, provincial governments, and all major political parties;

5. A double-majority requirement for legislation addressing the official languages of Canada;
6. Confirmation authority over certain executive appointments, a more active ombudsman role, and other institutional adjustments.

As previously discussed, many of these proposals have been inspired by the example of the British House of Lords. Other aspects of these proposals have been derived from the models provided by the second chambers of other relevant political systems. These proposals have been constructed with a strong awareness of the internal context of the Canadian social and political experience as well as the theoretical implications of upper houses in general, neo-institutional considerations, and practical political implications.

> As explained near the end of the previous chapter, those relevant sections of the Constitution Act of 1867 are double-indented with an extra space between those sections and the rest of the text. Those clauses that would be retained under this proposal are kept in a standard format.[1] *Those sections or clauses that would be newly added are indicated in italics.* ~~Sections, clauses, or language recommended for repeal are represented with crossed-out script~~.

Additional commentary relating to these theoretical constitutional proposals is provided between the various hypothetical clauses. This arrangement will be followed for the subsequent chapters as well. As already mentioned, this chapter will focus upon a consideration of those sections of the Constitution Act of 1867 that address the formal legislative powers of the Senate in relation to the government and the lower house.

The Suspensive Veto

> Constitution Act, 1867
> IV. Legislative Power
> 17. There shall be One Parliament for Canada, consisting of the Queen, an Upper House styled the Senate, and the House of Commons.
> 18. *(1)* The privileges, immunities, and powers to be held, enjoyed, and exercised by the Senate and by the House of Commons, and by the Members thereof respectively, shall be such as are from time to time defined by Act of the Parliament of Canada, but so that any Act of the Parliament of Canada defining such privileges, immunities, and powers shall not confer any privileges, immunities, or powers exceeding those at the passing of such Act held, enjoyed, and exercised by the Commons House of Parliament of the United Kingdom of Great Britain and Ireland, and by the Members thereof.
> *Power of the Senate in Relation to Money Bills*

Table 6.1 Effectiveness of Upper Houses Influence without Confidence Conditional Logit Analysis of Government Formation

All Systems	*Bicameral Systems*			
Independent Variables	*Model 1*	*Model 2*	*Model 3*	*Model 4*
Coalition with Upper-Chamber Majority	–	–	1.85	1.11
			(3.39)	(2.14)
Lower-Chamber Seat Share of Coalition			–	0.02
				(0.02)
Lower-Chamber Sear Share of Minority Coalition	–	–	–	11.80
				(2.57)
Minority Coalition	−0.87	−0.31	1.19	−4.31
	(−1.83)	(−0.40)	(1.34)	(−2.41)
Oversized Coalition	−0.92	−0.50	−0.60	−0.19
	(−2.89)	(−1.28)	(−1.51)	(−0.46)
Number of Parties in the Coalition	−0.26	−0.21	−0.18	−0.48
	(−1.55)	(−1.06)	(−0.89)	(−2.14)
Largest Party in the Coalition	0.99	1.22	1.00	−0.01
	(3.28)	(2.77)	(2.18)	(−0.03)
Median Party in the Coalition	0.10	0.06	−0.02	−0.21
	(0.43)	(0.18)	(−0.05)	(−0.17)
Ideological Divisions in the Coalition	−4.72	−3.27	−3.90	−4.90
	(−4.14)	(−2.26)	(−2.64)	(−3.17)
Ideological Divisions within Majority Opposition	1.04	−0.52	−2.45	−3.52
	(0.93)	(−0.33)	(−1.41)	(−2.06)
Previous Prime Minister in the Coalition	0.00	0.25	0.30	−0.01
	(0.02)	(0.63)	(0.77)	(−0.02)
Incumbent Coalition	1.69	1.63	1.62	1.56
	7.15)	(5.44)	(5.37)	(5.19)
Minority Coalition where Investiture Vote Required	−1.12	−0.95	−0.62	−0.86
	(2.97)	(−1.61)	(−1.02)	(−1.36)
Anti-System Presence in the Coalition	−17.05	−16.68	−17.27	−17.45
	(−4.59)	(−4.46)	(−4.50)	(−4.32)
Pre-Electoral Pact Associated with the Coalition	3.51	3.41	4.69	4.03
	(4.47)	(2.69)	(3.20)	(3.32)
Very Strong Party in the Coalition	1.12	0.70	0.85	0.51
	(2.32)	(0.99)	1.17	(0.66)
Merely Strong Party in the Coalition	0.34	0.37	0.25	0.63
	(1.02)	(0.86)	(0.56)	(1.45)
Merely Strong Party *Alone* in the Coalition	−1.19	−1.53	−2.00	−2.43
	(−1.75)	(−1.35)	(−1.70)	(−2.12)
Log-likelihood	−410	−264	−258	−248110
Number of Bargaining Situations	170	110	110	(13,852)
(Number of Coalitions)	(24.932)	(13,852)	(13,852)	

Note: Entries are unstandardized maximum likelihood coefficients with *t*-ratios in parentheses.
Source: Druckman, Martin, and Thies, p. 539.

(2) If a Money Bill, having been passed by the House of Commons and sent to the Senate at least 40 days before the end of the session, is not passed by the Senate without amendment within 40 days after it is so sent or if it is rejected by a vote of the whole Senate within that same time period, the Bill shall, unless the House of Commons direct to the contrary, be presented to the Governor General, on behalf of Her Majesty, and become an Act of Parliament upon the Royal Assent being signified, notwithstanding that the Senate has not consented to the Bill. Any amendments that are certified by the Speaker of the House of Commons and verified by the Governor General to have been made by the Senate during this 40-day period and accepted by the House of Commons shall be inserted in the Bill as presented for Royal Assent in pursuance of this section

(2) A Money Bill is defined as a Public Bill which, in the opinion of the Speaker of the House of Commons and confirmed by the Governor General, contains only provisions dealing with all or any of the following subjects: the imposition, repeal, remission, alteration, or regulation of taxation; the imposition for the payment of debt or other financial purposes; public supply; the appropriation, receipt, custody, issue or audit of accounts of public money; the raising or guarantee of any loan or its repayment; subordinate matters incidental to those subjects or any of them.

(3) Every Money Bill passed by the House of Commons shall include a certificate of the Speaker of the House of Commons that it is a Money Bill. The Governor General shall verify, prior to signifying the Royal Assent, that the certificate is valid in its designation of the bill as a Money Bill.

Powers of the Senate in Relation to Other Bills (Suspensive Veto)

(4) If any Public Bill (other than a Money Bill and a Bill pertaining to the Official Languages of Canada) is passed by the House of Commons in two successive sessions (whether of the same Parliament or not) and, having been sent to the Senate at least 40 days before the end of each session, is rejected or otherwise fails to be passed by the Senate in each of those sessions, that Bill shall, on its rejection for the second time by the Senate (unless the House of Commons direct to the contrary) be presented to the Governor General, on behalf of Her Majesty, and become an Act of Parliament on the Royal Assent being signified, notwithstanding that the Senate has not consented to the Bill. This provision shall not take effect unless one year has elapsed between the date of the second reading in the first of those sessions of the Bill in the House of Commons and the date on which it passes the House of Commons in the second of these sessions.

(5) When a Bill is presented to the Governor General for the Royal Assent in pursuance of the provisions of this section, the Speaker of the House of Commons shall provide a certificate that the Bill complies with provisions of this section, which the Governor General shall verify.

(6) A Bill shall be deemed to be rejected by the Senate if it is not passed by that chamber during the session in which it has been presented either without amendment or with such amendments only as the House of Commons and the Senate shall mutually agree.

(7) A Bill shall be deemed to be the same Bill as a former Bill sent to the Senate in the preceding session if it is identical with the former Bill or contains only such alterations as are certified by the Speaker of the House of Commons and verified by the Governor General to be necessary owing to the time which has elapsed since the date of the former Bill or to represent any amendments which have been made by the Senate in the former Bill during the preceding session. Any amendments that are certified by the Speaker of the House of Commons and verified by the Governor General to have been made by the Senate in the second session and accepted by the House of Commons shall be inserted in the Bill as presented for Royal Assent in pursuance of this section, provided that the House of Commons may, on the passage of such a Bill during the second session, suggest any further amendments without inserting the amendments in the Bill and any such suggested amendments shall be accepted by the Senate shall be treated as amendments made by the Senate and accepted by the House of Commons, though the exercise of this power by the House of Commons shall not affect the operation of this section in the event of the Bill being rejected by the Senate.
Enacting Formula
(10) Any Bill that shall become an Act of Parliament without the consent of the Senate under the provisions of section 18 shall be enacted with the following formula:

> *'Her Majesty, by and with the advice of the Senate of Canada and the advice and consent of the House of Commons of Canada (pursuant to the provisions of section 18 of the Constitution Act of 1867, as amended), enacts as follows/Sa majesté, sur l´avis du Sénat du Canada et sur l´avis et avec le consentement de la Chambre des communes du Canada (conformément aux dispositions de l´article 18 de la Loi constitutionelle de 1867, telle que modifiée), édicte.'*

This reform is modeled upon a similar formula found in Britain's Parliament Act of 1949, which modified the Parliament Act of 1911. It is a version of the suspensive veto scheme. But unlike many other proposed variations of this option, it is intended (like its British example) to extend beyond a single session of a Parliament *and* it requires a deliberate override on the part of the lower house (except for money bills) for the vetoed bill to be forwarded for the Royal Assent. Ironically, this requirement may impose an even greater sense of restraint upon the upper house in exercising such a suspensive veto, given the fact that it would require a positive action and public repudiation upon the popularly elected chamber and the government that it supports.[2]

The enacting clause not only would identify those bills that have become laws as a result of a lower house override but it also reinforces an aspect of the participation of the upper house that often is overlooked or underappreciated. The notion of "advice" as being distinct from "consent" also implies the significance of that former action. The rule of law is a principle that includes the idea that law not only follows an identifiable process but that the process is observable. This principle also is central to the broader tradition of positive law that requires the law to be knowable in order to be, ultimately, a legitimate "command of the sovereign." Public supervision and scrutiny can be as important as public approval within the democratic process and additional "advice," in this respect, can be as important as "consent" within this stage of the legislative process. That role is especially relevant when that extended advice includes expert investigation, additional public hearings, and enhanced publicity—all of which are functions that, as previously noted, are particular characteristics of upper houses (especially parliamentary ones) in general, including in relation to a liaison capacity.

Even upper houses that are constitutionally "weak," such as ones that possess only the power to delay legislation, have been found to have a notable degree of influence over government policies within parliamentary systems. They also can affect the effectiveness of governments in passing and enacting their legislative priorities. This influence has been found to exist regardless of whether or not the upper house is elected, though elected upper houses can have a much more disruptive effect upon the stability of parliamentary governments, including ones that have strong majority support within the lower house as well as minority and coalition governments.[3] In terms of the role of non-elected upper houses, that effect can be much more constructive.

The record of the House of Lords is instructive in this respect. The British upper house has, since the adoption of the Parliament Act of 1949, rejected scores of government bills that have been passed by the House of Commons. Most of this action has been taken against governments led by the Conservative Party, despite the fact that Conservative peers have dominated the chamber during this period. In fact, during the first administration under Margaret Thatcher, the House of Lords rejected 45 government bills sent to it by the lower house.[4] Most famously, the House of Lords rejected an early draft of the Local Government Bill (which would have eliminated, among other local authorities, the Labour Party–dominated Greater London Council) and only failed to reject a revised version of that bill in 1985 (the opposition to the bill being led by, among other members of that chamber, the Bishop of London) as a result of the Thatcher government packing the chamber with hereditary peers who had been transported to Westminster specifically for that purpose.[5]

The interesting point concerning these rejections is that in only four instances since 1949 has the Parliament Act of 1949 been invoked in order to complete the passage of legislation over the objections of the upper house and two of those instances represented bills that had passed the Commons as "free votes" without party discipline imposed.[6] Generally, the government will not resubmit a bill that has been rejected by the House of Lords, even though it could ensure its adoption by taking that action.[7] The pattern appears to have emerged that the House of Lords invokes its suspensive veto only in cases in which it involves a minor bill that is not considered part of the government's electoral mandate, a bill that is deemed to have serious technical flaws that it considers ought to be corrected with a new bill, a bill that appears to violate traditional principles of law (especially in the opinion of the Law Lords who sat in that chamber prior to the Reform Bill of 2009), or a bill that is strongly opposed by public opinion. Furthermore, the House of Lords has felt particularly emboldened to oppose government legislation when its majority is of the same political party as the government.

In fact, the House of Lords generally has adhered to the Salisbury Convention, which stipulates that it will not reject or, even, closely scrutinize bills passed by the House of Commons that are part of the current government's election manifesto—a convention that had been proceeded by a more general convention on respecting the popular mandate that had been violated in 1911, thus necessitating the first of the Parliament Acts.[8] Despite indications that it might choose to delay legislation of the Labour government that was elected in 1997, the British second chamber (which was, at that time, dominated by Conservative peers) generally restrained itself from serious disruption of the government's mandate, though its activities (through amendments and the defeat of less-central legislation) did spike during this period.[9] Similar speculation occurred that Labour peers would not honor the Salisbury Convention when the Conservatives returned to power (with the Liberal Democrats as coalition partners) in 2010[10] but, again, that outcome generally did not occur to an extent that seriously disrupted or challenged the government's mandate.[11]

Table 6.2 House of Lords Activities, 2001–2015

Year	*Tabled Amendments*	*Amendments Passed*	*Government Defeats*
2001–2002	8,813	2,557	57
2002–2003	9,782	2,996	83
2003–2004	5,519	1,795	32
2004–2005	3,306	913	36
2005–2006	10,143	3,249	61
2006–2007	5,559	1,911	43
2007–2008	7,259	2,625	29
2008–2009	6,363	1,824	21
2009–2010	2,031	565	10
2010–2012	1,402	366	5
2012–2013	2,589	846	27
2013–2014	3,627	1,301	14
2014–2015	2,599	927	34

Source: Parliament of the United Kingdom, House of Lords, "Public Bills Statistics," http://www.parliament.uk/business/publications/house-of-lords-publications/records-of-activities-and-membership/public-bills-statistics/

Table 6.3 Summary Information on Groups in the Lords 1999–2005

	Labour	*Conservative*	*Liberal Democrat*	*Crossbench*	*Bishop*
Size of group[a]	199	205	69	181	25
Average (mean) age[a]	66	69	64	70	60
Proportion of group new since 1997 (%)	67.0	27.9	67.1	42.0	84.0
Mean turnout in whipped votes (%)	53.2	34.2	51.3	10.1	3.2
Mean cohesiveness (rice index) in whipped votes (%)[b]	97.2	99.2	99.0	50.0	75.1
% placing themselves ideologically distant from party leader	53.2	46.1	17.0	n/a	n/a
% believing they have a duty to vote the party line	83.5	57.7	89.1	n/a	n/a
No. of defeats (of 283) where some in group voted against govt	105	282	264	283	137
No. of times (of 283) that abstention would have averted defeat[d]	3	278	179	47	3
No. of times (of 283) that govt support would have averted defeat	8	283	256	152	8

[a] At the end of 2004–2005 parliamentary session[b] Calculated for Labour, Conservative, Liberal Democrat, and Crossbench only on votes where more than 10 such members participated; for Bishops where more than two participated.[c] More than one point away on a 10-point left-right scale.[d] For Labour, impact of rebels only.*Source*: Russell and Sciara, table VII.

As previously emphasized, the Senate of Canada very seldom has made use of its absolute veto. Between 1867 and 1967, the Senate only defeated a total of ten bills passed by the House of Commons. Between 1985 and 1993, that rate increased but only to the extent that seven House of Commons bills were either blocked or were attempted to be blocked by the Senate. This pattern demonstrates a strong reluctance by the upper house to employ such a strong option against the elected chamber that delegates sovereign power to the government.[12] It does not account for informal expressions of concern or opposition by the Senate that result in the House of Commons withdrawing or altering bills before they proceed to final votes within that chamber, which does indicate a greater Senate influence over legislation than might, otherwise, be indicated by the formal record.[13] It does not necessarily account for actions such as the delaying of Bill C-130 (which sought to establish a free trade agreement between Canada and the United States) by the Canadian

Senate in 1988 in order to compel the Progressive Conservative government of Brian Mulroney to call an election in order to seek a mandate on that policy.[14] Nonetheless, the overall record indicates an upper house that is very reluctant to exercise its formal authority, regardless of the power that it technically possesses.

In comparison, the experience of the House of Lords indicates the effectiveness of a suspensive veto (particularly one requiring positive action to override it) in a parliamentary setting. The will of the lower house (and its popular mandate) cannot be thwarted if it has the resolve to pursue it. But the suspensive veto does not constitute a mere symbolic gesture as it places pressure on the government to justify its original position. It is, in a neo-institutional sense, an obstacle that can be easily overcome but only if other political conditions support it. Therefore, the upper house is constrained in its use of that suspensive veto by considerations of those same conditions. Furthermore, the suspensive veto does not need to be invoked in a politically hostile manner, especially when it is used for a genuine reconsideration of the specific construction of the legislation and not as a rejection of its substance. Of course, the proposal of amendments can serve that same purpose, which the upper house is well positioned to provide.

THE SUSPENSIVE VETO AND RESPONSIBLE GOVERNMENT

Even in non-parliamentary systems, such as the United States, the primacy of popular assemblies over budgetary matters has been upheld. For example, the

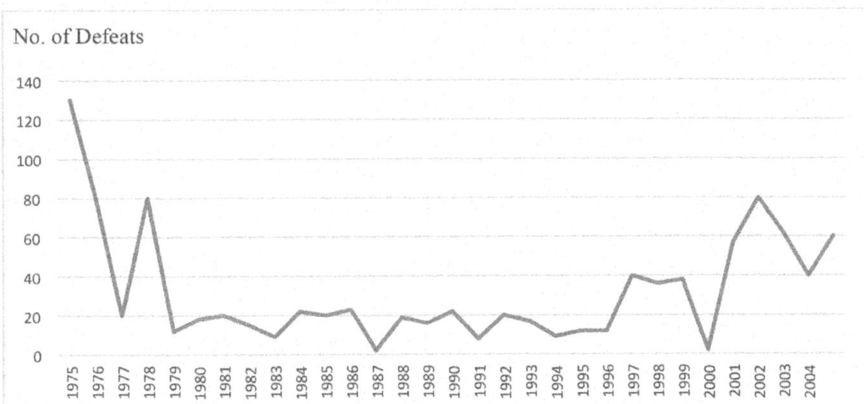

Figure 6.1 Government Defeats in the House of Lords, 1975–2004. Recreated by the author. Russell, "Reforming the British House of Lords."

House of Representatives must originate all money bills that are considered by Congress—a principle that was even more notable in this respect when American Senators were selected by their respective state legislatures, rather than directly elected.[15] All matters relating to revenue and spending in Canada have been considered to be the exclusive purview of the lower house and that principle ought not to be violated by a reformed Senate. It is a principle that is central to a liberal democratic ideal of sovereign authority that transcends the idea that elections, by themselves, convey legitimacy.

At the same time, though, the advantages of the upper house in its role of review should not be entirely dismissed in this respect. The Senate could offer improving amendments, technical corrections, or, simply, express concern in this area, particularly if it stems from an expert assessment or widespread apprehension. A capacity to delay, briefly, this sort of legislation could provide those advantages without seriously curtailing the authority of the lower house. Furthermore, public pressure should continue to make the Senate extremely reluctant (as it has been under the current scheme in which it possesses an absolute veto over these bills) to exercise even this limited action over money legislation, thus enhancing its effectiveness if and when it is temporarily invoked.

This approach is consistent with general theories of the parliamentary upper house. As previously addressed, these theories include the separation of the upper house from the government—an ideal that reflects a more liberal assumption concerning the concept of a separation of powers ensuring effectively limited government. That consideration merits reiteration, especially in connection with the relationship between the upper house and the lower house in terms of legislation regarding budgetary and other financial matters. The upper house, especially within a parliamentary system, generally is not required to provide legislative support for the legitimacy of the government of the day, thus allowing for a useful critique that provides a philosophically liberal challenge to a potentially unrestrained central role of government while, simultaneously, ensuring that it does not undermine it. Within both a liberal democratic context and, more narrowly, the Westminster model, this relationship is particularly pronounced as the support of the lower house is the determining factor in establishing that government. The principles of responsible government are grounded upon that relationship.[16]

The suspensive veto can have a liberating effect in this respect. It further emphasizes the distinct status of the upper house in contrast with the lower house upon which the government must depend for its existence. Opposition to any government legislation can be interpreted as opposition to the government, itself, and, thus, as an attack upon its very legitimacy. Under such circumstances, the upper house naturally should feel constrained in its actions. The suspensive veto allows the upper house and its members to become disentangled from the political pressures and constraints that the lower house and its members generally experience. As a result, party discipline becomes a less important influence upon political behavior within the upper house, unlike its role within the lower house, in which it is a required feature for parliamentary responsible government to be sustained.[17] The institutional presence of a suspensive veto provides a government with a working majority in the lower house and the authority to override objections of the upper house.

However, that institutional feature may not, by itself, assure the absence of partisan pressure within the legislative behavior of the upper house. Political patronage often accounts for initial nominations or appointments to that body and such members may be influenced by a sense of gratitude, long-term loyalty, or hope for future political advantage from their governmental and party leaders. Nonetheless, members of upper houses have been shown to be removed from the direct pressures exerted by the head of government. Therefore, members of that chamber, including members appointed from the government party, are freer to take actions that may not accord with current government policy and action without the risk that a "rebellion" would entail for their counterparts in the lower house.[18] That characteristic has been described as the capacity to "embarrass" the government (especially over initiatives that are not part of its electoral mandate and may meet with general public disapproval) and it has been noted as being particularly strong within non-elected chambers.[19] This condition creates opportunities for increased freedom of political activity, including of the legislative, publicity, and investigative sort associated with the theme of "specialized roles and functions."

This attribute of the upper house, especially from a parliamentary perspective, is a critical consideration for any reform plan. Unless the objective is to create an effective rival of the lower house and the government, the most truly effective role for an upper house is to address political activities that do not necessarily imitate or challenge but, instead, complement and enhance the overall legislative process. The suspensive veto is designed, primarily, to achieve that goal.

A potential difficulty with that particular reform is the popular perception of the upper house as a legislative body whose *de jure* internal activity is identical to the lower house. This perception is central to the utilitarian critique that the role of a parliamentary upper house is redundant and, thus, either a source of unnecessary conflict or, more generally, entirely supercilious. That characteristic can create an equally popular impression that the upper house ought to behave (in most, if not all, of its activities) in a manner that is functionally identical to the lower house, including possession of the same legislative powers and prerogatives—including the authority to reject government legislation and, even, require that government to resign or call new elections. That function and authority can be associated with the Italian

Senate, upon which parliamentary upper house the Italian government is dependent for its support equally with the House of Delegates—a factor that contributed to political deadlock and instability and that required major reform to alleviate it.[20]

The Triple-E goal of an "effective" Senate typically has been expressed in terms of a capacity to block the legislation of the government, including under circumstances in which the governing party has received a clear majority support within the House of Commons.[21] Of course, the current Senate of Canada has the *de jure* authority to reject *any* legislation, including bills that are derived from a popular government mandate. Meanwhile, the second "E" is based upon the assumption that a Senate with its own electoral mandate would legitimize such action, as opposed to currently appointed body. The Alberta Select Committee that originated this plan emphasized that the Senate should be able to exercise an outright veto over any legislation that affects provincial jurisdiction.[22] However, in recognition of the potential conflict with the principle of responsible parliamentary government, another Alberta select committee modified the final "E" by shifting to a suspensive veto the proposed powers of this reformed Senate over all ordinary (non-money) legislation except for ones that directly affect provincial jurisdiction.[23]

THE SUSPENSIVE VETO AND A NEO-INSTITUTIONAL ANALYSIS

Neo-institutional responses can be measured in terms of the anticipated efficacy of such reform, though it can be difficult to measure its effect in the absence of a clear example of that effect. One instance of that sort of measurement is the effect that the suspensive veto actually has had upon the House of Lords. Following the Reform Acts of the 19th century (which extended the British franchise) but prior to the enactment of the Parliament Act of 1949 (which refined the formal restrictions upon the upper house veto that had been established in 1911), the House of Lords had demonstrated, for decades, a strong reluctance to amend, let alone reject, legislation approved by the House of Commons. Since the introduction of the current suspensive veto in 1949, this sort of action by the House of Lords has proliferated—generally with the lower house accepting these amendments and without reintroducing the defeated legislation.[24] During the 2010–2011 parliamentary session, alone, the House of Lords (dominated by peers from the same parties as the ruling coalition government) defeated 23 government bills, most of which, ultimately, were either abandoned or reintroduced with substantial revisions.[25]

Not only did this institutional reform appear to liberate the behavior of these members of the upper house, it also imposed an indirect sense of constraint, when applied judiciously, upon the members of the lower house. This result is consistent with a neo-institutional rational choice model of political responses that prefer the least coercive methods to more coercive methods for achieving overall results.[26] Formal rules do not guide this behavior; informal expectations are the motivating factor—expectations that can be compared to the sense of a "national mood" which, though it can be difficult to gauge with tangible precision, nonetheless has been documented to provide a strong constraint on political processes and behavior.[27] As previously noted, those influences can treat institutions like a maze through which political actors (like "mice") must navigate to get to "a piece of cheese." The construction of the maze affects the behavior and, even, the preferences of the mouse. The construction of the political institutions also affects the behavior of the actors who must navigate it.[28]

The relationship between this approach and rational choice theory suggests a systemic tendency to seek alternative institutions for promoting certain political goals—which second chambers can provide.[29] A meaningful assessment of this claim requires additional data but the principles that it describes appear, even in the absence of that data, as a reasonable approach to exploring the potential affect that institutional reform may have upon political behavior. Some of that assessment can be derived from a consideration of other institutional factors, including the system of shared sovereignty that has been traditionally tied to the creation of the Senate of Canada. In that way, reform proposals can be based upon the actual performance of a reformed upper house, rather than an imagined claim of a performance that it "ought" to do.

Neo-institutional studies derive much of their usefulness from empirical observations, which can include case studies and surveys. The influence of comparative politics upon the development of institutionalism in general often has relied upon this emphasis.[30] A particularly good source of comparison is between the Canadian and British parliamentary systems and the reform of their respective upper chambers. Prior to 1949, the House of Lords's activity could be described as restrained. Since 1949, that activity has increased.[31] While the numbers in this respect are difficult to measure with precision, they do suggest a trend and a shift in self-perceived purpose and role for the British upper house.

RESPONSIBLE GOVERNMENT, LEGISLATIVE POWERS, AND THE BRITISH AND AUSTRALIAN EXAMPLES

Four reasons have been offered for this shift. First, the appointment method (which will be addressed in another chapter) has increasingly opened the British upper house to persons who have achieved that membership through merit. Second, the fact that the appointment process has been available to the input of all political parties (even while in opposition) has made that chamber more politically balanced, especially when considering the addition of truly non-partisan members who sit on the Cross Benches. Third, it is more reflective of ongoing shifts in public opinion, rather than relying upon an electoral mandate from a particular election held at a particular time. That flexibility has been instrumental in increasing public support for addressing otherwise unpopular government legislation. Fourth, the performance of that chamber since the reforms of the House of Lords Act of 1999 has demonstrated its capacity to make positive contributions to the parliamentary process without perceived obstructionism or ultimate challenge to the legitimacy of the government's support in the House of Commons.[32]

The British upper house, like its Canadian counterpart, behaves in a less overtly partisan fashion—an additional theme that will be addressed within another chapter. Again, this characteristic can be explained in neo-institutional ways. That behavior does not follow conventional patterns typically associated with legislative activity in representative chambers, especially parliamentary ones. Instead, the qualities that contribute to appointed second chambers appear to motivate more independent behavior, especially with the increase of potential "veto players" that can be attributed to this compositional element.[33]

Likewise, any discussion of the benefits of having an elected Canadian Senate ought to be compared to the example of the Australian Senate. The motivations that prompted the Governor-General's Crisis in Australia in 1975 offers, by itself, an important case study in this respect. That case study is, admittedly, singular. Unfortunately, as with other accounts of the upper house, the number of incidents does not provide sufficient mass to be quantifiably significant. Furthermore, the presence of correlation does not, automatically, result in the finding of causation.

Nonetheless, broader data on the behavior of the Senate of Australia provides inferences, if not actual statistical significance, of the unintended consequences of the sort of "democratic" reform that would result in an elected Senate of Canada, especially when not considered within a more critical liberal democratic context. For example, between 1991 and 2013, a total of 127 government bills were "negatived" by the Senate of Australia.[34] That figure provides an average of 5.52 outright defeats (as opposed to other "negatived" legislative maneuvers, such as bills that have been "discharged from the Notice Paper" or "laid aside by the House of Representatives") of government legislation introduced during each of those years. At the same time, though, those figures are incomplete and potentially misleading, reinforcing the limitations of this sort of analysis. Many of these bills could be considered relatively minor ones that have not challenged the government's

Table 6.4 Parliament of Australia, Senate Legislation, 1991–2000

	1991	*1992*	*1993**	*1994*	*1995*	*1996**	*1997*	*1998**	*1999*	*2000*
Bills passed by Senate	211	260	144	168	183	85	224	139	206	181
Bills passed by Senate then laid aside or discharged by Reps	3	3	1	5	2	2	6	3	-	-
Bills discharged from Senate *Notice Paper*	10	3	-	-	2	1	1	4	2	-
Bills negatived by Senate	1	2	2	4	1	-	7	2	2	6
Number of amendments moved to adoption of committee report*	-	-	-	-	-	5	7	6	5	8
Agreed to						2	5	4	2	4
Number of bills on which there were disagreements between the Houses	10	7	10	14	10	4	23	7	15	19
Number of bills referred to Senate committees	41	55	43	53	44	45	93	96^	74	78

* Indicates an election year +When all matters referred to a committee have been considered, the chair shall be directed to report to the Senate. Resolutions reported from a committee may be agreed to or disagreed to by the Senate, or agreed to with amendments. (*See Senate Standing Order 148*)^ This figure includes 10 bills which were referred in both the 38th and 39th parliaments.*Source*: Parliament of Australia, Legislation—general, 1991–2000, http://www.aph.gov.au/Parliamentary_Business/Statistics/statsnet/consolidations/19912000/~/~/~/~/~/link.aspx?_id=F8103DD7838C43C6BD661661EF2CCBFB&_z=z

Table 6.5 Parliament of Australia, Senate Legislation, 2001–2010

	*2001**	*2002*	*2003*	*2004**	*2005*	*2006*	*2007**	*2008*	*2009*	*2010*
Bills passed by Senate	171	154	155	156	167	172	184	164	140	156
Bills passed by Senate then laid aside or discharged by Reps	-	3	2	0	0	0	0	1	0	0
Bills discharged from Senate *Notice Paper*	-	2	2	0	0	4	2	2	3	0
Bills negatived by Senate	9	5	9	7	1	0	0	13	41	4
Number of amendments moved to adoption of committee report*	4	2	1	1	2	1	0	2	4	1
Agreed to	2	0	0	1	0	0	0	2	1	1
Number of bills on which there were disagreements between the Houses	12	12	25	23	8	1	1	10	9	5
Number of bills referred to Senate committees	44	55	68	68	65	100	71	92	112	109

*Indicates an election year

mandate, while other ones could be considered to be more significant, such as the Senate rejection of the Rudd government's carbon-trading system in 2009, which had been part of that government's electoral platform.[35] The difficulty of determining statistical relevance is a common one in assessing second chambers.

Nonetheless, it still may be revealing that the number of defeats per year increased, greatly, during years in which the primary Opposition party controlled either a majority or a near-majority of Senate seats—for example, in 2009, 41 government bills were "negatived" by the Senate during the tenure of the Labor Party government under Prime Minister Kevin Rudd while a majority of Senate seats were controlled by the Liberal-led Coalition. However, it is further significant that the defeats of that particular year coincided with the attempts by the government to enact the widely unpopular Resource Super Profit Tax[36] among other problems in popularity that the prime minister was facing.[37] Interestingly, those numbers did not correspond to a similar increase in the number of Senate amendments, especially ones that resulted in disagreement between it and the House of Representatives. Those numbers also have fluctuated between 1991 and 2013 with the highest numbers occurring in 1997 (23), 2003 (25), and 2004 (23)—the latter two dates occurring during Liberal governments in which it and its coalition partners controlled a near majority of seats in the Australian upper house.[38]

Overall, though, the participation of the Australian Senate within the broader parliamentary and political systems has demonstrated considerable constraint,[39] despite the conspicuous exception of the conflicts that precipitated the Governor-General's Crisis. Actual challenges to government legislation and policy on the part of the Australian Senate reflect a very small percentage of overall federal legislative activity in any given year.[40] If one excludes the particularly contentious year of 2009, the average number of bills that were negatived (including ones that were discharged) as the result of Senate action represents an average of only .034% of all government legislation. That figure provides an interesting comparison with the records of the British House of Lords.

As already noted, prior to 1911, the House of Lords very rarely rejected government bills that had been approved by the House of Commons, though formal records are not consistently available in this area. After 1911, the willingness of the House of Lords to oppose government legislation appeared to increase—though, again, outright defeats of government bills by the British upper house were extremely rare. Between 1911 and 1949, 12 major government bills were actively opposed by the upper house. After 1949, this frequency increased with 27 major government bills being actively opposed by the upper house.[41] Institutionally, these numbers might appear to be potentially meaningful in relation to the passing of the two Parliament Acts that allowed the House of Commons to override defeats on the part of the House of Lords. Admittedly, these numbers are too small to be statistically significant within a strict analytical context. They also do not take into account other, less dramatic activities, especially in the areas of "technical" amendments, oversight, research, and investigation. For example, qualitative features of this opposed legislation (whether it is important to the government's mandate, whether it has a politically vital purpose, or whether it affects the country as a whole or a very small sector of it) are not considered—factors that could be compared to similar behavior within the Canadian and Australian second chambers.

Indeed, in contrast to both of these Westminster-model second chambers, the Senate of Canada's activity has been less apparent. Outright rejection of government legislation passed by the Canadian House of Commons has been extremely rare in the history of that second chamber. Instead, that chamber has focused upon a mission to "scrutinize" legislation sent to it from the lower house or (more rarely) initiated, directly, by the government. Its activity has been, as a result, more narrowly focused upon the themes of "improvement" in relation to government bills and policies, as well as attention to private bills—many of which originate in the Senate.

During the period 2001–2012, this more parochial legislative activity has been particularly apparent. A total of 340 bills became Acts of Parliament and a total of 41 of them were subject to either Senate amendments or "observations" that recommended changes or other modifications to the legislation. These figures do not take into account the number of specific amendments present within each amended bill—for example, Bill C-2, in 2006, was an omnibus bill that addressed diverse proposals relating to the theme of government accountability. It was subject to 158 separate amendments.[42] Like the preponderance of Senate amendments, they frequently addressed parochial issues, technical improvements, or specific corrections to the original legislation. On average, the Senate took action, during this time period, on a little more than 12% of government bills that ultimately were adopted.

An apparent limitation with this sort of quantified information is that it lacks qualitative refinement. The extent to which amendments can be deemed to be "substantial" is difficult to determine without using a more detailed and lengthy series of case studies on a significant number of examples. Furthermore, the distinction between actual amendments, requiring a legislative response by the House of Commons, and observations that do not mandate a legislative response on the part of the lower house, frequently is obscure, as is the effectiveness of the latter action in its influence upon government legislation. Because of an absence of substantive institutional change within the Senate of Canada, throughout its history (constitutionally and, arguably, internally), any correlation between institutional change and legislative performance remains, necessarily, speculative.

Table 6.6 Parliament of Australia, Senate Legislation, 2011–2017

	2011	*2012*	*2013**	*2014*	*2015*	*2016*	*2017>*
Bills passed by Senate	188	207	146	135	181	102	47
Bills passed by Senate then laid aside or discharged by Reps	0	1	1	1	0	0	0
Bills discharged from Senate *Notice Paper*	4	2	4	2	2	0	1
Bills negatived by Senate	3	7	4	28	9	3	0
Number of amendments moved to adoption of committee report<	0	0	0	0	0	0	0
Agreed to	N/A	N/A	N/A	N/A	N/A	N/A	N/A
Number of bills on which there were disagreements between the Houses	0	2	1	4	3	5	1
Number of bills referred to Senate committees	123	100	99	122	109	72	26

*Indicates an election year
<When all matters referred to a committee have been considered, the chair shall be directed to report to the Senate. Resolutions reported from a committee may be agreed to or disagreed to by the Senate, or agreed to with amendments. (*See Senate Standing Order 148*)
> Figures for this column only cover January through May of this year.
Source: Parliament of Australia, Legislation—general, 2011–2020, http://www.aph.gov.au/Parliamentary_Business/Statistics/statsnet/consolidations/19912000/~/~/~/~/~/~/~/link.aspx?_id=2E54679D3B12418E9321D9BAA2191B83&_z=z

Therefore, a neo-institutional analysis that rests upon empirical evidence is compelled to consider the comparative example of other second chambers within the Westminster system. In that respect, the Senate of Australia could be deemed to be more "effective" in defeating government legislation while the House of Lords could be deemed to be more "effective" in amending it. The fact that the former upper house is an elected one, is formally permitted to defeat legislation passed by its lower house, and consists, overwhelmingly, of professional politicians while the latter upper house is appointed (though a hereditary element remains) may delay but not, ultimately, defeat legislation passed by its lower house (and includes large numbers of members from diverse and non-political backgrounds) may be significant in this respect. These institutional variables are extremely important but they are not the only ones that matter. Other variables, such as general political and social cultures, demographics, general institutional cultures, economic structures and conditions, public expectations, and many other factors also must be included.

A particularly challenging distinction is that, unlike the Senate of Australia, the House of Lords is more likely to express legislative opposition through the amendment process rather than through outright defeat of a substantive government bill. Government "defeats" as defined in this way have received a fair amount of attention and represent a potentially more meaningful insight into that chamber's institutional behavior. During the period of 2001 through 2012, for example, British peers tabled a total of 60,177 amendments of which a total of 18,801 were adopted. Of these amendments, a total of 377 were regarded as "government defeats."[43] Although 441 Acts of Parliament were passed within the United Kingdom during this period,[44] the scope of these amendments cannot be accurately assessed in that respect because many amendments undoubtedly were addressed to the same bill. Nonetheless, on the surface, that activity appears to be considerable.

By comparison, the "number of amendments moved to adoption of committee report" within the Senate of Australia during this same time period was 31, the total "number of bills on which there were disagreements between the Houses" was 119, and the total "number of bills referred to Senate committees" was 622, including 10 bills that were referred, twice, during two different parliamentary sessions. Therefore, the number of amendments moved to adoption of committee reports reflected only .02% of total legislation thus affected during this time period. Furthermore, the number of bills referred to committee reflected less than 35% of all legislation—compared with the activity of the House of Lords in which virtually all legislation appears to have been referred to committee.[45]

Another difficulty of applying a neo-institutional analysis to the Senate of Australia is that the absence of significant institutional change within this parliamentary arrangement denies a necessary catalyst for including the structure of the chamber as a variable. A potential contrast could be provided by the introduction of proportional representation for Senate elections, which was adopted in 1949. That institutional change was responsible for a greater diversity of political parties within the Australian upper house, thus increasing the motivation for increased partisanship, especially under conditions in which it was increasingly difficult for a single party to gain a majority of seats in that second chamber. In conjunction with the constitutional provision for dissolving both houses of the Australian Parliament in the event of a serious and irreconcilable difference over legislation, it also has been noted as a potentially significant example of institutional influence over the behavior of the parliamentary upper house.[46]

The presence of the "double dissolution" as a means of overcoming impasses between the two Australian parliamentary chambers was designed to address the dual desire of an "effective" upper house that would address the interests of the various Australian states and a mechanism for ensuring responsible government at the federal level. Section 57 of the Constitution of Australia allows for a simultaneous dissolution of both chambers in the event of a "deadlock" over legislation—thus providing a means of ensuring some vestige of the initiative of the parliamentary government (and the principle of responsible government) as well as the sovereign authority of the electorate.[47] It resulted from a compromise over the powers and role of the Senate that had reflected the contentious conflict of expectations.[48] It had been agreed, during the debates on creating a constitutional system for a new Commonwealth of Australia, that some sort of mechanism would be necessary to overcome potential conflicts in this area.[49] This constitutional convention was introduced in order to ensure that the Senate of Australia adheres to the expectation (as particularly emphasized by future Prime Minister Alfred Deakin) of an upper house that primarily would serve as a reviewing and revising chamber and that also would be capable of exercising some sort of "veto" power, though one that would be "limited in time."[50]

It may be significant that the use of the double dissolution occurred only once prior to the 1949 introduction of proportional representation in Senate elections[51] but five times since that institutional amendment.[52] Again, this sort of information provides a trend but the numbers are two small, too disparately timed, and too subject to the influence of other variables to constitute a truly significant correlation. It may provide a means for comparative analysis in this area that is not grounded purely upon superficial aspects of formal legalism but it does not overcome a tendency toward speculation in the absence of more substantial data and the ability to control for a wide array of other, potentially influential variables.

This example indicates both the promise and the limitation of a neo-institutional approach toward upper house reform, including within Canada. Precise data concerning voting patterns during much of the Australian Senate's history is difficult to find and collate and, as with the data since 1991, it also can be widely inconclusive. Thus, claims concerning the potential relationship between institutional reform and legislative behavior in this area also are difficult to determine. Certainly, a comparison of the Australian and Canadian upper chambers concerning the difference that elections would make to the behavior of the latter upper house is, understandably, challenging in this respect.

In other words, this sort of analysis suffers from two challenges that frequently can confront quantitative analysis: insufficient empirical evidence and too many variables. Therefore, a neo-institutional approach is not, necessarily, a panacea for arriving at choices that will produce desired or predictable results, especially when performed within the context of comparative politics and the tremendous diversity of variables that contrasting political systems, in general, provide. Nonetheless, merely attempting this approach can be highly useful. It compels prospective reformers to consider the true potential that institutional change can affect but, also, the limits of that potential. Rather than engaging in "wishful thinking," this approach, even when incomplete, encourages an analysis that may be more detached from broader political desires that can obscure the real effect that institutional change will produce.

A different source of analysis, therefore, that may be helpful in complementing that approach may be a return to certain normative considerations. For example, part of the inducement for restraint that is noted among these upper chambers also could be attributed to the influence of classic conservative norms over these institutional features. The evolution of the role of the upper house and the overall parliamentary system, while retaining their formal structure, is consistent with this desire to maintain a level of stability that can accommodate other broad political changes. This ideological principle is particularly relevant within the context of an unentrenched constitutional tradition (such as Britain) but also as applied to the partially entrenched constitutional norms of Canada's parliamentary system. These sorts of philosophical influences are reinforcing in relation to this broader institutional model and could help to explain this pattern of relatively restrained, yet constructive, behavior even further.

THE SUSPENSIVE VETO AS A PREFERRED OPTION

So this analysis returns to the theme of this particular clause of this model of constitutional amendment. The effectiveness of adopting a suspensive veto for the Senate of Canada appears to offer certain institutional advantages and a neo-institutional analysis can indicate, but not definitively support, this conclusion: 1) the suspensive veto deprives the upper house of certain express powers; 2) it also liberates that chamber in relation to increasing its informal powers. The authority to delay legislation, when exercised strategically, can impose a different form of accountability on the lower house and the government that derives its mandate from that elected chamber. By compelling the lower house to reaffirm its previous legislative decision, it also compels the government to renew its defense of the policy which that legislation enacts. Of course, if that policy and legislation constitutes a clear part of a government's platform and mandate, that exercise would be not only futile but, arguably, would constitute an unacceptable challenge to responsible parliamentary government in particular and liberal democratic norms in general. It would, at best, promote a sense of frustration among the electorate and within society as a whole. At worst, it would produce a constitutional crisis.

However, if the object of this exercise was directed toward a bill and policy that does not constitute a part of a government's election platform and mandate, if it were clearly unpopular with the electorate, if it represented a cynical "power grab" (or, even, an action of questionable propriety), if it offended constitutional principles, or if it was related to a controversial issue that would be addressed in an imminent election, a suspensive veto would be regarded very differently. The delay caused by the suspensive veto would, then, constitute a reasonable and legitimate requirement for a government to reaffirm its intention and resubmit that intention to national approval. In other words, the suspensive veto would represent a response to the lower house and government of "are you sure?" By committing that action, the upper house also would be making that question available for the electorate to ponder as well.

The suspensive veto is far more compatible with both the Westminster model of parliamentary government as it has evolved into the 21st century and the broader tradition of liberal democratic thought. It avoids the potential undermining of the parliamentary principle of responsible government while reinforcing the role of the upper house as a chamber of legislative and policy scrutiny and, thus, responding to potential utilitarian criticisms of redundancy. Under those conditions, the theme of "accountability" for the upper house assumes different dimensions, thus also challenging an important rationale for it to be an elected body. The following chapters will address that theme as well as other ones.

NOTES

1. The gender-specific language of the original constitutional texts also are retained, though it would be recommendable that they be updated in that respect, as generally proposed in Richard B. Saphire, "Judicial Review in the Name of the Constitution," *University of Dayton Law Review,* vol. 8 (1983), pp. 796–97.

2. Meg Russell and Richard Cornes, "The Royal Commission on Reform of the House of Lords: A House for the Future?" *Modern Law Review*, vol. 64, no. 1 (January 2001), pp. 84–88.

3. James N. Druckman, Lanny W. Martin, and Michael F. Thies, "Influence without Confidence: Upper Chambers and Government Formation," *Legislative Studies Quarterly*, vol. 30, no. 4 (November 2005), pp. 529–548.

4. Donald R. Shell, "The House of Lords and the Thatcher Government," *Parliamentary Affairs*, vol. 38, no. 1 (Winter 1985), p. 16.

5. Glenn Dymond and Hugo Deadmon, "The Salisbury Doctrine," (London: House of Lords Library Note, June 2006), pp. 39–42; Shell, pp. 26–29.

6. Rodney Brazier, "Appendix I: The Parliament Acts," *Constitution: Seventh Report* (London: House of Lords, 2006), http://www.publications.parliament.uk/pa/ld200506/ldselect/ldconst/ 141/14104.htm.

7. Richard Kelly, "The Parliament Acts," (London: Parliament and Constitution Centre, 2007), pp. 10–11.

8. Her Majesty's Government, *Reform of the House of Lords* (London: Her Majesty's Stationer's Office, 2007), p. 10.

9. Dymond and Deadmon, pp. 53–57.

10. Eamonn Butler, "The Future of the Salisbury Convention," Adam Smith Institute (June 2010), http://www.adamsmith.org/blog/politics-and-government/the-future-of-the-salisbury-convention

11. Meg Russell and Maria Sciara, "Why Does the Government get Defeated in the House of Lords?" The Lords, the Party System and British Politics 2 British Politics (2007), http://www.palgrave-journals.com/bp/journal/v2/n3/full/4200064a.html#tbl7

12. J. Lynch-Staunton, "The Role of the Senate in the Legislative Process," *Canadian Parliamentary Review* (Summer 2000), pp. 10–14.

13. J. A. Robertson, "Rejection of Bills by the Canadian Senate," Library of Parliament Research Paper (Ottawa: Parliament of Canada, 1990), pp. 3–8.

14. Jeffrey M. Ayres, "Political Process and Popular Protest: The Mobilization against Free Trade in Canada," *American Journal of Economics and Sociology*, vol. 55, no. 4 (October 1996), pp. 483–484.

15. Robert V. Remini, *The House: The History of the House of Representatives* (New York: Harper Collins, 2006), pp. 19–20.

16. Arend Lijphart, *Democracies: Patterns of Majoritarian and Consensus Government in Twenty-One Democracies* (New Haven, CT: Yale University Press, 1984), pp. 101–104, 219–220; K. C. Wheare, *Legislatures* (New York: Oxford University Press, 1963), pp. 205–206.

17. Peter H. Russell and Lorne Sossin, *Parliamentary Democracy in Crisis* (Toronto: University of Toronto Press, 2009), pp. 151–154; Torbjörn Bergman, Wolfgang C. Müller, Kaare Strøm, and Magnus Blomgren, "Democratic Delegation and Accountability: Cross-National Patterns," in *Delegation and Accountability in Parliamentary Democracies* (Oxford: Oxford University Press, 2003), pp. 179–184.

18. Russell, pp. 446–449.

19. Philip Norton, "Achieving Accountability," *The House Magazine*, vol. 28, no. 1,029 (March 2003), pp. 34–36.

20. Sergio Fabbrini, "Political Change without Institutional Transformation: What Can We Learn from the Italian Crisis of the 1990s?" *International Political Science Review*, vol. 21, no. 2 (April 2000), pp. 175–176, 191–192.

21. Legislative Assembly of Alberta, Special Committee on Senate Reform, *Strengthening Canada: Reform of Canada's Senate* (March 1985).

22. Peter McCormick, Ernest C. Manning, and Gordon Gibson, *Regional Representation: The Canadian Partnership* (Calgary: Canada West Foundation, 1981).

23. Canada West Foundation, *Renewal of Canada—Institutional Reform* (Calgary: Canada West Foundation, 1992), pp. 9, 12–14.

24. University College London Constitution Unit, School of Public Policy, http://www.parliament.uk/about/faqs/house-of-lords-faqs/lords-govtdefeats/

25. United Kingdom Government, House of Lords, http://www.ucl.ac.uk/constitution-unit/research/parliament/house-of-lords/lords-defeats

26. G. Bruce Doern and Richard Phidd, Canadian Public Policy (Toronto: Methuen, 1983), pp. 110–112; G. Bruce Doern and V. Seymour Wilson, "Conclusions and Observations," in Issues in Canadian Public Policy, G. Bruce Doern and V. Seymour Wilson, eds. (Toronto: Macmillan, 1974), pp. 339–340.

27. John W. Kingdon, Agendas, Alternatives, and Public Policies (New York: Harper Collins, 1995), pp. 146–149.

28. Charles M. Cameron, Albert D. Cover, Jeffrey A. Segal, "Senate Voting on Supreme Court Nominees: A Neoinstitutional Model," *American Political Science Review,* vol. 84, no. 2 (June 1990), pp. 527–528.

29. M. J. Trebilcock, D. G. Hartle, J. R. S. Pritchard, and D. N. Dewees, The Choice of Governing Instrument (Ottawa: Economic Council of Canada, 1982), pp. 22–25.

30. Alan S. Zuckerman, "Advancing Explanation in Comparative Politics: Social Mechanisms, Endogenous Processes, and Empirical Rigor," in *Comparative Politics: Rationality, Culture, and Structure* (Cambridge: Mark Irving Lichbach and Alan S. Zuckerman, eds. (Cambridge: Cambridge University Press, 2009), pp. 72–95.

31. David Butler and Gareth Butler, *Twentieth Century British Political Facts, 1900–2000* (London: Macmillan, 2000), p. 229.

32. Meg Russell, "Reforming the British House of Lords: How a Little Reform Can Go a Long Way," *Papers on Parliament,* no. 47 (Canberra, July 2007), http://www.aph.gov.au/About_Parliament/Senate/ Research_and_Education/pops/~/link.aspx?_id=25A63692B488497B9304A3697AA8A75D&_z=z

33. Meg Russell and Maria Sciara, "Why Does the Government get Defeated in the House of Lords?" The Lords, the Party System and British Politics 2 British Politics (2007), http://www.palgrave-journals.com/bp/journal/v2/n3/full/4200064a.html#tbl7

34. Parliament of Australia—Senate—Senate StatsNet, "Bills Negatived, 1991–2013," http://www.aph.gov.au/Parliamentary_Business/Statistics/Senate_StatsNet/legislation/negatived

35. "Australia's Carbon-Reduction Scheme Blocked by Senate," *Daily Telegraph*, August 13, 2009, http://www.telegraph.co.uk/earth/environment/climatechange/6019376/Australias-carbon-reduction-scheme-blocked-by-senate.html; "Australian Senate Rejects Carbon Trade Bill," *China Daily*, December 12, 2009, http://www.chinadaily.com.cn/world/2009-12/02/content_9101814.htm

36. "Mining Tax Faces One More Hurdle," *Brisbane Times*, February 6, 2012, http://news.brisbanetimes.com.au/breaking-news-national/mining-tax-faces-one-more-hurdle-20120206-1r1r3.html

37. Philip Coorey, "Rudd Fights to the Death," *Sydney Morning Herald*," June 24, 2010, http://www.smh.com.au/national/rudd-fights-to-the-death-20100623-yz8r.html

38. Parliament of Australia—Senate—Senate StatsNet, "Amendments Moved," http://www.aph.gov.au/Parliamentary_Business/Statistics/Senate_StatsNet/legislation/3ramendments

39. John Uhe, "Generating Divided Government: The Australian Senate," in *Senates: Bicameralism in the Contemporary World*, in Samuel C. Patterson and Anthony Mughan, eds. (Columbus: Ohio State Press University, 1999), pp. 110–112.

40. Parliament of Australia—Senate—Senate StatsNet, "Legislation—General, 1991–2000," http://www.aph.gov.au/Parliamentary_Business/Statistics/statsnet/consolidations/19912000/generallegislation

41. Butler and Butler, p. 229.

42. Parliament of Canada—The Senate, "Report on Activities, 2007," http://sen.parl.gc.ca/portal/AnnualReports/2006-2007/chapter_1-e.htm

43. House of Lords Information Office, "Work of the House of Lords—Current and Previous Editions," http://www.parliament.uk/mps-lords-and-offices/offices/lords/house-of-lords-information-office/work/

44. UK General Public Acts, http://www.legislation.gov.uk/ukpga

45. House of Lords Information Office, "Work of the House of Lords—Current and Previous Editions," http://www.parliament.uk/mps-lords-and-offices/offices/lords/house-of-lords-information-office/work/

46. John Uhr, "Generating Divided Government: The Australian Senate," in *Senates in the Contemporary World*, Samuel C. Patterson and Anthony Mughan, eds. (Columbus: Ohio State University Press, 1999), pp.93–119

47. Cheryl Saunders, *The Constitution of Australia: A Contextual Analysis* (Oxford: Hart, 2011), pp. 125–128.

48. Manning Clark, *A History of Australia* (Melbourne: Melbourne University Press, 1993), pp. 401–404.

49. *Official Record of the Debates of the National Austalasian Convention* (Sydney, 1897), pp. 584–585.

50. *Austalasian Convention*, p. 75.

51. W. Redmond Curtis, "The Origin and Genesis of the Deadlock Clause of the Australian Constitution," *Political Science Quarterly*, vol. 60, no. 3 (September 1945), pp. 418–420.

52. Consultative Group on Constitutional Change, *Resolving Deadlocks: The Public Response* (Canberra: Department of the Prime Minister and Cabinet, 2004), pp. 13–14.

Chapter 7

Constitutional Amendment Part II

Membership, Representation, and Federalism

SENATE REFORM AND MEMBERSHIP LIMITS

One of the constraints of Senate reform has been arriving at a precise ratio of seats within a finite limit and relatively small number of total seats. Another problem that historically has affected the effectiveness of this chamber has been a lack of consistent participation by its members. In an upper house with an absolute veto, these deficiencies can be a source of special concern.

NUMBER OF SENATORS

> 21. The Senate shall, subject to the Provisions of this Act, consist of ~~One Hundred and five Members~~, *an unlimited number of Members*, who shall be styled Senators.

This concept is one of the more theoretically attractive but, arguably, practically unrealistic ideals presented by the hypothetical constitutional amendment. Nonetheless, it addresses, at least in theory, one of the most perplexing problems confronting the effective representation of the Canadian upper house. It benefits from the comparative analysis that the British parliamentary upper house offers in this respect. It also can be explained in terms of a general theme of non-elected "representation" that may find some inspiration from both communitarian and republican thoughts, even though, in the latter case, it is applied to a distinctly non-republican system of government.

The unlimited number of peers that the House of Lords can accommodate has led to an expansion of its membership and, simultaneously, an expansion of the number of potential participants in its proceedings who possess specialized knowledge, special backgrounds, and useful expertise. More recent reforms have brought that number to a smaller size and future reforms could further reduce the number of eligible peers within that chamber.[1] Nonetheless, the fact that many peers do not participate in its proceedings on a regular basis has not been a historic impediment to its overall ability to function because of the reserve of available peers, though the opposite argument has been made.[2]

A hypothetical scenario of the removal of limits upon the number of potential Senators can be used to explain the advantages that could be possible for governments that have the luxury of being expansive in their approach to appointments. Under such an idealistic scenario, fewer trade-offs would be necessary for including persons and groups who are representative of the diversity of Canada and its political interests. While that actual result could be considered to be fantastical, it still offers a useful model for contemplating the themes of diversity and representation in conjunction with the theoretical principle of an upper house as a chamber that reflects a distinctly different interest than the lower house. Therefore, it could provide other sources of inspiration for contemplating potential options for non-constitutional reforms in the areas of appointment and inclusion, especially from the actual example of the House of Lords in this respect.

It would be expected, under such a hypothetical scheme, that a core group of committed Senators would continue to dominate the routine proceedings of that chamber, just as it has been the case in the House of Lords, which has an informal category popularly known as "Working Peers" who are expected to attend to political and party business within that chamber.[3] Given the guidelines that will be described for making appointments, those overall numbers would increase at a relatively slow rate, thus resulting in a number of Senators that will be practical as well as consistent with more inclusive goals. Again, though, because the necessary constitutional amendment to achieve such a result would be highly unlikely, this concept best serves as a model for theoretical principles that might, ultimately, be emulated in other, indirect ways.

As the comparative British example demonstrates, a lack of limits in membership permits other potential innovations, especially in terms of committee assignments. It also raises important questions regarding compensation. For example, rather than paying a salary, Senators could be compensated upon the basis of actual attendance and participation in parliamentary business. That practice was introduced to the House of Lords, ironically, in contrast to the *lack* of compensation that peers historically had experienced.[4] Arguably, it could provide a good setting for the Senate to attempt to limit corruption, though compensation for travel and other expenses would not be eliminated. Of course, it also could allow for an increased capacity for diversity in parliamentary appointments.

This particular reform may appear to be especially counterintuitive, given its departure from past expectations relating to limited and relatively precise (despite the constitutional allowance for as many as eight additional appointments) membership. Furthermore, it can be difficult to conceive of a Canadian second chamber in which membership can, potentially, exceed several hundred Senators. Certainly (as a minor housekeeping issue), it would necessitate the elimination of individual desks for Senators and their replacement with open benches. As a practical and more meaningful matter, though, it could alleviate the need for consistent participation on the part of most Senators, allowing them to be selective in this respect. The presence of a suspensive veto could complement this sort of result by making the implications of full participation for conducting the process of responsible government a less urgent matter, thus alleviating concerns regarding Senate membership and possible non-participation. Again, the example of the House of Lords (which has well-exceeded a 1,000 eligible members) offers a functioning comparative example for conceiving this sort of arrangement.

This approach could accommodate a communitarian theme in relation to the upper house. The expansive inclusivity that could be promoted through such a scheme would lend itself to a much broader understanding of participation within the legislative process while, simultaneously, declining to challenge the overall principle of representative government. Thus a venue for the sort of "social discourse" that is required for developing a true sense of the "common good" within a communitarian ideal of modern society[5] may be more readily established as a contribution to the policy and legislative processes while avoiding an overt challenge to the democratic will.

This approach also (and ironically, given this non-republican system of government) can be associated with a republican theme of the role of distinct institutions of government, especially in response to the theoretical principle of an upper house as a chamber that represents "something else" within a political system. This approach toward bicameralism seeks to avoid an identical structure between the lower and upper legislative chambers. Instead, it provides an opportunity for the institutional presence of a wider array of constituencies within society.[6] These approaches also are relevant to the theme of diverse representation that will be revisited within this chapter.

REGIONAL AND PROVINCIAL REPRESENTATION

As previously discussed, the theme of federalism is one that appears to be unavoidable within the context of Senate reform. It also is an area that almost certainly would require a formal constitutional amendment in order to be affected. Aside from the practical difficulty of successfully negotiating and navigating that extremely daunting path, finding a ratio of representation that could accommodate all provincial desires (and create a compromise between the themes of equal representation and representation by population) and satisfy the goals of the federal government severely undermines that aspiration. Therefore, this part of the hypothetical constitutional amendment offers a way to imagine a potential starting point for engaging in this sort of negotiation.

This problem of meaningful regional and provincial representation has not been confined to the issue of Canadian Senate reform. It has been noted that conventional expectations concerning the role of the cabinet in this respect have been diminished with the emergence of the tendency for governments to be dominated by a "court party" that effectively bypasses the strong role that diverse cabinet membership has traditionally provided.[7] That trend has exacerbated feelings of alienation among marginalized parts of the country, thus bolstering a desire to enhance the role of other institutions, such as the Senate, for representing, perhaps directly, the people and interests of these underrepresented constituencies.

Likewise, attempts to reform representation within the Canadian House of Commons appear to have floundered. Prime Minister Justin Trudeau established a House of Commons Special Committee on Electoral Reform to address, among other themes, the problem of underrepresentation of various segments of the Canadian population within the Commons. The recommendation of pursuing a proportional representation system was the most obvious attempt to address that situation.[8] However, the government's unwillingness to pursue that reform, further, indicated the severe difficulty of arriving at a national consensus in this area.[9] That result might potentially have reinforced the potential popularity of using other political institutions, such as the Senate, as a means of dealing with this representational issue. It did not address (at least not directly) concerns about provincial representation.

A potentially unlimited membership could create a potential lack of precision in terms of the ratio of representation among the various regions and provinces, which could, arguably, provide a constructive way to overcome that inherent difficulties of arriving at a precise, workable, and acceptable formula. This indefinite aspect of the hypothetical proposal in relation to the number of members also suggests considerations relating to other themes, such as the scope and arrangement of regional and provincial representation within the Senate. In particular, it can prompt an evaluation of its significance in relation to Canadian federalism.

Representation of Provinces in Senate

22. *(1)* In relation to the Constitution of the Senate, Canada shall be deemed to consist of ~~Four~~ *Five* Divisions:

> 1. Ontario; 2. Quebec; 3. The Maritime Provinces, Nova Scotia and New Brunswick, and Prince Edward Island *and Newfoundland*; 4. The Western Provinces of Manitoba, British Columbia, Saskatchewan, and Alberta; *5. The Federal Territories of the Northwest Territories, Nunavut, and the Yukon,* which ~~Four~~ *Five* Divisions shall (subject to the Provisions of this Act) be ~~equally~~ represented in the Senate ~~as follows: Ontario by twenty-four senators; Quebec by twenty-four senators; the Maritime Provinces and Prince Edward Island by twenty-four senators, ten thereof representing Nova Scotia, ten thereof representing New Brunswick, and four thereof representing Prince Edward Island; the Western Provinces by twenty-four senators, six thereof representing Manitoba, six thereof representing British Columbia, six thereof representing Saskatchewan, and six thereof representing Alberta; Newfoundland shall be entitled to be represented in the Senate by six members; the Yukon Territory and the Northwest Territories shall be entitled to be represented in the Senate by one member each.~~

It is possible to argue (and this model is based upon that premise) that federalism ought not to be the primary focus of consideration for upper house reform in Canada. However, given the centrality of federalism to Canadian politics and government in general, plus the strong connection between certain other Senate reform proposals (most notably the Triple-E concept) and federal-provincial relations, it is a difficult "elephant in the room" to ignore.[10] Furthermore, any sort of proposal in this area (and it is the case for most reform proposals) would absolutely require a constitutional amendment that would, in turn, require the approval of provincial governments. The role of federalism within this process cannot be ignored so attention to this aspect of that body's membership needs to be addressed as a constitutional option.

But the Senate was not constructed as a vehicle for the representation of provincial governments (as distinct from their respective provinces as constituencies) within the federal parliamentary system, though the need for Senators who would be connected to particular provinces and regions had been a consideration in its development.[11] Furthermore, the Senate's composition originally was divided according to regional boundaries. That arrangement suggested its role as an institution for the representation of the regions (rather than the individual provinces) of Canada at the federal level, although two of those "regions" corresponded to the individual Central Canadian provinces of Ontario and Quebec. Among the provinces of Western Canada and Atlantic Canada, regional interests have provided a source of mutual political, social, and economic perspectives and interests.[12] So it is impossible to ignore that one of the historically perceived roles of the Senate, at least informally, was the representation of regional interests and, consequently, the interests of the provinces within them.[13]

But a desire for equal representation might not be shared by Ontario and Quebec for obvious reasons—and the support of at least one of those provinces is necessary for a constitutional amendment.[14] Provinces such as British Columbia have demonstrated a desire to increase their representation within the Canadian upper house, especially in ways that reduce the representation of the Atlantic Provinces to match their much smaller population. Therefore, even among Western provinces, support for equal Senate representation may not prove feasible.[15]

As previously noted, a utilitarian critique is highly critical of the use of a national legislature for addressing the theme of federalism. That perspective emphasizes, instead, the greater utility of direct negotiation between different levels of shared sovereignty—in other words, a system of interstate, as opposed to intrastate federalism. Despite the evolution of federal-provincial relations in the direction, though, ignoring the intrastate approach to reform probably will remain a "non-starter" among many, if not most, provincial governments and the populations that they represent, especially in Western Canada. This context and relationship between the Canadian parliamentary upper house and federalism require, therefore, additional analysis in this broader theoretical respect.

THE RELEVANCE OF THE RELATIONSHIP BETWEEN THE SENATE AND FEDERALISM

In general, Canada's federal system initially was conceived as being fairly centralized, leading prominent scholars such as K. C. Wheare to describe it, during its early decades, as "quasi-federal." In certain respects, he denied that it qualified as a federal system at all, given the stronger example of federalism under the U.S. Constitution. In particular, the British North America Act created a distinctly hierarchical system of subordinate powers, beginning with British imperial authority, proceeding through the Canadian government and, finally, descending to the provincial governments.[16] This relationship was revealed through such arrangements as federally appointed and provincially administered courts, the presence of Crown representatives at all levels, and the federal power to "reserve" legislation to await a review and final decision on the part of the authority that had appointed them. Under those arrangements, it could be surmised, at least in theory, that the political decisions reached by one level of government could be disallowed by the level of government that existed "above" it.[17] At least in terms of their origins, the provinces (despite some initial demands and designs to the contrary) appeared to be delegated subordinate powers that lacked an ultimately true sense of sovereign authority to uphold them.[18]

This relationship would change as a result of a series of appeals to the Judicial Committee of the Privy Council (JCPC). Initially, appeals from both provincial and federal jurisdictions could, and often did, ultimately end with this imperial judicial body, which included, at the time, members of the Judicial Committee of the House of Lords who typically would serve as the final court for all domestic British appeals and controversies. Its authority in this respect superseded even the Supreme Court of Canada that had been conceived under the original constitutional settlement and formally created in 1875, further reinforcing this sense of hierarchical centralization. It was not difficult to assume that the JCPC was regarded as a juridical institution that would not be sympathetic to claims of shared sovereignty that provincial governments might bring to it, given the lack of experience and familiarity with federalism among its members and their greater familiarity with unitary British and imperial governance. It was, therefore, surprising and (among many federal politicians) a source of outrage when the JCPC began to make rulings that strengthened provincial claims to sovereign authority in certain significant areas.[19]

These appeals coincided with the growing interpretive significance of section 92 of the British North America Act of 1867, as it then was known. In particular, those clauses of that section addressing provincial control over internal resources not only expanded sovereign authority over policy making but, even more significantly, greatly increased the potential for provincial revenue enhancement, thus enhancing the potential "bargaining power" of provincial governments in their dealings with the federal government—primarily for those provinces that had resources (either natural or commercial) that provided increased economic self-sufficiency.[20]

One JCPC decision that is illustrative of this change in ways that are relevant to the Senate is the 1883 case of *Hodge vs. Regina*. This case addressed a controversy concerning the administration of laws pertaining to the sale of alcohol. The Province of Ontario had delegated part of that responsibility to the municipal authorities in Toronto and, under that authority, the Licence Commission of Toronto passed a related resolution and convicted a saloon owner of a violation of that resolution. The appeal of the subsequent conviction was based upon a contention that the municipal body had exceeded its authority by passing a resolution that was *ultra vires* the authority of municipal government because the provincial authority had legislated in an area that fell under the exclusive jurisdiction of the federal government.[21]

The JCPC ruled that the Ontario Legislative Assembly did have the proper authority to legislate in this area and to delegate that authority to the municipal level. Simultaneously, it admitted that this legislative and policy-making authority also belonged to the federal level. Therefore, the provincial regulations that were consistent with section 92 provisions "to make regulations in the nature of police or municipal regulations of a purely local character" did not, in reference to section 91, "interfere with the general regulation of trade and commerce which belongs to the Dominion Parliament."[22]

This decision was the origin of the "double aspect" doctrine of Canadian constitutional law. This doctrine acknowledged overlapping spheres of sovereign authority exercised by both federal and provincial authorities, even in relation to the same policy matter. In terms of federalism, it created conditions that have allowed for parallel areas of policy and legislative authority. In institutional terms, it challenged one of the principal purposes for the Senate as conceived under the original British North America Act. The role of the Senate as a federal legislative body that would represent regional and provincial interests could be associated with an assumption of a strongly centralized sovereign federal authority. However, if the provinces could exercise authority over a wider array of policies (particularly ones that are exercised in parallel with federal policies in similar areas), the need to have a direct representational presence within the federal legislature would become less urgent or, even, less germane.[23]

Therefore, the Judicial Committee of the Privy Council, by establishing this "double aspect" doctrine, strengthened the division of sovereign authority under the federal Canadian scheme and established the constitutional conditions that would lead to a more decentralized Canadian federal system.[24] In doing so, it also, indirectly and inadvertently, made the role of the Senate in relation to federalism and provincial input into the central government policies much less necessary and, even, less pertinent than might once have been envisioned. It also made it, arguably, less applicable to a constitutional vision that might continue to be held in that respect, including by proponents of Senate reform who made provincial representation within the Canadian upper house a central focus.

A consequence of this arrangement and its subsequent replacement was, again, the need for direct negotiations between federal and provincial governments, rather than through the indirect influence of provinces upon federal institutions, including Parliament. Furthermore, in terms of the Senate, this route for provincial input was further marginalized by the constitutional (as well as the *de facto*) prominence of the House of Commons in all budgetary matters. But even the role of the House of Commons became increasingly marginalized in this respect as the prominence of party discipline and the institutional advantages of the Prime Minister's Office advanced the ascendancy of executive federalism.[25] Thus the original vision of the Senate in relation to regional representation had become even more redundant.

Constitutional Patriation

During the 1960s and 1970s, tensions arose between federal governments that sought greater centralization of authority (especially under Prime Minister

Pierre Trudeau) and provincial governments that sought to enhance their authority in areas that they felt should belong to their proper sovereign jurisdiction. This period, described as "conflictual federalism," culminated with the struggle over constitutional patriation. Conflictual federalism, as a general concept, often is a product of the sort central direction represented by block grants. In Canada, it resulted in a situation in which the provinces found themselves in conflict with the federal government in terms of the funding of policy priorities and, thus, they increasingly resisted federal incursions (including federal spending on provincial programs) into provincial priorities and policy making.[26]

Western Canada's frustration concerning this relationship became acute and it served as the basis for its motivation to find ways to improve its political influence within the overall federal system. Consequently, one of the goals of the Triple-E proposal was expressed in terms of a "return" of the Senate of Canada to the representational role that allegedly had been envisioned for it within the British North America Act.[27] Indeed, this overall conflict influenced motivations for the patriation of the entirety of the British North America Act, which developed into an intense negotiation between the federal and provincial governments over the terms of a plan to entrench the constitutional arrangement (including a particularly controversial amending formula) that would become the Constitution Act of 1982. Conflict with Quebec and its separatist Parti Québécois government, under the leadership of René Levesque, was especially challenging.[28]

Senate reform was not part of this process and, instead, the emphasis remained upon the direct role of provincial governments within the overall federal system. That emphasis included the adoption of Section 33 of the Charter of Rights and Freedoms, known as the "notwithstanding clause," which would provide a mechanism for provincial governments to opt out of certain key provisions of the Charter, again emphasizing the direct relationship among governments, as would the amending formula, which was another essential feature of the Constitution Act of 1982.[29] Still, the relationship between the Canadian Senate and federalism (superficially similar to the U.S. Senate and, arguably, the Senate of Australia) remained an inextricable association, especially for reformers.[30]

EXECUTIVE FEDERALISM

This constitutional settlement was reached through an application of interstate federalism known as "executive federalism." Rather than the legislative process as the institutional path for greater inclusion of provincial interests within the Canadian system, the role of their premiers who dominate their respective parliamentary legislative assemblies has proven to be the most direct option for pursuing federal-provincial relations—even if it often has been frustrated. Nonetheless, "provincial premiers have direct access to the prime minister and do not hesitate to pursue an issue with him."[31] The use of the Privy Council Office as a central governmental focus for pursuing these relationships for major and minor provincial priorities remains dominant.

Granted, interstate federalism has not experienced unqualified success. The pursuit of executive federalism through First Ministers' meetings among prime ministers and provincial premiers, once commonly employed to negotiate federal-provincial agreements, have all but disappeared. The Meech Lake and Charlottetown Accords failed after lengthy and difficult intergovernmental bargaining. Prime Ministers such as Stephen Harper and Justin Trudeau have refused to engage in that often-acrimonious process. But a legislative process, using the Senate, to achieve success in these relations, would merely employ an indirect method for provincial premiers and their respective governments that arguably would require an unnecessary additional step to the overall process.[32]

Of course, the Triple-E model is based upon the premise that the ability of Senators, representing provincial interests and building coalitions with Senators from their own region or, perhaps, across regions, would put pressure on the federal government by frustrating (or threatening to frustrate) its legislation and policies. This sort of intrastate federal model assumes that the federal government would be open to that potential scenario and that it would achieve its goals through a method that the current, less formal process does not achieve. But the "mutual veto" within the bicameral Canadian system is not conducive to that outcome, nor is it necessarily consistent with the "collaborative federalism" that has tended to dominate this relationship between the Canadian federal and provincial governments since the late 1990s.[33] Meanwhile, it also is abundantly clear that the provincial governments, almost certainly, would not agree to any Senate reform if it did not include some sort of concession to the provinces.

Senate Reform, Interstate Federalism, and Intrastate Federalism

So it appears to be practically impossible to address constitutional reform of the Senate of Canada without including the provinces and, thus, the theme of federalism. Simultaneously, it appears to be practically impossible to address that reform in a manner that would, potentially, permit provinces to interfere, directly, in federal policy making and legislation. Therefore, while contemplating a role for provinces in terms of the theme of representation, it also is important to consider the most appropriate approach and venue in terms of the relationship of this central institution to this important Canadian political theme. Even from a highly idealized approach, the theoretical lessons provided by this hypothetical constitutional amendment illustrate the interplay of these considerations and theoretical model of reform for a parliamentary upper house under those sort of heightened political circumstances.

> 21. *(2) The Governor General, in the Queen's name and in respect of Canada, shall appoint, every four years, five representatives for each of the first four divisions, as specified in subsection (1), provided that for those divisions with multiple Provinces, no Province shall be denied an appointment during the course of a four-year period. Furthermore, the fifth division, as specified in subsection (1), shall receive one appointment, every four years, provided that no Federal Territory shall be denied an appointment during the course of a twelve-year period.*
>
> ~~In the Case of Quebec each of the Twenty-four Senators representing that Province shall be appointed for One of the Twenty-four Electoral Divisions of Lower Canada specified in Schedule A. to Chapter One of the Consolidated Statutes of Canada.~~
>
> *(3) Lieutenant Governors of each Province, in the Queen's name and in respect of each Province, shall appoint, each year, one representative to the Senate. Commissioners of each Federal Territory, in the Queen's name and in respect of each Federal Territory, shall appoint, every four years, one representative to the Senate.*

This specific clause attempts to straddle divergent aspirations and expectations relating to Senate reform. It is important to place that discussion within the context of the two general approaches (as explained within chapter 2) that have emerged and previously mentioned for addressing the overall relationship between Canada and its provinces: interstate federalism and intrastate federalism. Conferences of First Ministers have historically proven to be the most conspicuous expression of interstate federalism within Canada but other forms of federal-provincial cooperation have developed within the Canadian federal relationship that appear to supersede this role for the Senate. In fact, it has been suggested that plans for Senate reform that emphasize its role in federal relationships would prove to be a distraction from more effective means of addressing those relationships.[34]

Admittedly, the association between bicameralism and federalism is a comparatively consistent theme.[35] That association was an explicit focus within Canada of Bill C-60 in 1978 and its concept of replacing the Senate with a House of Federation. But the functional centrality of executive federalism among first ministers could be disrupted by enhancing the role of the Senate in intrastate federalism in ways that might not be appreciated until any such scheme actually was put into effect.[36] Because it would be impractical to expect that party politics could be entirely circumvented from this process (especially national parties), reform proposals that emphasize an intrastate role for the Senate to reflect provincial interests ultimately may not achieve their objectives because of the other partisan influences.[37]

Intrastate federalism has been considered a conventional response to address the competition inherent as part of shared sovereignty, especially within political systems that have a bicameral legislature.[38] The United States originally addressed this concern through the creation of an upper house of the national Congress in which Senators would represent state legislatures.[39] It also used this arrangement to reach a compromise concerning the basis for representation among smaller and larger states by providing representation by population for the lower House of Representatives and equal representation among the states, each of which would be represented by two Senators, regardless of the state's population.[40]

By the early 20th century, populist and progressive demands for reform of that chamber (including strong concerns over bribing of state legislators and the role of money, generally, in securing Senate seats) resulted in a constitutional amendment requiring popular election to the U.S. Senate.[41] Even before that time, though, U.S. Senators had long ceased to be considered to be national representatives of the state governments that had selected them but, instead, had become agents of their respective national party interests. Furthermore, the divided government that frequently resulted from the dominance of different legislative chambers by different political parties proved to be manageable, largely because the American political system was grounded upon a republican practice of non-responsible government in which the executive administration did not require legislative support in order to function, even if its policy priorities could not be enacted.[42]

Again, though, the promotion of this sort of intrastate federalism poses a different situation within parliamentary systems, especially ones derived from the Westminster model of responsible government. Because parliamentary governments need to maintain legislative support in order to survive, they require a sustainable process grounded upon party discipline—otherwise, governments of any effective tenure in office would be impossible to achieve. In the case of Canada, that attitude of acquiescence has prevailed.[43] Furthermore, given the fact that Canadian Senators would not need to face election and would be, ultimately, selected at the federal level, the representational role of that chamber quickly became both unfeasible and untenable, resulting (as previously discussed in relation to suspensive vetoes) in a chamber that would challenge the legislative will of the House of Commons and the government it sustained only under extremely rare circumstances.

Continuing the regional division (and expanding it to include the territories) for Senate appointments and the recognition of the provinces within them could be a first step in the process of appropriately addressing federalism within this overall reform proposal. Allowing the provincial governments a role in appointing some of these Senators would be an appropriate second step. These hypothetical reforms present a model of the sorts of calculations (and even trade-offs in a more crudely utilitarian sense) that could contribute toward a greater provincial willingness to participate in that constitutional process, especially as these reforms seek to retain a measure of representation for demographically smaller provinces that is greater than their populations would warrant under a strictly proportional scheme. In that sense, this part of the reform proposal imitates (at least superficially) the political settlement for the U.S. Senate that emerged from the so-called "Great Compromise" concerning the role of the American upper house in providing for asymmetrical federalism.[44] Meanwhile, this continued apportionment could remain acceptable to the largest two provinces by continuing to treat them as regions unto themselves. This asymmetrical arrangement could, therefore, accommodate the two, otherwise irreconcilable, representational goals of the larger and smaller provinces.[45]

It is important to reiterate the fact that this proposed reform specifies that the various Lieutenant Governors (and, consequently, the elected provincial Premiers) would select a large proportion of the members of the reformed Senate. Therefore, the policy interests and political goals of their respective provincial governments and electorate would be highly relevant to that process. As a tool of intrastate federalism, it may not be as robust as some critics would want. However, its significance in terms of acknowledging those provincial interests and offering a forum for advocating provincial priorities at the federal level ought not to be ignored.

Upper House Reform, Federalism, and the German Model

Some proponents of Canadian upper house reform since the end of the Second World War have noted, instead, the model of the German federal system. The members of the upper house of the German parliament, the Bundesrat, are appointed by their respective state (in German, *länder*) governments and, typically, that membership includes members of the *länder* cabinet, including the minister-president of each *länder*. Furthermore, voting for each *länder* is conducted upon the basis of bloc voting. If the electors for a particular *länder* are split, the entire vote for that *länder* representation is considered invalid.[46]

Another attractive feature of the Bundesrat as a model for Canadian Senate reform in this respect has been the fact that its activities are limited to policy matters that directly affect the *länder*, especially (but not exclusively) in relation to constitutionally identified concurrent powers, which refers to those areas of federal authority in which the *länder* are required to implement and administer federal policies. The number of such German bills originally was small but, more recently, a majority of German federal legislation (as a result of broadening interpretations of concurrent legislation) has been constitutionally classified in that way. In relation to all other legislation, the Bundesrat may exercise only a suspensive veto that may be overridden by an overall majority vote of the Bundesrat. This arrangement has been cited by some proponents of Canadian Senate reform as an obvious model to be based upon principles of intrastate federalism, especially in terms of the direct role that the governments of sovereign subunits of a federal system can influence that system and promote the interests of their respective governments.[47]

However, notable differences between the German and Canadian federal systems must be taken into account. German federalism was reestablished after World War II in order to counter the centralizing tendencies of German government that had predominated prior to that conflict and facilitated the Nazi rise to power.[48] No such imperative was responsible for the creation of Canadian federalism. Furthermore, the arrangement of shared sovereign authority within the German Federal Republic was designed in a functional manner to divide responsibilities between policy creation and policy implementation, while Canadian federalism ultimately was directed toward the creation of dual spheres of policy responsibility.[49] Therefore, intrastate cooperation is much more consistent with the overall scheme of German federalism than is ostensibly the case within the more overtly competitive environment of Canadian federalism.

Furthermore, and ironically, although the Bundesrat is an institution of intrastate federalism, the fact that its membership is dominated by cabinet members of the various *länder* (including minister-presidents) creates a situation in which it functionally serves as an example of executive interstate federalism. In the case of serious legislative disputes that require Bundesrat approval, the resolution of such disputes typically requires negotiations between federal ministers and their *länder* counterparts.[50] That arrangement has been criticized because it encourages political "deals" outside the formal legislative setting and its higher level of public scrutiny—perhaps not unlike criticisms of the workings of executive federalism within Canada.[51] Ultimately, the German federal model and its relationship to upper house reform provide an interesting comparison but, also, clear contrasts with Canadian experience and political culture.

SENATE REFORM AND DIFFERENT MODELS OF FEDERALISM

Intrastate federalism frequently assumes less overt forms, particularly in relation to attempts to include federal cabinet ministers from the various regions, though that practice has not been regarded as a truly effective vehicle for provincial input into the governmental process at that level. Likewise, it has been perceived to be a feature of the practical functioning of bureaucracies for implementing and shaping policy decisions. Implementation of federal policies and programs at the regional, provincial, and local levels is an opportunity for this sort of interaction, provided that the composition of the public service consciously reflects provincial representation.[52] But even when such arrangements have been made within the Canadian system, they have not necessarily resulted in an effective expression of the goals of intrastate federalism. "As in the case with the cabinet, the regional representativeness of the federal bureaucracy does not lead directly to regional sensitivity."[53] The fault, again, may not lie in the implementation of such strategies but with the true nature and culture of Canadian federalism, which has developed a distinctly interstate orientation, especially during the latter part of the 20th century.

Indeed, the perceived effectiveness and efficiency of executive federalism appears to have reinforced this historical trend toward addressing federal relations from an interstate, rather than an intrastate, perspective. It is perceived to be directly representative of provincial interests because it requires a direct diplomacy among the first ministers (both federal and provincial) who dominate their respective governments. It is this ability to "speak for" the electorate of their respective provinces that lends this process its sense of credibility. It further has been identified as possessing practical advantages for administrative actors and institutions.[54]

Executive federalism also appears to provide an effective platform for the promotion of "cooperative federalism." This approach accomplishes, through the collaboration of governments at both levels, an arguably greater source of influence for provincial goals and needs than its antithesis of "competitive federalism" that results in struggles for dominance that federal governments generally are better positioned to win, resulting in policy decisions that are, ultimately, unilateral.[55] Rather than rely upon other delegates to express provincial concerns, this approach to interstate federalism treats provincial governments (especially their premiers) as "privileged spokespersons" on behalf of their respective constituencies. It not only permits direct input and negotiation but often is preferred by smaller provinces because of this direct role and the tendency to treat intergovernmental federal interaction as a dialogue among institutional "equals."[56] That approach also appears to be consistent with a game-theory analysis of direct federal relationships in which even small provinces are projected to achieve their goals with greater effectiveness through direct negotiations than through intra-governmental arrangements.[57] While a reformed Senate (as well as a stronger role for all legislatures within Canada) might be able to offer a level of intra-governmental supervision over this process, it would not (and ought not) replace the impulse for the intergovernmental process that has become so firmly established within the Canadian federal system.[58]

PRESERVING INTERSTATE FEDERALISM

Many proposals for Canadian Senate reform are designed to reignite an element of intrastate federalism into the Canadian system. However, the purpose of such proposals often is to rein in the centralization of federal authority.[59] That emphasis, alone, makes such proposals non-starters in terms of support at the federal level and, arguably, among smaller provinces that are more economically dependent upon federal revenue sharing. Substantive Senate reform will require, at a minimum, consistent collaboration between federal and provincial governments and, almost certainly, a comprehensive consensus that would meet the requirements of attaining necessary constitutional amendments. Even a particular federal government that is sympathetic to these particular provincial goals is extremely unlikely to support them, given the fact that they could create more problems than they solve (from both a federal and a provincial perspective) and would permit provincial governments to influence and, potentially, frustrate the legislative process of responsible government at the federal level.[60]

In other words, federal governments are extremely unlikely to embrace the development of intrastate federalism in a manner that could result in the voluntary surrender of their own sovereign authority. The role and authority of the Bundesrat was, essentially, imposed upon Germany by the victorious Allies. Its creation did not, necessarily, reflect a conscious public desire at the subunit level of German government. Furthermore, even intrastate institutions such as the Bundesrat have tended to conduct their business through informal interactions and negotiations that are consistent with the practice of interstate, rather than intrastate, federalism.[61]

But, again (and, admittedly, *ad naseum*), it appears to be highly implausible that any attempt at Canadian Senate reform could succeed without some form of provincial input into the process of selecting Senators. The original purpose of the Senate as a body to represent regional interests is a constitutional reality that is difficult to ignore, as Pierre Trudeau tacitly acknowledged through his own reform proposals in this area.[62] Furthermore, provincial approval for any constitutional amendment in this area would, almost certainly, prove to be a non-starter if it failed to provide for some sort of meaningful provincial input, especially into the appointment of Senators.[63] Therefore, providing provincial governments with direct appointments to the Senate appears to be a politically necessary aspect of this reform, especially as any necessary constitutional amendment for Senate reform in Canada would require the approval of the provinces which would, in turn, almost certainly demand some sort of concession on the federal role of this parliamentary institution. In this way, reform of the Senate of Canada can reintroduce an element of intrastate federalism while not detracting, distracting, or diminishing from the evolving process of interstate federalism.

NOTES

1. Royal Commission on Reform of the House of Lords, *A House for the Future* (London: Her Majesty's Stationery Office, 2000), pp. 116–119.
2. Harold J. Laski, *Parliamentary Government in England* (London: George Allen and Unwin, 1938), p. 135.
3. Her Majesty's Government, *The House of Lords: Reform* (London: Her Majesty's Stationery Office, 2007), pp. 44–46.
4. "House of Lords Expenses," February 2014, http://www.parliament.uk/business/lords/whos-in-the-house-of-lords/house-of-lords-expenses/
5. Allen E. Buchanan, "Assessing the Communitarian Critique of Liberalism," *Ethics*, vol. 99, no. 4 (July 1999), pp. 852–882.
6. Andrew Lintott, *The Constitution of the Roman Republic* (Oxford: Oxford University Press, 2004), pp. 63–65; Wilfried Nippel, "Ancient and Modern Republicanism: 'Mixed Constitutions' and 'Ephors,'" in *The Invention of the Modern Republic* (Cambridge: Cambridge University Press, 1994), pp. 6–26.
7. Donald J. Savoie, "The Rise of Court Government in Canada," *Canadian Journal of Political Science*, vol. 32, no. 4 (December 1999), pp. 637–641.
8. House of Commons of Canada, Special Committee on Electoral Reform, *Strengthening Democracy in Canada: Principles, Process, and Public Engagement for Electoral Reform*. Ottawa: House of Commons (December 2016), pp. 69–77, 165–167.
9. Wherry, Aaron, "Trudeau's Promise of Electoral Reform: From 'We Can Do Better' to Accusations of Betrayal," *Canadian Broadcasting Corporation News*, February 5, 2017, http://www.cbc.ca/news/politics/wherry-trudeau-electoral-reform-promise-betrayal-1.3962386.
10. Serge Joyal, "The Senate as the Embodiment of the Federal Principle," in *Protecting Canadian Democracy: The Senate You Never Knew*, Serge Joyal, ed. (Montreal and Kingston, ON: McGill-Queen's University Press, 2003), pp. 272–274.
11. P. B. Waite, "Edward Whelan Reports from the Quebec Conference," *Canadian Historical Review* (March 1961), pp. 23–45.
12. Docherty, pp. 28–29.
13. George Ross, *The Senate of Canada: Its Constitutions, Duties, and Powers Historically Considered* (Toronto: Copp Clark, 1914), pp. 11–13.
14. Aaron Wherry, "Where the Province Stand on Senate Reform," *MacLean's*, June 12, 2015, http://www.macleans.ca/politics/where-the-provinces-stand-on-senate-reform/.
15. Keith Baldry, "Why Christy Clark is Rejecting Justin Trudeau's Reform of the Senate," *Global News*, December 3, 2015, http://globalnews.ca/news/2379480/why-christy-clark-is-rejecting-justin-trudeaus-reform-of-the-senate/.

16. K. C. Wheare, *Federal Government* (Oxford: Oxford University Press, 1970), pp. 18–20.

17. Garth Stevenson, *Unfulfilled Union: Canadian Federalism and National Unity* (Montreal and Kingston, ON: McGill-Queen's University Press, 2009), pp. 29–34.

18. W. R. Lederman, "Unity and Diversity in Canadian Federalism," *Canadian Bar Review,* vol. 53 (1975), pp. 597–620.

19. Alan Cairns, "The Judicial Committee and Its Critics," *Canadian Journal of Political Science*, vol. 4, no. 3 (1971), pp. 301–345.

20. Marsha A. Chandler, "Constitutional Change and Public Policy: The Impact of the Resource Amendment (Section 92A)," *Canadian Journal of Political Science*, vol. 19, no. 1 (March 1986), pp. 105–110.

21. [1883] UKPC 59.

22. Ibid., at 10–11.

23. Peter Hogg, *Constitutional Law of Canada* (Toronto: University of Toronto Press, 2007), 15.9(c); Peter C. Oliver, "The Busy Harbours of Canadian Federalism: The Division of Powers and Its Doctrines in the McLachlin Court," in *Public Law at the McLachlin Court: The First Decade*, David A. Wright and Adam M. Dodek, eds. (Toronto: Irwin, 2011), pp. 171–179.

24. John Saywell, *The Lawmakers: Judicial Power and the Shaping of Canadian Federalism* (Toronto: University of Toronto Press, 2002), pp. 83–85.

25. Ronald L. Watts, *Executive Federalism: A Comparative Analysis* (Kingston, ON: Institute of Intergovernmental Relations, 1989), pp. 11–12; David Cameron and Richard Simeon, "Intergovernmental Relations in Canada: The Emergence of Collaborative Federalism," *Publius*, vol. 32, no, 2 (Spring 2002), pp. 49–53.

26. Rand Dyck, *Canadian Politics: Critical Approaches* (Toronto: Nelson, 2012), pp. 416–420.

27. Kenneth H. Norrie, "Energy, Canadian Federalism, and the West," *Publius*, vol. 14, no. 1 (Winter 1984), pp. 83–88.

28. Raymond Hudon, "Intégration et diversité: Les Dilemmes de fédéralisme canadien, *Rervue Internationale de Science Politique*, vol. 5, no. 4 (1984), pp. 455–472.

29. Garth Stevenson, *Unfulfilled Union* (Montreal and Kingston, ON: McGill-Queen's University Press, 2004), pp. 49–65.

30. D. A. Soberman, "Canada's Institutional Deficit," *Queen's Law Journal,* vol. 6 (Spring 1983), pp. 205–207.

31. Savoie, pp. 638–639.

32. Donley T. Studlar and Kyle Christensen, "Is Canada a Westminster or Consensus Democracy? A Brief Analysis," *PS: Political Science and Politics*, vol. 39, no. 4 (October 2006), pp. 838–839; Herman Bakvis and Douglas Brown, "Policy Coordination in Federal Systems: Comparing Intergovernmental Processes and Outcomes in Canada and the United States," *Publius*, vol. 40, no. 3 (Summer 2010), pp. 492, 500–501.

33. Michael Lusztig, "Federalism and Institutional Design: The Perils and Politics of a Triple-E Senate in Canada," *Publius*, vol. 25, no. 1 (Winter 1995), pp. 41–42.

34. Herman Bakvis and Roselle Hryciuk, "An Experiment in Intrastate Federalism: The Cabinet Committee on Canadian Unity," in *Canada: The State of the Federation,*

1993, Ronald L. Watts and Douglas M. Brown, eds. (Kingston, ON: Institute on Intergovernmental Relations, 1993), pp. 137, 143–144.

35. George Tsebelis and Jeannette Money, *Bicameralism* (Cambridge: Cambridge University Press, 1997), pp. 33–34.

36. Donald V. Smiley, *Canada in Question: Federation in the Eighties* (Toronto: McGraw-Hill Ryerson, 1980), p. 85.

37. Franks, *Parliament of Canada*, p. 200.

38. Samuel L. LaSelva, "Federalism as a Way of Life: Reflections on the Canadian Experiment," *Canadian Journal of Political Science*, vol. 26, no. 2 (June 1993), pp. 221–222.

39. William H. Riker, "The Senate and American Federalism," *American Political Science Review*, vol. 49, no. 2 (June 1955), pp. 455–463.

40. Daniel Wirls and Stephen Wirls, *The Invention of the United States Senate* (Baltimore: Johns Hopkins University Press, 2004), pp. 71–80.

41. Wirls and Wirls, pp. 211–216.

42. Vik D. Amar, "The Senate and the Constitution," *Yale Law Journal*, vol. 97, no. 6 (May 1988), pp. 1116–1119.

43. Richard J. Van Loon and Michael S. Whittington, *The Canadian Political System: Environment, Structure, and Process* (Toronto: McGraw-Hill Ryerson, 1987), pp. 594–599, 627–628.

44. David Robertson, *The Original Compromise: What the Constitution's Framers Were Really Thinking* (New York: Oxford University Press, 2013), pp. 97–102.

45. Donald Smiley, "Central Institutions," in *Canada and the New Constitution: The Unfinished Agenda* (Montreal: Institute for Research on Public Policy, 1983), vol. 1, pp. 103–104.

46. David P. Conradt and Eric Lagenbacher, *The German Polity* (Lanham, MD: Rowman and Littlefield, 2013), pp. 228–233.

47. David Elton, Frederick C. Engelmann, and Peter McCormick, *Alternatives: Toward an Effective Federal System for Canada* (Calgary: Canada West Foundation, 1978), pp. 6–11; Frederick C. Engelmann, "A Prologue to Structural Reform of the Canadian Government," *Canadian Journal of Political Science*, vol. 19, no. 4 (December 1986), pp. 673–674; Smiley and Watts, pp. 54–58.

48. Hans-Georg Wehling, "The Bundesrat," *Publius*, vol. 19, no. 4 (Autumn 1989), pp. 55–56.

49. David P. Conradt and Eric Langenbacher, *The German Polity* (Lanham, MD: Rowman and Littlefield, 2013), pp. 228–233.

50. Uwe Thaysen, *The Bundesrat, the Länder, and German Federalism* (Washington, DC: American Institute for Contemporary German Studies, 1994), pp. 13–26.

51. Alison B. Alter, "Minimizing the Risks of Delegation: Multiple Referral in the German Bundesrat," *American Journal of Political Science*, vol. 46, no. 2 (April 2002), pp. 300–301, 313; Peter H. Merkl, "Executive-Legislative Federalism in West Germany," *American Political Science Review*, vol. 53, no. 3 (September 1959), pp. 735–737; Georg Vanberg, "Establishing Judicial Independence in West Germany: The Impact of Opinion Leadership and the Separation of Powers," *Comparative Politics*, vol. 32, no. 3 (April 2000), pp. 338–341.

52. Donald V. Smiley and Ronald L. Watts, *Intrastate Federalism in Canada* (Toronto: University of Toronto Press, 1985), pp. 85–89.

53. Smiley and Watts, p. 88.

54. Gregory J. Inwood, Carolyn M. Johns, and Patricia L. O'Reilly, *Intergovernmental Policy Capacity in Canada* (Montreal and Kingston, ON: McGill-Queen's University Press, 2011), pp. 40–52, 57–59.

55. Richard Simeon and Ian Robinson, *State, Society, and the Development of Canadian Federalism* (Toronto: University of Toronto Press, 1990), pp. 285–295.

56. Simeon and Robinson, pp. 262–268.

57. Richard Simeon, *Intergovernmental Relations* (Toronto: University of Toronto Press, 1985), pp. 33–65.

58. David Cameron, "Inter-Legislative Federalism," in *Reconsidering the Institutions of Canadian Federalism*, J. Peter Meekinson, Hamish Telford, and Harvey Lazar, eds. (Montreal and Kingston, ON: McGill-Queen's University Press, 2004), pp. 163–175.

59. David Cameron, "Inter-Legislative Federalism," in *Reconsidering the Institutions of Canadian Federalism*, J. Peter Meekinson, Hamish Telford, and Harvey Lazar, eds. (Montreal and Kingston, ON: McGill-Queen's University Press, 2004), pp. 163–175.

60. Franks, pp. 200–201.

61. Hans-Georg Wehling, "The Bundesrat," *Publius*, vol. 19, no. 4 (Autumn 1989), pp. 56, 58–62.

62. Vincent Lemieux, "La Representation et la gouverne," *Analyses des Politiques*, vol. 12 (fèvrier 1986), pp. 122–126.

63. Stevenson, *Unfulfilled Union* pp. 231–232.

Chapter 8

Constitutional Amendment Part III

Appointment, Partisanship, Diversity, Democratic Theory

The desire for an elected Senate of Canada has been motivated by claims that an elected chamber will be more accountable, representative, and responsive to the Canadian electorate.[1] These claims frequently appear to be based upon a populist democratic theory that may not consider, fully, the implications of parliamentary democracy. That expectation often has been blandly asserted as being a *prima facie* requirement of institutional reform within *any* democratic system. It also has claimed that it could address the problem of the lack of diversity in representation within the overall Canadian parliamentary system, provided that the election of Senators would be conducted through some form of proportional representation.[2]

Some of that critique has been thoughtful in acknowledging the complexity of the democratic process in this respect and the idea that adding elections to non-central institutions does not, automatically, improve democracy.[3] However, many other calls for an elected Senate appear to have treated this element of it in a largely symbolic manner,[4] as though assuming that elections automatically improve all institutions within a democratic society. Such an uncritical assertion neglects the important distinction between democracy as a simple method of politics and liberal democracy as an ideological tradition to which modern societies such as Canada adhere.

THE PROBLEM OF DEFERENCE AND POPULIST ASSUMPTIONS

Increasingly since the end of the Second World War, people have taken advantage of rising standards and conditions to become active participants within their political systems, resulting in rising expectations relating to those systems as materialist societies transition toward post-materialist ones. Consequently, it has been argued that citizens have become generally less deferential to established elites, especially appointed ones.[5] As these populations have assumed that material wants will be fulfilled, they increasingly emphasize, instead, the role of government in providing for the advancement of social values and the promotion of a better "quality of life." Part of that post-materialist expectation is that many members of 21st-century democratic societies are less deferential to established elites and more insistent upon direct electoral accountability.[6] A similar trend has been noted within Canada, where changes in political culture have affected overall confidence in governmental institutions.[7]

That trend may be responsible for the appeal of making as many government institutions as possible elected ones. While it predates the establishment of elected judges within the United States (or, indeed, the election of offices that, arguably, might better be based upon a non-partisan assessment of specific expertise, such as auditor or environmental engineer), the rationale that elections improve institutions is bolstered in a similar way by the assumption of accountability, though that assumption frequently is not realized in practice.[8] That approach is particularly appealing when guided by a belief that democratic government should reflect only the will of an electoral majority or plurality. That theme has been addressed within the chapter on the political theory of second chambers and it makes particularly sense in reference to an institution that can overturn legislation and policies approved by a representative chamber such as the Canadian House of Commons. But the role of an institution that may delay or recommend changes to (but not overturn) the popular will present a different sort of consideration, as noted elsewhere.

Nonetheless, this theme also emphasizes the objection that an unelected Senate simply defies the "spirit of the times" that demands that all public institutions must be directly accountable to the shifting popular will. The vast wave of populist movements that became particularly obvious in certain parts of the world in 2016 (and that characterized the Reform Party that would be part of the merged Conservative Party that would govern Canada under Prime Minister Stephen Harper) would indicate that a reformed but unelected Senate of Canada could not survive popular (if not populist) expectations and demands.[9] Under that rubric, the argument that an appointed upper house of parliament advances the cause of popular sovereignty (by removing a challenge to the democratically elected lower house) simply would "fall on deaf ears." That perspective offers a plausible objection, though it is dependent upon the contention that the point of this exercise and these recommendations is to outline the composition of an institution primarily upon its perceived popularity at a given point in time.

This book is basing its recommendations for reform upon instrumental arguments. In other words, it is proposed that reform should be based upon theories, evidence, and concepts that are consistent with an attempt to arrive at an ideal model for a parliamentary upper house rather than an immediately popular one. Furthermore, the interests that are served should address the broader needs and interests of a liberal democracy in a more profound sense—which also reflects the previously addressed principles of a polyarchy. A parallel example could be offered by those economists, political scientists, and public policy experts who continued, long after the referendum that authorized Great Britain's departure from the European Union, to argue for remaining within that union—not because the arguments would be popularly embraced by a population that had been motivated by other beliefs and assumptions but because a reasonable argument could be made that it was, nonetheless, the right decision to make, regardless of contrary popular sentiment.[10]

This chapter offers recommendations for a hypothetical amendment to Canada's Constitution Act of 1867 that attempt to address characteristics associated with a polyarchy. Those characteristics include alternatives to election (and, thus, competition with the elected parliamentary lower house), a lessening of partisanship within the legislative system, a greater representation of the diversity of society (demographically, geographically, and meritoriously), and alternatives to a belief that all institutions of democratic government require an electoral basis to achieve legitimacy. Those conclusions might not be popular within the context of a particular time and place but they still might lead to beneficial and, arguably, preferential results.

Independent Advisory Board

When Prime Minister Justin Trudeau instituted a new appointment process in 2016, he sought to implement a theme that this book also recommends. His goal was to create a system that would ignore partisan considerations and choose Senators, instead, upon the basis of merit. By 2017, an Independent Advisory Board for Senate Appointments was established. Its membership includes five members for every selection of a Senator, including three federal members (including the Chair) plus two members from the province (based upon consultations with the respective provincial government) that will be represented by that appointment. The staggered terms of two years were created to ensure both continuity and rotation, thus bolstering its nonpartisan nature.[11]

While its purpose reflects principles that are expressed within this section relating to non-partisanship, merit, and diversity,[12] it exists outside of the context of the wider array of reforms that would be necessary to make its effectiveness more persistent. The fact that this hypothetical constitutional amendment specifies that the federal government would retain a larger number of direct appointments, this process could offer an additional provincial input that might address desires for greater intrastate federalism within the overall process. Meanwhile, more specific guidelines also could clarify expectations in this respect.

This hypothetical constitutional amendment offered within this book recommends not only further formalizing that process of the Independent Advisory Board but, also, making it more systematic. A future government could dispense with that process, though it arguably might also pose an informal, yet powerful, constitutional convention that future governments will feel compelled to retain. Nonetheless, whether by constitutional or non-constitutional means, that formalized institutional structure has been proven to be not only feasible but, arguably, necessary for meaningful reform of the Senate as a whole, especially given the overall role that parliamentary upper houses ought to perform.

NON-PARTISAN REPRESENTATION IN THE SENATE

An interesting feature of the appointment of peers within the current British system is the practice of including appointees who have been nominated by the opposition parties (especially, but not exclusively, by the Leader of the Loyal Opposition) as well as by the Prime Minister. Additionally, non-political figures also are elevated to a peerage as a result of both government nominations and recommendations from other, non-partisan quarters. Government nominations (with the obvious approval of the governing party) evidently constitute the bulk of those appointments. Nonetheless, the inclusion of opposition nominees has reinforced theoretical characteristics of the upper house within Britain, especially in terms of its less contentiously partisan inner workings and public perceptions. As an idealized model, a hypothetical constitutional clause offers a way to contemplate the implications of this aspect of Senate reform.

Representation in Other Categories

(4) No more than half of the total number of Senators appointed during each four-year period by the Governor-General or Lieutenant Governor, in the name of the Queen, may be representatives or, otherwise, members of the same political party, nor may a Senator serve concurrently in any other legislative body in Canada.

(5) Provision shall be made in the Senate of Canada for the accommodation of Senators who have no formal party affiliation, including in terms of the

appointment of appropriate Parliamentary Officers to oversee their organizational and procedural interests.

The tendency to insist upon elections as the only means for conferring legitimacy upon institutions other than the one that directly supports the government is a phenomenon that could be characterized as the "Cool Whip effect." Classic advertisements for Cool Whip desert topping asserted that, in relation to any type of dessert, "everything is better with Cool Whip." Likewise, there often appears to be a strain of thought that insists that, in relation to any public institution of a liberal democracy, "everything is better when it is elected." But just as the concept of American judges elected upon the basis of their popular acceptability or the approval of the results of particular judicial decisions (as opposed to ones appointed upon the basis of an executive assessment and legislative confirmation of their professional qualifications) has been subject to challenge,[13] the belief in the automatic desirability of elected Senators also ought to be subject to a critical review.

While many British peerages have been awarded upon the basis of partisan service and loyalty in relation to a political party, many of them also are awarded upon the basis of non-partisan and non-political considerations—a category that has included the classification known as "Peoples' Peers."[14] This category of peers has reinforced those non-partisan and specialized characteristics of the British upper house in a manner that is instructive for Canada. One of the strongest objections to the election of Senators is a concern about the reinforcing of partisanship that elections would likely encourage. The cost of elections also could cause prospective Senators to require the institutional mechanism and support of organized political parties in order to achieve electoral success. Additionally, given the costs associated with achieving elected office within any democratic system (including Canada, particularly at the national level), it also could actually increase exposure to the influence of formal interest groups (which would provide financial backing in support of such candidacies) that has been an important complaint of current Senate practice, including Colin Campbell's seminal treatment of the subject.[15]

Independent Senators

A notable feature of the House of Lords has been its Cross Benches. Its presence has strengthened claims regarding the relative independence of that legislative body, especially in relation to the government and to the British party system. It also has provided a place and role for non-partisan peers (including former Speakers of the House of Commons who, thus, maintain the prestigious neutral procedural role that they achieved within the lower house) among other former officials. That arrangement has facilitated the participation of experts and specialists from various fields from outside the conventional political system, thus also strengthening that characteristic advantage of upper houses.[16]

The elected Senate of Australia also has a Cross-bench section. In that case, this section typically is reserved for elected members of minor parties (such as the Green Party of Australia) or for politicians who have been elected independently of any party affiliation. As all Australian Cross-bench Senators achieve that position as the result of contested elections, the concept of an "independent" Senator does not carry the same meaning or function as it does in a hereditary or (now overwhelmingly) appointed body such as the House of Lords.[17] This sort of requirement for Canada could have multiple advantages in this respect. The concept of "no party affiliation" could be a difficult one to determine and, in some cases, could be subject to challenge if it were to be abused. Yet the principle could be reasonably expected to be followed in an honest and faithful manner, especially given the conventions of parliamentary government that, ultimately, are intended to guide all Westminster-model systems, including the Canadian one.

The concept of this sort of section has interesting philosophical implications as well. In the absence of partisan affiliation, members of society who do not identify with a particular political party can feel indirectly disenfranchised, especially within a parliamentary system that so strongly relies upon the role of parties in establishing responsible government. This form of inclusion (especially in terms of providing a means to advance broad and diverse social discourse) is highly consistent with aspects of communitarian thought, even though it might have the consequence of reducing such a body to an instrumental status of governmental convenience.[18] Republican principles offer another way to think about this accommodation, even though Canada is not a republic. By providing a Cross Bench section, an additional institutional presence (though one that is located within a larger and more structurally distinctive body) is made available for the inclusion of yet another distinct "constituency" of society. This principle is entirely consistent with a republican approach toward the role of a legislative upper house in the modern sense.[19] It also can be expressed, as addressed within chapter 3, as a manifestation of the principle of "virtual representation," thus providing an additional presence for underrepresented yet important constituent groups within Canadian society.

A practical consideration of this system would be the physical accommodation of both increased numbers of Senators and a Cross Bench section. The current allocation of desks within that chamber (as also is provided within the House of Commons) almost certainly could not be continued. The use of benches (as found within the current House of Lords) might provide a good example of a practical solution, especially if consistent attendance on the part of all Senators were not to be expected. When a particularly large attendance is expected, the pragmatic arrangements that typically are made within both legislative chambers of the Royal Palace of Westminster could provide a useful model. In any event, furniture is not destiny and meaningful parliamentary reform certainly would never be a slave to surmountable physical impediments, despite the status that might be attached to Senators having individual desks as conveniences.

SENATE REFORM AND CANADIAN DIVERSITY

A characteristic of any upper house (particularly a parliamentary one) is its capacity to provide for the representation of distinctive constituencies that are not determined through a scheme of representation by population—in other words, the representation of "something else." Although legislative chambers often overrepresented certain dominant groups and professions (and the Canadian House of Commons is an excellent example of this problem as its elected members are, as a whole, overwhelmingly white, male, and middle aged[20]), an appointed upper house frequently is well-positioned to redress that problem. However, a truly successful application of that principle often requires a conscious effort, leading to a consistent practice and a commitment to these values within a system's political culture.

> 21. *(6) In addition to Senators appointed pursuant to subsections (2) and (3) and notwithstanding the restrictions imposed by subsection (4), the following persons shall be automatically appointed (provided that they meet all other qualifications pursuant to sections 23 and 31 of this Act) as Senators: former Governors General of Canada, former Lieutenant Governors of the several Provinces, former Commissioners of the Federal Territories, former Speakers of the House of Commons, former Speakers of the legislatures of the several Provinces, former Speakers of the several Assemblies of the Federal Territories, former Clerks of the Queen's Privy Council for Canada, former occupants of the post of senior civil servant for each of the several Provinces and Federal Territories, former Presidents of the Council of First Nations, Companions of the Order of Canada, former Governors of the Bank of Canada, former Ambassadors of Canada to the United Nations, former Commissioners of the Royal Canadian Mounted Police, former Governors of the Canadian Broadcasting Corporation/Radio Canada, former Directors of the National Gallery of Canada, former Chiefs of Staff of the Armed Forces of Canada, former Commissioners of the Human Rights Commission of Canada, any person who has been conferred the title of Right Honorable in respect of Canada and who is not, otherwise, occupying an elected or otherwise official public post or office.*

(7) In the name of the Queen, the Governor General shall be entitled to appoint one additional Senator per year without regard to region, province, or territory, the several Lieutenant Governors may appoint one additional Senator, each, per every four-year period, and the several Commissioners of Federal Territories may appoint one additional Senator per every eight-year period. None of the Senators appointed under this category shall be a member of a political party and all Senators appointed under this category shall have distinguished themselves in fields of endeavor that may include, but should not be limited to: education, the natural and physical sciences, medicine, the performing and visual arts, the literary arts, the military, police, international diplomacy, business, philanthropy, athletics, journalism, humanist and social science scholarship, and other professional and non-professional fields.

(8) The Governor General, the several Lieutenant Governors, and the several Commissioners of Federal Territories, in the name of the Queen, shall seek to appoint Senators in a manner consistent with the preservation and enhancement of the multicultural heritage of Canadians.

(9) Senators who are serving in the Senate at the time of the adoption of subsections (2) and (3) shall continue to serve in that Chamber, pursuant to the requirements and conditions specified in this Act.

This hypothetical constitutional amendment offers one theoretical response to a desire to increase, within such an electoral system, the presence and input of diverse groups within a society through various expressions of consociational democracy that are consistent with communitarian political thought and strategy.[21] The classic definition of this concept provided by scholars such as Arend Lijphart emphasizes the collaboration of ruling elites of a fragmented political culture designed to provide necessary stability. More limited applications of this concept are designed to enhance democratic participation among social and political subcultures.[22]

This characteristic has been particularly noteworthy in connection with the House of Lords. While its membership was, historically, tied to the landed aristocracy, the introduction of life peerages in 1958 had a dramatic effect upon its composition. Previous attempts (most notably under Prime Minister John the Earl Russell in 1869) to allow for the creation of Life Peers (especially among persons who had distinguished themselves in the civil service, the military, the judiciary, science, literature, and the arts, as well as politics) had been rejected.[23] But even prior to the eventual adoption of a life peerage system, appointment to the British upper house had been expanded and made more open by the trend of awarding hereditary peerages to persons upon the basis of having distinguished themselves in some notable way—the mathematical physicist Lord Kelvin (who used his parliamentary position to advocate for the British adoption of the metric system) is but one (the first one from the natural and physical sciences) example.[24]

This trend became more pronounced during the 20th century and it has been reinforced by the House of Lords Appointments Commission, which is responsible for advocating and vetting such appointments. The commission was one of the most conspicuously adopted proposals that emerged from the Royal Commission on the Reform of the House of Lords, though it did not replace the role of the Prime Minister in the actual process as originally suggested.[25] That commission is chaired by a Cross-bench peer and it provides non-binding but highly influential advice upon these appointments, including in terms of suitability and potential conflicts of interest.[26] Although the commission has expressed disappointment in not being as successful as it would like in attracting an even greater diversity among nominees (especially in terms of more female peers),[27] it has been lauded by critics for its non-partisan and publicly useful approach.[28]

The House of Lords otherwise has been notable for advancing (at least somewhat more than the House of Commons) parliamentary representation of otherwise underrepresented groups within British society.[29] An anecdotal yet particularly notable and instructive example was the elevation of the civil rights activist David Pitt, in 1975, to the second chamber as Lord Pitt of Hampstead. This appointment made him the first person of African descent to have been a member of either chamber of the British parliament.[30] Many other such appointments have been made in an effort to increase the diversity of Parliament. Another anecdotal example occurred when Laurence Olivier was elevated to the House of Lords as Baron Olivier of Brighton and became the first actor so honored. Politically, that move was regarded as important to the promotion of the arts in Britain, as he also had been Director of the National Theatre and the Labour government at that time wanted to pursue a more expansive legislative agenda concerning the performing and fine arts within Parliament. That aspect of the strategy seemed to be appropriate as that chamber had been playing a pivotal role in amending legislation in that area.[31] It also was designed to enhance the role of the upper house as an institution that can express the expertise, as well as the opinions, of distinct constituencies of various categories, including demographically, professionally, socially, and culturally. That role is indicative of a broader theoretical role of second chambers that may particularly resonate in Canada.

A HOUSE OF EXPERTS

An upper house can be oriented in such a way that appointments are perceived to be based upon a theme of merit. This interpretation can address concerns about a negative public perception of "elitism" in relation to this chamber and the process of appointing its members.[32] It also can serve as a means for promoting the appointment of truly distinguished representatives of the various groups that comprise Canadian society.

Diversity can be expressed not only in terms of the traditional categories of ethnicity, gender, religion, and similar characteristics but, also, in professional terms. This reflection is appropriate within the context of an industrialized economy with a diverse professional base. The relationship between the Canadian government and various sectors of its economy provides an additional impetus for enhancing this particular feature of the country's diversity.

The current Senate of Canada includes members who have been appointed from a variety of professional backgrounds. This professional diversity is a historical trend that was noted by F. A. Kunz in his seminal 1965 critique of the Senate of Canada, especially in terms of business interests.[33] Although still not tremendously diverse in this respect, appointments to this body have included persons with distinctive professional backgrounds. This fact has been noted by a former Clerk of the Privy Council and Secretary to the Cabinet.

> The people appointed to the Senate were not usually professional politicians. They had actually done something with their lives. They were small business people, senior managers in big business, heads of NGOs or professionals with real-world experience. They were the kind of people who wanted to make a difference and contribute to Canada, without subjecting themselves to the contact sport of elected politics. How to attract such people to public life without making them run for office? Appoint them.[34]

This diversity may be more significant when considered within the context of its limited size (due to the current constitutional limits imposed upon its maximum numbers) and its use for rewarding politicians of the governmental parties, including former members of the lower house. Still, the composition of the Senate of Canada elicits a consideration of its potential for even greater representative diversity in this area. "There is no doubt that in much of the literature, the institution is viewed as the lower order of an upper chamber. Yet the same literature occasionally acknowledges a representative function for the Senate; MacKay himself discusses Senate membership in light of minorities (linguistic, religious, and ethnic), occupations, and age, while Kunz supplements this material and adds education."[35] This observation may not be unique but it could be even more prescient in suggesting the further possibilities in this area that the right sort of institution reform of the Canadian upper house could provide.

Nonetheless, it is consistent with the historical evolution of the parliamentary upper house that members of such chambers often have a more specialized professional background than their colleagues in the lower house. The early history of the Canadian Senate suggests this influence in terms of both its relatively diverse professional composition (especially in relation to the business community, which was a relatively less represented constituency at that time, though it now might be considered to be overrepresented) and its expression of particular expertise over a range of policy areas.[36] Unlike members of the House of Commons (who were, increasingly, professional politicians), Senators are not distracted by the need to secure election to their tenured parliamentary positions nor are they as likely to be engaged in party and other partisan activities as their lower house colleagues. Although members of the Senate of Canada have not yet developed the sort of social and professional diversity that characterizes the House of Lords, a modest distinction within the Canadian upper house in this respect is, still, notable.[37]

APPOINTMENT AND DEMOCRATIC THEORY

Democratic theory and practice are more complex than a simple application of elections upon all institutions and decisions. Procedural democracy is, therefore, an appropriate manifestation of this desire to reflect and protect the will and interests of the ancient Greek concept of the *demos* as a comprehensive whole as addressed within chapter 3. As previously noted, procedural democracy is predicated upon the ideal that the *demos* remain in possession of the *ultimate* political will. Political preferences and decisions do not need to be derived, directly, from an electoral mandate, provided that those decisions are capable of being subordinated to the overall popular will.[38] A problem may occur, though, when democratic preferences are found to be in procedural conflict with each other. Furthermore, that conflict can undermine the expert advice and transformation of will into action that non-elected actors can provide. The lack of an electoral mandate does not, in itself, negate the democratic role than non-elected officials and institutions may contribute. Lastly, democratic decisions tend to be imperfectly reflected. They typically do not represent the will of all and sometimes do not even truly indicate the will of the majority.[39]

As intimated within chapter 3, the ancient interpretation of democratic theory did not enjoy the positive association with popular sovereignty that it embraced during the modern period. In fact, Aristotle characterized democracy as a functionally "bad" form of government, associated with a form of self-destructive mob rule. Instead, he insisted that a "good" version of a "government of the many" should be tempered by the features of a mixed system that included monarchical and aristocratic elements.[40] That Aristotelian approach to the role of the *demos* was, therefore, a circumspect one.[41] From that perspective, a legislative body that does not directly represent the popular will offers a particular role in response to a popular (such as an elected) governmental body[42] and it is consistent with some of the attributes associated with the evolution of the legislative upper house.

The rise of liberal ideology altered the perceived role of both individual persons and citizens in general within the political process and, subsequently, the concept of democracy. The functional values that arose from the market place became the normative values of liberalism and liberal societies. Those values would emphasize not only the practices that are necessary for a market economy to function[43] but, also, the relationship between freedom and individual property interests (especially as articulated through the modern concept of civil rights and liberties) that would have a profound effect upon the understanding of the role of government in general.[44]

In that sense, as previously stated, the upper house becomes a check upon the executive (rather than upon the lower house of the legislature) and the executive's potential threat to the liberal property rights of citizens.[45] A meaningful understanding of the significance of democratic institutions within this context would be based upon the distinction between elections as ends in themselves and a true institutional expression of a recognizable and unchallenged popular will. Adding the democratic process to every government position (such as the judiciary and the civil service) does not necessarily reinforce democratic principles. In fact, it may badly confuse and undermine them. Also in that sense, procedural democracy relies upon a parochial expression of the will of the *demos*. A wider application of that process, especially through widespread election of specialized positions, can have the ironic consequence of undermining that will. Robert Dahl has provided an eloquent comment on that particular danger.

> [P]robably no one who believes that full procedural democracy is a relevant aspiration thinks that it must hold for all matters, including judgments on highly technical, judicial, and administrative matters of every kind. Rhetorical assertions that seem to make procedural democracy the only proper method of making decisions have again and again been shown to be illusory and self-defeating. Yet as with the problem of inclusion, there is an exceptionally tricky problem here, one that can be dealt with only summarily in this article by stipulating a fifth criterion, *that of final control by the* demos ("popular sovereignty"). That is, the scope, domain, and procedures for making decisions other than by full procedural democracy are subject to decisions made by full procedural democracy.[46]

This understanding of democratic theory strongly indicates the inadvisability of conferring electoral legitimacy upon more than one political institution, particularly when it could affect the democratic legitimacy of the state as a whole.[47] Two particular objections are suggested in this respect. First, the substitution of mass popularity for individual expertise is a potentially disastrous consequence in many instances.[48] The belief that the electoral process for decision making of this sort results in a superior outcome may be based upon both anti-elite and anti-intellectual biases that have been especially associated with the American populist tradition.[49] Second, the reference to the role of "full" procedural democracy as a safeguard and ultimate arbiter relating to the policies that these particular expert decisions represent (especially within societies that experience socio-political cleavages) implies a distinction between sovereign electoral authority and other and, arguably, lesser forms of electoral expression.[50]

The "full" manifestation of the electoral will is intended to provide an assertion of the delegation of the sovereign authority of a democratic populace. While it is not an expression of every individual will, it does signify the prime expression of the collective sovereign will, even if only imperfectly. Therefore, a challenge to that expression by a competing institutional expression (such as additional bodies and officials whose legitimacy rests, primarily, upon their election) arguably undermines the role of the "full" body as the supreme expression of the sovereign will. In simpler terms, elected bodies, representing distinct constituencies (even when drawn from the same population), compete against each other in a dueling claim of legitimacy that can undermine both of them but can undermine, more seriously, the body that is intended to be the ultimate reflection of the sovereign will.[51]

THE LESSONS OF THE AUSTRALIAN GOVERNOR-GENERAL'S CRISIS

One of the most important case studies related to this theme is the so-called Australia Governor-General's Crisis. In 1975, the Parliament of Australia found itself at an impasse. The Labor Party government of Gough Whitlam had a majority in the House of Representatives (the lower house of the Australian Parliament) as a result of the general elections of 1972 and 1974. However, it did not command a majority in the Australian Senate. That particular upper house of parliament is elected and, upon the basis of its own electoral mandate within that chamber and constitutional powers that allow it to veto the legislation of the lower house (including government policy), the opposition Liberal Party and its allies within the Senate decided to block government appropriations that had been approved by the House of Representatives.

Prime Minister Whitlam attempted to break this impasse by having the Governor-General, Sir John Kerr, call for an election of half of the seats in the Senate. Instead, the Governor-General opted to dismiss Whitlam and appoint the Leader of the Opposition, Malcolm Fraser, in his place. This action created a political crisis that was not resolved, even after subsequent elections provided a majority in both parliamentary chambers to the Liberal Party. Despite the constitutional option of invoking a "double dissolution" of both houses of parliament and calling new elections for both of them (which may well have resulted in the same dueling majorities in any event), the Governor-General invoked his reserve powers in a controversial decision to allow the position of the elected Senate to determine the issue.[52]

Many constitutional, political, and fiscal issues contributed to this crisis, not the least of which was the dubious interpretation and application of the Governor-General's reserve powers that disregarded the advice of the current prime minister. Nonetheless, even many of those Australians who were partisans of the opposition parties that precipitated the immediate crisis were disturbed by the perception of an overall breach of constitutional convention. The fact that the Senate of Australia is an elected body clearly played a significant role in the decision of opposition Senators to deny approval of government appropriations and force a crisis in which a parliamentary majority of the lower house, upon which the government mandate is based, was thwarted by elected representatives claiming a similar electoral mandate in the upper house.[53] That fact emboldened Australian Senators and legitimized a political move that led to the dismissal of a parliamentary government that possessed a working majority within that lower house that was ultimately responsible for its mandate.

> It has never authoritatively been laid down that a government must resign *merely because it has failed to obtain appropriation.* The convention derived from Westminster is that a government must resign *if it loses the confidence of the House of Commons.* Failure to obtain appropriations from the Commons is one of the indicia of loss of such confidence, and refusing appropriation is also a sanction for ensuring that a government will not be able to carry on in defiance of the will of the Commons. The reconciliation of these principles with the existence of an *elected* upper house systematically capable of having a political majority differing from that of the lower house, has never been satisfactorily worked out in terms of the Westminster conventions.[54]

The Constitution of Australia permits the parliamentary upper house to block government legislation that has been approved by the lower house, including appropriations. This sort of impasse could be prevented simply by denying the upper house an absolute veto in such areas. The constitutional strategy of a double dissolution also might have reconciled this conflict, though the fact that each Australian state has an equal number of representatives in the Senate, regardless of population, makes such an electoral reconciliation far from certain. Again, though, the sense of electoral legitimacy among Senators contributed to their ultimate course of action.

Therefore, this example, though admittedly anecdotal, does illustrate one of the potential consequences of an elected Senate of Canada. The fact that this sort of impasse occurred within Australia but has not occurred between the Canadian parliamentary chambers suggests the difficulty of reconciling the presence of two elected chambers within a single parliamentary system. Therefore, it is important to revisit the underlying rationale behind desires to reform the Senate of Canada by making it, like the Canadian House of Commons, an elected body.

CANADIAN SENATE ELECTIONS IN ACTION

Despite the constitutional difficulties of amending the Constitution Act of 1867 in this (or any related) area (as demonstrated by the attempt to adopt Bill C-20, which was intended to provide a method for the federal government to be advised on Senate appointments by an electoral process within each province), the governments of Prime Minister Brian Mulroney and, particularly, Prime Minister Stephen Harper adopted an informal and indirect electoral approach that would be presented to the Supreme Court of Canada as part of the Senate Reference case in the form of "consultative elections" that will be addressed within chapter 9. In that spirit, Alberta created special elections for selecting "Senators in Waiting." Stanley Waters was appointed by the Mulroney government while Bert Brown and Betty Unger were appointed by the Harper government. Alberta conducted a special election for the purpose of nominating "preferred" candidates to be appointed from that province to the Senate of Canada in 1989, 1998, 2004, and 2012. The two leading candidates who emerged from the 2004 election (of a field of 13 candidates) were Bert Brown and Betty Unger, who tied for first place in that election with 14.3% of the vote, each.[55] In the 2012 election, the leading candidate, Douglas Black, received a total of 15.9% of the vote while the second leading candidate, Scott Tannas, received 13.1% of the total vote and the third place candidate, Mike Shaikh, received 11.5% of the total vote.[56]

Interestingly, all of these candidates had profiles that are remarkably similar not only to their current colleagues in the Canadian upper house but, also, as part of a pattern that has been historically noted within that chamber. Of the 11 leading candidates from the first four election cycles (Bert Brown was elected and "reelected" during two different cycles) for "Senators in Waiting," 10 of them were white, 10 of them were male, all of them were middle aged, and 9 of them have had backgrounds in business and as professional politicians: Betty Unger also has a background as a nurse as well as in business, while Ted Morton is a university professor and Stan Waters was a career military officer who later entered the business world.[57] Two of these elected "Senators in Waiting" offer interesting demographic and professional case studies. Senator Douglas Black is male, white, and is a lawyer with particular expertise in the energy sector. Senator Scott Tannas also is a white male who has considerable experience in business, particularly as founder and president of the Western Financial Group.[58] All of them have represented the Progressive Conservative Party (with recent strong challenges from the Alberta-based Wildrose Party)[59] except Bill Code, who represented the Liberal Party.[60]

These cases are, of course, anecdotal. They present, nonetheless, certain indications of the challenges of the electoral process for addressing matters of diversity (both professional and demographic) that some proponents of Senate reform have advocated.[61] The small percentage of the vote that the leading candidates received also raises potential concern over the democratic legitimacy that this process has sought to instill into Senate appointments. Finally, these campaigns required the same tools that all electoral contests require, including monetary expenditures—the 2012 special Senate election reportedly cost $2,100,000.00.[62] Nonetheless, these examples offer interesting initial indications regarding the overall role of elections within the larger democratic context of the Canadian parliamentary system.

PARLIAMENTARY DEMOCRACY AND AN APPOINTED UPPER HOUSE

The relationship between the Senate of Canada and its parliamentary system has been noted in several places within this book. Nonetheless, it is a theme that merits an additional summarization—if only because it is so crucial for understanding the strength of the underlying argument in favor of an appointed, rather than an elected, upper house. Therefore, despite the risk of redundancy, the appropriateness of that relationship between that vision of the Senate and the Canadian parliamentary system should be reiterated.

Canada consciously chose to become a parliamentary democracy—specifically consistent with the Westminster model of Great Britain. That choice was based upon both tradition and a rejection of the trade-off that republican democracy provides. Parliamentary democracy is, by contrast, grounded upon a unified institutional expression of democratic sovereignty. Both executive and legislative powers ultimately are invested in procedural control of the legislature. Therefore, the government depends upon the support of the legislature in order to function. This fact encourages "party discipline" (in which members of political parties are expected to vote, uniformly, in support of their respective party positions on legislation) that ensures the consistent support of the legislature for the government's policy agenda and major legislative choices. The ultimate result is government based upon a broad constituency that promotes efficacy over limited political authority.[63]

As noted within chapter 4, the fact that Canada is a parliamentary democracy is extremely significant in this respect. The legitimacy of the central government is entirely dependent (consistent with this tradition) upon the legislative support of the lower house of the Canadian government. That lower chamber, the House of Commons, is dependent for its legitimacy, in turn, upon the election of its members. That arrangement is at the core of the concept of "responsible government" that defines parliamentary democracy. The demonstration of a government's legitimacy is inextricably tied to its capacity to deliver on its electoral promises. A government that cannot enact its major policy proposals has failed to demonstrate its control of the legislature and, thus, must be compelled to seek a renewal of that legitimacy through the electoral process.[64]

The partisanship of the lower house is a necessary feature of a legitimate and functional parliamentary democracy. For other institutions of that system, partisanship can be detrimental to that democratic ideal. Appointed bodies may not be entirely free of such partisan considerations. However, elections can have a strong reinforcing effect upon partisanship. Furthermore, elections can create difficulties (especially when based upon a non-proportional system) for advancing a more diverse presence within the overall governmental process.

An appointment process also can have benefits for managing federal relations. Federal units are sovereign within their own spheres. Therefore, a process that encourages interference through the insertion of elected officials into the institutions of these respective levels of sovereign federal authority can be unnecessarily confrontational. Interstate federalism has been a strong resource for the negotiations that are essential to effective federal-provincial relations within Canada. An elected upper house could exacerbate tensions in this respect and not only at the national level. It is entirely possible that elected Senators could vote against the positions of their respective provincial governments upon the basis of their own distinct "mandate," thus contradicting claims of provincial democratic authority and legitimacy over certain key issues.

An appointed Senate of Canada with unlimited (or, at least, indefinite) numbers of members that allows for input in the appointment process at the provincial level and provides directive criteria for promoting diversity does not guarantee that these goals will be achieved. However, they are much less likely to achieve the opposite effect. It is important to consider the unintended consequences of institutional change within the process of institutional reform. This part of the hypothetical constitutional amendment is intended to be particularly instructive of these theoretical considerations, especially in warning against the unintended consequences of alternative approaches to Senate reform that may not contemplate them.

NOTES

1. David E. Smith, *The Canadian Senate in Bicameral Perspective* (Toronto: University of Toronto Press, 2004), pp. 53–61.

2. Roger Gibbins, "A New Senate for a More Democratic Canada," Canada West Foundation, March 2010, pp. 5–6.

3. Serge Joyal, *Protecting Canadian Democracy: The Senate You Never Knew* (Montreal and Kingston, ON: McGill-Queen's University Press, 2003), pp. 140–141.

4. Michael Lusztig, "Federalism and Institutional Design: The Perils and Politics of a Triple-E Senate in Canada," *Publius*, vol. 25, no. 1 (Winter 1995), pp. 35–36, 50.

5. Karl W. Deutsch, "Social Mobilization and Political Development," American Political Science Review, vol. 55, no. 3 (1964), pp. 493–514.

6. Ronald Inglehart and Christian Welzel, "Changing Mass Priorities: The Link Between Modernization and Democracy," *Perspectives on Politics*, vol. 8, no. 2 (June 2010), pp. 551–567.

7. Neil Nevitte, *The Decline of Deference: Canadian Value Change in Cross-National Perspective* (Toronto: University of Toronto Press, 1996), pp. 49–64.

8. Claire S. H. Lim, "Preferences and Incentives of Appointed and Elected Public Officials: Evidence from State Court Trial Judges," *American Economic Review*, vol. 103, no. 4 (June 2013), pp. 1,360–1,397.

9. David Laycock, "Populism and Democracy in Canada's Reform Party," in Cass Mudde and Cristóbal Rovira Kaltwasser, eds., *Populism in Europe and the Americas: Threat or Corrective for Democracy?* Cambridge: Cambridge University Press, 2013), pp. 48–49, 53–54, 60.

10. Andrew Soergel, "How Britain Could Undo the Brexit," US News and World Report, June 26, 2016, https://www.usnews.com/news/articles/2016-06-28/how-britain-could-undo-the-brexit.

11. Government of Canada, Independent Advisory Board for Appointment of Senators, https://www.canada.ca/en/campaign/independent-advisory-board-for-senate-appointments.html.

12. Government of Canada, Prime Minister's Office, "Prime Minister Announces Intention to Recommend the Appointment of Nine New Senators." October 27, 2016, http://pm.gc.ca/eng/news/2016/10/27/prime-minister-announces-intention-recommend-appointment-nine-new-senators; Alex Boutlier, "Liberals are Expected to Appoint 20 New Senators within Weeks," *Toronto Star*, September 20, 2016, https://www.thestar.com/news/canada/2016/09/21/liberals-are-expected-to-appoint-20-new-senators-within-weeks.html.

13. Stephen J. Choi, Mitu Gilati, and Eric A. Posner, "Professionals or Politicians: The Uncertain Empirical Case for an Elected Rather than an Appointed Judiciary," John M. Olin Law and Economics Working Paper No. 1831 (Chicago: University

of Chicago, 2006); Joanna M. Shepherd, "The Influence of Retention on Judges' Voting," *Journal of Legal Studies*, vol. 38, no. 1 (January 2009); F. Andrew Hanssen, "The Effect of Judicial Institutions on Uncertainty and the Rate of Litigation: The Elections versus Appointment of State Judges," *Journal of Legal Studies*, vol. 28, no. 1 (January 1999).

14. http://lordsappointments.independent.gov.uk/how-to-apply.aspx

15. Colin Campbell, *The Canadian Senate: A Lobby from Within* (Toronto: MacMillan, 1978), pp. 125–133.

16. http://www.crossbenchpeers.org.uk/

17. John Uhr, *Deliberative Democracy in Australia* (Cambridge: Cambridge University Press, 1998), pp. 98–99.

18. William M. Sullivan, "Institutions and the Infrastructure of Democracy," in *New Communitarian Thinking: Persons, Virtues, Institutions, and Communities*, Anitai Etzioni, ed. (Charlottetown: University Press of Virginia, 1995), pp. 170–171, 175–177.

19. Jean Yarbrough, "Representation and Republicanism: Two Views," *Publius*, vol. 9, no. 2 (Spring 1979), pp. 77–98.

20. Smith, p. 81.

21. T. K. Oommen, "New Nationalisms and Collective Rights: The Case of South Asia," in *Ethnicity, Nationalism, and Minority Rights*, Stephen May, Tariq Modood, and Judith Squires, eds. (Cambridge: Cambridge University Press, 2004), pp. 126–127.

22. Arend Lijphart, "Consociational Democracy," *World Politics*, vol. 21, no. 2 (January 1969), pp. 211–219; Jürg Steiner, "The Consociational Theory and Beyond," *Comparative Politics*, vol. 13, no. 2 (April 1981), pp. 339–346.

23. Olive Anderson, "The Wensleydale Peerage Case and the Position of the House of Lords in the Mid-Nineteenth Century," *English Historical Review*, vol. 82, no. 324 ((July 1967), pp. 486–502.

24. Bernard Semmel, "Parliament and the Metric System," *Isis*, vol. 54, no. 1 (March 1963), pp. 130–131.

25. Meg Russell and Richard Cornes, "The Royal Commission on Reform of the House of Lords: A House for the Future?" *Modern Law Review*, vol. 64, no. 1 (January 2001), pp. 95–96.

26. http://lordsappointments.independent.gov.uk/

27. House of Lords Appointment Commission, "Nominations from Women: A Note by the Secretariat," (Mary 2005), http://www.bbc.co.uk/blogs/opensecrets/HOLAC.pdf

28. House of Commons, Public Administration Select Committee, *Work of the Committee in 2007* (London: Her Majesty's Stationery Office, 2008), pp. 11–13.

29. Meg Russell, *The Contemporary House of Lords: Westminster Bicameralism Revived* (Oxford: Oxford University Press, 2013), pp. 76–79.

30. "Peer from the West Indies," *British Medical Journal*, vol. 2, no. 6203 (December 1979), pp. 1,486–1,487.

31. "Laurence Olivier Takes His Seat in the House of Lords," *The News and Courier* (Charleston, SC), March 25, 1971, p. A12.

32. "Liberating the Senators," *The Economist*, January 31, 2014, http://www.economist.com/ blogs/americasview/2014/01/canadian-politics

33. F. A. Kunz, *The Modern Senate of Canada* (Toronto: University of Toronto Press, 1965), pp. 66, 212.

34. Mel Cappe, "In Defence of an Appointed Senate," *Globe and Mail*, June 17, 2013, A17.

35. Smith, p. 81.

36. James T. McHugh, *In Another Place: Three Case Studies in the Development of the Upper House of Parliament within the Westminster Model of Government* (Edinburgh: University of Edinburgh M.Litt Thesis, 1986), pp. 98–112.

37. David Coletto, "Is the British House of Lords Model Viable for Canada's Senate?" *Abacus Data Insider*, June 17, 2013, http://abacusinsider.com/politics-public-affairs/canadian-senate-house-lords-model-viable-canada/

38. Jack Donnelly, "Human Rights, Democracy, and Development," *Human Rights Quarterly*, vol. 21, no. 3 (August 1999), pp. 615–618.

39. Philippe C. Schmitter and Terry Lynn Karl, "What Democracy Is . . . And Is Not," in *Democracy: A Reader*, Larry Diamond and Marc F. Plattner, eds. (Baltimore: Johns Hopkins University Press, 2009), pp. 3–16.

40. Aristotle, pp. 189–192, 229–241.

41. Andrew Lintott, "Aristotle and Democracy," *Classical Quarterly*, vol. 42, no. 1 (1992), pp. 124–126.

42. Clifford Bates, *Aristotle's Best Regime: Kingship, Democracy, and the Rule of Law* (Baton Rouge: Louisiana State University Press, 2003), pp. 97–102.

43. Stephen Gardbaum, "Liberalism, Autonomy, and Moral Conflict," *Stanford Law Review*, vol. 48, no. 2 (January 1996), pp. 385–417.

44. Charles Larmore, "Political Liberalism," *Political Theory*, vol. 18, no. 3 (August 1990), pp. 339–360.

45. Meg Russell, "What are Second Chambers For?" *Parliamentary Affairs,* vol. 54 (2001), pp. 451–453.

46. Robert Dahl, "On Removing Certain Impediments to Democracy in the United States," *Political Science Quarterly*, vol. 92, no. 1 (Spring 1977), p. 12—emphasis found within the original quote.

47. Robert Dahl, *On Democracy* (New Haven, CT: Yale University Press, 2000), pp. 83–99.

48. John Higley and Michael Burton, *The Elite Foundations of Liberal Democracy* (Lanham, MD: Rowman and Littlefield, 2006), pp. 1–5.

49. Richard Hofstadter, *Anti-Intellectualism in America* (New York: Vintage, 1966), pp. 3–24.

50. Arend Lijphart, "Constitutional Designs for Divide Societies," in Diamond and Plattner, eds., pp. 139–152.

51. David Fisk, "Superfluous or Mischievous: Evaluating the Determinants of Government Defeats in Second Chambers," *Legislative Studies Quarterly*, vol. 36, no. 2 (May 2011), pp. 231–253; Heller, William B. 2007. "Divided Politics: Bicameralism, Parties, and Policy in Democratic Legislatures," *Annual Review of Political Science*, vol. 10, no. 2 (2007), pp. 245–269.

52. John Uhr, "Generating Divided Government: The Australian Senate," in *Senates: Bicameralism in the Contemporary World*, in Samuel C. Patterson and Anthony Mughan, eds. (Columbus: Ohio State Press University, 1999), pp. 110–112.

53. Frank G. Clarke, *The History of Australia* (Westport, CT: Greenwood Press, 20002), pp. 164–167.

54. Geoffrey Sawer, "Constitutional Issues in Australian Federalism," *Publius*, vol. 7, no. 3 (Summer 1977), p. 27.

55. Elections Alberta, *Report of the Chief Electoral Officer on the Senate Nominee Election* (Edmonton: Government of Alberta, 2004), pp. 8–10.

56. Elections Alberta, *Report of the Chief Electoral Officer on the Senate Nominee Election* (Edmonton: Government of Alberta, 2012), pp. 9–12.

57. Parliament of Canada, Senators and Members, Stanley Waters, http://www.parl.gc.ca/ Parlinfo/Files/Parliamentarian.aspx?Item=5309ceb5-be13-4e5b-a255-a8969bae7674&Language=E&Section=FederalExperience; Parliament of Canada, Senators and Members, Bert Brown, http://www.parl.gc.ca/parlinfo/Files/Parliamentarian.aspx?Item=22124571-ff5b-4d12-bccf-50f78cbe2b3d&Language=E&Sec tion=ALL; Parliament of Canada, Senators and Members, Betty Unger, http://www.parl.gc.ca/Parlinfo/ Files/Parliamentarian.aspx?Item=5309ceb5-be13-4e5b-a255-a8969bae7674&Language=E&Section=FederalExperience; Parliament of Canada, Senators and Members, Cliff Breitkreuz, http://www.parl.gc.ca/parlinfo/Files/Parliamentarian.aspx?Item=1b89db3a-1e68-4db6-90fe- e9939bac441e&Language=E& Section=ALL; Parliament of Canada, Senators and Members, Stanley Waters, http://www.parl.gc.ca/Parlinfo/Files/Parliamentarian.aspx?Item=5309ceb5-be13-4e5b-a255-a8969bae7674&Language=E&Section=FederalExperience; "Mike Shaikh for Senate," http://www.mikeforsenate.ca/; "Immigrants of Distinction Award Recipients: Business Award," http://www. immigrantservicescalgary.ca/ida/recipients; Josh Wingrove, "Ted Morton: Alberta's Charisma-Challenged Firebrand Takes His Shot," *Globe and Mail*, August 5, 2011, http://www.theglobeandmail.com/news/politics/ted-morton-albertas-charisma-challenged-firebrand-takes-his-shot/article589611/

58. Parliament of Canada, "Current Members," Scott Tanis, http://www.parl.gc.ca/SenatorsMembers/Senate/SenatorsBiography/ISenator.asp?Language=E; Parliament of Canada, "Current Members," Douglas Black, http://www.parl.gc.ca/ Senators-Members/Senate/SenatorsBiography/isenator_det.asp?senator_id=3567&sortord=N&Language=E&M=M

59. Eric Grenier, "Wildrose or PQ Senators? Welcome to an Elected Red Chamber," *Globe and Mail*, February 3, 2013, http://www.theglobeandmail.com/news/politics/wildrose-or-pq-senators-welcome-to-an-elected-red-chamber/article8127059/

60. Patrick Malcolmson, "Reflections on Canada's First Senate 'Election,'" *Canadian Parliamentary Review*, vol. 14, no. 3 (1991).

61. Roger Gibbins, "A New Senate for a More Democratic Canada," Canada West Foundation, March 2010, pp. 5–6.; F. A. Kunz, *The Modern Senate of Canada* (Toronto: University of Toronto Press, 1965), pp. 66, 212.

62. Government of Alberta, International and Intergovernmental Relations, "Alberta Senate Nominee Elections," http://www.international.alberta.ca/592.cfm

63. Patrick Malcolmson and Richard Myers, *The Canadian Regime: An Introduction to Parliamentary Government in Canada* (Toronto: University of Toronto Press, 2012), pp. 37–57.

64. Munroe Eagles and Sharon A. Manna, "Politics and Government," in *Canadian Studies in the New Milennium*, Patrick James and Mark Kasoff, eds. (Toronto: University of Toronto Press, 2008), pp. 70–77.

Chapter 9

Constitutional Amendment Part IV

Official Language Protection, Nomination Oversight, and Structural Features

Rather than become a democratic challenger to the supremacy of the House of Commons, it is preferable for the Canadian upper house to fulfill a different role. Given the emphasis upon group and collective identity within Canadian society, specific authority could be assigned to the Canadian Senate in specific areas that reflect the diversity of Canadian society. This role, instead of placing the Senate in direct conflict with the elected House of Commons (and the government that it supports), could complement that democratic purpose.

As addressed elsewhere within this book, a meaningful democracy requires a commitment to the rights, needs, and interests of all members of society and not, merely, of the majority (or, frequently, a plurality) of those persons who actually participate in the electoral process. A simple majoritarian system often is not able to reflect the diversity needs and interests of a society. Courts that exercise a constitutional mandate (such as the Charter of Rights and Freedoms reinforces for the Canadian judicial system), while protecting all citizens, can provide particular protections for members of a political system's minority. But the effective input of the variety of group interests within a society as diverse as Canada could benefit from additional institutional avenues for this sort of expression.[1] It may be possible to assign specific powers to the Canadian parliamentary upper house of this purpose.

OFFICIAL LANGUAGES AND THE "DOUBLE MAJORITY"

In particular, it may be advisable to apply this reform to specific areas of public policy. One such area of authority that has been raised within other Senate reform proposals has been in terms of the pivotal Canadian theme of language identity and rights. Another relevant area can be oversight of executive appointments. Both of these themes will be addressed in terms of the hypothetical and idealized amendment to the Constitution Act of 1867.

Powers of the Senate in Relation to Official Languages Bills

IV. 18. *(8) Any Bill pertaining to the Official Languages of Canada must be approved by both the House of Commons and the Senate in order to be presented to the Governor General, on behalf of the Queen, for the Royal Assent, notwithstanding any other conditions specified within this section and pursuant to the requirements specified within section 36 of this Act.*

(9) A bill pertaining to the Official Languages of Canada will not be deemed to have passed the Senate unless it receives, within that body, the support of a majority of Senators who are formally designated as English-speaking and a majority of Senators who are formally designated as French-speaking.

(10) The status of a Senator as English-speaking or French-speaking will be certified by the Speaker of the Senate and affirmed by the Governor General.

This clause refers to the idea of the "double majority" that has been a prominent feature of other reform proposals, including the House of Federation and Charlottetown variations.[2] Its inclusion could be deemed necessary for the participation of Quebec in any constitutional (or, even, non-constitutional) adoption of Senate reform. It also serves to provide supplemental legislative and constitutional protection for the official languages of Canada, thus appealing to those interests that support this policy as a central feature of Canadian identity.

The underlying rationale for including this concept is tied to the constitutional status of Canada's two official languages, English and French. The bilingual character of the country has been a perpetual fact of its political existence since the colonial period and it is the most conspicuous manifestation of this historical duality between Anglophone and Francophone Canada.[3] The acquisition of New France following its successful prosecution of the French and Indian War resulted in British control over a French-speaking population that also was overwhelmingly Catholic. Language, in particular, was a distinguishing feature of identity for the people of this colony and a source of concern for British colonial authorities as they sought to ensure control over it and its neighboring territories within North America, including during the struggle of the American colonies for their independence.[4] The division of colonial Canada into Lower Canada and Upper Canada reflected this fundamental cleavage. Following rebellions in both colonial divisions in 1837, the now-famous report of Lord Durham on these rebellions, their causes, and a proposed British response advocated an imperial policy of assimilation as a means of "eliminating" this linguistic cleavage. His proposal to unite Upper and Lower Canada into a single province that would experience increased immigration of Anglophone settlers from Britain was intended gradually to eliminate the volatile presence of Francophone culture and language within British North America.[5]

But such an approach could not be sustained and the Francophone population of British North America persisted, not only within Quebec but within other colonies (such as New Brunswick) where the Francophone population constituted a conspicuous minority. The achievement of self-governance, through negotiations that resulted in the British North America Act of 1867 (now the Constitution Act of 1867), was accomplished within an environment that recognized the permanence of this feature of the new country.[6] Nonetheless, bilingualism was not officially recognized within the country until, in the wake of the Royal Commission on Bilingualism and Biculturalism in 1966, the Official Languages Act of 1969 was adopted by the federal government. However, this legislation was not constitutionally binding because Canada had no patriated constitution. As the Francophone population of the country continued to decline relative to the overall population of the country, the securing of language rights became an important concern, especially within Quebec. The negotiation that led, in 1982, to the patriation of the British North America Act of 1867 and the adoption of the Constitution Act of 1982 featured, therefore, this crucial consideration, despite the fact that Quebec ultimately withheld its consent to the constitutional settlement.[7]

LANGUAGE PROTECTION AND THE ACCOMMODATION OF QUEBEC

This hypothetical constitutional change reflects that ongoing concern. It also reflects the importance of securing agreement from Quebec in relation to obtaining the necessary constitutional assent for such change. The constitutional agreement concerning Canada's official languages was a crucial feature of the Constitution Act of 1982 as well as a central focus of the identity not only of Canada and Quebec but of provinces such as New Brunswick and Ontario as well.[8] Therefore, this protection of the official languages offered by the "double majority" provision is consistent with the overall character of Canadian national identity and is not relevant merely to Quebec.[9] It also strongly suggests that any reform in this area would have to be constitutionally sanctioned so this hypothetical proposal might reasonably offer not only a theoretical model against which more pragmatic policy proposals can be measured but, potentially, a potential basis for actual constitutional negotiation in this area.

As previously noted, the concept of a "double majority" for language legislation and constitutional amendments has been included within other proposals for Canadian Senate reform.[10] In part, these inclusions have reflected concern over the persistence of the separatist movement within Quebec. Various factors have spurred support for this movement and for the sense of Quebec national identity that serves as its foundation. However, the one factor that ties all of them together is the French language and its central place in that national identity.

Hostility to bilingualism outside Quebec exacerbated a sense of its French language and culture being "under siege."[11] The rise of the Parti Québécois, beginning in 1968, mobilized these resentments and sentiments toward greater collective action, including the ultimately unsuccessful separatist referenda of 1980 and 1995 and the 1977 adoption of *La Charte de la langue française*.[12] The failures of constitutional accommodations through the unsuccessful Meech Lake Accord and Charlottetown Accord have reinforced feelings of resentment and vulnerability among the French-speaking populations of Canada, especially (but not entirely) within Quebec, though other factors also have influenced those political sentiments.[13]

The inclusion of a "double majority" clause within a Senate reform amendment cannot, by itself, compensate for the wider array of constitutional concessions and accommodations that many people within Quebec (separatists and federalists, alike) have sought.[14] But it could serve a useful role in that respect, even if only symbolically. It could reinforce the sense of permanent commitment concerning the official languages of Canada that the Constitution Act of 1982 has enshrined. Conceivably, it could have an unintended consequence when dealing with languages other than French and English (especially the languages of Canada's First Nations)[15] but, arguably, its value in terms of promoting political unity within Canada would outweigh any restrictions that it might present within an unforeseen future circumstance. Furthermore, and again, the "double majority" as part of Senate reform could facilitate the support of Canadians for whom the bilingual character of the country is a defining feature, as well as address the concerns of Quebec and other French-speaking Canadians.

CONFIRMATION OF EXECUTIVE NOMINATIONS

The capacity of the prime minister to appoint government officials without the express consent of Parliament (especially through the use of Orders in Council) is a powerful one. It is one of the features that have been associated with the perception of the Canadian prime minister becoming increasingly "presidential" in style and authority.[16] Although that characterization might be misplaced (considering the evolution of parliamentary leadership), concerns about that sort of concentration of authority (especially given strong party discipline within the Canadian system)[17] suggest a potential role for Canadian Senators in this sort of reform.

Powers of the Senate in Relation to Nominations

IV. 18. *(11) Any nominee of an executive agency that has national regulatory responsibility and authority over the economic, diplomatic, and cultural policies of Canada may be subject to review by the Senate, prior to final confirmation of those appointments. Any such review must be initiated by the Speaker of the Senate (in accordance with the internal rules of that House) within 20 days following the issuing of the relevant Order in Council or other official announcement of that nomination and the proceedings may not extend beyond 40 days following the official announcement of that nomination. The Senate may, upon its own discretion, make non-binding recommendations relating to the qualifications and appropriateness of these nominees. Prior to the initiation and conclusion of a Senate review, nominees may serve in that nominated position in an acting capacity, subject to immediate change upon the issuing of a recommendation, the expiration of 20 days without the initiation of a Senate review, or, in the event that a review is initiated, the conclusion of the 40-day period following the official announcement of that nomination.*

Some reform proposals have recommended that the Senate of Canada should have outright authority to confirm or reject executive nominees in certain categories.[18] Such authority almost certainly could not be delegated through non-constitutional means. Nonetheless, this activity is consistent with a general public oversight that is associated with a liaison role that often has been served by second chambers.[19] Nonetheless, this model suggests that this sort of role should not result in the Senate having an outright veto over actions of the government. It could, however, suggest conditions under which a government can experience public pressure. Should the Senate of Canada recommend against the appointment of a controversial nominee under such an arrangement, it would not prevent an executive appointment but it could result in final approval becoming politically untenable. Thus, the Senate could exercise influence without outright authority. Furthermore, the Senate could opt not to initiate a review, thus tacitly approving or acquiescing in that nomination.

The delegation of this sort of authority to an upper house in relation to executive nominations is not unique. It exists, for example, within the U.S. Senate and it has been used with conspicuous (and, arguably, obstructing) effect.[20] Of course, that body is not part of a system of parliamentary democracy. In this instance, the power to review and confirm appointments is derived from republican principles of government, stretching back to Aristotle's admonitions concerning the need for a "mixed government" to avoid a concentration of power.[21] That approach is especially pertinent to the influence of republican principles as developed within the modern period.

However, the extent this role for the Senate of Canada ought to assume within the non-republican Canadian system of parliamentary democracy is debatable. It is appropriate, therefore, to consider the implication of this sort of reform from that theoretical perspective, especially in contrast to more traditional parliamentary understandings. Its most important value may reside in the theoretical role of the upper house as a body of advice and oversight that does not interfere with the mandate of a government. Thus this particular reform proposal emphasizes the non-binding nature of the recommendation and the fact that appointees may serve in an acting capacity while the Senate investigates and evaluates the nomination during a reasonable time period. If there is a valid objection to a particular nominee, pressure from the political system as a whole (as well as the spirit of constitutional convention relating to the functioning of the parliamentary system as a whole) ought to be sufficient to elicit an appropriate response.

Confirmation Authority and the Role of the Ombudsman

The political role of the ombudsman (the etymology of the word is derived from the Old Norse word *umboðsmaðr*, meaning "representative" and it does not refer to a particular gender, though some applications of it prefer to use "ombudsperson") is both relatively recent and ancient and its experience might offer an additional function for a reformed Senate of Canada that advances this goal of diversity and a pluralist democracy. In the modern sense, it has been traced to 19th-century Sweden (though its political presence extends over many centuries[22]) and it offers a function that enhances political access beyond the role of legislative representatives. In the Western tradition, this sort of role also could be associated with the office of Tribune within the ancient Roman Republic. That official, acting on behalf of the Plebian class of Roman citizens, would monitor the proceedings of the Roman Senate as well as the activities of municipal officials (including the supreme executive officers who served as Consuls) and could bring charges against corrupt officials or other powerful persons who were deemed to be abusing their authority or, otherwise, violating the principles of republican government.[23]

But it was the parliamentary expression of this role that came to define it in its modern sense and application. The Swedish Parliamentary Ombudsman was an outcome of the Instrument of Government of 1809, which established a clear distinction in terms of the accountability of government ministers. It succeeded the earlier Office of the Supreme Ombudsman, established during the early 18th century as an instrument of royal enforcement to ensure that administrators and jurists acting on behalf of the king would be performing their roles, properly. Otherwise, the Supreme Ombudsman could prosecute these officials on behalf of the monarch.[24] Thus the role of the Ombudsman became intricately associated with upholding the will of Parliament on behalf of the nation, including in terms of its central role in establishing legitimate government and an expression of an increasingly democratic sovereign will. It also has provided a forum for expressing the interests of citizens who are members of important but smaller groups that might, otherwise, be ignored by elected representatives.[25]

That office and its functions have relevance for Canada. Given the liaison functions that the Senate of Canada traditionally has exercised,[26] the promotion of that function within that body could provide the sort of forum that it has served within other political systems. The Swedish experience might be related to the Canadian context in a general way. Its expression could have very positive implications for promoting a wider consensus of support for the function of the governmental system in general as well as the parliamentary system through a process of indirect representation and oversight on the part of Senators. In its confirmation authority (even if that authority is, ultimately, only advisory), the Senate can provide the sort of broader input that historically has been a concern of public trust in the political system.[27] Although presented as part of this overall hypothetical constitutional amendment, this sort of proposal easily could be advanced through non-constitutional and, even, informal avenues.

SUMMONS, TENURE, AND THE INTERNAL PROCEDURES OF THE SENATE

The qualifications for a Canadian Senator are a product of the historical context in which that institution was created. In the spirit of the unentrenched parts of the Canadian constitutional tradition, it has been possible to develop those requirements in relation to the evolution of Canadian society. Nonetheless, as part of a broader model of idealized reforms, it would seem to be advisable to engage in a certain amount of practical institutional "housekeeping" (the Constitution Act of 1965 demonstrates that this sort of constitutional change could be feasibly enacted, unilaterally, by the federal government) in this area as well, which also offers potential insight into the implications of wider constitutional reform of the Senate.

Qualifications of Senator

23. The Qualifications of a Senator shall be as follows:

(1) He shall be of the full age of Thirty Years:

(2) He shall be either a natural-born Subject of the Queen, or a Subject of the Queen naturalized by an Act of ~~the Parliament of Great Britain, or of the Parliament of the United Kingdom of Great Britain and Ireland, or of the Legislature~~

of One of the Provinces of Upper Canada, Lower Canada, Canada, Nova Scotia, or New Brunswick, before the Union, or of the Parliament of Canada after the Union:

(3) He shall be legally or equitably seised as of Freehold for his own Use and Benefit of Lands or Tenements held in Free and Common Socage, or seised or possessed for his own Use and Benefit of Lands or Tenements held in Franc-alleu or in Roture, within the Province for which he is appointed, of the Value of Four thousand Dollars, over and above all Rents, Dues, Debts, Charges, Mortgages, and Incumbrances due or payable out of or charged on or affecting the same:

(4) His Real and Personal Property shall be together worth Four thousand Dollars over and above his Debts and Liabilities:

(5) He shall be resident in the Province for which he is appointed:

(6) In the Case of Quebec he shall have his Real Property Qualification in the Electoral Division for which he is appointed, or shall be resident in that Division.

When Sr. Peggy Butts was recognized for her lifetime service as a religious leader and educator with an appointment to the Senate of Canada, she was initially unable to serve because of her religious vow of poverty as a nun. It was only after her order deeded a parcel of property to her for that purpose that she was able to accept that appointment. While the property qualification in its stated terms (as opposed to its real terms through the conversion of 1867 Canadian dollars to today's equivalent value) no longer appears to be onerous, this anecdote highlights the conflict between the traditional role of the upper house in terms of representing a particular socio-economic status and the more evolved ideal of the upper house.[28] In fact, the Supreme Court of Canada, in the Senate Reference case, specified that this sort of constitutional change is, indeed, one area that the federal government could perform, unilaterally, except in the case of Quebec.[29]

The New Democratic Party has, historically, opposed property qualifications because of its financially based restriction on legislative participation as well as its implied comment on class status within Canada. It also has opposed the Senate in general—in part because its role in representing the provinces has been perceived to be an impediment to effective national policies that advance greater economic equality.[30] The House of Lords has been traditionally associated with the British class system and, as a result, a good deal of opposition to that body has been based upon lingering reactions to that symbolic impression, despite the fact that life peers, in particular, no longer reflect that historic role of this chamber as a protector of aristocratic (especially agrarian) interests.[31] The elimination of all references to property qualifications would not only be helpful in that respect but also would be consistent with liberal democratic principles in general. It may appear to be an anachronism but it contributes to a wider negative perception and a broad constitutional effort to reform the Senate could take advantage of that process to address this issue as well.

Other aspects of the internal procedures of the Senate also can be addressed through this model. In some cases, these alternations would reflect other facets of the overall reform, such as the idealized concept of constitutionally sanctioning an indefinite number of members. In other cases, the formal rules that already exist could be maintained without affecting the spirit or letter of this sort of reform.

> Summons of Senator
>
> 24. The Governor General shall from Time to Time, in the Queen's Name, by Instrument under the Great Seal of Canada, summon qualified Persons to the Senate; and, subject to the Provisions of this Act, every Person so summoned shall become and be a Member of the Senate and a Senator.
>
> Addition of Senators in certain cases
>
> 26. ~~If at any Time on the Recommendation of the Governor General the Queen thinks fit to direct that Four or Eight Members be added to the Senate, the Governor General may by Summons to Four or Eight qualified Persons (as the Case may be), representing equally the Four Divisions of Canada, add to the Senate accordingly.~~
>
> Reduction of Senate to normal Number
>
> 27. ~~In case of such Addition being at any Time made, the Governor General shall not summon any Person to the Senate, except on a further like Direction by the Queen on the like Recommendation, to represent one of the Four Divisions until such Division is represented by Twenty-four Senators and no more.~~
>
> ~~Maximum Number of Senators~~
>
> 28. ~~The Number of Senators shall not at any Time exceed One Hundred and thirteen.~~
>
> Tenure of Place in Senate
>
> 29. ~~(1) Subject to subsection (2),~~ a Senator shall, subject to the provisions of this Act, hold his place in the Senate for life.
>
> ~~Retirement upon attaining age of seventy-five years~~
>
> ~~(2) A Senator who is summoned to the Senate after the coming into force of this subsection shall, subject to this Act, hold his place in the Senate until he attains the age of seventy-five years.~~
>
> Resignation of Place in Senate
>
> 30. A Senator may by Writing under his Hand addressed to the Governor General resign his Place in the Senate, and thereupon the same shall be vacant.
>
> Disqualification of Senators
>
> 31. The Place of a Senator shall become vacant in any of the following Cases:
>
> (1) If for Two consecutive Sessions of the Parliament he fails to give his Attendance in the Senate:
>
> (2) If he takes an Oath or makes a Declaration or Acknowledgment of Allegiance, Obedience, or Adherence to a Foreign Power, or does an Act whereby he

becomes a Subject or Citizen, or entitled to the Rights or Privileges of a Subject or Citizen, of a Foreign Power:

~~(3) If he is adjudged Bankrupt or Insolvent, or applies for the Benefit of any Law relating to Insolvent Debtors, or becomes a public Defaulter~~:

(4) If he is attainted of Treason or convicted of Felony or of any infamous Crime:

(5) If he ceases to be qualified in respect of Property or of Residence; provided, that a Senator shall not be deemed to have ceased to be qualified in respect of Residence by reason only of his residing at the Seat of the Government of Canada while holding an Office under that Government requiring his Presence there.

Summons on Vacancy in Senate

32. When a Vacancy happens in the Senate by Resignation, Death, or otherwise, the Governor General shall by Summons to a fit and qualified Person fill the Vacancy.

Questions as to Qualifications and Vacancies in Senate

33. If any Question arises respecting the Qualification of a Senator or a Vacancy in the Senate the same shall be heard and determined by the Senate.

Appointment of Speaker of Senate

34. The Governor General may from Time to Time, by Instrument under the Great Seal of Canada, appoint a Senator to be Speaker of the Senate, and may remove him and appoint another in his Stead.

Quorum of Senate

35. Until the Parliament of Canada otherwise provides, the Presence of at least Fifteen Senators, including the Speaker, shall be necessary to constitute a Meeting of the Senate for the Exercise of its Powers.

Although it is presented as part of a broader hypothetical constitutional amendment, many of these alterations to internal procedures of the chamber (such as the quorum and Speaker), can be related to the unexpressed constitutional provisions—ones that are derived from the unentrenched principles of the parliamentary process. It is possible that these alterations could be included within an informal approach to Senate reform. This non-constitutional approach is addressed within the following chapter but certain preliminary considerations also ought to be broached at this point in relation to that option.

The issue of partisanship is relevant to this non-constitutional route. A parliamentary chamber that is organized along partisan lines includes assigned leaders from the government and opposition parties as well as party whips and spokespersons for various portfolios, including both government and "shadow" government representatives. A less highly partisan chamber (such as Justin Trudeau suggested with his removal of Liberal Senators from his party's parliamentary caucus, though that unilateral move was not reciprocated by other parliamentary parties and it applied to Senators who had, previously, been accustomed to serving in a formally partisan capacity[32]) has different needs, especially in terms procedural efficiency and fairness. A good example of this latter sort of organization is the Cross Benches of the House of Lords. That section of the second chamber could be guided by a Convener. Whips are not necessary as there is no party discipline to be enforced. Instead, the Convener is selected upon the basis of other factors, including a reputation for even-handed care of the procedural interests of the other members. That person facilitates the participation of members who wish to contribute to various aspects of the parliamentary process, including motions, debates, committee assignments, and similar matters.[33] The position of Chairman of Committees within the House of Lords performs a similar non-partisan role.[34]

The British upper chamber does not extend automatic membership within the respective party caucus for members who declare a particular party affiliation. Instead, that membership is extended only to peers who have specific functions within the upper chamber, including government and opposition leaders of that house and any government ministers or shadow cabinet members who happen to belong to it instead of the House of Commons.[35] That more limited party presence contributes to a less divisive environment among peers in general. That fact contributes to the role of the Lord Speaker (prior to 2006, a role performed by the Lord High Chancellor) as far less active in supervising the proceedings of that house, especially in comparison with the Speaker of the House of Commons. Instead, the members of the House of Lords are far more self-governing in their behavior, which often contributes to a more constructive atmosphere in its parliamentary business.[36]

These sorts of features are a product of the institutional culture of the British upper house.[37] Advancing a similar institutional culture for the Senate of Canada is not a simple matter but, arguably, it can be achieved, given their shared cultural, political, and parliamentary history. Furthermore, it offers a potentially less strenuous path toward reform than constitutional amendment presents within the Canadian political system. That path requires political will and collaboration, which is required for any meaningful reform effort. This option, though, may provide a more positive spirit for that purpose.

A MODEST INTERPRETATION OF THE ROLE OF THE CANADIAN UPPER HOUSE

The specific proposals of this chapter emphasize both a spirit of cooperation and a sense of the more modest role that a second chamber theoretically should perform as part of a parliamentary system. Therefore, it also reemphasizes a key consideration in response to the principles of parliamentary democracy. The definition of "effective" is not, necessarily, tied to legislative power, especially in relation to the government. But it can be tied to a capacity to perform functions that the lower house is either unable or disinclined to perform.

The "double majority" is an indicator of that potential role. As a guarantor of compromise over a politically and constitutionally difficult theme, the Senate can serve as a means of diminishing potential ill will and controversy. While not necessarily a non-partisan role, it can be perceived as a fair one that ensures that one of Canada's most significant controversies is not altered or addressed in an imprudent manner. Likewise, the advice provided by an oversight role relating to executive nominations offers a potentially stabilizing role for the Canadian upper house, especially in terms of improving public awareness.

The chamber of "sober second thought" can be especially useful when performing these functions. A reformed Senate of Canada need not be a competitor with the House of Commons in order to perform a truly complementary or supplementary role within Parliament. Yet, arguably, the Senate already operates that way, especially in its performance in amending and improving (especially technically) the legislation that is sent to it from the lower house.[38] That interpretation deserves additional consideration, especially within the context of reform, or restraint from reform, in relation to the Canadian parliamentary upper house.

NOTES

1. Rein Taagepera and Matthew Soberg, *Seats and Votes: The Effects and Determinants of Electoral Systems* (New Haven, CT: Yale University Press, 1989, pp. 273–275.

2. Charlottetown Proposal, p. 5.

3. José Woehrling, "La Reconnaissance du Québec comme société distincte et la dualité linguistique du Canada: Conséquences juridiques et constitutionnelles," *Analyse de Poliiques* vol. 14 (septembre 1988), pp. S43–S62.

4. Fred Anderson, *Crucible of War: The Seven Years' War and the Fate of Empire in British North America, 1754–1756* (New York: Vintage Books, 2000), pp. 410–456; Laurent Veyssière, *La Nouvelle-France en heritage* (Paris: Armand Colin, 2013), pp. 298–308.

5. Ged Martin, *The Durham Report and British Policy: A Critical Essay* (Cambridge: Cambridge University Press, 2008), pp. 29–41.

6. Desmond Morton, *A Short History of Canada* (Toronto: McClelland and Stewart, 2006), pp. 88–98.

7. Barry L. Strayer, *Canada's Constitutional Revolution* (Edmonton: University of Alberta Press, 2013), pp. 279–281.

8. Julie Auger, "Le Français au Québec à l'aube de vingt et unième siècle," *French Review*, vol. 77, no. 1 (octobre 2003), pp. 88–93.

9. Sylvia Bashevkin, *True Patriot Love: The Politics of Canadian Nationalism* (Oxford: Oxford University Press, 1991), pp. 5–12.

10. Beaudoin-Dobie Report, pp. 52–55; Government of Canada, *Shaping Canada's Future—Together* (Ottawa: Queen's Printer, 1991); Jean-Luc Pepin and John Roberts, *Report on the Task Force on Canadian Unity* (Ottawa: Queen's Printer, 1979).

11. Léon Dion, "The Mystery of Quebec," *Daedalus*, vol. 117, no. 4 (Fall 1988), pp. 286–297.

12. Michel Plourde, *La Politique linguistique du Québec, 1977–1987* (Québec: Institut Québécois du Recherche sur la culture, 1988), pp. 2–23; Hudson Meadwell, "The Politics of Nationalism in Quebec," *World Politics*, vol. 45, no. 2 (January 1993), pp. 203–241.

13. Paul Howe, "Rationality and Sovereignty Support in Quebec," *Canadian Journal of Political Science*, vol. 31, no. 1 (March 1998), pp. 31–59.

14. Léon Dion, *Le Duel constitutionnel Québec-Canada* (Montréal: Boréal, 1995), pp. 1–30.

15. Joseph Errington, "Getting Language Rights: The Rhetorics of Language Endangerment and Loss," *American Anthropologist*, vol. 105, no. 4 (December 2003), pp. 727–728.

16. Stephen Azzi and Norman Hillmer, "Evaluating Prime Ministerial Performance: The Canadian Experience," in *Understanding Prime Ministerial Performance: Comparative Perspectives*, Paul Strangio, Paul 'T Hart, and James Walter, eds. (Oxford: Oxford University Press, 2013), pp. 243–253.

17. Donald J. Savoie, "The Rise of Court Government in Canada," *Canadian Journal of Political Science*, vol. 32, no. 4 (December 1999), pp. 658–660.

18. Donald V. Smiley and Ronald L. Watts, *Intrastate Federalism in Canada* (Toronto: University of Toronto Press, 1985), pp. 89–91; Molgat-Cosgrove Report, p. 34.

19. L. C. Reif, *The Ombudsman, Good Governance, and the International Human Rights System* (Leiden, The Netherlands: Martin Nijhoff, 2004), pp. 4–5.

20. William MacKay and Charles W. Johnson, *Parliament and Congress: Representation and Scrutiny in the Twenty-First Century* (Oxford: Oxford University Press, 2010), pp. 150–153.

21. Aristotle, *Politics*, Book 4, pt. XIV; Philip Petit, *Republicanism: A Theory of Freedom and Government* (Oxford: Oxford University Press, 1997), pp. 171–205.

22. Gabriele Kucsko-Stadlmayer, *European Ombudsman-Institutions: A Comparative Legal Analysis Regarding the Multifaceted Realisation of an Idea* (New York: SpringerWien, 2008), pp. 409–417; L. C. Reif, *The Ombudsman, Good Governance, and the International Human Rights System* (Leiden, The Netherlands: Martin Nijhoff, 2004), pp. 4–5; H. Yueh-Chin, "Role and Responsibility of the Control Yuan," in *The Ombudsman Concept*, L. C. Reif, ed. (Edmonton: International Obudsman Institute, 1995), p. 23.

23. Christopher S. Mackay, *Ancient Rome: A Military and Political History* (Cambridge: Cambridge University Press, 2007), pp. 35–36, 131.

24. International Ombudsman Institute, *Australasia and Pacific Ombudsman Institutions: Mandates, Competences, and Good Practices* (New York: Springer, 2013), pp. 3–4.

25. James T. Ziegenfuss, Jr. and Patricia O'Rourke, *The Ombudsman Handbook: Designing and Managing an Effective Problem-Solving Program* (Jefferson, NC: McFarland, 2010), pp. 29–46.

26. Parliament of Canada, "On the Job with a Senator," About Parliament, http://www.parl.gc.ca/ About/Parliament/OnTheJobSenate/index-e.asp

27. Harold D. Clarke, Allan Kornberg, and Marianne C. Stewart, "Parliament and Political Support in Canada," *American Political Science Review*, vol. 78, no. 2 (June 1984), pp. 453–458; Kenneth Kernaghan, "Power, Parliament, and Public Servants in Canada," *Canadian Public Policy*, vol. 5, no. 3 (Summer 1979), pp. 393–395.

28. CBC Archives, "Canada's Upper House: Do We Need the Senate?" http://web.archive.org/web/20071016103302/http://www.cbc.ca/newsinreview/apr98/senate/consitut.htm

29. *In re Reform of the Senate*, 2014 SCC 32, paras. 84–94.

30. David E. Smith, *The Canadian Senate in Bicameral Perspective* (Toronto: University of Toronto Press, 2003), p. 58.

31. Dell G. Hitchner, "The Labour Government and the House of Lords," *Western Political Quarterly*, vol. 1, no. 4 (December 1948), pp. 426, 427–428.

32. James Cudmore, "Justin Trudeau Removes Senators from Liberal Caucus," CBC News-Politics, January 29, 2014, http://www.cbc.ca/news/politics/justin-trudeau-removes-senators-from-liberal-caucus-1.2515273

33. Meg Russell, *The Contemporary House of Lords: Westminster Bicameralism Revived* (Oxford: Oxford University Press, 2013), pp. 69–70.

34. J. C. Sainty, *The Origins of the Office of Chairman of Committees in the House of Lords* (London: House of Lords Records Office, 1974).

35. Russell, pp. 96–98.

36. Ibid., pp. 209–223.

37. Vernon Bogdanor, *The New British Constitution* (Portland, OR: Hart, 2009), pp. 150–153.

38. Paul G. Thomas, "Comparing the Lawmaking Roles of the Senate and the House of Commons," in *Protecting Canadian Democracy: The Senate You Never Knew*, Serge Joyal, ed. (Montreal and Kingston, ON: McGill-Queen's University Press, 2003), pp. 189–228.

Part III

OBSERVATIONS AND NON-CONSTITUTIONAL REFORM

Chapter 10

Scandal and its Constitutional Aftermath

The assumption that some sort of reform to the Senate of Canada is necessary has become pervasive. Like all assumptions, though, it could benefit from further and more critical scrutiny. The Senate appears to be criticized as much for the things it does not do as for the things that it does. It also appears to be criticized, sometimes, for not solving a variety of pervasive problems, frustrations, and slights that are reflected within the wider Canadian political system.

Therefore, when the institution is challenged by scandalous incident or subject to a concerted effort to amend or abolish it, attention returns to those criticisms. That negative attention was particularly acute as a result of an episode that came to the public attention beginning in 2012. In partial response to that episode, an effort to impose a relatively rapid package of reforms was initiated, resulting in a reference case brought by the government before the Supreme Court of Canada. While both of these events might, in retrospect, appear to have been much less significant than enthusiastic critics of the Senate might have contended, they reinforced many of the themes surrounding Senate reform, including, perhaps ironically, the theoretical groundings that suggest a different approach toward that reform than many of its traditional critics might prefer.

SCANDAL

In 2012, investigations were initiated against four Senators, all involving allegations of improprieties concerning reimbursement of their expenses. Three of these Senators had been relatively recent appointments of the government of Prime Minister Stephen Harper and were members of the caucus of the

Conservative Party, while the remaining Senator was a Liberal who had been appointed in 2003. The subsequent investigations and actions taken in these cases attracted a great deal of public notice and prompted additional debate concerning the Senate and its potential reform.[1]

Senators are required to have an official residence in the province that they represent through their appointment. If that residence is their primary one and it is more than 100 kilometers from Ottawa, they are permitted to claim reimbursement for expenses related to it. The definition of certain terms, such as "primary" residence, as well as the amount of time Senators are expected to spend at that domicile in order to qualify for this reimbursement, had been found to be ambiguous.[2] Nonetheless, a recognized abuse of the reimbursement system ultimately had been observed relating to several Senators and four of them were subject to investigation and audit with three of them eventually facing criminal charges for fraud and a different combination of three of them being suspended from the Canadian upper house as a result.[3]

Senator Mac Harb had been a Member of Parliament and a civic official in Ottawa before being appointed to the Senate as a member of the Liberal caucus. He had claimed reimbursement for housing expenses for a home that he had purchased in Pembroke, Ontario (just beyond 100 kilometers from Ottawa), soon after his appointment as a Senator from Ontario. He previously had lived in Ottawa and the 2012 investigation alleged that he rarely, if ever, visited his Pembroke residence but continued to reside, primarily, in Ottawa, thus improperly receiving reimbursement for the residence that he maintained in Ottawa.[4] After initially disputing that he had not committed any impropriety, he repaid $Can 231,649.07 in expenses in 2013 and retired from the Senate, being eligible to claim lifetime retirement compensation.[5] In 2014, he was charged with one count of fraud by the Royal Canadian Mounted Police and challenged the charges by pleading not guilty.[6]

Senator Pamela Wallin is a prominent former journalist and diplomat who became a Senator in 2008 as a member of the Conservative caucus. She was found to have received reimbursement for travel expenses that included her claimed primary residence in Saskatchewan, for which province she was appointed. It included travel that occurred directly between Wadena, Saskatchewan and Ottawa and travel that included overnight stops in Toronto (where she owns a condominium) while traveling between Saskatchewan and Ottawa as well as to other destinations.[7] Some of those reimbursed expenses were found to include travel to Guelph, Ontario, where she was serving as Chancellor of the University of Guelph and which was not considered to be the sort of "official government-related business" that normally would qualify for reimbursement.[8] Although she challenged the fairness of the subsequent audit process that determined that she had improperly claimed these expenses, she repaid reimbursements totaling $Can 121,348.00 in 2013.[9]

Senator Patrick Brazeau is a member of the Algonquin nation who became active in the politics of Canadian indigenous peoples, ultimately rising to become Chief of the Congress of Aboriginal Peoples, leading a well-publicized campaign to amend section 67 of the Human Rights Act that allowed communal features of the Indian Act to supersede individual human rights claims for aboriginal people in Canada. He subsequently was appointed for Quebec as a member of the Conservative caucus and the youngest member of the Senate, at age 41, in 2008, eventually resigning as Chief following criticism for drawing two simultaneous public salaries.[10] Additionally (though unrelated to the expenses investigation), he has faced charges of sexual assault and cocaine possession (on which he eventually was granted an unconditional discharge by the court),[11] as well as accusations of general alcohol abuse, violent behavior, and inappropriate behavior.[12] His claims for expenses regarding his home near Ottawa were based upon claiming primary residence in a house in Maniwaki, Quebec that is owned by his father. Following an investigation and audit, he was ordered by the Senate to repay $Can 48,745.00 in reimbursements, though it was established that he had lived at least part of the time covered by the payment of expense in Maniwaki, which has been recovered through salary garnishing.[13] In 2014, he was charged with fraud to which he pleaded not guilty.[14]

Senator Mike Duffy was a prominent television journalist who was appointed for Prince Edward Island and became a member of the Conservative caucus. He was investigated for improper expense claims when it was alleged that he seldom lived in, or even visited, the house he maintains in Cavendish, Prince Edward Island and claimed as a primary residence. Although he disputed the allegations and asserted that his reimbursements were proper under Senate rules, he nonetheless paid back $Can 90,172.00 in 2013.[15] As the investigation into improprieties related to reimbursements continued, additional allegations were made that a representative from the Prime Minister's Office, Chief of Staff Nigel Wright, had provided Senator Duffy with a personal check to cover that payment upon the alleged basis of a letter of understanding drafted by Benjamin Perrin, Special Adviser and Legal Counsel to the Prime Minister[16]—that lat.ter claim was, later, dropped, as was a criminal investigation concerning Nigel Wright.[17] Senator Duffy also claimed that he had been prompted by the Prime Minister's Office to accept the check as part of a plan to bring an end to the controversy—a charge that was strongly denied and became part of Duffy's subsequent trial for fraud, breach of trust, and bribery.[18]

All three Conservative Senators subsequently left that party´s caucus, either voluntarily or through expulsion. The Senate Standing Committee on Internal Economy, Budgets, and Administration ultimately determined that all four of the accused Senators had obtained reimbursements for which they were not entitled.[19] The full Senate voted to suspend the three Senators who remained members of that chamber without pay (but while retaining certain benefits, such as health insurance) in November 2013 for the duration of that parliament.[20] Liberal Senators protested that the vote to suspend had been designed, primarily, to shelter the Conservative Party from the political repercussions of the scandals and, consequently, its members largely refused to support the suspension motions.[21]

The Auditor General filed a report in June 2015 that released the results of a comprehensive audit that the Senate had requested to determine the extent to which individual Senators may have used public funds for personal or private purposes. The Auditor General found that oversight and transparency in Senate rules and procedures in this area were very inadequate and that 30 Senators had made inappropriate claims for funds and recommended that nine of them (mostly concerning reimbursements regarding living expenses while maintaining alleged primary residences outside of Ottawa) be referred to police investigation. Ambiguities relating to travel, residence, and the factors that constitute "primary residence" also were noted.[22]

This scandal attracted a great deal of the attention of the Canadian public during that time.[23] It also elicited a great deal of commentary and criticism concerning the Senate of Canada and prompted increased demands for reform or, even, abolition of that parliamentary chamber.[24] Some of those demands were based upon a belief that these scandals indicated that the Canadian upper house was, by its very nature, irredeemably corrupt as a result of its own institutional nature.[25] Of course, that conclusion is based upon a logical fallacy: after all, members of elected institutions (including the Canadian House of Commons) historically have been investigated for similar accusations of misdeeds yet abolition of those bodies generally has not been suggested as the only solution for that problem.[26] Therefore, the scandal also prompted renewed contemplation among members of that body for internal reforms, especially in terms of clearer rules and better oversight of personal expenses.[27]

A distinction should be made between those aspects of this scandal that may have been isolated to the specific personalities and circumstances and those aspects that can be directly attributed to the characteristics and role of the Canadian upper house as a political institution. For example, a claim that appointment, as opposed to election, of Senators invites the sort of corrupt behavior that may be associated with the activity of political patronage should be closely considered. The general issue of "accountability" also has been raised in that respect.[28] It is reasonable that any reform of the Senate of Canada should consider these themes. Responses to those themes, however, may be more relevantly a reflection of general politics than the current or potential future institutional features of that body.

SOURCES OF CORRUPTION

The appearance of scandal within a political institution can, sometimes, reveal deep and profound flaws that can be remedied only through extensive reconstruction or abolition of that body. Often, though, the fault lies not in the institution but in the inevitable fallibility of humans, especially when they act in the capacity of "political animals."[29] Any exposure to political power can result in such an outcome and political institutions are, after all, merely a manifestation of politics and the power that accompanies it. As Lord Acton famously observed, "power corrupts and absolute power corrupts, absolutely."[30] Even modest power (such as the Senate of Canada is perceived to exercise) can be noted as being potentially subject to that maxim.

A recommendation for reform of any institution ideally ought to be directed by the belief that it can be improved in order to achieve a greater good, rather than destroyed in order to eliminate a perceived evil. Therefore, the appropriate neo-institutional question that must be addressed is whether the problem lies within the institution, itself, or in other factors, such as the culture that guides its behavior or the persons who become its members. The actual answer seldom is as simple as an act of retributive denunciation.

Political corruption can be found within all systems of government. It is more pervasive within non-liberal democratic states (especially dictatorships) but it exists anywhere that power and its potential for abuse also exist. One response toward political corruption is a belief that elected office is less vulnerable to corrupt practices because of the presence of electoral accountability: a corrupt official may be recalled at the next election or, depending upon the specific rules of the system, impeached or otherwise removed from office. Closely tied to this belief is the conviction that appointed political positions may be subject to the temptation of patronage in exchange for direct compensation (such as a pay-off), or in order to place political loyalists in a position to support the political goals of the appointers, or as a reward for political services. These reasons often have convinced many observers (though often uncritically) that political positions should, generally, all be subject to the electoral mandate, including the requirement for reelection.

> Key to these different outcomes was the sequence by which different countries reformed their bureaucracies relative to the moment they opened up their political systems to wider democratic contestation. Those countries that created strong bureaucracies while they were still authoritarian, like Prussia, created enduring autonomous institutions that survived subsequent changes of regime into the present. On the other hand, countries that democratized before a strong state was in place, such as the United States, Greece, and Italy, created clientelistic systems that then had to be reformed. The United States succeeded in this; Greece did not, and Italy was only partially successful.[31]

The U.K. parliamentary expenses scandal of 2009 offers an excellent example of the applicability of this sort of corruption among both elected and non-elected parliamentary officials. It began with a request, under that country's Freedom of Information Act, for information relating to the expenses of Members of Parliament.[32] After considerable attempts to oppose the fulfillment of that request, the House of Commons released the information on expenses but not after the documents were released to, and published by, a British newspaper.[33]

The result was a revelation of alleged abuses of reimbursements for housing expenses when primary residences were outside of London and other travel expense improprieties that were remarkably similar to the Canadian scandal. Ultimately, criminal charges were brought against six elected Members of Parliament and two members of the House of Lords.[34] Beyond the criminal charges, the scandal involved scores of MPs but only three additional peers, resulting in resignations of cabinet ministers as well as the Speaker of the House of Commons.[35] The scandal damaged the political standing of the governing Labour Party and prompted large numbers of independent candidacies for the next general election (as well as demands for parliamentary reform) yet ultimately did not appear to have nearly as strong of an effect upon the prospects of these elected parliamentarians during the next general election as initially was predicted.[36]

Unlike the British scandal, the Canadian example did not involve Members of Parliament. Although claims of lack of electoral accountability were alleged as underlying reasons for this result, other causes (derived from a broader understanding of the nature of political corruption) should be addressed. Indeed, the fact that the British scandal did not appear to have as strong as an electoral consequence as initially projected suggests that the electoral approach toward Canadian Senate reform also might not have this intended effect in terms of promoting greater accountability in response to expense and other potential scandals. This phenomenon has been empirically noted in terms of other democratic parliamentary systems and tends to undermine the assumption that electoral accountability provides a strong safeguard against corruption, scandal, and other forms of political misbehavior among elected parliamentarians and other officials, especially when other considerations (such as the performance of the economy) prove to be more directly relevant to voters.[37]

Nonetheless, it remains fair to note that the Canadian expenses scandal did not involve elected Members of Parliament. The reasons for this discrepancy merit further speculation. Reasons that this sort of scandal occurred among these particular Canadian non-elected parliamentary officials could, hypothetically, be the result of:

1. The relative absence of party discipline that otherwise would be imposed upon elected representatives;
2. The subsequent lack of authority and oversight upon the activities of elected representatives wielded by parliamentary officers such as Party Whips;
3. A general lack of effective bureaucratic oversight of general expense processes as a result of less intense partisanship, leading to lax internal safeguards;
4. Lack of structure and oversight regarding the appointment process for these officials, resulting in the selection of more potentially corrupt officials.

The Senate has been notorious for its patronage appointments, thus adding credence to reform proposals that would seek to promote elections or merit-based nomination systems in its place. Ironically, appointments of persons such as Patrick Brazeau also may have been motivated by a desire to enhance the diversity of the chamber (though with someone who would be deemed to be reliably partisan in a manner that may not be easy to find among members of a particular group)[38] while the appointment of a prominent celebrity journalist such as Mike Duffy might have been intended to reassure the public with a person regarded as "trustworthy" who, simultaneously, could effectively communicate a particular party message.[39]

However, despite the presence of "cronyism" within this process (as Stephen Harper once charged),[40] the belief that elections, themselves, eliminate internal political favoritism has not been truly scrutinized. There is no evidence that elected Senators would have been less prone to this sort of scandal than appointed ones. Indeed, electoral accountability did not serve as an effective check on this sort of behavior among elected British parliamentarians.[41] Furthermore, in terms of the British scandal, the political and electoral consequences for many of the Members of Parliament who were involved were not nearly as severe as predicted.[42] The powers of the Senate also appear to be irrelevant to this outcome. Cronyism can be as pervasive to the selection process for party nominations to electoral districts as they can be to appointments to non-elected political offices. Most of the scholarly literature on political corruption addresses systemic problems associated with governments, rather than the actions of specific officials within particular political bodies.[43] Institutional culture typically is shaped by practice, rather than structure.[44] Corrupt governments can, and do, have strong democratic features such as regular elections, extensive bureaucracies, and accountability and, yet, they can become and remain overwhelmingly corrupt.[45] In this case, individual Senators may have taken advantage of vague rules that cost Canadian taxpayers as much as $Can 1,000,000.00 (a not inconsiderable sum)—a sum that was determined after spending nearly $Can 23,000,000.00 (a significantly even more considerable sum) to uncover and investigate those expenses.[46]

Nonetheless, it is appropriate to contemplate specific lessons that may be learned from the episode of the Canadian Senate expenses scandal. They may provide direction in terms of reform proposals that could seek to avoid its repetition, especially in terms of internal reforms regarding the supervision of compensation and expenses as well as the vetting process for recommending appointments to that body. Potential constitutional amendments also could be advanced to clarify issues such as the meaning of "residency" in relation to representation that could be as relevant for MPs from districts outside Ottawa as they are for Senators who are appointed to "represent" the various regions and provinces of Canada.[47]

FORMAL CONSTITUTIONAL AMENDMENT: THE SENATE REFERENCE CASE

An immediate consequence of the Senate expense scandal was to prompt further aggressive activity in favor of advancing Senate reform. The Harper government had argued, long before the Senate expenses scandal, that it could proceed with unilateral reform of the Senate by the federal government and proposed ways that it could be achieved.[48] That eventual attempt ultimately resulted in a definitive statement by the Supreme Court of Canada regarding the constitutional obstacles (beyond the conventional political ones) that would need to be overcome before substantive changes to the constitutional structure of the Senate of Canada could become a reality.

The Harper Government specifically proposed that certain reforms, such as "consultative elections" (in which Senatorial elections within provinces would be deemed to provide, technically, "advice" on nomination to the Prime Minister), as well as defined terms and term limits for Senators could be enacted through simple federal legislation rather than requiring a constitutional amendment. A few of these sorts of "elections" had, already, occurred, as detailed within chapter 7. The basis for this claim for unilateral reforms in these areas was that they would alter only the internal mechanisms of the Senate. For example, the government argued that appointments of Senators following consultative elections would not, fundamentally, revise the Senate's constitutional structure because the Governor-General would continue to appoint Senators, though through the indirect advice of provincial voters.[49] The government also inquired into the possibility of outright abolition of the Senate, developing an argument for unilateral constitutional change by the federal government in that area as well, though it eventually would choose not to pursue it, politically.[50] Following strenuous objections from some provinces to this sort of unilateral action, the government submitted the scheme to the scrutiny of the judicial system through the constitutional device of a reference case.[51]

The federal government wanted to avoid resorting to the complex constitutional amendment process as articulated within the Constitution Act of 1982. The government argued that these reforms merely constituted variations to the powers of that body, consistent with allowances provided within section 42 of the Constitution Act of 1982.[52] But the Supreme Court's 2014 decision on this reference case rejected that line of argument, directly and unambiguously. For example, its unanimous opinion clearly required that any change that would result in *de facto* elimination of the Senate would have to be conducted within the parameters of the constitutional amendment formula that would require provincial, as well as federal, approval.

> Abolition of the Senate is not merely a matter relating to its "powers" or its "members" under s. 42(1)(*b*) and (*c*) of the *Constitution Act, 1982*. This provision captures Senate *reform*, which implies the continued existence of the Senate. Outright abolition falls beyond its scope. To interpret s. 42 as embracing Senate abolition would depart from the ordinary meaning of its language and is not supported by the historical record. The mention of amendments in relation to the powers of the Senate and the number of Senators for each province presupposes the continuing existence of a Senate and makes no room for an indirect abolition of the Senate. Within the scope of s. 42, it is possible to make significant changes to the powers of the Senate and the number of Senators. But it is outside the scope of s. 42 to altogether strip the Senate of its powers and reduce the number of Senators to zero. ... Abolition of the Senate would therefore fundamentally alter our constitutional architecture—by removing the bicameral form of government that gives shape to the *Constitution Act, 1867*—and would amend Part V, which requires the unanimous consent of Parliament and the provinces under s. 41(*e*) of the *Constitution Act, 1982*.[53]

This opinion did not consider the political wisdom of the proposed or potential reforms of that institution that a constitutional amendment might provide.[54] For example, the Supreme Court considered those reforms only from the perspective of the authority of the federal government to act upon them and not upon the basis of their merits—deeming that question to remain one that the political system (ideally through the process of constitutional amendment) and public opinion should answer.[55] The Supreme Court further ruled that almost all such changes as the government contemplated (including basing appointments upon consultative elections) would have a constitutionally central affect upon the Senate and the parliamentary system.

> Introducing a process of consultative elections for the nomination of Senators would change our Constitution´s architecture, by endowing Senators with a popular mandate which is inconsistent with the Senate´s fundamental nature and role as a complementary legislative chamber of sober second thought. The view that the consultative elections proposal would amend the Constitution of Canada is supported by the language of Part V of the *Constitution Act, 1982*. The words employed in Part V are guides to identifying the aspects of our system of government that form part of the protected content of the Constitution. Section 42(1)(b) provides that the general amending procedure (s. 38(1)) applies to constitutional amendments in relation to "the method of selecting Senators." This broad wording includes more than the formal appointment of Senators by the Governor General and covers the implementation of consultative elections. By employing this language, the framers of the *Constitution Act, 1982* extended the constitutional protection provided by the general amending procedure to the entire process by which Senators are "selected." Consequently, the implementation of consultative elections falls within the scope of s. 42(1)(b) and is subject to the general amending procedure, without the provincial right to "opt out." It cannot be achieved under the unilateral federal amending procedure. Section 44 is expressly made subject to s. 42—the categories of amendments captured by s. 42 are removed from the scope of s. 44.[56]

The Supreme Court determined that reforms that would not alter the "fundamental nature" of the Senate could be made, unilaterally, such as changes to the property qualification to determine the eligibility of Senators—though that qualification in relation to Quebec would require the approval of that province because it would affect determinations in reference to the districts for which Quebec Senators would be appointed.[57] But in terms of more profound changes, unilateral action would violate the Constitution, including in terms of its spirit and the ways in which parliamentary upper houses have been intended to fit within the overall political system.

> The framers sought to endow the Senate with independence from the electoral process to which members of the House of Commons were subject, in order to remove Senators from a partisan political arena that required unremitting consideration of short-term political objectives.
>
> Correlatively, the choice of executive appointment for Senators was also intended to ensure that the Senate would be a *complementary* legislative body, rather than a perennial rival of the House of Commons in the legislative process. Appointed Senators would not have a popular mandate—they would not have the expectations and legitimacy that stem from popular election. This would ensure that they would confine themselves to their role as a body mainly conducting legislative review, rather than as a coequal of the House of Commons.[58]

These passages are particularly instructive because they indicate that the justices of the Supreme Court of Canada appear to have grasped the broader purpose and theoretical nature of the parliamentary upper house:

1. The principle that it should not serve as a rival to the legitimacy of the lower house (especially from a democratic perspective);
2. The role that election plays in conferring that legitimacy upon the lower house and the government it supports;
3. The concept of a different constituency that an upper chamber typically is designed to reflect;
4. The specialized functions that can be delegated to an upper house.

Beyond a narrow application of the amending formula of the Constitution Act of 1982, this ruling also identified the constitutional role of the Senate. That identity was not only rooted in Canada's history and political culture but, also, in a distinct institutional purpose that the Westminster model gradually has conferred upon its bicameral manifestations.[59] It also is critical to note that the Supreme Court objected, specifically, to an appointment process that involved elections; the Court did not indicate any objections to the non-electoral advice that a Prime Minister might seek from other political figures (such as provincial premiers, members of prominent organizations or groups, or leaders of other political parties) for recommending appointments to the Governor-General.

An entrenched constitutional system is distinguished not by the written documents that frame it but by the formal process that ratifies it and provides a method for future fundamental changes. The amending formula of the U.S. Constitution is an excellent comparative example. It requires the approval of two-thirds of both legislative chambers of the U.S. Congress (or the approval of a specially assembled constitutional convention) and the approval of three-quarters of the American states, either through their respective state legislatures or through specially convened state conventions. It is a process that has been deliberately designed to be very difficult to navigate, successfully, and those obstacles have resulted in a constitution that has been successfully amended only 27 times (with the first ten of those amendments having been adopted, together) during the first two and a quarter centuries of its existence.[60]

The amending formula stipulated by the Constitution Act of 1982 meets that standard of legal and political rigor. It requires, in most cases, the approval of the Parliament of Canada and the approval of at least seven provincial legislatures, provided that the population of the approving provinces represents at least 50% of the country's population—requiring, as a practical matter, that at least either Ontario or Quebec must be one of the approving provinces. However, a select category of constitutional changes requires a unanimous consent among the federal and provincial governments—including, according to the Supreme Court, abolition of the Senate.[61]

That amending formula has produced three notable political consequences. First, it has made the process of changing the constitutional system and its political institutions challenging to achieve. Second, it has compelled greater federal-provincial cooperation in contemplating, negotiating, and arranging constitutional change. Third, it has made constitutional change correspondingly rare—in fact, no major constitutional changes have yet been achieved since this formula was adopted, despite notable attempts. The failure to adopt the proposed constitutional amendment that emerged from the Meech Lake Accord in 1987 and the Charlottetown Accord in 1992 are particular prominent examples of those consequences.[62]

It is, therefore, possible that the Supreme Court was providing a reminder, through this reference case, of the potentially monumental consequences that the sorts of reforms that the government had presented it. That reminder arguably includes a caution about the unintended consequences of pursuing those sorts of changes. In that way, the Court may have been prompted by classic conservative instincts to warn against action that might appear to be merely political but is, in fact, more essentially constitutional than its advocates might appreciate. Ultimately, though, the Supreme Court affirmed that truly substantive reform of the Senate must rely upon an extremely high level of consensus. It did not exclude the possibility of reforms that might originate from within the institution and rely upon its own mechanisms, behavior, and capacity for political compromise, especially if they are consistent with the spirit of Canada's constitutional heritage.[63]

REFLECTION

It has been tempting for some commentators to attribute broad implications from both the Canadian Senate expenses scandal and the Senate Reference case.[64] In reality, it is plausible to conclude that these episodes achieved little more than to highlight the persistent potential for individual corruption (especially when the rules in that area are ambiguous) within *any* political institution. That assessment arguably is true for practically any political institution, regardless of its composition and the political system upon which it rests and the obvious need (especially within a liberal democracy) to achieve constitutional consensus in order to affect substantive institutional and cultural change within a political system.[65]

Simultaneously, these episodes also may serve to reinforce the relevance of the theories on the nature, underlying values, and roles of parliamentary upper houses addressed within Part I of this book. The features that characterize the parliamentary upper house, particularly within the Westminster model, provide a different forum for legislative and other political behavior. Both the causes and solutions of particular events and activities must be understood from that theoretical perspective if subsequent reactions to them are to be addressed in a meaningful way.

As the Supreme Court noted, the Senate of Canada was not intended to mirror the House of Commons in either its structure or its role and attempts to reform it without appreciating that distinction can have unintended consequences that could undermine not only the effectiveness of the upper house but the legitimacy of the lower house and the effective performance of the overall political system. For that reason, constitutional change in this area ought to be difficult to achieve. Also for that reason, informal political change of this sort of institution should be pursued with deliberateness and care and be guided the ideal framework that these theoretical principles provide.

NOTES

1. Ian Austen, "Canadian Senators' Expenses Under Investigation After Auditor´s Report," *New York Times*, June 9, 2015, http://www.nytimes.com/2015/06/10/world/americas/ canadian-senators-expenses-under-investigation-after-auditors-report.html?_r=0
2. Auditor General of Canada, "Report of the Auditor General of Canada to the Senate of Canada: Senator's Expenses," Ottawa, Ministry of Public Works and Government Services, 2015, p. 23.
3. "Key Moments in the Senate Expense Scandal," *Toronto Star*, June 9, 2015, http://www.thestar.com/news/canada/2015/06/09/key-moments-in-the-senate-expense-scandal.html
4. Kim Mackrael, "Senator Mac Harb Selling House Amid Expenses Scrutiny," *Globe and Mail*, May 7, 2013, http://www.theglobeandmail.com/news/politics/senator-mac-harb-selling-house-amid-expenses-scrutiny/article11777222/
5. "Senator Mac Harb Pays Back $231,000 in Expenses, Retires," CBC News-Politics, August 26, 2013, http://www.cbc.ca/news/politics/senator-mac-harb-pays-back-231-000-in-expenses-retires-1.1308485
6. Glen McGregor, "RCMP Charge Mac Harb and Patrick Brazeau in Senate Expenses Investigation," *Ottawa Citizen*, May 20, 2014, http://ottawacitizen.com/news/local-news/rcmp-charge-mac-harb-and-patrick-brazeau-in-senate-expenses-investigation
7. Pamela Wallin, "Wadena Is My Home, the Senate Is My Job," (op-ed), *Globe and Mail*, February 13, 2013, http://www.theglobeandmail.com/globe-debate/pamela-wallin-wadena-is-my-home-the-senate-is-my-job/article8535391/
8. "Pamela Wallin´s, "Expense Claims Sought from 3 More Organizations," CBC News-Politics, March 31, 2015, http://www.cbc.ca/news/politics/pamela-wallin-s-expense-claims-sought-from-3-more-organizations-1.3016760

9. Joanna Smith, "Senate Expenses Scandal: Pamela Wallin Repaid Money, Mac Harb Owes $231K, Tkachuk Confirms," *Toronto Star*, June 12, 2013, http://www.thestar.com/ news/canada/2013/06/12/senate_expanses_wallin_repaid_money_tkachuk_confirms.html

10. J. Patrick Boyer, *Our Scandalous Senate* (Toronto, Dundurn, 2014), pp. 41–46.

11. Tom Spears, "Given Absolute Discharge, Patrick Brazeau Vows to Return to Senate," *Ottawa Citizen*, October 29, 2015, http://ottawacitizen.com/news/local-news/brazeau-granted-absolute-discharge-on-assault-cocaine-charges

12. Laura Stone, "Patrick Brazeau Back to Rehab After Arrest on Alcohol-Related Charges," Global News, October 14, 2014, http://globalnews.ca/news/1613102/patrick-brazeau-reportedly-arrested-on-alcohol-related-charges/

13. Deloitt, LLP, "Examination of Senator Brazeau's Primary and Secondary Residence Status," Ottawa, Senate of Canada, 2013, pp. 3, 19–20.

14. "Patrick Brazeau Court Date Set on Senate Fraud, Breach of Trust Charges," *CBC News-Politics*, September 15, 2014, http://www.cbc.ca/news/politics/patrick-brazeau-court-date-set-on-senate-fraud-breach-of-trust-charges-1.2766553

15. Deloitt, LLP, "Examination of Senator Duffy´s Primary and Secondary Residence Status," Ottawa, Senate of Canada, 2013, p. 13.

16. Andrea Janus, "PM´s Former Legal Adviser Arranged Deal for Wright to Give Duffy $90K," CTV News, May 20, 2013, http://www.ctvnews.ca/politics/pm-s-former-legal-adviser-arranged-deal-for-wright-to-give-duffy-90k-1.1289718

17. Rachel Mendleson, "Case Closed on Lawyers in Mike Duffy-Nigel Wright Affair," *Toronto Star*, October 25, 2014, http://www.thestar.com/news/canada/2014/10/26/case_closed_on_lawyers_in_mike_duffynigel_wright_affair.html

18. Mark Gollom, "Mike Duffy Says He Resisted PMO Plan for Housing Expense Repayment 'at Every Opportunity,'" *CBC New-Politics*, December 14, 2015, http://www.cbc.ca/news/politics/mike-duffy-trial-crrown-defence-expenses-1.3363639

19. Senate of Canada Standing Committee on Internal Economy, Budgets, and Administration, "Twenty-Seventh Report of the Committee," Ottawa, Parliament of Canada, August 13, 2013, http://www.parl.gc.ca/Content/SEN/Committee/411/ciba/rep/rep27aug13-e.htm; Senate of Canada Standing Committee on Internal Economy, Budgets, and Administration, "Twenty-Sixth Report of the Committee," Ottawa, Parliament of Canada, May 29, 2013, http://www.parl.gc.ca/Content/SEN/Committee/411/ciba/ rep/rep26may13-e.htm; Senate of Canada Standing Committee on Internal Economy, Budgets, and Administration, "Twenty-Fourth Report of the Committee," Ottawa, Parliament of Canada, May 9, 2013, http://www.parl.gc.ca/Content/SEN/Committee/411/ciba/ rep/rep24may13-e.htm; Senate of Canada Standing Committee on Internal Economy, Budgets, and Administration, "Twenty-Third Report of the Committee," Ottawa, Parliament of Canada, May 9, 2013, http://www.parl.gc.ca/Content/SEN/Committee/411/ciba/ rep/rep23may13-e.htm

20. Leslie MacKinnon, "Senate Votes to Suspend Brazeau, Duffy, Wallin,"*CBC News-Politics*, November 5, 2013, http://www.cbc.ca/news/politics/senate-votes-to-suspend-brazeau-duffy-wallin-1.2415815

21. MacKinnon, http://www.cbc.ca/news/politics/senate-votes-to-suspend-brazeau-duffy-wallin-1.2415815

22. Auditor General of Canada, "Report of the Auditor General of Canada to the Senate of Canada: Senator's Repayment Status," Ottawa, Ministry of Public Works and Government Services, 2015, http://sen.parl.gc.ca/portal/Reporting/AG/index-e.htm

23. Laura Payton, "Senate Scandal Puts Harper's Brand at Risk, Poll Suggests," *CBC News-Politics*, November 1, 2015, http://www.cbc.ca/news/politics/senate-scandal-puts-harper-s-brand-at-risk-poll-suggests-1.2304444

24. Anne McIlroy, "Ottawa´s Senate Expense Scandal Is Anything But a Dull Affair," *The Guardian*, November 8, 2013, http://www.theguardian.com/world/2013/nov/08/canada-senate-duffy-wallin-harper

25. Campbell Clark, "As Senate Expense Scandal Grows, Why Hasn't Ottawa Cut Off the Money?" *The Globe and Mail*, June 6, 2015, http://www.theglobeandmail.com/news/politics/as-senate-expense-scandal-grows-why-hasnt-anyone-cut-off-the-money/article24833462/; Bob Vrbanac, "The True Cost of Canada´s Senate Expense Scandal," *Kitchner Post*, June 17, 2015, http://www.kitchenerpost.ca/opinion-story/5910835-the-true-cost-of-canada-s-senate-expense-scandal/; "Time to Abolish the Senate?" (letters to the editor) *Toronto Star*, June 13, 2015, http://www.thestar.com/opinion/letters_to_the_editors/2015/06/13/time-to-abolish-the-senate.html

26. Kenneth M. Gibbons, "The Political Culture of Corruption in Canada," in *Political Corruption in Canada: Cases, Causes, and Cures*, Kenneth M. Gibbons and Donald C. Rowat, eds. (Toronto: McClelland and Stewart, 1976), pp. 231–249.

27. Mark Kennedy, "Most Canadian Want the Senate Reformed, Not Abolished: Poll," *National Post*, December 30, 2015, http://news.nationalpost.com/news/canada/most-canadians-want-senate-reformed-not-abolished-poll

28. Jesse Kline, "What the Senate Expense Scandal Teaches Us About Reform," *National Post*, August 14, 2012, http://fullcomment.nationalpost.com/2013/08/14/jesse-kline-what-the-senate-expense-scandal-teaches-us-about-reform/

29. Aristotle, *The Politics and the Constitution of Athens*, Stephen Everson, ed. (Cambridge: Cambridge University Press, 1996), pp. 13, 70.

30. John Dalberg-Acton, "Letter to Bishop Mandell Creighton, April 5, 1887," in *Historical Essays and Studies*, J. N. Figgis and R. V. Laurence, eds. (London: Macmillan, 1907).

31. Francis Fukuyama, *Political Order and Political Decay: From the Industrial Revolution to the Globalization of Democracy* (New York: Farrar, Strauss, and Giroux, 2014), p. 65.

32. Emma Griffiths, "Expenses Details 'Intrude' on MPs," *BBC News*, February 7, 2008, http://news.bbc.co.uk/2/hi/uk_news/politics/7233560.stm; Ben Worthy, "Freedom of Information and the MPs´ Expenses Crisis," in *The Political Costs of the 2009 British MPs´ Expenses Scandal*, Jennifer vanHeerde-Hudson, ed. (New York: Palgrave MacMillan, 2014), pp. 27–42.

33. "Expenses: How MPs Expenses Became a Hot Topic," *Daily Telegraph*, January 6, 2016, http://www.telegraph.co.uk/news/newstopics/mps-expenses/5294350/Expenses-How-MPs-expenses-became-a-hot-topic.html

34. Simon Hattenstone, "MPs' Expenses Scandal: What Happened Next?" *The Guardian*, May 11, 2012, http://www.theguardian.com/politics/2012/may/11/

mps-expenses-scandal-what-next; Jennifer vanHeerde-Hudson and Orlanda Ward, "The 2009 British MPs´ Expenses Scandal: Origins, Evolution, and Consequences," in vanHeerde-Hudson, ed., pp. 1–26.

35. Stephen Wright and James Chapman, "Shaming of the 389 Greedy MPs Who Went Too Far," *Daily Mail*, February 5, 2010, http://www.dailymail.co.uk/news/article-1248648/MP-expenses-Shaming-389-greedy-politicians-went-far.html; vanHeerde and Ward, in vanHeerde, ed., pp. 1–16.

36. Charles Pattie and Ron Johnston, "The Impact of the Scandal on the 2015 General Election," in vanHeerde, ed., pp. 88–110.

37. Staffan Kumlin and Peter Esaiasson, "Scandal Fatigue? Scandal Elections and Satisfaction with Democracy in Western Europe, 1977–2007," *British Journal of Political Science*, vol. 42, no. 2 (April 2012), pp. 263–282.

38. Ira Basen, "Patrick Brazeau: Harper's Strategic Aboriginal Appointment," *CBC News-Politics*, February 13, 2013, http://www.cbc.ca/news/canada/patrick-brazeau-harper-s-strategic-aboriginal-appointment-1.1411015; "Brazeau not ´Legitimate Representative' of First Nations: Ontario Chiefs," *APTN National News*, February 9, 2011, http://aptn.ca/news/2011/02/09/brazeau-not-legitimate-represenative-of-first-nations-ontario-chiefs-2/

39. Jennifer Ditchburn, "Duffy Says Harper Appointed Him to the Senate to Gain Canadians´Trust," *Globe and Mail*, December 8, 2015, http://www.theglobeandmail.com/news/ politics/mike-duffy-pleads-in-his-own-defence-at-trial/article27642013/

40. Bruce Livesey, "Why Harper Corrupted the Senate," *National Post*, August 27, 2015, http://www.nationalobserver.com/2015/08/27/news/why-harper-corrupted-senate

41. Nick Vivyan, Markus Wagner, and Jessica Tarlov, "Where Did Electoral Accountability Fail? MP Misconduct, Constituent Perceptions and Vote Choice," in vanHeerde, ed., pp. 111–131.

42. Nicholas Allen and Sarah Birch, "Tempests and Teacups: Politicians' Reputations in the Wake of the Expenses Scandal," in vanHeerde, ed., pp. 132–152.

43. Frank Anachiaricho and James B. Jacobs, *The Pursuit of Absolute Integrity: How Corruption Control Makes Government Ineffective* (Chicago: University of Chicago Press, 1996), pp. 4–7; Michael Johnston, *Syndromes of Corruption: Wealth, Power, and Democracy* (Cambridge: Cambridge University Press, 2005), pp. 1–15; Susan Rose-Ackerman, *Corruption and Government: Causes, Consequences, and Reform* (Cambridge: Cambridge University Press, 1999), pp. 111–176.

44. Elinor Ostrom, *Understanding Institutional Diversity* (Princeton, NJ: Princeton University Press, 2005), pp. 125–131.

45. Jana Kunicová and Susan Rose-Ackerman, "Electoral Rules and Constitutional Structures as Constraints on Corruption," in *Corruption, Development, and Institutional Design*, J. Kornai, L. Mátyás, and G. Roland, eds. (London: Palgrave Macmillan, 2009), pp. 3–23; Michael Parenti, *Democracy for the Few* (Boston: Wadsworth, 2011), pp. 151–154; Jonathan Mendilow, "Introduction: Political Finance, Corruption, and the Future of Democracy," in *Money, Corruption, and Political Competition in Established and Emerging Democracies*, Jonathan Mendilow, ed. (Lanham, MD: Lexington Books, 2012), pp. 1–16.

46. Josh Dehaas, "RCMP Senate Investigations Could Cost Millions on Top of $21M Audit," *CTV News*, May 20, 2015, http://www.ctvnews.ca/politics/rcmp-senate-investigations-could-cost-millions-on-top-of-21m-audit-1.2383422

47. Don Hays, "Updating Some Antiquated Constitutional Provisions Relating to the Senate," *Canadian Parliamentary Review*, vol. 32, no. 1 (2009).

48. Nadia Verelli, "Harper´s Senate Reform: An Example of Open Federalism," Kingston, ON: Institute of Intergovernmental Relations, 2008, pp. 1–2.

49. "A Primer on Reforming the Senate: Questions and Answers," *National Post*, June 20, 2011, p. A4.

50. Susan Delacourt, "Forget Killing the Senate Says PM: Harper Rejects NDP Bid for Vote on Abolishing ´Sober Second Thought'," *Toronto Star*, March 2, 2011, p. A6.

51. Daniel LeBlanc, "Ottawa to Press Court on Senate: Conservatives Make Risky Bet on Supreme Court Reference to Clear the Path to Elected, Fixed-Term Senators," *Globe and Mail*, September 17, 2012, p. A1.

52. Ted Morton, "No Statecraft, Questionable Jurisprudence: How the Supreme Court Tried to Kill Senate Reform," *School of Public Policy Research Papers*, vol. 8 , no. 21 (April 2015), pp. 2–4.

53. *In re Reform of the Senate*, 2014 SCC 32, para. 8.

54. 2014 SCC 32; Lorraine Snyder, "Reference *re* Senate Reform (2014): The Supreme Court Clarifies the Senate Reform Process," *Centre for Constitutional Studies*, June 20, 2014, http://ualawccsprod.srv.ualberta.ca/ ccs/index.php/constitutional-issues/federalism/767-reference-re-senate-reform-2014-the-supreme-court-clarifies-the-senate-reform-process

55. Emmett Macfarlane, "Did the Supreme Court Just Kill Senate Reform?" *Maclean's*, April 25, 2014, http://www.macleans.ca/politics/did-the-supreme-court-just-kill-senate-reform/

56. *In re Reform of the Senate*, 2014 SCC 32, p. 6.

57. Ibid., pp. 84–94.

58. Ibid., p. 57–58, emphasis in the original.

59. Ibid., p. 13–16.

60. Sanford Levinson, ed., *Responding to Imperfection: The Theory and Practice of Constitutional Amendment* (Princeton, NJ: Princeton University Press, 1995), pp. 3–36.

61. David E. Smith, "The Canadian Senate: What Is to Be Done?" in Essential Readings in Canadian Constitutional Politics, Christian Leuprecht and Peter H. Russell, eds. (Toronto: University of Toronto Press, 2011), pp. 44, 46.

62. Peter H. Russell, "Constitutional Odyssey: Can Canadians Become a Sovereign People?" (Toronto: University of Toronto Press, 2004), pp. 127–153, 275–302.

63. Gordon Gibson, "Challenges in Senate Reform: Conflicts of Interest, Unintended Consequences, New Possibilities," *Public Policy Sources,* vol. 83 (September 2004), pp. 28–29; Emmett Macfarlane, "Senate Reform: The Good, the Bad, and the Unconstitutional," *Policy Options*, September 21, 2015, http://policyoptions.irpp.org/issues/september-2015/the-future-of-the-senate/senate-reform-the-good-thebad-and-the-unconstitutional/

64. Ian Greene and Garrett MacSweeney, "The Ethics of Senate Reform," Paper Presented to the Annual Conference of the Canadian Political Science Association, Ottawa, June 4, 2015, https://www.assocsrv.ca/cpsa-acsp/2015event/Greene-MacSweeney.pdf

65. Andrei S. Markovits and Mark Silverstein, eds., *The Politics of Scandal: Power and Politics in Liberal Democracies* (Teaneck, NJ: Holmes and Meier, 1989), pp. 1–6.

Chapter 11

The Senate as It Is, Could Be, and Ought to Be

Non-Constitutional Reform

The ancient Greek principle of *archē* establishes an ideal that is not expected to be experienced but only realized as a theoretical absolute.[1] Given the considerable difficulties of gaining any constitutional consensus within Canada as well as navigating the demanding requirements of the constitutional amending formula, a constitutional amendment on Senate form is, by itself, a daunting prospect. Even more daunting would be the acceptance of reforms that would, while theoretical sound and consistent with the institutional and cultural foundations of parliamentary upper houses, challenge conventional beliefs or previously established proposals. Therefore, it may be advisable to treat a proposed constitutional reform scheme as presented within this book as an example of that ancient Greek principle—an ideal against which more attainable proposals may be measured and assessed.

The hypothetical constitutional amendment that has been presented within this book provides such a model. Meanwhile, less formal options appear to have a much better chance of being implemented (especially given the ruling of the Supreme Court of Canada in the Senate Reference case) and, indeed, policy makers, parliamentarians, and politicians have actively contemplated and advocated that approach. In addition to internal administrative and procedural reforms, the Canadian Senate also has the option of negotiating an agreement with the government and the House of Commons that, while not constitutionally or, even, legally binding could have an effect upon the political culture and behavior of the Senate that could prove to be just as binding, especially given the strong institutional norms that have guided Canada's Westminster parliamentary system and its partially unentrenched constitutional principles.

This process should begin with a review of the Senate of Canada as it currently exists and functions. Any belief that the Senate of Canada does nothing would be not only unfair but wildly inaccurate. If its activities are compared to Canada's House of Commons, then, admittedly, it is far less active and assertive. However, that lesser activity is far from no activity. Furthermore, within the context of a parliamentary democracy, that more limited activity ought to be preferred to the alternative of potentially frustrating the overall process of parliamentary government that depends upon the supremacy of the elected lower house. Nonetheless, this upper house appears to have attracted a good deal of animosity of a sort that often seeks confirmation of its alleged inadequacy and contemptible nature.

This book has approached the subject of Canadian Senate reform from, hopefully, a more positive and constructive perspective. It has resulted in recommendations that seek to place that institution within the wider context of its parliamentary heritage. The hypothetical constitutional amendment that has been presented as a theoretical model has emphasized the modification (but not replacement) of the appointment system (with a particular emphasis upon appointment based upon merit and the promotion of diversity) along with an indefinite (though not indiscriminate) number of Senators. It also has stressed the concept a suspensive veto as a means of emboldening the Senate in taking constructive legislative action. Concepts such as the "double majority" relating to language legislation and more general promotion of the diversity of the country (including in an ombudsman role) has been added to these recommendations, as have other ideas concerning the supervisory, informational, and advocacy role of the Canadian upper house. In all of these recommendations, the role of the Senate within the context of Canadian federalism has not been forgotten and, indeed, aspects of the hypothetical examples of greater involvement of provincial leaders as part of the appointment process, the promotion of enhanced representation for previously underrepresented regions and territories of Canada, and other suggestions have been particularly cognizant of this factor.

THE APPEAL OF CONVENTION

As previously noted, the fact that Canada's constitutional tradition is not wholly grounded upon entrenched documents is a key feature that often is underappreciated. The function of Canada's parliamentary system is dependent upon these unentrenched features. The role of these features is the basis for the conventions of the Canadian constitutional tradition and it also provides important guidance for its non-constitutional reform, especially as informed by both its political and institutional cultures.[2]

The Westminster system upon which this aspect of the Canadian constitutional tradition is based is guided by traditions, habits, guidelines, and customs. Under this system, political actors understand and relate to other political actors and the overall political system.[3] Much of that activity is implicitly understood, rather than explicitly articulated.[4] As a result, the Westminster model is based upon conventions that are not only honored by custom but, also, required in order for the system to function.[5] A failure to abide by a constitutional convention (such as a government that lost a "vote of confidence" and, subsequently, refused to resign or ask the head of state to call new elections) ultimately could make the entire system unpredictable and, thus, unworkable.[6] Therefore, the uses of convention to shape institutional reform, including the Senate of Canada, is a logical and practical, as well as a necessary, approach to political and legal change within the Canadian system.[7] That approach also informs and directs all political behavior through political institutions that cannot be understood, properly, unless they are analyzed within that constitutional context,[8] as the Supreme Court of Canada, itself, contends.[9]

As previously explained, the Salisbury Convention offers an excellent example of a convention that was achieved through deliberate negotiation and explicit, though informal, agreement.[10] This convention resulted from negotiations between the Conservative Party majority in the House of Lords and the Labour Party Government that was elected in the aftermath of World War II. As a result of this convention, the British upper house will not reject, amend the substance of, or, even, closely scrutinize bills passed by the House of Commons that are recognized as part of the Government's election manifesto.[11] This convention persists, despite occasional concerns about upper house discontent with a particular government.[12]

While an overt political agreement of this nature has never existed within Canada, the Senate has shown a willingness to conform to a similar convention. As a result, the Senate has been extremely restrained in the use of its absolute veto, especially in relation to government policies and legislation that are related to its electoral mandate.[13] This restraint does not include expressions of concern or resistance by the Senate that result in the House of Commons withdrawing or altering bills before they proceed to final votes within that chamber.[14] Nonetheless, the overall record indicates a Canadian upper house that operates in a manner consistent with convention.

Therefore, it is possible to argue that meaningful Senate reform can be achieved in a similar manner. Non-constitutional reform, in this context, may be something of a misnomer. It actually may reflect change with constitutional ramifications that does not require a formal amendment of entrenched constitutional documents. Nonetheless, the effect can be just as profound as a formal constitutional change but without the politically disruptive element that the constitutional amendment process typically may engender. That approach to reform of the Canadian Senate could be, ultimately, both appealing and satisfying.

NON-CONSTITUTIONAL REFORM

As David Smith has noted, the Senate can achieve meaningful reform without the need to resort to constitutional amendment. In its committee system, its investigative function, and its capacity to provide public information, it can mobilize the Canadian populace, caution the government, deter indiscriminate actions, and publicize the workings of the political system. Internal improvements to the Senate and its business can enhance a performance that already makes a positive contribution to Canadian politics.[15] Shifting the actual function of advising the Governor-General on Senate appointments from the Prime Minister to some other, less partisan source offers another example of this sort of non-constitutional reform that is constitutionally acceptable, provided that it does not entail some form of election as its means of nomination. If nothing else, these changes can improve the positive functions that already take place within the Canadian second chamber while, simultaneously, addressing some of the concerns and grievances that often have prompted other proposals for its reform or abolition.

> When the subject of the Senate arises, it is essential for reformers to recognize the complementary relationship that currently (and necessarily) exists between the two chambers. Reform proposals that do not acknowledge this fact and at the same time offer no alternative constitutional justification for what they propose are destined to fail. In any case, institutional redesign of this magnitude will not happen because conflicting interests, lack of coherent purpose, and an absence of commitment to change stand in its way. It is difficult to say which of these three is the greatest impediment to reformers' success, but it needs to be emphasized that without public commitment, specific reforms are unlikely to happen.[16]

As Prime Minister Justin Trudeau's reforms have indicated, an effective method for advancing non-constitutional reform involves the appointment process. Those reforms demonstrate that it is possible to encourage appointments of Senators in a non-electoral manner (as stipulated by the Supreme Court of Canada in the Senate Reference case[17]) upon the basis of non-partisan considerations, especially as directed toward honoring accomplished Canadians from a variety of professional and personal backgrounds. Nonetheless, those reforms can be deepened. Aside from structural means of pursuing this sort of non-constitutional reform, though, it is even more important to achieve a level of political will that would facilitate this overall goal. Ideally, if a political consensus were to be achieved (not only within the Senate but, more generally, within the political system) regarding that goal, it could develop into an unentrenched constitutional convention that would guide the spirit of the appointment process for Senators, rather than relying upon the letter of formal constitutional or legislative settlements.

Likewise, the Senate of Canada could decide, collectively, to pursue internal reforms to its organization and procedures. Its members could limit the presence of party officials and, also, agree that its members who are affiliated with particular parties would not automatically become participants in their respective parliamentary caucuses. Senators could agree to replace partisan offices, such as whips, with conveners or other facilitators of its parliamentary business. Ultimately, the structure and function of the Senate, including in terms of committee assignments and procedure, could be designed to reflect a role that is not intended to emulate the House of Commons but, instead, complement and supplement the efforts of that lower house and the government whose legitimacy it supports, especially as a contrast to the particularly partisan nature of the Canadian House of Commons and the political parties that dominate it.[18]

If nothing else, these sorts of encouragements may alter popular perceptions of the Senate by acknowledging the work that it does and the even more productive work that it can do. Some of these changes can occur through political action outside of the second chamber. Much of it, though, will depend upon the willingness of the Senate to take command of its own destiny in a manner that is both constructive and conspicuous, thus demonstrating to its critics and the general public its value as a constitutionally unreformed parliamentary institution.[19] This hypothetical accord is presented, piecemeal, within the next several sections of this chapter, identified by a different font in a double-indented format. It starts with a reaffirmation of a *convention that already exists in practice*: a commitment not to interfere with the electoral mandate of the government.

Many of the general principles expressed by this hypothetical agreement reflect aspects of the reforms that Justin Trudeau already has implemented. In particular, his creation of an Independent Advisory Board for the Appointment of Senators is similar to the recommended Advisory Commission. Like this hypothetical agreement, it offers the prospect of a non-constitutional action that could become an informal, yet powerful, constitutional convention within the partially entrenched Canadian constitutional tradition. But this recommendation suggests ways that it can be improved, thus advancing an even broader path toward comprehensive reform of the Senate of Canada, especially in terms of placing more of the control over its destiny within its own institutional domain. Those similarities and differences will be noted through the explanation and commentary relating to this proposal.

An Agreement on Practices Relating to the Senate of Canada

The Senate and the House of Commons of Canada have unanimously approved of the following declaration of principles and practices that they are publicly committed to putting into effect as expeditiously and as reasonably as possible and are, furthermore, committed to maintaining on an ongoing basis.

Declaration of Non-Interference with Government Mandate

> The Senate of Canada will issue a public declaration that it will honor the electoral mandate of any elected government by guaranteeing the passage of any legislation that is related to the clear electoral manifesto and unambiguous publicly-declared campaign promises of the political party that will be summoned to lead that government as a result of such an election. That commitment will include governments that are supported by a political party that has elected a majority of members of the House of Commons and those governments that are supported by a minority of members of that chamber. However, this commitment will not be regarded as deterring the Senate from offering amendments designed to improve legislation or policy implementation or to correct technical or other errors in relation to them. Furthermore, the Senate will retain the prerogative of rejecting legislation that is not deemed to be derived from an express electoral mandate or which, otherwise, clearly appears to be contrary to both the electoral mandate of the government and the public will and interest. This declaration will be confirmed upon the basis of the unanimous approval of the Senate but it will not be subject to statutory confirmation.

Non-constitutional agreement may be derived purely from conventional practice or from express agreement. In the latter case, it often represents a conscious political desire to reinforce implicit understandings through explicit declarations. In certain respects, the Salisbury Convention reflects that latter path, even though long-standing practice has been more common within the British experience. Likewise, the Canadian political system also could make use of a more explicit recognition and affirmation of principles that would assume the form of constitutional convention in terms of the Senate of Canada and its relationship to the broader parliamentary and political system. Such an agreement may or may not be supported by subsequent legislation but its express parameters could assume the form of an accord.

This sort of arrangement could allow for a retained place and role for partisan appointments. Rather than abandoning the role of parties, entirely, it could accommodate their presence while, also, committing partisan Senators to a far less adversarial and far more constructive role within the parliamentary process. Most importantly, it would allow the Senate to retain that option and rely upon its initiative in such matters, rather than through executive institutions such as the Privy Council or Prime Minister's Office.

Appointment (Advising) Process

As the Trudeau reforms have demonstrated, one of the most conspicuous themes relating to non-constitutional reform has been recommendations to make changes to the appointment process. That sort of non-constitutional change would not include either an alteration to the number of Senators within that chamber or elections of any sort so it would be, necessarily, constrained in its scope, especially for promoting greater diversity within that chamber. Yet it is, arguably, the category of non-constitutional Senate reform that has the most potential for success in capitalizing upon the institutional features of that chamber (rather than relying upon the Prime Minister) to enhance its role and influence within the overall Canadian political system.

> Appointment Advisory Commission
>
> A Commission will be established for the purpose of providing advice relating to future appointments to the Senate of Canada. This Appointment Advisory Commission will examine nominations proposed by the Government and offer an opinion on the suitability of those nominations in terms of the following criteria: 1) the perceived qualifications and high standards of propriety for holding such an important and distinguished office; 2) actual or potential conflicts of interest that might undermine the fair performance of the senatorial duties of the nominated persons; 3) general considerations relating to the integrity of the Senate, the ethical norms of the Parliament of Canada, and the public interest.
>
> The Commission also will, from time to time, offer advice relating to persons who could be considered for potential nomination to the Senate, particularly of persons who shall not have formal party affiliation and are deemed to be appropriate candidates because of their distinguished backgrounds, meritorious service to the country, or strong and specific public approbation, including recommendations submitted to the Commission by Canadian citizens.

This recommendation is similar to the actual Independent Advisory Board that Prime Minister Justin Trudeau implemented in 2016.[20] However, it is not identical. Its principle distinctions are that this version would be created through the auspices of the Senate (thus conferring additional responsibility upon it to guarantee that it remains independent of the government of the day), it will have a more distinctive mandate in terms of specifying the qualifications expected of a Senate appointee, and its composition (as will be indicated within the continuation of this clause) will be broader and more directly responsible to the legislature and the judiciary, rather than the solely executive authority. Furthermore, this status should provide greater assurance that it will be less susceptible to the immediate influence of different governments as they are elected, especially given the role that the respective Speakers of the two chambers will exercise. Thus it arguably has a greater likelihood of becoming an enduring feature of the Canadian political system.

Despite previous claims to the contrary, changing the appointment process did *not* required constitutional amendment[21] as the Justice Department confirmed to Prime Minister Justin Trudeau when he explored the potential implementation of his Independent Advisory Board.[22] Those claims largely were based upon a misunderstanding of the actual power that is being exercised through the appointment process. Section 24 of the Constitution Act of 1867 merely indicates that the Governor-General, on behalf of the monarch, "shall ... summon qualified Persons to the Senate."[23] That exclusive formal authority is reiterated in section 26 (relating to the appointment of "four or eight" additional Senators)[24] of that entrenched constitutional document. Non-constitutional reform of the appointment process would not actually change that constitutional power or procedure. The Governor-General would continue to appoint Senators, exclusively, as the Constitution Act of 1867 indicates.

The action that *has* changed (and would further change) is the manner in which the Governor-General is *advised*, during the process. According to the guidance that the Supreme Court provided within the Senate Reference case, so long as that advice is not based upon some sort of electoral process (including "consultative elections"), the advice provided to a Prime Minister in this area should be unrestricted.[25] Constitutionally, the head of state is not *formally* obliged to accept *any* advice on that subject, even from the Prime Minister. The fact that the Governor-General consistently acts upon the advice of the Prime Minister is because of the unentrenched conventions of Canada's parliamentary system, which are very much part of the overall Canadian constitutional tradition but are not part of the entrenched constitutional documents that require constitutional amendment to change it. Instead, varying the advising process merely constitutes an informal political change that could become an established convention, consistent with the Westminster model of parliamentary government from which the Canadian political system is derived. Therefore, it is essential to stress that non-constitutional reform in this area is oriented toward the process of advice, rather than actual appointment. In that context, a great deal of latitude for reform is both possible and desirable.

This category of potential reform is, yet, another example of the strong usefulness of the House of Lords as a model for Canada and its Westminster-style parliamentary and political system. From a formal-legal perspective, the monarch may create *anyone* as a peer. In actuality, any creation of a new peerage is the result of a recommendation by the British Prime Minister. That recommendation is not directed by any formal edict but it is strongly guided by practical, and strong, political constraints that have been recognized as binding conventions, consistent with the unenumerated British constitutional tradition.

Again, it may be possible to retain a role for political parties within the Senate and its appointment scheme. Much of the success for the appointment process regarding the House of Lords has been tied to these long-standing conventions. One of them is a practice of shared nominations, especially (but not exclusively) between Government and Opposition parties. Although the party that constitutes the government of the day invariably recommends the creation of peerages that favors members of its own party, peers from opposition parties also are created and proposals for reform of the upper house in Britain have stressed greater parity in this respect. Furthermore, peers who have been elevated because of meritorious service and distinction in a wide variety of fields and backgrounds have become a conspicuous feature of this process and have led to recommendations for a specified ration of non-partisan, merit-based peerage creations. Therefore, recommendations for this British reform have tended to emphasize a strengthening and institutionalization of this historical trend.[26]

Constitutional conventions of this sort often revolve around a fundamental sense of "fairness" in terms of both the process and the broader political system. That context is not entirely grounded upon political idealism. It also is based upon pragmatic considerations relating to the effective functioning of the overall system.[27] In the absence of a sense of trust that the government will not overtly abuse this process or exclude opposition and independent nominations for peerages, the political system could degenerate into an unworkable state of oppressiveness, retaliation, and immobility (much like the American concept of "gridlock") that can undermine both its effectiveness and its public legitimacy, as observed within a variety of parliamentary systems (both Westminster and non-Westminster) and in relation to various institutional relationships, including legislative composition and powers.[28]

As a result, informal understandings relating to the inclusion of nominations from interests outside of the current government assume, in practice, a status akin to formal agreement, except that these understandings benefit from a level of flexibility. That political culture provides an enormous advantage in situations in which precise formulas (such as exact ratios of Government-to-Opposition nominations) are not only difficult to ascertain but, also, a potential source of additional friction—as well as contrary to the spirit of constitutional conventions that permits the unentrenched features of a parliamentary democracy to function, effectively. Those sorts of factors need to be remembered when engaging in agreements on new conventions in this area.[29]

Appointment Advisory Commission

As previously stated, this Advisory Commission is similar, but not identical, to the one that Justin Trudeau established in 2016. An important distinction is its framework to provide a broader and even more independent institutional forum for vetting, approving, and advancing nominations. Another important distinction, again, is its reliance upon legislative and judicial appointments, as well as executive appointments, for its commissioners. This sort of forum was established by the British government in 2000 as part of its overall reform of the House of Lords. It consists of peers from the major political parties, Cross-bench peers, and a non-parliamentary member. Its role is: "to recommend individuals for appointment as non-party-political life peers; to vet nominations for life peers, including those nominated by the UK political parties, to ensure the highest standards of propriety."[30] It also provides a forum for members of the public to nominate potential peers, provided that the nominees are not active members of a political party.[31]

This process was credited with uncovering the "Cash for Peerages" scandal of the government under Prime Minister Tony Blair in 2006 (in which it was discovered that certain peerages had been connected to campaign contributions and other benefits) and averting "cronyism" relating to the creation of certain Labour Party peerages.[32] While similar processes have not been adopted within other parliamentary systems, it provides a highly useful model for the potential creation of a similar system within Canada. Whether such a body ultimately would be a committee of the Senate, an extra-parliamentary body, or assume some other form, it could be created by legislation, an Order-in-Council, or through less formal means that would not require constitutional amendment.

Appointment Advisory Commission (continued)

This commission will be comprised of 18 members who are appointed according to the following formula: three members appointed, each, by the Prime Minister, the Speaker of the House of Commons, the Chief Justice of Canada, and the Clerk of the Privy Council and six members nominated by the Speaker of the Senate. Appointments to this commission will be confirmed by a vote of the Senate of Canada. The commission will be responsible for maintaining its own schedule and agenda and will be provided a budget and institutional support for its activities as determined by appropriate parliamentary statute.

This Commission may not reject or, otherwise, interfere with the actual nomination process of Canadian Senators. The Commission will confine its activities to offering advice to the Prime Minister and the Governor General. That advice will be publicly made and the proceedings of the Council will be transparent and open to public scrutiny.

Again, it is important to stress that this process would not result in actual nominations. Instead, it would offer advice and express opinions relating to potential and actual nominees. However, it also would impose potentially enormous political pressure upon any government that might choose to ignore its public pronouncements and persist in nominating someone to the Governor-General for appointment to the Senate. The power of convention would provide a very strong role within this overall process, even though it would be, ultimately, an informal one.

This process could improve public confidence in the independence and appropriateness of the Senate nomination process. It also might enhance the prestige of Senators who are appointed as a result of this expression of well-informed approval. Its informality and the fact that it does not bind a Prime Minister's final decision also appear to conform to constitutionally acceptable guidelines. That outcome could provide yet another benefit in terms of the overall quest to achieve non-constitutional reform of the Senate and enhance the general effectiveness of Senators.

Distinctive Status

A significant difference between Canadian Senators and British peers is the level of prestige that typically is attached to these respective appointments. A British peerage has been a mark of distinction for millennia within the British archipelago and it has been tied to the dominance of tribal and clan leadership, aristocratic privilege, class hegemony, and social status. These features of the peerage and its political representation within the House of Lords served as a distinctive feature of that parliamentary institution well into the 20th century.[33]

> Senatorial Honors
>
> The Department of Canadian Heritage will be asked to develop recommendations for additional and enhanced symbols of status and protocol relating to Senators of Canada. These recommendations will not include any matters of remuneration, legal privileges, or other individual advantages that are not of a purely symbolic nature. The recommendations of the Department of Canadian Heritage will be delivered to the Queen for her consideration and action upon her own authority in right of Canada.

The rise and eventual dominance of liberal democratic values and political practices gradually, subtly, and permanently changed the purpose (if not always the popular image) of the peerage, especially by the end of the 20th century. Nonetheless, the prestige of the peerage remained a dominant feature, though that prestige increasingly became associated with political service and, more importantly, meritorious achievement. The fact that most hereditary peers were excluded from participating in parliamentary activity as a result of the Parliament Act of 1999 did not diminish the particular distinction that the granting of a peerage, including above the rank of Baron (those higher ranks remain exclusively hereditary and are ineligible from automatic inclusion in the House of Lords), continues to bestow, even in the opinion of people outside of the United Kingdom. A Life Peerage provides recognition for favorable partisan performance but it also is an honor of particular distinction for such a person to be addressed, permanently, as "My Lord."[34] That status confers particular recognition upon persons who have achieved distinction and accomplishments in a wide variety of professional (including artistic) fields and socio-economic backgrounds, thus also enhancing the diversity of that body.[35]

That factor is comparatively pertinent in connection with the procedures for vetting recipients of Companions of the Order of Canada. The criteria for eligibility and appointment as Companions, though broadly drawn, provide a useful guideline to the caliber of Canadian who might be considered appropriate for appointment to the Senate: "Appointments of persons as Companions and honorary Companions shall be made in recognition of their outstanding achievement and merit of the highest degree, especially in service to Canada or to humanity at large."[36] The composition and procedures of the Advisory Council likewise offer a guideline in this area, including high-ranking and conventionally non-partisan officials[37] who typically reach their decisions through consensus, rather than an actual vote.[38]

This sort of non-constitutional reform could be more difficult to affect than other changes in relation to the Senate of Canada because it might require a change in political and social culture, popular attitude, and perspective among the general Canadian populace. It also could inspire the Senate to assume a role as part of a new national honors system. Therefore, it is not a reform that could be expected to be legislated in a conventional manner. It would need to be part of the broader rehabilitation of the Senate within the collective imagination of the country. By affecting other reforms (such as the appointment process, itself), the status and dignity of Senators might be, accordingly, enhanced as well.

Numerical Constraints

The process within Britain is greatly facilitated by the fact that the number of peerages and, therefore, the number of potential appointments remains, theoretically, unlimited. It permits a continuous process of adding members to the British upper house that facilitates improvements in its diversity, non-partisan membership, and the inclusion of members from all major political parties. Changes to the total number of Senators would, of course, require a constitutional amendment so this aspect of potential reforms to the appointment system cannot realistically be included within the category of "non-constitutional" reform options. But the constitutional allowance for additional ("four or eight") Senate appointments could be applied, at the discretion of the Prime Minister, to the appointment of notable persons, such as former prime ministers, former House of Commons speakers, former Governors-Generals, or other distinguished previous office holders.

Although this process might be intended to promote an environment of "fair play" and trust within the system, that goal could be promoted and, eventually, augmented by the inclusion of an effective and independent vetting procedure. The institutional body that would provide that oversight could result from a separate creation or it could be sanctioned within the parliamentary upper house, itself, as it has been done for the British political system. However, it is fair to note that, despite the implementation of this sort of reform within Britain, its system for the appointment of peers certainly has not abandoned its role in providing political patronage, especially for the government. Therefore, it also may well be unreasonable to expect an abandonment of partisan and patronage appointments within the Canadian system. Nonetheless, it could be highly possible to reduce some level of public cynicism involving such appointments, especially when introduced in conjunction with the creation and maintenance of an effective vetting process in relation to it.

> Additional Senators as Non-Partisan Appointments
>
> The Government of Canada will make a commitment to restrict any requests for the creation of additional Senators under section 26 of the Constitution Act of 1867 to persons who have had no party affiliation and who would be expected to participate in a politically independent manner as Senators. The Governor General will be apprised of this agreement whenever such a request for additional Senators (beyond the constitutionally-established normal number) is submitted under the provisions of that section. The Appointment Advisory Commission will be consulted prior to requests for additional Senators being formally submitted to the Governor General and may investigate and offer advice in relation to it.

While the Independent Advisory Board established by Justin Trudeau is pledged to making non-partisan appointments (and he personally removed Liberal Senators from the parliamentary party caucus), there is no guarantee that partisanship would never influence the process in the future.[39] One way to promote greater integrity in this respect could be to reinforce that commitment by providing a hypothetical enumeration of appointments during a typical session of parliament. If, during such a session, a total of nine vacancies became available (for example, as the result of Senators resigning their seats, accepting a different appointment, or reaching the mandatory retirement age of 75), it might be possible to reach, by convention, an informal understanding that four of those vacancies would be filled by Senators from the Government party, three vacancies would be filled from the Opposition parties, and two vacancies would be filled by non-partisan appointments who were nominated upon the basis of merit. Such an arrangement might require an understanding derived from a formula that would result from an explicit convention (much like the Salisbury Convention) or some other negotiated process.

Compensation

If appointment to the Senate increasingly is perceived to be a distinctive and high honor, more than a political position or sinecure, then it may be possible to alter the manner in which Senators are remunerated for their official activities. The fact that salaries are not formally addressed within the Constitution Acts provides additional opportunity to advance non-constitutional reform that could solicit public support for an adjustment that could be regarded as making Senators directly accountable for their work, as well as being more cost-effective. But general salaries for members of unpopular political institutions can exacerbate public resentment and undermine their sense of legitimacy, even when they are shown to be cost-effective.

> Compensation of Senators
>
> The remuneration of Senators of Canada will no longer be provided by salary (with the exception of Government ministers and parliamentary officers) but through compensation based upon actual attendance and participation in the parliamentary business of that chamber, including its committees. Senators also may be compensated for reasonable expenses that they incur in the performance of their parliamentary duties, including travel and lodging expenses. The precise terms, conditions, and levels pertaining to this compensation will be determined by statute.

Paying and reimbursing participants in a political process for their specific activities (instead of providing a salary for their general holding of an office) is not an entirely uncommon practice. Among certain state governments within the United States, that practice has been employed, especially given the absence of full-time participation that is experienced within many state legislatures.[40] But Canadian Senators are paid full salaries, regardless of actual service.

Again, the House of Lords provides a conspicuous example of this practice. A daily allowance is given to each peer who participates in legislative activity, including committee assignments. Historically, peers were not compensated for their parliamentary activities except if they served as Government ministers or parliamentary officers. Therefore, allowances have not replaced salaries but have been used, instead, to encourage participation.[41] Despite concerns that some peers may take advantage of this provision by claiming compensation for minimal participation, it has continued to be pursued.[42]

Constitutionally, Canadian Senators only need to attend one legislative sitting every two sessions in order to retain their position[43] and, by extension, its salary. This sort of reform could alter the perception of the Senate as a patronage-driven sinecure by attaching compensation directly to participation without altering the constitutional retention of a Senator's status as a Senator for attending the chamber once every two years. It also would not require a formal constitutional amendment, especially as this area of policy is consistent with section 42 (1) of the Constitution Act of 1982.

Independent Senators

The Cross Benches of the British House of Lords offer a highly interesting institutional example of a non-partisan role for the parliamentary upper house. This section of that chamber is particularly appropriate for persons whose elevation to a peerage is tied to non-partisan activity, such as former Governors of the Bank of England or former Presidents of the Trades Union Congress. Reform efforts for this chamber consistently have included a determination to retain this feature.[44] It also provides a forum for peers who have achieved this rank as a result of distinctive service or merit in a variety of fields of endeavors. Creating both a category and physical space for members of the upper house who are not affiliated with a particular political party has facilitated broader and less partisan parliamentary participation.[45]

> Independent Senators
>
> A category of Senators who are not members of a political party and are considered to be politically independent will be accommodated within the Senate. That accommodation will include the creation and maintenance of Conveners for the purpose of organizing and protecting their parliamentary participation (especially in terms of debate and committee assignments) and privileges.

Although the Independent Advisory Commission has recommended this arrangement, this agreement would more formally institutionalize it while retaining the possibility of Senators who wish to retain partisan loyalties and affiliations. The Australian Senate also offers an interesting and relevant example in this area, particularly in relation to additional partisan considerations. As previously noted, the Cross Benches serve as a venue within the Australian Senate for Senators who have been elected from a minor-party status (such as the Green Party of Australia) or for politicians who have been elected independently of any party affiliation. As all Australian Senators achieve their position as the result of contested elections, the concept of an "independent" Senator does not carry the same meaning as it does in an appointed body.[46] Nonetheless, this sort of requirement for Canada could have multiple advantages in this respect, even though the concept of "no party affiliation" could be a difficult one to determine and, in some cases, could be subject to challenge if it were to be abused. Yet the principle could be reasonably expected to be followed in an honest and faithful manner, especially given the conventions of parliamentary government that, ultimately, are intended to guide all Westminster model systems, including the Canadian one.

The promotion of an active role for non-partisan and other categories of independent Senators can be achieved through non-constitutional means. That promotion can be facilitated through internal adjustments within that chamber, as well as previously addressed changes regarding advising the appointment process that will lead to an increased acceptance of the potential contributions of these Senators to the parliamentary process. It also can enhance the diversity of that chamber (thus increasing parliamentary diversity, overall) and, thus, complement the role that the Canadian upper house can perform and the contributions it can make within the overall political system.

Federalism and Provincial Input

Many proposals for Canadian Senate reform, including the Triple-E Senate, are designed to address the role and relationship of the provinces with the federal government. While many of these proposals ostensibly seek to emphasize an element of intrastate federalism within the Canadian system, they often are recognized as attempts to rein in the centralization of federal authority, which inevitably would result in resistance at the federal level.[47] Substantive Senate reform will require, at a minimum, consistent collaboration between federal and provincial governments. Even a particular federal government that is sympathetic to particular provincial goals relating to Senate reform may be unlikely to support them (despite previous Harper Government's support for "consultative elections"), given the fact that they could create more problems than they solve (from both a federal and a provincial perspective) and would permit provincial governments to influence and, potentially, frustrate the legislative process of responsible government at the federal level.[48]

> Provincial Consultation
>
> The Government of Canada will publicly commit itself to consult with, and be advised by, the several provincial and (at the discretion of the Prime Minister of Canada) territorial governments of Canada in relation to nominating appropriate persons to the Senate. The various First Ministers will negotiate this process of consultation and advice among themselves. These governments are expected to demonstrate good faith in arriving at a consensus in this respect. First Ministers will provide a list of recommended persons from which the Prime Minister may select nominees to recommend to the Governor General, though the Prime Minister retains final discretion in making such recommendations.

Some proponents of Canadian upper house reform since the end of the Second World War have expressed an attraction for the model of the German federal system in this respect. That model has been mentioned in general terms within chapter 6 but its actual method for selecting members has not been specified in detail. The members of the upper house of the German parliament, the Bundesrat, are appointed by their respective state (in German, *länder*) governments and, typically, that membership includes members of the *länder* cabinet, including the minister-president of each *länder*. Furthermore, balloting for each *länder* is conducted upon the basis of bloc voting. If the electors for a particular *länder* are split, the entire vote for representation is considered invalid.[49] As a result, intrastate arrangements of institutions such as the Bundesrat have tended to be conducted through interactions and negotiations that more accurately reflect the practice and goals of interstate federalism.[50] That experience is, ultimately, one that is particularly distinctive in terms of contrasting the German and Canadian contexts for addressing federalism, including in terms of the appropriate role of the upper house.[51]

The Canadian experience suggests that indirect and informal non-constitutional arrangements might serve as a preferential method for addressing federalism within the context of the Senate of Canada. Other substantive reform would necessitate formal constitutional change. Instead, a non-constitutional process of informal negotiation could be introduced. Provincial governments could be permitted a role in advising the nomination of a substantive number of Senators, though not to the extent that it would eclipse the federal role in this process. This method would be a variation on the overall non-constitutional approach to reforming the advising process in support of Senate appointments. Otherwise, additional non-constitutional reform in the area of federalism probably will need to rely upon negotiations between the federal and provincial level, especially as an extension of executive federalism.

The final sentence of this proposed passage is important from the perspective of the Supreme Court of Canada's ruling in its Senate Reference case. While the Court specified the general unconstitutionality of basing nominations upon an electoral process, it also noted that, by convention, the actual nomination sent to the Governor-General must remain within the absolute discretion of the Prime Minister.[52] The Court specified its objection to language that appeared to compel such a choice on the part of the Prime Minister in relation to "consultative elections" that it found objectionable in this respect.[53] Therefore, this agreement would respond to that constitutional concern in two ways: by requiring First Ministers to provide a list of potential nominees, rather than a single, preferred nominee; by emphasizing that the Prime Minister is not compelled to choose from that list, though it might be considered to be extremely politically expedient to do so. The ultimate goal would be provincial and territorial input.

Internal Senate Procedural Reforms

Procedural issues that are internal to any legislative body can have a potentially profound effect upon themes such as alleviating partisanship, improving performance, and enhancing public visibility and trust. It can establish a highly constructive tone that not only improves the activities of the chamber but can have a positive effective upon the public perception and appreciation of its functions as well. Pragmatic adjustments to the rules that govern the chamber may not be conspicuous or dramatic but they can perform a utilitarian role in improving its efficiency and effectiveness, especially in areas in which the chamber already performs a highly useful purpose.

> Procedural Initiatives
>
> The Senate of Canada will commit itself to form a Standing Committee on Procedural Reform for the purpose of developing and maintaining internal procedures and practices that are designed to enhance its parliamentary business in a reasonably fair, non-partisan, and constructive manner. These procedural improvements may include, but not be limited to, changes to the presence and role of party officers within the chamber (including party whips), more effective rules and oversight regarding compensation for expenses, improved public access to Senators and Senate committees, the development of liaison services, and alterations to the rules of debate and committee membership and participation for the purpose of promoting these same goals. These changes will be performed entirely within the Senate and be subject to its own discretion and initiative.

Justin Trudeau's decision to remove Senators of his Liberal Party from the party caucus has offered a way to conceptualize this sort of reform.[54] Although the manner in which it was accomplished might have been differently achieved (in a manner less subject to initial confusion and misunderstanding[55]), the idea behind it remains consistent with the overall goal of achieving non-constitutional Senate reform. By removing Liberal Senators from the party caucus (though not from party membership), he sought to emphasize a parliamentary role for them that is distinct from the role of the party's members in the House of Commons. That sort of reform, if pursued even further, could have a particular effect in changing the perspective of Senators relating to their parliamentary roles and, ultimately, the institutional culture of the chamber. It could change public perception as well.[56]

It is essential to note that isolated changes of the sort that Justin Trudeau introduced concerning the removal of Liberal Senators from that party's caucus do not achieve instant success. A central purpose of all institutional reform is to affect institutional culture, which requires time and familiarization. Even comprehensive reforms will not achieve "overnight success." The accumulation of reforms that transformed the institutional culture and practice of the current House of Lords required, in some instances, decades to achieve. Introducing less partisan practices also requires the long-term agreement and cooperation of all political parties. However, as part of a concerted and cooperative effort, even internal procedural changes ultimately can have a positive and lasting effect.

Other internal procedural changes could be made to the Senate that could promote similar outcomes. Limiting or, even, eliminating the role of party whips is one potential example. Providing procedural officers for non-party affiliated Senators might not only facilitate the role of that category of Senator but, also, could shift the overall emphasis of the chamber from partisanship to procedural efficacy.[57] The Senate also could improve its internal administration to enhance the openness and constructiveness of debate, institutional decorum, its oversight of the expenditures of its members, and access to research and other resources. This sort of reform not only does not require formal constitutional amendment but it also could be affected by the Senate, itself, as a purely self-motivated and self-contained initiative, separate from legislation or other formal political intervention. Furthermore, the success of such initiatives could inspire even broader non-constitutional reforms.

Summarizing the Observations

This book has drawn certain conclusions as derived from varying approaches to this overall theme of Senate reform. While these conclusions have included the theoretical constitutional amendment that has been used as an ideal model within the preceding chapters, they also have suggested that the unreformed Senate of Canada possesses characteristics that are constructive and reflect some of the best features of the upper house as a general institution of parliamentary government, especially within the tradition of the Westminster model. Therefore, they propose that, in the absence of more drastic reform, the Senate of Canada plays a role that contributes, positively, to the political life of Canada—a role that can be enhanced, given the right sort of emphasis.

Conclusions within this book relating to the theoretical context of upper houses in general have focused upon themes such as reduced partisanship, targeted constituencies, specialization and expertise, separation from government, elevated prestige, and a special role as guardians of constitutional guarantees and human rights. These theoretical assessments, though not exhaustive, certainly are not foreign to the Senate of Canada. Furthermore, they indicate both performance and potential in terms of the role that the upper house plays and can continue to play within the broader Canadian political system.

It also is important to note that the parliamentary upper house (particularly, though not exclusively, within the Westminster model) can be explained in terms of multiple philosophical and ideological traditions that should guide considerations relating to its reform or non-reform. The Canadian parliamentary system is the product of specific philosophical heritage that, though it is not homogeneous, provides traditions, values, and trends that are especially relevant to that system and, particularly, relevant to the workings of its parliamentary upper house. Liberal (including liberal democratic) and communitarian ideals have informed the true purpose and reform of that institution, especially in terms of complementing, but not obstructing, the sovereign will as it has been established by the parliamentary lower house.

Federalism is a perpetual focus of Canadian politics and should not be ignored in relation to Senate reform. However, while acknowledged and respected, it should not necessarily dominate those considerations.[58] Many proposals for Senate reform insist that the Senate's primary role *must* revolve around federalism, either because regional representation was a foundational characteristic of that institution, or because of its contrast with the nationwide representative role of the Canadian House of Commons, or because of frustrations associated with the influence of certain provinces. But these sorts of reforms are rife with unintended consequences, not least of which would be the tendency to confuse interstate federalism with intrastate federalism in a manner that could undermine the overall process of provincial-federal relations. While regional and provincial interests must be included within this process, they should not overwhelm it. The regional representational role of the Senate declined for a reason and its subsequent development in that respect should be appreciated, more critically. Involving provincial governments, directly, in the appointment process can be a positive move in that respect—and one that could be embraced in a non-constitutional manner. The adoption of a suspensive veto, through which legislation can be delayed but not, ultimately, prevented is another positive move that also can advance that goal.

The emphasis should be taken away from electoral recommendations for Senate reform. The Canadian parliamentary system has, at the federal level, an elected lower house that establishes democratic legitimacy for the government. Contesting that authority with another elected parliamentary chamber could lead to unsettling and unnecessary consequences. A Canadian second chamber that complements, rather than challenges, the legislative role of the House of Commons is best developed through means other than simply adding an electoral process to it. In fact, elections for secondary institutions actually can undermine the primary institutions of democratic systems, especially parliamentary ones. Making parliamentary upper chambers elected is an excellent example of this potential problem that should not be uncritically embraced. Improving appointments, however, might not only be a positive reform but one that could be affected without necessitating a constitutional amendment.

Reform of the Senate of Canada needs to be understood and appreciated within the context of the actual institutional parameters and the very real consequences (intended and unintended) that alterations of that nature can cause. Greater neo-institutional scrutiny could shift that perspective. The starting point for that shift and change in approach is an assessment of the institution in itself. Contrasting the way it *actually* functions with optimal ways that it *could* ideally function offer a constructive understanding of this issue and the possibilities that it presents. Neo-institutional approaches and techniques offer a crucial component of constructive reform of the Senate of Canada that also could be addressed in terms of internal behavior and adjustments, rather than the often-unchallenged assumption that only substantive structural changes can achieve such results.

Furthermore, by better reflecting the pluralism of Canadian society, either through the appointment process, in an ombudsman function, or through other legislative and extra-legislative activities, the Senate of Canada can address the omnipresent theme of the country's diversity, including in terms of multiculturalism. That emphasis would complement the democratic purpose of the Senate by attempting to reflect the contributions of *all* members of Canadian society, rather than merely its most dominant members. A majoritarian system often is not able to reflect the diversity of a society but a Canadian upper house that is reformed in a manner that is cognizant of this desirable goal should find greater success. Again, formal or, even, informal constitutional reform might not be necessary to achieve much of that purpose. Internal reforms to the procedures of the Senate and policy inducements by the government also could advance this ideal that is particularly relevant to Canadian society, including its bilingual and multicultural heritage—a factor that could have particular relevance for Quebec as well as the country as a whole.

When in Doubt

The recommendations for reform of the Senate of Canada, both constitutional and non-constitutional, that have been presented within this book may appear to be "unorthodox" in an ironic way, especially as many of its ideas draw upon a British model that has been more associated with the past than with the future. However, an arguably more unorthodox recommendation might be even more stunning: *do nothing*. That simpler alternative is based upon both theoretical and pragmatic considerations and it is offered from the perspective of the critical assessment that also serves as the basis for the more complex alternative that this book has advanced. In particular, it acknowledges the very intimidating obstacle of seeking constitutional consensus on this issue. Regardless of whether the approval of seven provinces (representing at least 50% of the country's population) or all of the provinces is necessary to secure a constitutional amendment, describing that path to reform as "daunting" is a gross understatement.[59] If for that reason, alone, the prospect of doing nothing (in an oxymoronically "constructive" way) ought to be considered.

Ultimately, the unreformed Senate of Canada truly does no real harm. Furthermore, it does provide some degree (and, arguably, a fair amount) of good. It amends laws, makes policy recommendations, provides liaison with the public, brings attention to important (if sometimes unglamorous) policies, provides technical improvements to policies, and supervises the public policy and legislative processes. Its committee activities, in particular, offer a constructive forum for bridging the divide between government activity and citizen understanding and involvement: "Les membres siégant aux comités acquierraient la certitude de voir les rapports d'un Sénat médiateur server de points de référence pour les discussions entre le gouvernement fédéral et les citoyens."[60] Given its relatively modest budget when compared to other institutions of Canadian government, it also appears to be relatively cost-effective. That role is not only a constructive (though, arguably, another modest) one but it also is one that also can be encouraged to continue and be improved in its functioning.

A Final Word

The Senate of Canada has greater potential as a political institution than many observers might recognize or admit. That potential has a modest scope but that modesty is appropriate under the circumstances. The Senate not only does no harm; it also might do more good than many, if not most, people (especially Canadian citizens) realize.

The Senate of Canada is the heir of a long evolution of a wider history of parliamentary development. The focus of that development has shifted, appropriately, to the lower house and, more recently, the executive government that depends upon the support of that lower house for its delegated authority. The legitimacy of the government is established by the approval of the sovereign people as imperfectly reflected through the electoral process. It needs no competitors and, certainly, the upper house should not serve as an elected opponent. However, like the judicial system, it can impose certain political constraints that are very compatible with the concept of a liberal democratic polity and the Westminster model of parliamentary government.

Therefore, Senate reform should aim to enhance and not confront. It should complement and not restrict. The parliamentary upper house should be subservient in that respect. Above all, Senate reform, and not just the Senate, should seek to do no harm. This book has argued in favor of that path, either through "unorthodox" changes, non-constitutional adjustments, or (at least externally) no change at all. Hopefully, that advice will be taken in the constructive spirit in which it has been offered. The Senate of Canada is very imperfect but it also is a practical, beneficial, responsive, complementary, and (in its own way) reasonably effective institution of parliamentary government. It ought to stay that way.

NOTES

1. William Keith Chambers Guthrie, *A History of Greek Philosophy* (Cambridge: Cambridge University Press, 2000), pp. 55, 77.
2. Peter Russell, *Constitutional Odyssey: Can Canadians Become a Sovereign People?* (Toronto: University of Toronto Press, 2004), pp. 15–16, 38–39.
3. R.A.W. Rhodes, John Wanna, and Patrick Weller, Comparing Westminster (Oxford: Oxford University Press, 2009), pp. 45–77.
4. A. V. Dicey, Introduction to the Study of the Law of the Constitution (Indianapolis: Liberty Fund, 1982), pp. 277–315.
5. Jeffrey Jowell, "The Rule of Law Today," in *The Changing Constitution*, Jeffrey Jowell and Dawn Oliver, eds. (Oxford: Clarendon Press, 1989), pp. 3–23; Fredeick Maitland, The Constitutional History of England (Cambridge: Cambridge University Press, 1948), pp. 281–288; Margaret H. Ogilvie, Historical Introduction to Legal Studies (Toronto: Carswell, 1982), pp. 203–266; Owen Hood Phillips and Paul Jackson, Constitutional and Administrative Law (London: Sweet and Maxwell, 1987), pp. 41–82; S. A. de Smith, Constitutional and Administrative Law (London: Longman, 1971), pp. 43–66.
6. Geoffrey Marshall, Parliamentary Sovereignty and the Commonwealth (Oxford: Clarednon Press, 1984), pp. 3–18.
7. Peter Hogg, Constitutional Law of Canada (Toronto: Carswell, 1977), pp. 196–197.
8. Andrew Heard, *Canadian Constitutional Conventions: The Marriage of Law and Politics* (Oxford: Oxford University Press, 1991), pp. i–vii, 3–15; Gregory S. Mahler, "Canada: Two Nations, One State?" in *Political Culture and Constitutionalism: A Comparative Approach*, Daniel P. Franklin and Michael J. Baun, eds. (Armonk, NY: M. E. Sharpe, 1995), pp. 56–76.
9. *In re Reform of the Senate*, 2014 SCC 32, pp. 29, 50.
10. Andrew McDonald and Robert Hazell, "What Happened Next? Constitutional Change under New Labour," in *Reinventing Britain: Constitutional Change under New Labour* (Berkeley: University of California Press, 2007), pp. 23–24.
11. Her Majesty's Government, *Reform of the House of Lords* (London: Her Majesty's Stationer's Office, 2007), p. 10.
12. Glenn Dymond and Hugo Deadmon, "The Salisbury Doctrine (London: House of Lords Library Note, June 2006), pp. 53–57.

13. J. Lynch-Staunton, "The Role of the Senate in the Legislative Process," *Canadian Parliamentary Review* (Summer 2000), pp. 10–14.

14. J. A. Robertson, "Rejection of Bills by the Canadian Senate," Library of Parliament Research Paper (Ottawa: Parliament of Canada, 1990), pp. 3–8.

15. David E. Smith, "The Improvement of the Senate by Non-Constitutional Means," in *Protecting Canadian Democracy: The Senate You Never Knew*, Serge Joyal, ed. (Montreal and Kingston, ON: McGill-Queen's University Press, 2003), pp. 231–233.

16. Smith, p. 230.

17. *In re Reform of the Senate*, 2014 SCC 32, p. 6.

18. Christopher Garner and Natalia Letki, "Party Structure and Backbench Dissent in the Canadian and British Parliaments," *Canadian Journal of Political Science*, vol. 38, no. 2 (June 2005), pp. 464–469; Franks, C. E. S., *The Parliament of Canada* (Toronto: University of Toronto Press, 1987), pp. 100–114.

19. Robert A. MacKay, *The Unreformed Senate of Canada* (Toronto: McClelland and Stewart, 1963), pp. 170–173.

20. Government of Canada, Independent Advisory Board for Appointment of Senators, https://www.canada.ca/en/campaign/independent-advisory-board-for-senate-appointments.html.

21. Stéphane Dion, "Le plan Trudeau pour un Sénat moins partisan et plus indépendant n'exige pas de changement constitutionnel," *Le Huffington Post (Québec)*, May 17, 2014, http://quebec. huffingtonpost.ca/stephane-dion/senat-plan-trudeau-constitution_b_5339170.html?utm_hp_ref=politique

22. "Justin Trudeau's Senate Appointments Plan Backed by Advice from Justice Officials," *CBC News-Politics*, October 28, 2015, http://www.cbc.ca/news/politics/justin-trudeau-s-senate-appointments-plan-backed-by-advice-from-justice-officials-1.3292533

23. Canada, Constitution Act, 1867, part IV, sec. 24.

24. Ibid., sec. 26.

25. *In re Reform of the Senate*, 2014 SCC 32, p. 6.

26. Royal Commission on Reform of the House of Lords, *The House of Lords: Reform* (London: Her Majesty's Stationery Office, 2007), pp. 26–27.

27. Meg Russell and Richard Cornes, "The Royal Commission on Reform of the House of Lords: A House for the Future?" *Modern Law Review*, vol. 64, no. 1 (January 2001), pp. 95–99.

28. Richard Albert, "The Fusion of Presidentialism and Parliamentarism," *American Journal of Comparative Law*, vol. 57, no. 3 (Summer 2009), pp. 562–564.

29. House of Lords and House of Commons Joint Committee on Conventions, *Conventions of the UK Parliament* (London: Her Majesty's Stationery Office, 2006), pp. 2–3.

30. House of Lords Appointment Commission, "About Us," http://lordsappointments.independent. gov.uk/about_us.aspx

31. House of Lords Appointment Commission, "Nominations for Non-Political Membership of the House of Lords," http://lordsappointments.independent.gov.uk/how-to-apply.aspx

32. BBC News, "No Charges on "Cash-for-Honours," July 20, 2007, http://news.bbc.co.uk/ 2/hi/uk_news/politics/6907594.stm

33. S. A. de Smith, "Reform of the Lords: Report of the Joint Committee on House of Lords Reform," *Modern Law Review*, vol. 26, no. 3 (May 1963), pp. 289–291.

34. David Cannadine, *The Decline and Fall of the British Aristocracy* (New York: Vintage Books, pp. 680, 697–708.

35. Ian Inglis, "The Politics of Stardust or the Politics of Cool: Popular Music and the British Honours System," *International Review of the Aesthetics and Sociology of Music*, vol. 41, no. 1 (June 2010), pp. 51–52.

36. Constitution of the Order of Canada, sec 11.

37. Ibid., sec 7.

38. Christopher McCreery, *The Order of Canada: Its Origins, History, and Developments* (Toronto: University of Toronto Press, 2005), p. 250.

39. Bill Curry, "Trudeau's Senate Appointments Spark Debate on Political Allegiance," *The Globe and Mail*, November 20, 2016, http://www.theglobeandmail.com/news/politics/trudeaus-senate-appointments-spark-debate-on-political-allegiance/article32953017/.

40. Washington Citizen's Commission on Salaries for Elected Officials, "Comparisons of the Salaries of Legislatures Nationally by Time Required to Do the Job," *State of Washington*, http://www.salaries.wa.gov/documents/ComparisonofTimeSalariesofLegislaturesNationally_001.pdf

41. U.K. Parliament, About Parliament, "Members of the Lords: Allowances," http://www.parliament.uk/about/mps-and-lords/about-lords/lords-allowances/

42. Rosa Prince, "House of Lords: Peers to Get Up to £30,000 Tax Free Plus Allowances," *The Daily Telegraph*, November 27, 2009, http://www.telegraph.co.uk/news/newstopics/mps-expenses/6663162/House-of-Lords-peers-to-get-up-to-30000-tax-free-plus-allowances.html

43. Canada. Constitution Act, 1867, sec. 31(1).

44. Her Majesty's Government, *House of Lords: Reform* (London: Office of the Deputy Prime Minister, 2007), pp. 13, 46.

45. David Coletto, "Is the British House of Lords Model Viable for Canada's Senate?" *Abacus Data Insider*, June 17, 2013, http://abacusinsider.com/politics-public-affairs/canadian-senate-house-lords-model-viable-canada/

46. John Uhr, *Deliberative Democracy in Australia* (Cambridge: Cambridge University Press, 1998), pp. 98–99.

47. David Cameron, "Inter-Legislative Federalism," in *Reconsidering the Institutions of Canadian Federalism*, J. Peter Meekinson, Hamish Telford, and Harvey Lazar, eds. (Montreal and Kingston, ON: McGill-Queen's University Press, 2004), pp. 163–175.

48. Franks, pp. 200–201.

49. David P. Conradt and Eric Lagenbacher, *The German Polity* (Lanham, MD: Rowman and Littlefield, 2013), pp. 228–233.

50. Hans-Georg Wehling, "The Bundesrat," *Publius*, vol. 19, no. 4 (Autumn 1989), pp. 56, 58–62.

51. Jörg Broschek, "Historical Institutionalism and the Varieties of Federalism in Germany and Canada," *Publius*, vol. 42, no. 4 (Fall 2012), pp. 662–687.

52. *In re Reform of the Senate*, 2014 SCC 32, p. 62.
53. Ibid., p. 61.
54. Stéphane Dion, "Liberal Plan is Best Path to a Functional Senate," *Toronto Star*, May 15, 2014, http://www.thestar.com/opinion/commentary/2014/05/15/stphane_dion_liberal_plan_is_best_path_to_a_functional_senate.html
55. "Trudeau's Senate Plans and Angry Veterans," *The National*, January 30, 2014, http://www.cbc.ca/thenational/content/analysis/atissue/trudeaus_senate_plan_angry_veterans.html
56. Christina Spencer, "Justin Trudeau Kicks All 32 Liberal Senators Out of Caucus in Bid for Reform," *National Post*, January 29, 2014, http://news.nationalpost.com/2014/01/29/justin-trudeau-kicks-senators-out-of-liberal-caucus-in-bid-to-show-hes-serious-about-cleaning-up-red-chamber/; Martha Hall Findlay, "Spin Overtakes Best of Trudeau's Attempt at Senate Reform," *Huffington Post (Canada)*, February 4, 2014, http://www.huffingtonpost.ca/martha-hall-findlay/trudeau-senate-reform_b_4724979.html
57. Howard Cody, "Lessons from Australia in Canadian Senate Reform," *Canadian Parliamentary Review*, vol. 18, no. 2 (1995), pp. 22–23.
58. Serge Joyal, "The Senate as the Embodiment of the Federal Principle," in Joyal, ed., pp. 272–274.
59. Christopher P. Manfredi, "Institutional Design and the Politics of Constitutional Modification: Understanding Amendment Failure in the United States and Canada," *Law and Society Review*, vol. 31, no. 1 (1997), pp. 122–126.
60. Normand Grimard, *L'indispensable Sénat: defense d'une institution mal aimée* (Hull, QC: Vents d'Ouest, 1993), pp. 159–160.

Appendix A

Constitution Act of 1867 in Respect of the Senate of Canada as Amended

CONSTITUTION ACT, 1867

IV. Legislative Power

17. There shall be One Parliament for Canada, consisting of the Queen, an Upper House styled the Senate, and the House of Commons.

18. (1) The privileges, immunities, and powers to be held, enjoyed, and exercised by the Senate and by the House of Commons, and by the Members thereof respectively, shall be such as are from time to time defined by Act of the Parliament of Canada, but so that any Act of the Parliament of Canada defining such privileges, immunities, and powers shall not confer any privileges, immunities, or powers exceeding those at the passing of such Act held, enjoyed, and exercised by the Commons House of Parliament of the United Kingdom of Great Britain and Ireland, and by the Members thereof.

POWER OF THE SENATE IN RELATION TO MONEY BILLS

(2) If a Money Bill, having been passed by the House of Commons and sent to the Senate at least 40 days before the end of the session, is not passed by the Senate without amendment within 40 days after it is so sent or if it is rejected by a vote of the whole Senate within that same time period, the Bill shall, unless the House of Commons direct to the contrary, be presented to the Governor General, on behalf of Her Majesty, and become an Act of Parliament upon the Royal Assent being signified, notwithstanding that the Senate has not consented to the Bill. Any amendments that are certified by the Speaker of the House of Commons and verified by the Governor General

to have been made by the Senate during this 40-day period and accepted by the House of Commons shall be inserted in the Bill as presented for Royal Assent in pursuance of this section

(2) A Money Bill is defined as a Public Bill which, in the opinion of the Speaker of the House of Commons and confirmed by the Governor General, contains only provisions dealing with all or any of the following subjects: the imposition, repeal, remission, alteration, or regulation of taxation; the imposition for the payment of debt or other financial purposes; public supply; the appropriation, receipt, custody, issue or audit of accounts of public money; the raising or guarantee of any loan or its repayment; subordinate matters incidental to those subjects or any of them.

(3) Every Money Bill passed by the House of Commons shall include a certificate of the Speaker of the House of Commons that it is a Money Bill. The Governor General shall verify, prior to signifying the Royal Assent, that the certificate is valid in its designation of the bill as a Money Bill.

POWERS OF THE SENATE IN RELATION TO OTHER BILLS (SUSPENSIVE VETO)

(4) If any Public Bill (other than a Money Bill and a Bill pertaining to the Official Languages of Canada) is passed by the House of Commons in two successive sessions (whether of the same Parliament or not) and, having been sent to the Senate at least 40 days before the end of each session, is rejected or otherwise fails to be passed by the Senate in each of those sessions, that Bill shall, on its rejection for the second time by the Senate (unless the House of Commons direct to the contrary) be presented to the Governor General, on behalf of Her Majesty, and become an Act of Parliament on the Royal Assent being signified, notwithstanding that the Senate has not consented to the Bill. This provision shall not take effect unless one year has elapsed between the date of the second reading in the first of those sessions of the Bill in the House of Commons and the date on which it passes the House of Commons in the second of these sessions.

(5) When a Bill is presented to the Governor General for the Royal Assent in pursuance of the provisions of this section, the Speaker of the House of Commons shall provide a certificate that the Bill complies with provisions of this section, which the Governor General shall verify.

(6) A Bill shall be deemed to be rejected by the Senate if it is not passed by that chamber during the session in which it has been presented either without amendment or with such amendments only as the House of Commons and the Senate shall mutually agree.

(7) A Bill shall be deemed to be the same Bill as a former Bill sent to the Senate in the preceding session if it is identical with the former Bill or contains only such alterations as are certified by the Speaker of the House of Commons and verified by the Governor General to be necessary owing to the time which has elapsed since the date of the former Bill or to represent any amendments which have been made by the Senate in the former Bill during the preceding session. Any amendments that are certified by the Speaker of the House of Commons and verified by the Governor General to have been made by the Senate in the second session and accepted by the House of Commons shall be inserted in the Bill as presented for Royal Assent in pursuance of this section, provided that the House of Commons may, on the passage of such a Bill during the second session, suggest any further amendments without inserting the amendments in the Bill and any such suggested amendments shall be accepted by the Senate shall be treated as amendments made by the Senate and accepted by the House of Commons, though the exercise of this power by the House of Commons shall not affect the operation of this section in the event of the Bill being rejected by the Senate.

ENACTING FORMULA

(10) Any Bill that shall become an Act of Parliament without the consent of the Senate under the provisions of section 18 shall be enacted with the following formula:

> "Her Majesty, by and with the advice of the Senate of Canada and the advice and consent of the House of Commons of Canada (pursuant to the provisions of section 18 of the Constitution Act of 1867, as amended), enacts as follows/Sa majesté, sur l´avis du Sénat du Canada et sur l´avis et avec le consentement de la Chambre des communes du Canada (confornément aux dispositions de l´article 18 de la Loi constitutionelle de 1867, telle que modifiée), édicte."

NUMBER OF SENATORS

21. The Senate shall, subject to the Provisions of this Act, consist of an unlimited number of Members, who shall be styled Senators.

REPRESENTATION OF PROVINCES IN SENATE

22. (1) In relation to the Constitution of the Senate, Canada shall be deemed to consist of Five Divisions:

1. Ontario; 2. Quebec; 3. The Maritime Provinces, Nova Scotia and New Brunswick, and Prince Edward Island and Newfoundland; 4. The Western Provinces of Manitoba, British Columbia, Saskatchewan, and Alberta; 5. The Federal Territories of the Northwest Territories, Nunavut, and the Yukon, which Five Divisions shall (subject to the Provisions of this Act) be represented in the Senate.

(2) The Governor General, in the Queen's name and in respect of Canada, shall appoint, every four years, five representatives for each of the first four divisions, as specified in subsection (1), provided that for those divisions with multiple Provinces, no Province shall be denied an appointment during the course of a four-year period. Furthermore, the fifth division, as specified in subsection (1), shall receive one appointment, every four years, provided that no Federal Territory shall be denied an appointment during the course of a twelve-year period.

(3) Lieutenant Governors of each Province, in the Queen's name and in respect of each Province, shall appoint, each year, one representative to the Senate. Commissioners of each Federal Territory, in the Queen's name and in respect of each Federal Territory, shall appoint, every four years, one representative to the Senate.

REPRESENTATION IN OTHER CATEGORIES

(4) No more than half of the total number of Senators appointed during each four-year period by the Governor-General or Lieutenant Governor, in the name of the Queen, may be representatives or, otherwise, members of the same political party, nor may a Senator serve concurrently in any other legislative body in Canada.

(5) Provision shall be made in the Senate of Canada for the accommodation of Senators who have no formal party affiliation, including in terms of the appointment of appropriate Parliamentary Officers to oversee their organizational and procedural interests.

(6) In addition to Senators appointed pursuant to subsections (2) and (3) and notwithstanding the restrictions imposed by subsection (4), the following persons shall be automatically appointed (provided that they meet all other qualifications pursuant to sections 23 and 31 of this Act) as Senators: former Governors General of Canada, former Lieutenant Governors of the several Provinces, former Commissioners of the Federal Territories, former Speakers of the House of Commons, former Speakers of the legislatures of the several Provinces, former Speakers of the several Assemblies of the Federal Territories, former Clerks of the Queen's Privy Council for Canada, former occupants of the post of senior civil servant for each of the several Provinces and Federal Territories, former Presidents of the Council of First Nations, Companions

of the Order of Canada, former Governors of the Bank of Canada, former Ambassadors of Canada to the United Nations, former Commissioners of the Royal Canadian Mounted Police, former Governors of the Canadian Broadcasting Corporation/Radio Canada, former Directors of the National Gallery of Canada, former Chiefs of Staff of the Armed Forces of Canada, former Commissioners of the Human Rights Commission of Canada, any person who has been conferred the title of Right Honorable in respect of Canada and who is not, otherwise, occupying an elected or otherwise official public post or office.

(7) In the name of the Queen, the Governor General shall be entitled to appoint one additional Senator per year without regard to region, province, or territory, the several Lieutenant Governors may appoint one additional Senator, each, per every four-year period, and the several Commissioners of Federal Territories may appoint one additional Senator per every eight-year period. None of the Senators appointed under this category shall be a member of a political party and all Senators appointed under this category shall have distinguished themselves in fields of endeavor that may include, but should not be limited to: education, the natural and physical sciences, medicine, the performing and visual arts, the literary arts, the military, police, international diplomacy, business, philanthropy, athletics, journalism, humanist and social science scholarship, and other professional and non-professional fields.

(8) The Governor General, the several Lieutenant Governors, and the several Commissioners of Federal Territories, in the name of the Queen, shall seek to appoint Senators in a manner consistent with the preservation and enhancement of the multicultural heritage of Canadians.

(9) Senators who are serving in the Senate at the time of the adoption of subsections (2) and (3) shall continue to serve in that Chamber, pursuant to the requirements and conditions specified in this Act.

POWERS OF THE SENATE IN RELATION TO OFFICIAL LANGUAGES BILLS

IV. 18. (8) Any Bill pertaining to the Official Languages of Canada must be approved by both the House of Commons and the Senate in order to be presented to the Governor General, on behalf of the Queen, for the Royal Assent, notwithstanding any other conditions specified within this section and pursuant to the requirements specified within section 36 of this Act.

(9) A bill pertaining to the Official Languages of Canada will not be deemed to have passed the Senate unless it receives, within that body, the support of a majority of Senators who are formally designated as English-speaking and a majority of Senators who are formally designated as French-speaking.

(10) The status of a Senator as English-speaking or French-speaking will be certified by the Speaker of the Senate and affirmed by the Governor General.

POWERS OF THE SENATE IN RELATION TO NOMINATIONS

(11) Any nominee of an executive agency that has national regulatory responsibility and authority over the economic, diplomatic, and cultural policies of Canada may be subject to review by the Senate, prior to final confirmation of those appointments. Any such review must be initiated by the Speaker of the Senate (in accordance with the internal rules of that House) within 20 days following the issuing of the relevant Order in Council or other official announcement of that nomination and the proceedings may not extend beyond 40 days following the official announcement of that nomination. The Senate may, upon its own discretion, make non-binding recommendations relating to the qualifications and appropriateness of these nominees. Prior to the initiation and conclusion of a Senate review, nominees may serve in that position in an acting capacity, subject to immediate change upon the issuing of a recommendation, the expiration of 20 days without the initiation of a Senate review, or, in the event that a review is initiated, the conclusion of the 40-day period following the official announcement of that nomination.

QUALIFICATIONS OF SENATOR

23. The Qualifications of a Senator shall be as follows:

(1) He shall be of the full age of Thirty Years:

(2) He shall be either a natural-born Subject of the Queen, or a Subject of the Queen naturalized by an Act of the Parliament of Canada.

(3) He shall be resident in the Province for which he is appointed:

SUMMONS OF SENATOR

24. The Governor General shall from Time to Time, in the Queen's Name, by Instrument under the Great Seal of Canada, summon qualified Persons to the Senate; and, subject to the Provisions of this Act, every Person so summoned shall become and be a Member of the Senate and a Senator.

TENURE OF PLACE IN SENATE

29. (1) A Senator shall, subject to the provisions of this Act, hold his place in the Senate for life.

RESIGNATION OF PLACE IN SENATE

30. A Senator may by Writing under his Hand addressed to the Governor General resign his Place in the Senate, and thereupon the same shall be vacant.

DISQUALIFICATION OF SENATORS

31. The Place of a Senator shall become vacant in any of the following Cases:

(1) If for Two consecutive Sessions of the Parliament he fails to give his Attendance in the Senate:

(2) If he takes an Oath or makes a Declaration or Acknowledgment of Allegiance, Obedience, or Adherence to a Foreign Power, or does an Act whereby he becomes a Subject or Citizen, or entitled to the Rights or Privileges of a Subject or Citizen, of a Foreign Power:

(3) If he is attainted of Treason or convicted of Felony or of any infamous Crime:

(4) If he ceases to be qualified in respect of Property or of Residence; provided, that a Senator shall not be deemed to have ceased to be qualified in respect of Residence by reason only of his residing at the Seat of the Government of Canada while holding an Office under that Government requiring his Presence there.

SUMMONS ON VACANCY IN SENATE

32. When a Vacancy happens in the Senate by Resignation, Death, or otherwise, the Governor General shall by Summons to a fit and qualified Person fill the Vacancy.

QUESTIONS AS TO QUALIFICATIONS AND VACANCIES IN SENATE

33. If any Question arises respecting the Qualification of a Senator or a Vacancy in the Senate the same shall be heard and determined by the Senate.

APPOINTMENT OF SPEAKER OF SENATE

34. The Governor General may from Time to Time, by Instrument under the Great Seal of Canada, appoint a Senator to be Speaker of the Senate, and may remove him and appoint another in his Stead.

QUORUM OF SENATE

35. Until the Parliament of Canada otherwise provides, the Presence of at least Fifteen Senators, including the Speaker, shall be necessary to constitute a Meeting of the Senate for the Exercise of its Powers.

Appendix B

An Agreement on Practices Relating to the Senate of Canada

WHEREAS improvements to the function of the Senate of Canada is deemed to be a constructive endeavor that is supported by a large part of the citizenry of Canada;

AND WHEREAS certain improvements are recognized as being consistent with the principles of parliamentary democracy that have guided Canada throughout its history;

AND WHEREAS formal constitutional amendments to the Canada Act of 1867 are deemed to be unnecessary and impractical for achieving those improvements;

AND WHEREAS these improvements are deemed to be achievable, as much as possible, through non-statutory and informal agreement;

NOW THEREFORE, the Senate and the House of Commons of Canada have unanimously approved the following declaration of principles and practices that they are publicly committed to putting into effect as expeditiously as reasonably possible and are, furthermore, committed to maintaining on an ongoing basis.

DECLARATION OF NON-INTERFERENCE WITH GOVERNMENT MANDATE

The Senate of Canada will issue a public declaration that it will honor the electoral mandate of any elected government by guaranteeing the passage of any legislation that is related to the clear electoral manifesto and unambiguous, publicly-declared campaign promises of the political party that will be summoned to lead that government as a result of such an election. That commitment will include governments that are supported by a political party that has elected a majority of members of the House of Commons and those governments that are supported by a minority of members of that chamber. However, this commitment will not be regarded as deterring the Senate from offering amendments designed to improve legislation or policy implementation or to correct technical or other errors in relation to them. Furthermore, the Senate will retain the prerogative of rejecting legislation that is not deemed to be derived from an express electoral mandate or which otherwise clearly appears to be contrary to both the electoral mandate of the government and the public will and interest. This declaration will be confirmed upon the basis of the unanimous approval of the Senate but it will not be subject to statutory confirmation.

APPOINTMENT ADVISORY COMMISSION

A Commission will be established for the purpose of providing advice relating to future appointments to the Senate of Canada. This Appointment Advisory Commission will examine nominations proposed by the Government and offer an opinion on the suitability of those nominations in terms of the following criteria: 1) the perceived qualifications and high standards of propriety for holding such an important and distinguished office; 2) actual or potential conflicts of interest that might undermine the fair performance of the senatorial duties of the nominated persons; 3) general considerations relating to the integrity of the Senate, the ethical norms of the Parliament of Canada, and the public interest.

The Commission also will, from time to time, offer advice relating to persons who could be considered for potential nomination to the Senate, particularly of persons who shall not have formal party affiliation and are deemed to be appropriate candidates because of their distinguished backgrounds, meritorious service to the country, or strong and specific public approbation, including recommendations submitted to the Commission by Canadian citizens.

This Commission may not reject or, otherwise, interfere with the actual nomination process of Canadian Senators. The Commission will confine its activities to offering advice to the Prime Minister and the Governor-General. That advice will be publicly made and the proceedings of the Council will be transparent and open to public scrutiny.

This commission will be comprised of 18 members who are appointed according to the following formula: three members appointed, each, by the Prime Minister, the Speaker of the House of Commons, the Chief Justice of Canada, and the Clerk of the Privy Council and six members nominated by the Speaker of the Senate. Appointments to this commission will be confirmed by a vote of the Senate of Canada. The commission will be responsible for maintaining its own schedule and agenda and will be provided a budget and institutional support for its activities as determined by appropriate parliamentary statute.

SENATORIAL HONORS

The Department of Canadian Heritage will be asked to develop recommendations for additional and enhanced symbols of status and protocol relating to Senators of Canada. These recommendations will not include any matters of remuneration, legal privileges, or other individual advantages that are not of a purely symbolic nature. The recommendations of the Department of Canadian Heritage will be delivered to the Queen for her consideration and action upon her own authority in right of Canada.

ADDITIONAL SENATORS AS NON-PARTISAN APPOINTMENTS

The Government of Canada will make a commitment to restrict any requests for the creation of additional Senators under section 26 of the Constitution Act of 1867 to persons who have had no party affiliation and who would be expected to participate in a politically independent manner as Senators. The Governor-General will be apprised of this agreement whenever such a request for additional Senators (beyond the constitutionally-established normal number) is submitted under the provisions of that section. The Appointment Advisory Commission will be consulted prior to requests for additional Senators being formally submitted to the Governor-General and may investigate and offer advice in relation to it.

COMPENSATION OF SENATORS

The remuneration of Senators of Canada will no longer be provided by salary (with the exception of government ministers and parliamentary officers) but through compensation based upon actual attendance and participation in the parliamentary business of that chamber, including its committees. Senators also may be compensated for reasonable expenses that they incur in the performance of their parliamentary duties, including travel and lodging expenses. The precise terms, conditions, and levels pertaining to this compensation will be determined by statute.

INDEPENDENT SENATORS

A category of Senators who are not members of a political party and are considered to be politically independent will be accommodated within the Senate. That accommodation will include the creation and maintenance of Conveners for the purpose of organizing and protecting their parliamentary participation (especially in terms of debate and committee assignments) and privileges.

PROVINCIAL CONSULTATION

The Government of Canada will publicly commit itself to consult with, and accept the advice of, the several provincial and (at the discretion of the Prime Minister of Canada) territorial governments of Canada in relation to nominating appropriate persons to the Senate. The various First Ministers will negotiate this process of consultation and advice among themselves. These governments are expected to demonstrate good faith in arriving at a consensus in this respect.

PROCEDURAL INITIATIVES

The Senate of Canada will commit itself to form a Standing Committee on Procedural Reform for the purpose of developing and maintaining internal procedures and practices that are designed to enhance its parliamentary business in a reasonably fair, non-partisan, and constructive manner. These procedural improvements may include, but not be limited to, changes to the presence and role of party officers within the chamber (including party whips), improved public access to Senators and Senate committees, the development of liaison services, and alterations to the rules of debate and committee membership and participation for the purpose of promoting these same goals. These changes will be performed entirely within the Senate and be subject to its own discretion and initiative.

Bibliography

"Australian Senate Rejects Carbon Trade Bill." *China Daily*. December 12, 2009. Available: http://www.chinadaily.com.cn/world/2009-12/02/content_9101814.htm.

"House of Lords Expenses." February 2014. Available: http://www.parliament.uk/business/lords /whos-in-the-house-of-lords/house-of-lords-expenses/.

"Immigrants of Distinction Award Recipients: Business Award." Available: http://www. immigrantservicescalgary.ca/ida/recipients.

"Laurence Olivier Takes His Seat in the House of Lords." *The News and Courier*. Charleston, SC. March 25, 1971.

"Liberating the Senators." *The Economist*. January 31, 2014. Available: http://www.economist.com/ blogs/americasview/2014/01/canadian-politics.

"Mike Shaikh for Senate." Available: http://www.mikeforsenate.ca/.

"Mining Tax Faces One More Hurdle." *Brisbane Times*. February 6, 2012. Available: http://news.brisbanetimes.com.au/breaking-news-national/mining-tax-faces-one-more-hurdle-20120206-1r1r3.html.

"Senate Memoranda to His Excellency the Governor General." Ottawa, 1873.

"Senate Reform in Canada." Available: http://www.rhondaparkinson.com/senate-reform.htm.

"Timeline: Key Dates in the Evolution of the Senate Expense Claim Controversy." *Global News*. August 13, 2013. Available: http://globalnews.ca/news/568714/a-look-at-key-dates-in-the-evolution-of-the-senate-expense-claim-controversy/.

"Trudeau's Senate Plans and Angry Veterans." *The National*. January 30, 2014. Available: http://www.cbc.ca/thenational/content/analysis/atissue/trudeaus_senate_plan_angry_veterans.html.

Adams, Howard. "The Roots of Separatism." *History of Education Quarterly*, vol. 8, no. 1 (Spring 1968).

Adamson, Christopher R., Peter C. Findlay, Michael K. Oliver, Janet Solberg. "The Unpublished Research of the Royal Commission on Bilingualism and Biculturalism." *Canadian Journal of Political Science*, vol. 7, no. 4 (December 1974).

Albert, Richard. "The Fusion of Presidentialism and Parliamentarism." *American Journal of Comparative Law*, vol. 57, no. 3 (Summer 2009).

Albinski, Henry S. "The Canadian Senate: Politics and the Constitution." *American Political Science Review*, vol.57, no. 2 (June 1963).

Almond, Gabriel A. and James S. Coleman. *The Politics of the Developing Areas.* Princeton, NJ: Princeton University Press, 1960.

Alter, Alison B. "Minimizing the Risks of Delegation: Multiple Referral in the German Bundesrat." *American Journal of Political Science*, vol. 46, no. 2 (April 2002).

Amar, Vik D. "The Senate and the Constitution." *Yale Law Journal*, vol. 97, no. 6 (May 1988).

Anastakis, Dmitry and Penny Bryden. *Framing Canadian Federalism.* Toronto: University of Toronto Press, 2009.

Anderson, Fred. *Crucible of War: The Seven Years' War and the Fate of Empire in British North America, 1754–1756.* New York: Vintage Books, 2000.

Anderson, Olive. "The Wensleydale Peerage Case and the Position of the House of Lords in the Mid-Nineteenth Century." *English Historical Review*, vol. 82, no. 324 (July 1967).

Andrain, Chalres F. and David E. Apter. *Political Protest and Social Change.* New York: New York University Press, 1995.

Aristotle. *The Politics and the Constitution of Athens.* edited by Stephen Everson. Cambridge: Cambridge University Press, 1996.

———. *The Politics.* Translated by Benjamin Jowett, edited by H. W. C. Davis. Mineola, NY: Dover, 2000.

Atkinson, Michael M. and Maureen Mancuso. "Do We Need a Code of Conduct for Politicians? The Search for an Elite Political Culture of Corruption in Canada." *Canadian Review of Canadian Studies*, vol. 18, no. 3 (September 1985).

Aucoin, Peter. "Regionalism, Party, and National Government." In *Party Government and Regional Representation in Canada,* edited by Peter Aucoin, 137. Toronto: University of Toronto Press, 1985.

Auger, Julie. "Le Français au Québec à l'aube de vingt et unième siècle." *French Review*, vol. 77, no. 1 (October 2003).

Ayres, Jeffrey M. "Political Process and Popular Protest: The Mobilization against Free Trade in Canada." *American Journal of Economics and Sociology*, vol. 55, no. 4 (October 1996).

Azzi, Stephen and Norman Hillmer. "Evaluating Prime Ministerial Performance: The Canadian Experience." In *Understanding Prime Ministerial Performance: Comparative Perspectives*, edited by Paul Strangio, Paul T. Hart, and James Walter, 242–263. Oxford: Oxford University Press, 2013.

Bach, Stanley. *Politics and Platypus: The Australian Senate in Theory and Practice.* Canberra: Australian Senate, 2003.

Bagehot [editorial board]. "A Democratic Embarrassment." *The Economist*, June 13, 2015, http://www.economist.com/news/britain/21654084-house-lords-aged-overcrowded-and-increasingly-effective-democratic-embarrassment.

Bagehot, Walter. *The English Constitution.* Oxford: Oxford University Press, 2001.

Bailey, Sidney, ed. *The Future of the House of Lords.* London: Hansard Society, 1954.

Bakvis, Herman and Roselle Hryciuk. "An Experiment in Intrastate Federalism: The Cabinet Committee on Canadian Unity." In *Canada: The State of the Federation, 1993*, edited by Ronald L. Watts and Douglas M. Brown. Kingston. ON: Institute on Intergovernmental Relations, 1993.

Bakvis, Herman, and Douglas Brown. "Policy Coordination in Federal Systems: Comparing Intergovernmental Processes and Outcomes in Canada and the United States." *Publius*, vol. 40, no. 3 (Summer 2010).

Baldry, Keith. "Why Christy Clark is Rejecting Justin Trudeau's Reform of the Senate." *Global News*, December 3, 2015. http://globalnews.ca/news/2379480/why-christy-clark-is-rejecting-justin-trudeaus-reform-of-the-senate/.

Bashevkin, Sylvia. *True Patriot Love: The Politics of Canadian Nationalism.* Oxford: Oxford University Press, 1991.

Bates, Clifford. *Aristotle's Best Regime: Kingship, Democracy, and the Rule of Law.* Baton Rouge: Louisiana State University Press, 2003.

BBC News. "No Charges on "Cash-for-Honours." *BBC News.* July 20, 2007. Available: http://news.bbc.co.uk/ 2/hi/uk_news/politics/6907594.stm.

Bell, Robert Bruce, John Newton, and Sandford Fleming. *Report on a General Scheme of Improvements for the Harbour of Montreal.* Montreal: Commission of Engineers, 1877.

Berger, Suzanne and Michael J. Piore. *Dualism and Discontinuity in Industrial Societies.* Cambridge: Cambridge University Press, 1980.

Bergman, Torbjörn, Wolfgang C. Müller, Kaare Strøm, and Magnus Blomgren. "Democratic Delegation and Accountability: Cross-National Patterns." In *Delegation and Accountability in Parliamentary Democracies.* Oxford: Oxford University Press, 2003.

Bevir, Mark and R. A. W. Rhodes. *The State as Cultural Practice.* Oxford: Oxford University Press, 2010.

Bill Curry. "Trudeau's Senate Appointments Spark Debate on Political Allegiance." *The Globe and Mail*, November 20, 2016, http://www.theglobeandmail.com/news/politics/trudeaus-senate-appointments-spark-debate-on-political-allegiance/article32953017/.

Bill, James A. and Robert L. Hardgrave, Jr. *Comparative Politics: The Quest for Theory.* Washington, DC: University Press of America, 1981.

Blackburn, Robin. *Ideology in Social Science.* New York: Pantheon, 1972.

Bluhm, William T. "The Place of the 'Polity' in Aristotle's Ideal State." *Journal of Politics*, vol. 24, no. 4 (November 1962).

Bogdanor, Vernon. *The New British Constitution.* Portland, OR: Hart, 2009.

Bonenfant, Jean-Charles. *Le Senat dans le federalism canadien.* Ottawa: Commission Royale d'Enquete sur le Bilingusime et le Biculturalisme, 1966.

Boutlier, Alex. "Liberals are Expected to Appoint 20 New Senators within Weeks." *Toronto Star.* September 20, 2016, https://www.thestar.com/news/canada/2016/09/21/liberals-are-expected-to-appoint-20-new-senators-within-weeks.html.

Brazier, Rodney. "Appendix I: The Parliament Acts." *Constitution: Seventh Report.* London: House of Lords, 2006. Available: http://www.publications.parliament.uk/pa/ld200506/ldselect/ldconst/ 141/14104.htm.

Brione, Patrick. "Survation Polling for *Daily Mirror* Shows Support for the House of Lords but Also Reform." *Survation*, July 30, 2015, http://survation.com/public-still-support-reform-for-house-of-lords/.

British Columbia. *Constitutional Proposals: Reform of the Canadian Senate.* Victoria, 1978.

Broderick, Albert. *The French Institutionalists: Marice Hariou, Georges Renard, Joseph T. Delos.* Cambridge, Ma: Harvard University Press, 1970.

Broschek, Jörg. "Historical Institutionalism and the Varieties of Federalism in Germany and Canada." *Publius*, vol. 42, no. 4 (Fall 2012).

Browne, G. P., ed. *Documents on the Confederation of British North America.* Toronto: University of Toronto Press, 1969.

Brugger, Bill. *Republican Theory in Political Thought: Virtuous or Virtual?* London: Macmillan, 1999.

Buchanan, Allen E. "Assessing the Communitarian Critique of Liberalism." *Ethics*, vol. 99, no. 4 (July 1999).

Buckner, Phillip Alfred. *The Transition to Responsible Government.* Westport, CT: Greenwood Press, 1985.

Bulpitt, Jim. *Territory and Power in the United Kingdom.* Manchester: Manchester University Press, 1983.

Burke, Edmund. *Reflections on the Revolution in France*, edited by J. G. A. Pocock. Indianapolis: Hackett, 1987.

Burton, Pierre. *The National Dream.* Montreal: McClelland and Stewart, 1971.

Butler, David and Gareth Butler. *Twentieth Century British Political Facts, 1900–2000.* London: Macmillan, 2000.

Butler, Eamonn. "The Future of the Salisbury Convention." *Adam Smith Institute.* June 2010. Available: http://www.adamsmith.org/blog/politics-and-government/the-future-of-the-salisbury-convention.

Bybee, Jay S.(1997)."Ulysses at the Mast: Democracy, Federalism, and the Sirens' Song of the Seventeenth Amendment. *Northwestern University Law Review*, vol. 91, no. 1 (1997).

Cairns, Alan C. "Alternative Styles in the Study of Canadian Politics." *Canadian Journal of Political Science*, vol. 7, no. 1 (March 1974).

———. "The Judicial Committee and Its Critics." *Canadian Journal of Political Science*, vol. 4, no. 3 (1971).

Cameron, Charles M., Albert D. Cover, Jeffrey A. Segal. "Senate Voting on Supreme Court Nominees: A Neoinstitutional Model." *American Political Science Review*, vol. 84, no. 2 (June 1990).

Cameron, David and Richard Simeon. "Intergovernmental Relations in Canada: The Emergence of Collaborative Federalism." *Publius*, vol. 32, no. 2 (Spring 2002).

Cameron, David. "Inter-Legislative Federalism." In *Reconsidering the Institutions of Canadian Federalism*, J. Peter Meekinson, Hamish Telford, and Harvey Lazar, eds. (Montreal and Kingston, ON: McGill-Queen's University Press, 2004), pp. 163–175.

Campbell, Colin. *The Canadian Senate: A Lobby from Within.* Toronto: MacMillan, 1978.

Canada 2000 Task Force. *Senate Reform and Constitutional Change.* Calgary: Canada West Foundation, 1992.

Canada West Foundation. *Renewal of Canada—Institutional Reform.* Calgary: Canada West Foundation, 1992.

Canada, *Report of the Special Joint Committee of the Senate and of the House of Commons on Senate Report* (Molgat Cosgrove Report). Ottawa: Queen's Printer, 1984.

Canada. Constitution Act, 1867, part IV, sec. 24

Canada. Constitution Act, 1867, part IV, sec. 26.

Canada. Constitution Act, 1867, sec. 31(1).

Cannadine, David. *The Decline and Fall of the British Aristocracy.* New York: Vintage Books.

Cappe, Mel. "In Defence of an Appointed Senate." *Globe and Mail.* June 17, 2013.

Careless, J. M. S. *Brown of the Globe.* Toronto: Macmillan, 1963.

Carr, Craig L. *Liberalism and Pluralism: The Politics of E Pluribus Unum.* New York: Palgrave Macmillan, 2010.

CBC Archives. "Canada's Upper House: Do We Need the Senate?" Available: http://web.archive.org/web/20071016103302/http://www.cbc.ca/newsinreview/apr98/senate/consitut.htm.

Chandler, Marsha A. "Constitutional Change and Public Policy: The Impact of the Resource Amendment (Section 92A)." *Canadian Journal of Political Science*, vol. 19, no. 1 (March 1986).

Chilcote, Ronald H. *Comparative Inquiry in Politics and Political Economy.* Boulder, CO: Westview, 2000.

———. *Theories of Comparative Political Economy.* Boulder, CO: Westview, 2000.

Choi, Stephen J., Mitu Gilati, and Eric A. Posner. "Professionals or Politicians: The Uncertain Empirical Case for an Elected Rather than an Appointed Judiciary." John M. Olin Law and Economics Working Paper No. 1831. Chicago: University of Chicago, 2006.

Cicero, Marcus Tullius. *Selected Works.* Translated by Michael Grant. London: Penguin, 1971.

Clark, Manning. *A History of Australia.* Melbourne: Melbourne University Press, 1993.

Clark, William Roberts, Matt Golder, and Sona L. Golder. *Principles of Comparative Politics.* London: Sage, 2013.

Clarke, Frank G. *The History of Australia.* Westport, CT: Greenwood Press, 2002.

Clarke, Harold D., Allan Kornberg, and Marianne C. Stewart. "Parliament and Political Support in Canada." *American Political Science Review*, vol. 78, no. 2 (June 1984).

Clarke, Harold D., Colin Campbell, and Arthur Goddard, eds. *Parliament, Policy, and Representation.* Toronto: Methuen, 1980.

CO 42: Dufferin to Kimberly, dispatch no. 302. December 29, 1873.

Cockburn, A. P. *Political Annals of Canada.* London: Stanley Paul, 1909.

Cody, Howard. "Lessons from Australia in Canadian Senate Reform." *Canadian Parliamentary Review*, vol. 18, no. 2 (1995).

Coletto, David. "Is the British House of Lords Model Viable for Canada's Senate?" *Abacus Data Insider.* June 17, 2013. Available: http://abacusinsider.com/politics-public-affairs/canadian-senate-house-lords-model-viable-canada/.

Conradt, David P. and Eric Lagenbacher. *The German Polity.* Lanham, MD: Rowman and Littlefield, 2013.

Consultative Group on Constitutional Change. *Resolving Deadlocks: The Public Response.* Canberra: Department of the Prime Minister and Cabinet, 2004.

Coorey, Philip. "Rudd Fights to the Death." *Sydney Morning Herald.* June 24, 2010. Available http://www.smh.com.au/national/rudd-fights-to-the-death-20100623-yz8r.html.

Coucill, Irma. *Canada's Prime Ministers, Governors General, and Fathers of Confederation.* Markham, ON: Pembroke, 2005.

Cowen, Zelman. "The Office of Governor General." *Daedalus*, vol. 114, no. 1 (Winter 1985).

Crick, Bernard. *Democracy: A Very Short Introduction.* Oxford: Oxford University Press, 2002.

Crowder, George. *Isaiah Berling: Liberty, Pluralism, and Liberalism.* Cambridge: Polity, 2004.

Curtis, W. Redmond. "The Origin and Genesis of the Deadlock Clause of the Australian Constitution." *Political Science Quarterly*, vol. 60, no. 3 (September 1945).

Daalder, Hans. "The Rise of Parties in Western Democracies." In *Political Parties and Democracy*, edited by Larry Diamond and Richard Gunther. Baltimore: Johns Hopkisn University Press, 2001.

Dahl, Robert. "On Removing Certain Impediments to Democracy in the United States." *Political Science Quarterly*, vol. 92, no. 1 (Spring 1977).

———. *A Preface to Democratic Theory.* Chicago: University of Chicago Press, 2006.

———. *On Democracy.* New Haven, CT: Yale University Press, 2000.

———. *Polyarchy: Participation and Opposition.* New Haven, CT: Yale University Press, 1972.

Dalberg-Acton, John. "Letter to Bishop Mandell Creighton, April 5, 1887." In *Historical Essays and Studies*, edited by J. N. Figgis and R. V. Laurence. London: Macmillan, 1907.

Dalton, Russell J. and Martin P. Wattenberg. "Unthinkable Democracy: Political Change in Advanced Industrial Democracies." In *Parties without Partisans: Political Change in Advanced Industrial Democracies*, edited by Russell J. Dalton and Martin P. Wattenberg. Oxford: Oxford University Press, 2002.

Dangerfield, George. *The Strange Death of Liberal England.* London: Paladin, 1972.

Daniels, William J. "The Geographic Factor in Appointments to the United States Supreme Court, 1789–1976." *Western Political Quarterly*, vol. 31, no. 2 (June 1978).

David, L. O. *L'Histoire du Canada depuis la Confederation.* Montreal: Librarie Beauchemin, 1909.

Debates and Proceedings of the Senate of the Dominion of Canada, March 19, 1877 (Ottawa: Queen's Printer for Canada, 1877).

Debates and Proceedings of the Senate, April 28, 1877.
Debates and Proceedings of the Senate, April 3, 1871.
Debates and Proceedings of the Senate, April 3, 1876.
Debates and Proceedings of the Senate, April 4, 1871.
Debates and Proceedings of the Senate, April 5, 1876.
Debates and Proceedings of the Senate, April 6, 1875.
Debates and Proceedings of the Senate, April 7, 1875.
Debates and Proceedings of the Senate, June 11, 1872.
Debates and Proceedings of the Senate, June 4, 1869.
Debates and Proceedings of the Senate, March 20, 1876.
Debates and Proceedings of the Senate, March 21, 1871.
Debates and Proceedings of the Senate, March 21, 1878.
Debates and Proceedings of the Senate, March 30, 1876.
Debates and Proceedings of the Senate, March 31, 1876.
Debates and Proceedings of the Senate, May 23, 1874.
Debates and Proceedings of the Senate, May 28, 1872.
Debates and Proceedings of the Senate, May 9, 1878.
Debates and Proceedings of the Senate. February 18, 1875.
Debates and Proceedings of the Senate. March 10, 1875.
Debates and Proceedings of the Senate. March 6, 1876.
Debates and Proceedings of the Senate. March 7, 1876.
deKiewiet, W. and F. H. Underhill, eds. *Dufferin/Carnarvon Correspondence*. Toronto: Champlain Society, 1955.
Deutsch, Karl W. "Social Mobilization and Political Development." *American Political Science Review*, vol. 55, no. 3 (1964).
Dicey, A. V. *Introduction to the Study of the Law of the Constitution*. Indainapolis: Liberty Fund, 1982.
Dion, Léon. "The Mystery of Quebec." *Daedalus*, vol. 117, no. 4 (Fall 1988).
———.. *Le Duel constitutionnel Québec-Canada*. Montréal: Boréal, 1995.
Dion, Stéphane. "Le plan Trudeau pour un Sénat moins partisan et plus indépendant n'exige pas de changement constitutionnel." *Le Huffington Post (Québec)*. May 17, 2014. Available: http://quebec.huffingtonpost.ca/stephane-dion/senat-plan-trudeau-onstitution_b_5339170.html ?utm_hp_ref=politique.
———. "Liberal Plan is Best Path to a Functional Senate." *Toronto Star*. May 15, 2014. Available: http://www.thestar.com/opinion/commentary/2014/05/15/stphane_dion_liberal_plan_is_best_path_to_a_functional_senate.html.
Docherty, David C. "The Canadian Senate: Chamber of Sober Second Reflection or the Loony Cousin Best Not Talked About?" *Journal of Legislative Studies*, vol. 8, no. 3 (April 2002).
Doern, G. Bruce and Richard Phidd. *Canadian Public Policy*. Toronto: Methuen, 1983.
Doern, G. Bruce and V. Seymour Wilson. "Conclusions and Observations." In *Issues in Canadian Public Policy*, edited by G. Bruce Doern and V. Seymour Wilson. Toronto: Macmillan, 1974.
Donnelly, Jack. "Human Rights, Democracy, and Development." *Human Rights Quarterly*, vol. 21, no. 3 (August 1999).

Dorey, Peter and Alexandra Kelso. *House of Lords Reform since 1911.* New York: Palgrave Macmillan, 2011.

Dorey, Peter. *The Labour Party and Constitutional Reform.* Baingstoke, England: Palgrave Macmillan, 2008.

Druckman, James N., Lanny W. Martin, and Michael F. Thies. "Influence without Confidence: Upper Chambers and Government Formation." *Legislative Studies Quarterly*, vol. 30, no. 4 (November 2005).

Dunleavy, Patrick and Brendan O'Leary. *Theories of the State: The Politics of Liberal Democracy.* New York: New Amsterdam Books, 1998.

Dyck, Rand. *Canadian Politics: Critical Approaches.* Toronto: Nelson, 2012.

Dymond, Glenn and Hugo Deadmon. *The Salisbury Doctrine* London: House of Lords Library Note, June 2006.

Eagles, Munroe and Sharon A. Manna. "Politics and Government." In *Canadian Studies in the New Milennium*, edited by Patrick James and Mark Kasoff. Toronto: University of Toronto Press, 2008.

Eggerston, Thráinn. *Economic Behavior and Institutions.* Cambridge: Cambridge University Press, 1990.

Eisenstadt, S. N. and L. Roniger, Patrons. *Clients, and Friends: Interpersonal Relations and the Structure of Trust in Society.* Cambridge: Cambridge University Press, 1984.

Elections Alberta. *Report of the Chief Electoral Officer on the Senate Nominee Election* (Edmonton: Government of Alberta, 2004).

———. *Report of the Chief Electoral Officer on the Senate Nominee Election* (Edmonton: Government of Alberta, 2012).

Elton, David and Peter McCormick. *A Blueprint for Senate Reform.* Calgary: Canada West Foundation, 1990.

Elton, David, Frederick C. Engelmann, and Peter McCormick. *Alternatives: Toward an Effective Federal System for Canada.* Calgary: Canada West Foundation, 1978.

Emy, Hugh V. *The Politics of Australian Democracy.* Melbourne: Macmillan, 1974.

Engelmann, Frederick C. "A Prologue to Structural Reform of the Government of Canada." *Canadian Journal of Political Science*, vol. 19, no. 4 (December 1986).

Engelmann, Frederick C., Peter McCormick, and David Elton. *Alternatives: Towards the Development of an Effective Federal System for Canada.* Calgary: Canada West Foundation, 1978.

Errington, Joseph. "Getting Language Rights: The Rhetorics of Language Endangerment and Loss." *American Anthropologist*, vol. 105, no. 4 (December 2003).

Evans, Peter B., Dietrich Rueschemeyer, and Theda Skopcol. "On the Road Toward a More Adequate Understanding of the State." In *Bringing the State Back*, edited by Peter B. Evans, Dietrich Rueschemeyer, and Theda Skopcol. Cambridge: Cambridge University Press, 1999.

Fabbrini, Sergio. "Political Change without Institutional Transformation: What Can We Learn from the Italian Crisis of the 1990s?" *International Political Science Review,* vol. 21, no. 2 (April 2000).

Findlay, Martha Hall. "Spin Overtakes Best of Trudeau's Attempt at Senate Reform." *Huffington Post (Canada).* February 4, 2014. Available: http://www.huffingtonpost.ca/martha-hall-findlay/trudeau-senate-reform_b_4724979.html.

Finer, Herman. *The Theory and Practice of Modern Government.* London: Methuen, 1962.

Fisk, David. "Superfluous or Mischievous: Evaluating the Determinants of Government Defeats in Second Chambers." *Legislative Studies Quarterly*, vol. 36, no. 2 (May 2011).

Forsey, Eugene. "Alexander Mackenzie's Memoranda on the Appointment of Extra Senators." *Canadian Historical Review*, vol. 27, no. 2 (June 1946).

Franks, C. E. S. "Not Dead Yet But Should It Be Resurrected? The Canadian Senate." In *Senates:Bicameralism in the Contemporary World,* edited by S. C. Patterson and A. Mughan. Columbus: Ohio State University Press, 1999.

———. *The Parliament of Canada.* Toronto: University of Toronto Press, 1987.

Gagnon, Alain-G. *Le Fédéralisme canadien contemporain: Fondemants traditions institutions.* Montréal: Les Presses de l'Université de Montréal, 2006.

Gardbaum, Stephen. "Liberalism, Autonomy, and Moral Conflict." *Stanford Law Review*, vol. 48, no. 2 (January 1996).

Garner, Christopher and Natalia Letki. "Party Structure and Backbench Dissent in the Canadian and British Parliaments." *Canadian Journal of Political Science*, vol. 38, no. 2 (June 2005).

Gibbins, Roger and Robert Roach. *A New Senate for a More Democratic Canada.* Calgary: Canada West Foundation, 2010.

Gibbins, Roger. *A New Senate for a More Democratic Canada.* Calgary: Canada West Foundation, 2010.

Gibbons, Kenneth M. "The Political Culture of Corruption in Canada." In *Political Corruption in Canada: Cases, Causes, and Cures*, edited by Kenneth M. Gibbons and Donald C. Rowat. Toronto: McClelland and Stewart, 1976.

Gibbons, Kenneth M. and Donald C. Rowat, eds. *Political Corruption in Canada:Cases, Causes, and Cures.* Toronto: McClelland and Stewart, 1976.

Gibson, Gordon. "Challenges in Senate Reform: Conflicts of Interest, Unintended Consequences, New Possibilities." *Public Policy Sources,* vol. 83 (September 2004).

Gould, Lewis L. *The Most Exclusive Club.* New York: Basic Books, 2006.

Government of Alberta, International and Intergovernmental Relations. "Alberta Senate Nominee Elections." Available: http://www.international.alberta.ca/592.cfm.

Government of Canada. *Charlottetown Accord*, 1992, p. 5.

Government of Canada. Independent Advisory Board for Appointment of Senators, https://www.canada.ca/en/campaign/independent-advisory-board-for-senate-appointments.html.

Government of Canada, Prime Minister's Office. "Prime Minister Announces Intention to Recommend the Appointment of Nine New Senators." October 27, 2016, http://pm.gc.ca/eng/news/2016/10/27/prime-minister-announces-intention-recommend-appointment-nine-new-senators.

Government of Canada. *Shaping Canada's Future—Together.* Ottawa: Queen's Printer, 1991.

Grenier, Eric. "Wildrose or PQ Senators? Welcome to an Elected Red Chamber." *Globe and Mail.* February 3, 2013. Available: http://www.theglobeandmail.com/news/politics/wildrose-or-pq-senators-welcome-to-an-elected-red-chamber/article8127059/.

Grimard, Normand. *L'indispensable Sénat: defense d'une institution mal aimée*. Hull, QC: Vents d'Ouest, 1993.

Gwyn, Richard. *Nation Builder: Sir John A. Macdonald: His Life, Our Times, vol II: 1867–1891*. Toronto: Random House, 2011.

Hall, Peter A. and Rosemary C. R. Taylor. "Political Science and the Three New Institutionalisms." *Political Studies*, vol. 44, no. 5 (May 2011).

Hamilton-Temple-Blackwood, Frederick, Marquis of Dufferin, and Henry Herbert. Earl of Carnarvon. *Dufferin/Carnarvon Correspondence: 1874–1878*. edited by C. W. deKewiet and F. H. Underhill. Toronto: Champlain Society, 1955.

Hammond, Thomas H. and Gary J. Miller. "The Core of the Constitution." *American Political Science Review*, vol. 81 (1987).

Hansard. House of Lords, Third Series, February 19, 1867.

Hanssen, F. Andrew. "The Effect of Judicial Institutions on Uncertainty and the Rate of Litigation: The Elections versus Appointment of State Judges." *Journal of Legal Studies*, vol. 28, no. 1 (January 1999).

Hayes, Alan L. *Anglicans in Canada: Controversies and Identity in Historical Perspective*. Urbana: University of Illinois Press, 2004.

Heard, Andrew. *Canadian Constitutional Conventions: The Marriage of Law and Politics*. Oxford: Oxford University Press, 1991.

Heller, William B. "Divided Politics: Bicameralism, Parties, and Policy in Democratic Legislatures." *Annual Review of Political Science*, vol. 10, no. 2 (2007).

Her Majesty's Government. *Reform of the House of Lords*. London: Her Majesty's Stationer's Office, 2007.

———. *The House of Lords: Reform*. London: Her Majesty's Stationery Office, 2007.

Herman, Michael John. "The Founding of the Supreme Court of Canada and the Abolition of the Appeal to the Privy Council." *Ottawa Law Review*, vol. 8, no. 7 (Winter 1976).

Higley, John and Michael Burton. *The Elite Foundations of Liberal Democracy*. Lanham, MD: Rowman and Littlefield, 2006.

Hitchner, Dell G. "The Labour Government and the House of Lords." *Western Political Quarterly*, vol. 1, no. 4 (December 1948).

Hobbes, Thomas. *Leviathan*, ch. XXV.

Hofstadter, Richard. *Anti-Intellectualism in America*. New York: Vintage, 1966.

Hogg, Peter. *Constitutional Law of Canada*. Toronto: Carswell, 1977.

Hollis, Martin and Steve Smith. "Roles and Reasons in Foreign Policy Decision Making." *British Journal of Political Science*, vol. 16 (1986).

Hopkins, Angus. "Parliamentary Government' and Victorian Political Parties, c. 1830-c. 1880." *English Historical Review*, vol. 104, no. 412 (July 1989).

House of Commons of Canada, Special Committee on Electoral Reform, *Strengthening Democracy in Canada: Principles, Process, and Public Engagement for Electoral Reform*. Ottawa: House of Commons, December 2016.

House of Commons, Public Administration Select Committee. *Work of the Committee in 2007*. London: Her Majesty's Stationery Office, 2008.

House of Lords and House of Commons Joint Committee on Conventions. *Conventions of the UK Parliament*. London: Her Majesty's Stationery Office, 2006.

House of Lords Appointment Commission. "About Us." Available from http://lordsappointments.independent. gov.uk/about_us.aspx.

———. "Nominations for Non-Political Membership of the House of Lords." Available: http://lordsappointments.independent.gov.uk/how-to-apply.aspx.

———.. "Nominations from Women: A Note by the Secretariat." May 2005. Available: http://www.bbc.co.uk/blogs/opensecrets/HOLAC.pdf.

House of Lords Information Office. "Work of the House of Lords—Current and Previous Editions." Available: http://www.parliament.uk/mps-lords-and-offices/offices/lords/house-of-lords-information-office/work/.

Howe, Paul. "Rationality and Sovereignty Support in Quebec." *Canadian Journal of Political Science*, vol. 31, no. 1 (March 1998).

Howlett, Michael. "The Politics of Constitutional Change in a Federal System: Negotiating Section 92A of the Canada Constitution Act (1982)." *Publius*, vol. 21, no. 1 (Winter 1991).

Hudon, Raymond. "Intégration et diversité: Les Dilemmes de fédéralisme canadien." *Rervue Internationale de Science Politique*, vol. 5, no. 4 (1984).

Inglehart, Ronald, and Christian Welzel. "Changing Mass Priorities: The Link Between Modernization and Democracy." *Perspectives on Politics*, vol. 8, no. 2 (June 2010).

Inglis, Ian. "The Politics of Stardust or the Politics of Cool: Popular Music and the British Honours System." *International Review of the Aesthetics and Sociology of Music*, vol. 41, no. 1 (June 2010).

International Ombudsman Institute. *Australasia and Pacific Ombudsman Institutions: Mandates, Competences, and Good Practices.* New York: Springer, 2013.

Inwood, Gregory J., Carolyn M. Johns, and Patricia L. O'Reilly. *Intergovernmental Policy Capacity in Canada.* Montreal and Kingston, ON: McGill-Queen's University Press, 2011.

Ipsos MORI, House of Lords Survey, December 13, 2007, https://www.ipsos-mori.com/researchpublications/researcharchive/250/House-of-Lords-Survey.aspx.

Jackson, Robert J. and Michael M. Atkinson. *The Canadian Legislative System.* Toronto: Macmillan, 1974.

———. *The Canadian Legislative System.* Toronto: macmillan, 1974.

Jenkins, Barbara. "Reexamining the 'Obsolescence Bargain': A Study of Canada's National Energy Program." *International Organization*, vol. 40, no. 1 (Winter 1986).

Jennings, Bruce. "The Institutionalization of Ethics in the U.S. Senate." *Hastings Center Report*, vol. 11, no. 1 (February 1981).

Jennings, Ivor. *The Approach to Self-Government.* Cambridge: Cambridge University Press, 1956.

Jowell, Jeffrey. "The Rule of Law Today." In *The Changing Constitution*, edited by Jeffrey Jowell and Dawn Oliver. Oxford: Clarendon Press, 1989.

Joyal, Serge. "The Senate as the Embodiment of the Federal Principle." In *Protecting Canadian Democracy: The Senate You Never Knew*, edited by Serge Joyal. Montreal and Kingston, ON: McGill-Queen's University Press, 2003.

———. *Protecting Canadian Democracy: The Senate You Never Knew.* Montreal and Kingston, ON: McGill-Queen's University Press, 2003.

Kamrava, Mehran. *Understanding Comparative Politics: A Framework.* New York: Routledge, 1996.

Keat, Russell and John Urry. *Social Theory as Science.* New York: Routledge, 2011.

Kelly, Richard. "The Parliament Acts." London: Parliament and Constitution Centre, 2007.

Kelso, Alexandra. "Reforming the House of Lords: Navigating Representation, Democracy, and Legitimacy at Westminster." *Parliamentary Affairs*, vol. 59 (2006).

Kernaghan, Kenneth. "Power, Parliament, and Public Servants in Canada." *Canadian Public Policy*, vol. 5, no. 3 (Summer 1979).

Kingdon, John W. *Agendas, Alternatives, and Public Policies.* New York: Harper Collins, 1995.

Kirk, Russell. *The Conservative Mind: From Burke to Eliot.* Washington, DC: Regnery, 1985.

Klassen, Thomas R. and Steffen Schneider. "Similar Challenges, Different Solutions: Reforming Labour Market Policies in Germany and Canada During the 1990s." *Canadian Public Policy*, vol. 28, no. 1 (March 2002).

Kline, Jesse. "What the Senate Expense Scandal Teaches Us About Reform." *National Post.* August 14, 2012. Available: http://fullcomment.nationalpost.com/2013/08/14/jesse-kline-what-the-senate-expense-scandal-teaches-us-about-reform/.

Knopf, Rainer and F. L. Morton. *Charter Politics.* Scarborough, ON: Nelson, 1991.

Kramer, Matthew H. *John Locke and the Origins of Private Property.* Cambridge: Cambridge University Press, 1997.

Krouse, Richard W. "Polyarchy and Participation: The Changing Democratic Theory of Robert Dahl." *Polity*, vol. 14, no. 3 (Spring 1982).

Kucsko-Stadlmayer, Gabriele. *European Ombudsman-Institutions: A Comparative Legal Analysis Regarding the Multifaceted Realization of an Idea.* New York: SpringerWien, 2008.

Kunz, F. A. *The Modern Senate of Canada.* Toronto: University of Toronto Press, 1965.

Kylie, Edward. "Constitutional Developments, 1840–1867." In *Canada and Its Provinces.* Toronto: University of Toronto Press, 1914.

Lackoff, Sanford. "Tocqueville, Burke, and the Origins of Liberal Conservatism." *Review of Politics*, vol. 60, no. 3 (Summer 1998).

Lacoursière, Jacques. *Histoire populair de Québec, 1896–1960.* Sillery, PQ: Septentrion, 1997.

Lane, Jan-Erik and Svante Ersson. *The New Institutional Politics: Performance and Outcomes.* New York: Routledge, 2000.

Larmore, Charles. "Political Liberalism." *Political Theory*, vol. 18, no. 3 (August 1990).

LaSelva, Samuel L. "Federalism as a Way of Life: Reflections on the Canadian Experiment." *Canadian Journal of Political Science,* vol. 26, no. 2. (June 1993).

Laski, Harold J. *Parliamentary Government in England.* London: George Allen and Unwin, 1938.

Lawson, Robert J. "Understanding Alienation in Western Canada: Is 'Western Alienation' the Problem? Is Senate Reform the Cure?" *Journal of Canadian Studies*, vol. 39, no. 2 (Spring 2005).

Laycock, David. "Populism and Democracy in Canada's Reform Party." In *Populism in Europe and the Americas: Threat or Corrective for Democracy?* edited by Cass Mudde and Cristóbal Rovira Kaltwasser. Cambridge, Cambridge University Press, 2013

Lederman, W. R. "Unity and Diversity in Canadian Federalism." *Canadian Bar Review* vol. 53 (1975).

Legislative Assembly of Alberta, Special Committee on Senate Reform, *Strengthening Canada: Reform of Canada's Senate.* March 1985.

———. *Strengthening Canada:Report of the Alberta Select Special Committee on Senate Reform.* Edmonton: Government of Alberta, 1985.

Lemieux, Vincent. "La Representation et la gouverne." *Analyses des Politiques*, vol. 12 (February 1986).

Letter to the Editor. *Le Canadien.* March 6, 1865.

Levinson, Sanford, ed. *Responding to Imperfection: The Theory and Practice of Constitutional Amendment.* Princeton, NJ: Princeton University Press, 1995.

Levmore, Saul. "Bicameralism: When Are Two Decisions Better than One?" *International Review of Law and Economics,* 12 (1992).

Lijphart, Arend. "Consociational Democracy." *World Politics*, vol. 21, no. 2 (January 1969).

———. "Constitutional Designs for Divided Societies." In *Democracy: a Reader,* edited by Larry Diamond and Marc F. Plattner. Baltimore, Johns Hopkins University Press, 2009.

———. *Democracies: Patterns of Majoritarian and Consensus Government in Twenty-One Democracies.* New Haven, CT: Yale University Press, 1984.

———. *Patterns of Democracy.* New Haven, CT: Yale University Press, 1999.

Lim, Claire S. H. "Preferences and Incentives of Appointed and Elected Public Officials: Evidence from State Court Trial Judges." *American Economic Review*, vol. 103, no. 4 (June 2013).

Lintott, Andrew. "Aristotle and Democracy." *Classical Quarterly*, vol. 42, no. 1 (1992).

Loewenberg, Gerhard and Samuel C. Paterson. *Comparing Legislatures.* Boston: Little, Brown, 1979.

Lusztig, Michael. "Federalism and Institutional Design: The Perils and Politics of a Triple-E Senate in Canada." *Publius*, vol. 25, no. 1 (Winter 1995).

Lynch-Staunton, J. "The Role of the Senate in the Legislative Process." *Canadian Parliamentary Review* (Summer 2000).

Ma, Shu-Yun. "Political Science at the Edge of Chaos? The Paradigmatic Implications of Historical Institutionalism." *International Political Science Review,* vol. 28, no. 1 (January 2007).

Macfarlane, Emmett. "Did the Supreme Court Just Kill Senate Reform?" *Maclean's.* April 25, 2014. Available: http://www.macleans.ca/politics/did-the-supreme-court-just-kill-senate-reform/.

MacGregor, Robert Dawson and Norman Ward. *Dawson's The Government of Canada.* Toronto: University of Toronto Press, 1987.

Mackay, Christopher S. *Ancient Rome: A Military and Political History.* Cambridge: Cambridge University Press, 2007.

MacKay, R. H. "To End or Mend the Senate?" *Queen's Quarterly*, vol. 71 (1964).

MacKay, Robert A. *The Unreformed Senate of Canada.* Toronto: McClelland and Stewart, 1963.

———. *The Unreformed Senate of Canada.* Toronto: McClelland and Stewart, 1963.

MacKay, William and Charles W. Johnson. *Parliament and Congress: Representation and Scrutiny in the Twenty-First Century.* Oxford: Oxford University Press, 2010.

Mackie, Gerry. "Schumpeter's Leadership Democracy." *Political Theory*, vol. 37, no. 1 (February 2009).

MacKinnon, Leslie. "Senate Votes to Suspend Brazeau, Duffy, Wallin." *CBC News:Politics.* November 5, 2013. Available: http://www.cbc.ca/news/politics/senate-votes-to-suspend-brazeau-duffy-wallin-1.2415815.

MacLachlan, Donald F. *The Esquimalt & Nanaimo Railway—The Dunsmuir Years: 1884–1905.* Vancouver:British Columbia Historical Railway Association, 1986.

MacNeil, Neil and Richard A. Baker. *The American Senate:An Insider's History.* New York: Oxford University Press, 2013.

Madison, James. "Federalist No. 51." In *The Federalist Papers,* edited by Alexander Hamilton, James Madison, and John Jay. New York: SoHo, 2010.

Mahler, Gregory S. "Canada: Two Nations, One State?" In *Political Culture and Constitutionalism: A Comparative Approach*, edited by Daniel P. Franklin and Michael J. Baun. Armonk, NY: M. E. Sharpe, 1995.

Maitland, Frederick. *The Constitutional History of England.* Cambridge: Cambridge University Press, 1948.

Malcolmson, Patrick and Richard Myers. *The Canadian Regime.* Toronto: University of Toronto Press, 2012.

Malcolmson, Patrick. "Reflections on Canada's First Senate 'Election.'" *Canadian Parliamentary Review*, vol. 14, no. 3 (1991).

Malkin, Bonnie. "Australia's Carbon-Reduction Scheme Blocked by Senate." *Daily Telegraph.* August 13, 2009. Available: http://www.telegraph.co.uk/earth/environment/climatechange/6019376/ Australias-carbon-reduction-scheme-blocked-by-senate.html.

Manfredi, Christopher P. "Institutional Design and the Politics of Constitutional Modification: Understanding Amendment Failure in the United States and Canada." *Law and Society Review*, vol. 31, no. 1 (1997).

March, James and Johan P. Olsen. *Rediscovering Institutions: the Organizational Basis of Politics.* New York NY, Free, 1989.

———. "The New Institutionalism: Organizational Factors in Political Life." *American Political Science Review,* vol. 78 (1984).

Marshall, Geoffrey. *Constitutional Conventions: The Rules and Forms of Political Accountability.* Oxford: Clarendon Press, 1986.

———. *Parliamentary Sovereignty and the Commonwealth.* Oxford: Clarednon Press, 1984.

Martin, Ged. *The Durham Report and British Policy: A Critical Essay.* Cambridge: Cambridge University Press, 2008.

Matthew, Colin.*The Nineteenth Century: The British Isles, 1815–1901.* Oxford: Oxford University Press, 2000.

McCormick, Peter, Ernest C. Manning, and Gordon Gibson. *Regional Representation: The Canadian Partnership.* Calgary: Canada West Foundation, 1981.

McCreery, Christopher. *The Order of Canada: Its Origins, History, and Developments.* Toronto: University of Toronto Press, 2005.

McDonald, Andrew and Robert Hazell. "What Happened Next? Constitutional Change under New Labour." In *Reinventing Britain: Constitutional Change under New Labour.* Berkeley: University of California Press, 2007.

McHugh, James T. *Comparative Constitutional Traditions.* New York: Peter Lang, 2003.

———. *In Another Place: Three Case Studies in the Development of the Upper House of Parliament within the Westminster Model of Government.* Edinburgh: University of Edinburgh M. Litt. Thesis, 1986.

Meadwell, Hudson. "The Politics of Nationalism in Quebec." *World Politics*, vol. 45, no. 2 (January 1993).

Merkl, Peter H. "Executive-Legislative Federalism in West Germany." *American Political Science Review*, vol. 53, no. 3 (September 1959).

Meyer, John W., John Boli, and George M. Thomas. "Ontology and Rationalization in the Western Cultural Account." In *Institutional Environments and Organizations*, edited by W. Richard Scott and John W. Meyer. London: Sage, 1994.

Meynell, Robert. *Canadian Idealism and the Philosophy of Freedom: C. B. Macpherson, George Grant, and Charles Taylor.* Montreal and Kingston, ON: McGill-Queen's University Press, 2011.

Michels, Robert. *Political Parties: A Sociological Study of the Oligarchical Tendencies of Modern Democracies.* New York: The Free Press, 1968.

Mill, John Stuart. *Considerations on Representative Government.* New York: Harper and Brothers, 1862.

Montesquieu. *De l'esprit des lois,* edited by Victor Goldschmidt. Paris: Flammarion, 1993.

Morton, Desmond. *A Short History of Canada.* Edmonton: Hurtig, 1985.

———. *A Short History of Canada.* Toronto: McClelland and Stewart, 2006.

Morton, W. L. *Monck Letters and Journals, 1863–1868.* Toronto: McClelland and Stuart, 1970.

Mouritsen, Per. "Four Models of Republican Liberty and Self-Government." In *Republicanism in Theory and Practice*, edited by Iseult Honohan and Jeremy Jennings. London: Routledge, 2005.

Muller, Jerry Z. *Conservatism.* Princeton, NJ: Princeton University Press, 1997.

Nevitte, Neil. *The Decline of Deference: Canadian Value Change in Cross-National Perspective.* Toronto: University of Toronto Press, 1996.

Norrie, Kenneth H. "Energy, Canadian Federalism, and the West." *Publius*, vol. 14, no. 1 (Winter 1984).

Norton, Philip. "Achieving Accountability." *The House Magazine*, vol. 28, no. 1,029 (March 2003).

Oborne, Peter. "Ed Miliband's Plan for an Elected House of Lords Would Mean an Upper House Dominated by Ukip." *The Telegraph*, November 3, 2014. http://www.telegraph.co.uk/ news/politics/ukip/11205797/Ed-Milibands-plan-for-an-elected-House-of-Lords-would-mean-an-upper-house-dominated-by-Ukip.html.

Official Record of the Debates of the National Austalasian Convention. Sydney, 1897.

Olgilvie, Margaret H. *Historical Introduction to Legal Studies*. Toronto: Carswell, 1982.

Oliver, Peter C. "The Busy Harbours of Canadian Federalism: The Division of Powers and Its Doctrines in the McLachlin Court." In *Public Law at the McLachlin Court: The First Decade*, edited by David A. Wright and Adam M. Dodek. Toronto: Irwin, 2011.

Order of Canada. *Constitution of the Order of Canada*.

Ouchi, William G. and Alan L. Wilkins. "Organizational Culture." *Annual Review of Sociology*, vol. 11 (1985).

Pangle, Thomas L. *Montesquieu's Theory of Liberalism: A Commentary on the Spirit of the Laws*. Chicago: University of Chicago Press, 1973.

Pantich, Leo. "The Role and Nature of the Canadian State." In *The Canadian State: Political Economy and Political Power*, edited by Leo Panitch. Toronto: University of Toronto Press, 1977.

Parkin, George R. *The Makers of Canada: Sir John A. MacDonald*. Charleston: Bibliobazzar, 2009.

Parliament of Australia—Senate—Senate StatsNet. "Amendments Moved." Available: http://www.aph.gov.au/Parliamentary_Business/Statistics/Senate_StatsNet/legislation/3ramendments.

———. "Bills Negatived, 1991–2013." Available: http://www.aph.gov.au/Parliamentary_Business/Statistics/Senate_StatsNet/legislation/negatived.

———. "Legislation—General, 1991–2000." Available: http://www.aph.gov.au/Parliamentary_Business/Statistics/statsnet/consolidations/19912000/generallegislation.

Parliament of Canada, Special Joint Committee on a Renewed Canada. *Report of the Special Joint Committee on a Renewed Canada (Beaudoin-Dobbie Report), 1992*.

Parliament of Canada. "Current Members." Douglas Black, http://www.parl.gc.ca/SenatorsMembers/Senate/SenatorsBiography/isenator_det.asp?senator_id=3567&sortord=N&Language=E&M=M

———. "On the Job with a Senator." About Parliament. Available: http://www.parl.gc.ca/ About/Parliament/OnTheJobSenate/index-e.asp.

———. *Current Members, Scott Tanis*. Available: http://www.parl.gc.ca/ Senators-Members/Senate/ SenatorsBiography/ISenator.asp?Language=E.

———. *Senators and Members, Bert Brown*. Available: http://www.parl.gc.ca/ parlinfo/Files/Parliamentarian.aspx?Item=22124571-ff5b-4d12-bccf-50f78cbe2b3d&Language =E&Section=ALL.

———. *Senators and Members, Betty Unger*. Available: http://www.parl.gc.ca/Parlinfo/ Files/Parliamentarian.aspx?Item=5309ceb5-be13-4e5b-a255-a8969bae7674&Language=E&Section =FederalExperience.

———. *Senators and Members, Cliff Breitkreuz*. Available: http://www.parl. gc.ca/parlinfo/Files/Parliamentarian.aspx.?Item=1b89db3a-1e68-4db6-90fe- e9939bac441e&Language=E&Section=ALL.

———. *Senators and Members, Stanley Waters*. Available: http://www.parl.gc.ca/ Parlinfo/Files/Parliamentarian.aspx?Item=5309ceb5-be13-4e5b-a255-a8969bae7674&Language= E&Section=FederalExperience.

———. *Senators and Members, Stanley Waters*. Available: http://www.parl.gc.ca/Parlinfo/Files/Parliamentarian.aspx?Item=5309ceb5-be13-4e5b-a255-a8969bae7674&Language=E&Section=FederalExperience.

Parliament of Canada—The Senate. "Report on Activities, 2007." Available: http://sen.parl.gc.ca/portal/AnnualReports/2006-2007/chapter_1-e.htm.

Parliamentary Debates on the Subject of the Confederation of the British North American Provinces:Third Session, Eighth Provincial Parliament of Canada. Quebec: 1865.

Patterson, S. C. and A. Mughan, eds., *Senates:Bicameralism in the Contemporary World.* Columbus: Ohio State University Press, 1999.

Peffer, W. A. "The United States Senate: Its Privileges, Powers, and Functions, Its Rules and Methods of Doing Business." *North American Review*, vol. 167, no. 501 (August 1898).

Pepin, Jean-Luc and John Robarts. *Report on the Task Force on Canadian Unity.* Ottawa: Queen's Printer, 1978.

Peters, B. Guy. *Institutional Theory in Political Science: The New Institutionalism.* London: Continuum, 2005.

———. *Strategies for Comparative Research in Political Science.* New York: Palgrave Macmillan, 2012.

Petit, Philip. *Republicanism: A Theory of Freedom and Government.* Oxford: Oxford University Press, 1997.

Phillips, Owen Hood and Paul Jackson. *Constitutional and Administrative Law.* London: Sweet and Maxwell, 1987.

Pitt, David. "Peer from the West Indies." *British Medical Journal*, vol. 2, no. 6203 (December 1979).

Plourde, Michel. *La Politique linguistique du Québec, 1977–1987.* Québec: Institut Québécois du Recherche sur la culture, 1988.

Pollard, A. F. *The Evolution of Parliament.* London: Russell and Russell, 1964.

Pollard, Bruce G. "Canadian Energy Policy in 1985:Toward a Renewed Federalism?" *Publius*, vol. 16, no. 3 (Summer 1986).

Pope, Joseph. *Documents on the Confederation of British North America,* edited by G. P. Browne. Toronto: McClelland and Stewart, 1969.

———. *Memoirs of the Right Honourable Sir John Alexander Macdonald, GCB.* London: Edward Arnold, 1894.

Raaflaub, Kurt A. and Robert W. Wallace. "'People's Power' and Egalitarian Trends in Archaic Greece." In *Origins of Democracy in Ancient Greece*, edited by Kurt A. Raaflaub and Josiah Ober. Berkeley: University of California Press, 2007.

Reif, L. C. *The Ombudsman, Good Governance, and the International Human Rights System.* Leiden, The Netherlands: Martin Nijhoff, 2004.

Remini, Robert V. *The House: The History of the House of Representatives.* New York: Harper Collins, 2006.

Report of the Special Joint Committee on Senate Reform. Ottawa: Queen's Printer, 1984.

Rhodes, R.A.W., John Wanna, and Patrick Weller. *Comparing Westminster.* Oxford: Oxford University Press, 2009.

Riggs, Fred W. "Presidentialism *versus* Parliamentarism: Implications for Representativeness and Legitimacy." *International Political Science Review*, vol. 18, no. 3 (July 1997).

Riker, William H. "The Justification of Bicameralism." *International Political Science Review*, vol. 13, no. 1 (January 1992).

———. "The Senate and American Federalism." *American Political Science Review*, vol. 49, no. 2 (June 1955).

Roberts, B. J. "Canada's Budgetary System." *Annals of the American Academy of Political and Social Science,* vol. 107 (May 1923).

Robertson, David. *The Original Compromise: What the Constitution's Framers Were Really Thinking.* New York: Oxford University Press, 2013.

Robertson, J. A. "Rejection of Bills by the Canadian Senate." Library of Parliament Research Paper (Ottawa: Parliament of Canada, 1990).

———. "Rejection of Bills by the Canadian Senate." Library of Parliament Research Paper. Ottawa: Parliament of Canada, 1990.

Rokkan, Stein and Derek Urwin. "Centres and Peripheries in Western Europe." In *The Politics of Territorial Identity*, edited by Stein Rokkan and Derem Urwin. London: Sage, 1982.

Ross, George. *The Senate of Canada: Its Constitutions, Duties, and Powers Historically Considered.* Toronto: Copp Clark, 1914.

Royal Commission on Reform of the House of Lords. *The House of Lords: Reform.* London: Her Majesty's Stationery Office, 2007.

Royal Commission on the Canadian Pacific Railway. *Report.* "Papers of Sir John A. Macdonald Connected with the Awarding of Section Fifteen of the Canadian Pacific Railway." Ottawa, 1877.

Royal Commission on the Reform of the House of Lords. *A House for the Future.* London: Her Majesty's Stationery Office, 2000.

Rush, Michael. "The Canadian Parliament and the Federal System." In *Canadian Federalism: Past, Present, and Future,* edited by Michael Burgess. Leicester: Leicester University Press, 1990.

Russell, Meg and Maria Sciara. "Why Does the Government get Defeated in the House of Lords? The Lords, the Party System and British Politics." *British Politics,* vol. 2 (2007).

Russell, Meg and Richard Cornes. "The Royal Commission on Reform of the House of Lords: A House for the Future?" *Modern Law Review*, vol. 64, no. 1 (January 2001).

Russell, Meg. "Reforming the British House of Lords: How a Little Reform Can Go a Long Way." *Papers on Parliament*, no. 47. Canberra, July 2007.

———. "Responsibilities of Second Chambers: Constitutional and Human Rights Safeguards." In *Second Chambers,* edited by Nicholas D.J. Baldwin and Donald Shell, Abingdon, Oxfordshire, Frank Cass, 2001.

———. "What are Second Chambers For?" *Parliamentary Affairs,* vol. 54 (2001).

———. *Reforming the House of Lords.* New York: Oxford University Press, 2000.

———. *Reforming the House of Lords: Lessons from Overseas.* Oxford: Oxford University Press.

———. *The Contemporary House of Lords: Westminster Bicameralism Revived.* Oxford: Oxford University Press, 2013.

Russell, Peter H. and Lorne Sossin. *Parliamentary Democracy in Crisis.* Toronto: University of Toronto Press, 2009.

Russell, Peter H. *Constitutional Odyssey: Can Canadians Become a Sovereign People?* Toronto: University of Toronto Press, 2004.

Sainty, J. C. *The Origins of the Office of Chairman of Committees in the House of Lords.* London: House of Lords Records Office, 1974.

Saphire, Richard B. "Judicial Review in the Name of the Constitution." *University of Dayton Law Review,* vol. 8 (1983).

Saunders, Cheryl. *The Constitution of Australia: A Contextual Analysis.* Oxford: Hart, 2011.

Savoie, Donald J. "The Rise of Court Government in Canada." *Canadian Journal of Political Science*, vol. 32, no. 4 (December 1999).

Sawer, Geoffrey. "Constitutional Issues in Australian Federalism." *Publius*, vol. 7, no. 3 (Summer 1977).

Saywell, John. *The Lawmakers: Judicial Power and the Shaping of Canadian Federalism.* Toronto: University of Toronto Press, 2002.

Scarfe, Brian L. "Redistributing Elected Senate Seats for Regional Balance." *Canadian Public Policy*, vol. 10, no. 2 (June 1984).

Schapiro, J. Salwyn. "John Stuart Mill, Pioneer of Democratic Liberalism in England." *Journal of the History of Ideas*, vol. 4, no. 2 (April 1943).

Scott, W. Richard. *Institutions and Organizations: Ideas and Interests.* London: Sage, 2008.

Searing, Donald D. "Roles, Rules, and Rationality in the New Institutionalism." *American Political Science Review*, vol. 85, no. 4 (December 1991).

Seidle, F. Leslie. "Senate Reform and the Constitutional Agenda: Conundrum or Solution?" In *Canadian Constitutionalism, 1791–1991*, edited by Janet Ajzenstat. Ottawa: Canadian Study of Parliament Group, 1992.

———. "Strengthening Canadian Democracy." Institute for Research on Public Policy. Available: http://www.irpp.org/research/research_project.php?page=2&ResearchCode=Strengthening%20Canadian%20Democracy.

Selznick, Philip. "Institutionalism 'Old' and 'New.'" *Administrative Science Quarterly,* vol. 41 (1996).

Semmel, Bernard. "Parliament and the Metric System." *Isis*, vol. 54, no. 1 (March 1963).

Shell, Donald R. "The House of Lords and the Thatcher Government." *Parliamentary Affairs*, vol. 38, no. 1 (Winter 1985).

Shepherd, Joanna M. "The Influence of Retention on Judges' Voting." *Journal of Legal Studies*, vol. 38, no. 1 (January 2009) .

Shepsle, Kenneth A. "Studying Institutions: Some Lessons from the Rational Choice Approach." *Journal of Theoretical Politics,* vol. 1 (1989).

Simeon, Richard and Ian Robinson. *State, Society, and the Development of Canadian Federalism.* Toronto: University of Toronto Press, 1990.

———. *Intergovernmental Relations.* Toronto: University of Toronto Press, 1985.

Skinner, Quentin. "Hobbes on Sovereignty: An Unknown Discussion." *Political Studies* vol. 13 (1965).

Skopcol, Theda. *Social Revolutions in the Modern World.* Cambridge: Cambridge University Press, 1997.

———. *States and Social Revolution.* Cambridge: Cambridge University Press, 1979.

Smethurst, S. E. "Cicero and the Senate." *The Classical Journal,* vol. 54, no. 2 (1958).

Smiley, Donald V. and Ronald L. Watts. *Intrastate Federalism in Canada.* Toronto: University of Toronto Press, 1985.

———. *Canada in Question: Federation in the Eighties.* Toronto: McGraw-Hill Ryerson, 1980.

———. "Central Institutions." In *Canada and the New Constitution: The Unfinished Agenda.* Montreal: Institute for Research on Public Policy, 1983.

Smith, David E. "The Canadian Senate: What Is to Be Done?" In *Essential Readings in Canadian Constitutional Politics*, edited by Christian Leuprecht and Peter H. Russell. Toronto: University of Toronto Press, 2011.

———. "The Improvement of the Senate by Non-Constitutional Means." In *Protecting Canadian Democracy: The Senate You Never Knew*, edited by Serge Joyal. Montreal and Kingston, ON: McGill-Queen's University Press, 2003.

———. *The Canadian Senate in Bicameral Perspective.* Toronto: University of Toronto Press, 2003.

Smith, Jennifer. "Informal Constitutional Development: Change by Other Means." In *Canadian Federalism,* edited by Herman Bakvis and Grace Skogstad. Oxford: Oxford University Press, 2002.

Smith, Peter J. "The Ideological Origins of Canadian Confederation." *Canadian Journal of Political Science*, vol. 20, no. 1 (March 1987).

Smith, S. A. de. "Reform of the Lords: Report of the Joint Committee on House of Lords Reform." *Modern Law Review*, vol. 26, no. 3 (May 1963).

———. *Constitutional and Administrative Law.* London: Longman, 1971.

Snyder, Lorraine. "Reference *re* Senate Reform (2014):The Supreme Court Clarifies the Senate Reform Process." *Centre for Constitutional Studies.* June 20, 2014. Available: http://ualawccsprod.srv.ualberta.ca/ ccs/index.php/constitutional-issues/federalism/767-reference-re-senate-reform-2014-the-supreme-court-clarifies-the-senate-reform-process.

Soberman, D. A. "Canada's Institutional Deficit." *Queen's Law Journal,* vol. 6 (Spring 1983).

Soergel, Andrew. "How Britain Could Undo the Brexit." *US News and World Report*, June 26, 2016, https://www.usnews.com/news/articles/2016-06-28/how-britain-could-undo-the-brexit.

Spencer, Benjamin. "Jurisdiction to Adjudicate: A Revised Analysis." *University of Chicago Law Review*, vol. 73, no. 2 (Spring 2006).

Spencer, Christina. "Justin Trudeau Kicks All 32 Liberal Senators Out of Caucus in Bid for Reform." *National Post.* January 29, 2014. Available: http://news.

nationalpost.com/2014/01/29/justin-trudeau-kicks-senators-out-of-liberal-caucus-in-bid-to-show-hes-serious-about-cleaning-up-red-chamber/.

Steiner, Jürg. "The Consociational Theory and Beyond." *Comparative Politics*, vol. 13, no. 2 (April 1981).

Steinmo, Sven and Kathleen Thelen. *Structuring Politics: Historical Institutionalism in Comparative Analysis.* Cambridge: Cambridge University Press, 1992.

Stevenson, Garth. *Ex Uno Plures: Federal-Provincial Relations in Canada, 1867–1896.* Montreal and Kingston, ON: McGill-Queen's University Press, 1993.

———. *Unfulfilled Union: Canadian Federalism and National Unity.* Montreal and Kingston, ON: McGill-Queen's University Press, 2009.

Stitchcombe, Arthur L. *Information and Organizations.* Berkeley: University of California Press, 1990.

Strayer, Barry L. *Canada's Constitutional Revolution.* Edmonton: University of Alberta Press, 2013.

Stubbs, William. *The Constitutional History of England.* Oxford: Clarendon Press, 1887.

Swinton, Katherine. "Amending the Canadian Constitution: Lessons from Meech Lake." *University of Toronto Law Journal*, vol. 42, no. 2 (Spring 1992).

Taagepera, Rein and Matthew Soberg. *Seats and Votes: The Effects and Determinants of Electoral Systems.* New Haven, CT: Yale University Press, 1989.

Taylor, Charles. "No Community, No Democracy." In *The Communitarian Reader: Beyond the Essentials*, edited by Amitai Etzioni, Andrew Volmert, and Elanit Rothschild. Oxford: Rowman and Littlefield, 2004.

Taylor, W. A. *Crown Land Grants: A History of the Esquimalt and Nanaimo Railway Land Grants, the Railway Belt, and the Peace River Block.* Victoria: British Columbia Crown Land Registry Services, 1997.

Thaysen, Uwe. *The Bundesrat, the Länder, and German Federalism.* Washington, DC: American Institute for Contemporary German Studies, 1994.

The Globe. April 8, 1876.

The Independent Crossbenchers. Available: http://www.crossbenchpeers.org.uk/.

Thelen, Kathleen and Sven Steinmo. "Historical Institutionalism in Comparative Politics." In *Structuring Politics: Historical Institutionalism in Comparative Analysis*, edited by Sven Steinmo, Kathleen Thelen, and Frank Longstreth. Cambridge: Cambridge University Press, 1992.

Thomas, Paul G. "Comparing the Lawmaking Roles of the Senate and the House of Commons." In *Protecting Canadian Democracy: The Senate You Never Knew*, edited by Serge Joyal. Montreal and Kingston, ON: McGill-Queen's University Press, 2003.

Thomson, Dale C. *Jean Lesage et la Révolution tranquille.* Québec: Trécarré, 1984.

Todd, Alpheus. *Parliamentary Government in the Colonies.* London: Longmans, Green, and Company, 1929.

Trebilcock, M. J., D. G. Hartle, J. R. S. Pritchard, and D. N. Dewees. *The Choice of Governing Instrument.* Ottawa: Economic Council of Canada, 1982.

Trigg, Stephanie. *Shame and Honor: A Vulgar History of the Order of the Garter.* Philadelphia: University of Pennsylvania Press, 2012.

Tsebelis, George and Jeannette Money. *Bicameralism.* Cambridge: Cambridge University Press, 1997.

Tsebelis, George. "Decision Making in Political Systems: Veto Players in Presidentialism, Parliamentarism, Multicamearlism, and Multipartyism." *British Journal of Political Science*, vol. 25, no. 3 (July 1995).

Tully, James and Quentin Skinner. *An Approach to Political Philosophy: Locke in Contexts.* Cambridge: University of Cambridge Press, 1993.

Tupper, Charles. *Recollections of Sixty Years in Canada.* London: Cassell, 1914.

Uhr, John. "Generating Divided Government: The Australian Senate." In *Senates: Bicameralism in the Contemporary World*, edited by Samuel C. Patterson and Anthony Mughan. Columbus: Ohio State Press University, 1999.

———. *Deliberative Democracy in Australia.* Cambridge: Cambridge University Press, 1998.

UK General Public Acts. Available: http://www.legislation.gov.uk/ukpga.

United Kingdom Government. *House of Lords.* Available: http://www.ucl.ac.uk/constitution-unit/research/parliament/house-of-lords/lords-defeats

United Kingdom Parliament. *About Parliament, Members of the Lords: Allowances.* Available: http://www.parliament.uk/about/mps-and-lords/about-lords/lords-allowances/.

University College London Constitution Unit, School of Public Policy. Available: http://www.parliament.uk/about/faqs/house-of-lords-faqs/lords-govtdefeats/.

Van Loon, Richard J. and Michael S. Whittington. *The Canadian Political System: Environment, Structure, and Process.* Toronto: McGraw-Hill Ryerson, 1987.

Vanberg, Georg. "Establishing Judicial Independence in West Germany: The Impact of Opinion Leadership and the Separation of Powers." *Comparative Politics*, vol. 32, no. 3 (April 2000).

Vaughan, Frederick. *The Canadian Federalist Experience.* Montreal and Kingston, ON: McGill-Queen's University Press, 2003.

Veyssière, Laurent. *La Nouvelle-France en heritage.* Paris: Armand Colin, 2013.

Waite, P. B. "Edward Whelan Reports from the Quebec Conference." *Canadian Historical Review*, vol. 42, no. 1 (March 1961).

———. *Macdonald: His Life and World.* Toronto: McGraw-Hill Ryerson, 1975.

———. *The Charlottetown Conference.* Ottawa: Canadian Historical Association, 1970.

Wallace, W. S. "Edward Blake's Aurora Speech." *Canadian Historical Review*, vol. 2, no. 2 (July 1921).

Ward, Lee. "Locke on Executive Power and Liberal Constitutionalism." *Canadian Journal of Political Science*, vol. 38, no. 3 (September 2005).

Warwick, Paul. *Government Survival in Parliamentary Democracies.* Cambridge: Cambridge University Press, 1994.

Washington Citizens' Commission on Salaries for Elected Officials. "Comparisons of the Salaries of Legislatures Nationally by Time Required to Do the Job." State of Washington. Available: http://www.salaries.wa.gov/documents/ComparisonofTimeSalariesofLegislaturesNationally_001.pdf.

Watts, Ronald L. *Executive Federalism: A Comparative Analysis.* Kingston, ON: Institute of Intergovernmental Relations, 1989.

Weber, Max. *The Theory of Social and Economic Organization.*.edited by Talcott Parsons. New York: Free Press, 1964.

Wehling, Hans-Georg. "The Bundesrat." *Publius*, vol. 19, no. 4 (Autumn 1989).

Wheare, K. C. *Federal Government.* Oxford: Oxford University Press, 1970.

———. *Legislatures.* New York: Oxford University Press, 1963.

Wherry, Aaron, "Trudeau's Promise of Electoral Reform: From 'We Can Do Better' to Accusations of Betrayal." *Canadian Broadcasting Corporation News*, February 5, 2017, http://www.cbc.ca/news/politics/wherry-trudeau-electoral-reform-promise-betrayal-1.3962386.

———. "Where the Province Stand on Senate Reform." *MacLean's*, June 12, 2015, http://www.macleans.ca/politics/where-the-provinces-stand-on-senate-reform/.

White, Randall. *Voice of Region: The Long Journey to Senate Reform in Canada.* Toronto: Dundurn Press, 1990.

Wingrove, Josh. "Ted Morton: Alberta's Charisma-Challenged Firebrand Takes His Shot." *Globe and Mail.* August 5, 2011. Available: http://www.theglobeandmail.com/news/politics/ted-morton-albertas-charisma-challenged-firebrand-takes-his-shot/article589611/.

Winthrop, Delba. "Aristotle on Participatory Democracy." *Polity*, vol. 11, no. 2 (Winter 1978).

Wirls, Daniel and Stephen Wirls. *The Invention of the United States Senate.* Baltimore: Johns Hopkins University Press, 2004.

Woehrling, José. "La Reconnaissance du Québec comme société distincte et la dualité linguistique du Canada: Conséquences juridiques et constitutionnelles." *Analyse de Poliiques,* vol. 14 (September 1988).

Wood, Gordon S. *The Creation of the American Republic, 1776–1787.* Durham: University of North Carolina Press, 1998.

World Directory of Parliaments. Geneva: Inter-Parliamentary Union, 1999.

Yarbrough, Jean. "Representation and Republicanism: Two Views." *Publius*, vol. 9, no. 2 (Spring 1979).

Yueh-Chin, H. "Role and Responsibility of the Control Yuan." In *The Ombudsman Concept*, edited by L. C. Reif. Edmonton: International Obudsman Institute, 1995.

Ziegenfuss, James T., Jr. and Patricia O'Rourke. *The Ombudsman Handbook: Designing and Managing an Effective Problem-Solving Program.* Jefferson, NC: McFarland, 2010.

Zoch, Paul A. *Ancient Rome: An Introductory History.* Norman: University of Oklahoma Press, 1998.

Zuckerman, Alan S. "Advancing Explanation in Comparative Politics: Social Mechanisms, Endogenous Processes, and Empirical Rigor." In *Comparative Politics: Rationality, Culture, and Structure,* edited by Mark Iriving Lichbach and Alan S. Zuckerman. Cambridge: Cambridge University Press, 2009.

Zywicki, Todd J. "Beyond the Shell and Husk of History: The History of the Seventeenth Amendment and its Implications for Current Reform Proposals." *Cleveland State Law Review*, vol. 45, no. 1 (1997).

Index

About the Author

James T. McHugh is professor and former chair in the Department of Political Science and a fellow and director of Academic Planning for the Ray C. Bliss Institute of Applied Politics at the University of Akron, as well as an adjunct lecturer in the Department of Political Science at the University of Vermont. Dr. McHugh has previously served at Roosevelt University in Chicago, American University in Washington, DC (in which city he later was a Public Policy Scholar for the Canada Institute of the Woodrow Wilson International Center for Scholars), and Queen's University in Kingston, Ontario (where he earned his doctorate), as well as having been a Fulbright Distinguished Chair for North American Integration at Carleton University in Ottawa. A widely published scholar in political theory, comparative politics, public law, and other fields, he is, currently, president of the Association for Canadian Studies in the United States.

Lightning Source UK Ltd.
Milton Keynes UK
UKOW04n1305181017
311182UK00008B/234/P

9 781498 547932